TRADING PSYCHOLOGY 2.0

Founded in 1807, John Wiley & Sons is the oldest independent publishing company in the United States. With offices in North America, Europe, Australia and Asia, Wiley is globally committed to developing and marketing print and electronic products and services for our customers' professional and personal knowledge and understanding.

The Wiley Trading series features books by traders who have survived the market's ever changing temperament and have prospered—some by reinventing systems, others by getting back to basics. Whether a novice trader, professional or somewhere in-between, these books will provide the advice and strategies needed to prosper today and well into the future.

For more on this series, visit our website at www.WileyTrading.com.

TRADING PSYCHOLOGY 2.0

From Best Practices to Best Processes

Brett N. Steenbarger, PhD

WILEY

Published by John Wiley & Sons, Inc., Hoboken, New Jersey.
Published simultaneously in Canada.

For general information on our other products and services or for technical support, please contact our Customer Care Department within the United States at (800) 762-2974, outside the United States at (317) 572-3993 or fax (317) 572-4002.

Wiley publishes in a variety of print and electronic formats and by print-on-demand. Some material included with standard print versions of this book may not be included in e-books or in print-on-demand. If this book refers to media such as a CD or DVD that is not included in the version you purchased, you may download this material at http://booksupport.wiley.com. For more information about Wiley products, visit www.wiley.com.

Library of Congress Cataloging-in-Publication Data

Steenbarger, Brett N.
    Trading psychology 2.0 : from best practices to best processes / Brett N Steenbarger, Ph.D.
        pages cm.—(Wiley trading series)
    Includes index.
    ISBN 978-1-118-93681-8 (hardback)—ISBN 978-1-118-93683-2 (ePDF)—ISBN 978-1-118-93682-5 (epub)
    1.   Stocks—Psychological aspects. 2.   Speculation—Psychological aspects.
3.   Investments—Psychological aspects.   I.   Title.
    HG6041.S762 2015
    332.6401'9—dc23

                                                                    2015016663

Cover Design: Wiley
Cover Images: Business growth graph ©iStock.com/Violka08; Black Chess King and lying Pawns on board ©iStock.com/Dominik Pabis

Printed in the United States of America
SKY10087395_100924

EPIGRAPH

If you don't have time to do it right, when will you have time to do it over?

John Wooden

CONTENTS

Successful efforts to master markets lead us down paths of self-mastery. This book is one guide to those paths.

Market participants have traditionally defined self-mastery as *discipline*—controlling the emotions that all too often distort information processing and trigger impulsive behavior. To be sure, discipline is required for any great undertaking, whether it is pursuing an Olympic medal, a business startup, or a medical breakthrough. But discipline, while necessary for success, is never sufficient. Discipline does not substitute for skill, talent, and insight. Strict, disciplined adherence to mediocre plans can only lock in mediocre results. If it were otherwise, there would be no losing automated trading systems.

I've followed and traded markets since the late 1970s. During the past decade, I have served as a full-time performance coach at two trading firms—Kingstree Trading in Chicago and Tudor Investment Corp. in Greenwich, Connecticut—and worked with many other trading organizations on a consultative basis. Through the TraderFeed blog and three prior trading books, I've had the honor of interacting with thousands of traders around the world. If there's one thing this whirlwind of experience has taught me, it's that there is far more to market mastery than controlling emotions and impulses. Sustained success requires the cultivation of a host of positive performance elements: creativity, productivity, adaptation to change, and psychological well-being. The good news is that recent research in psychology and related fields has profoundly deepened our understanding of these contributors to human performance. The bad news is that most of us in the money management world, immersed in the day-to-day challenges of keeping up with news flows and market movements, have little opportunity to sift through and apply this knowledge. As a consequence, we tend to work hard, but not smart. From the organization of our daily routines to our reviews of performance, we rarely optimize learning, independent thought, and productivity.

The unfortunate tendency to substitute quantity of effort for quality ensures that we will face a yawning gap between our real and ideal selves: between who we are and who we're capable of becoming. *Trading Psychology 2.0* seeks to bridge that gap by breaking trading success down to four essential processes. In the coming pages, you will learn a simple ABCD:

A   How to dynamically Adapt to changing market conditions
B   How to identify and Build on your distinctive trading strengths
C   How to Cultivate creative processes and generate fresh market perspectives
D   How to Develop best practices that help you sustain productivity and effectiveness in your work routines

Most of all, this book is about taking best practices—the ingredients of your trading success—and weaving them into best processes. The goal is not to change you but to help you more consistently tap into the drivers of your success.

In hindsight, it's not difficult to see that *Trading Psychology 2.0* is a natural extension of my previous books. The first of these, *The Psychology of Trading*, focused on the emotional problems faced by traders and how these mirror common life challenges. It introduced a solution-focused framework to trading: identifying the patterns that underlie our success and becoming more consistent in enacting those. My second book, *Enhancing Trader Performance*, adopted a developmental view of trading success, emphasizing expertise development as an ongoing process of deliberate practice that matches skills, talents, and challenges. An important implication of that work was that there are many forms of trading, each requiring unique skills and learning processes. I continue to find that many of the emotional problems faced by developing traders are the result of bolting generic learning processes onto very specific performance domains, creating frustration and suboptimal performance. Finally, my most recent text, *The Daily Trading Coach*, created a cookbook of psychological techniques and approaches to help traders overcome common performance challenges. An overarching theme of that book is that a primary goal of trading psychology is self-coaching. By becoming better self-observers and catching best and worst practices as they occur, we can overcome market noise with enhanced self-determination.

Trading Psychology 2.0 differs from these books in one key respect: It breaks trading success down into those four ABCD processes and explores research-based ways of maximizing them in our personal and professional lives. The book's aim is to move trading psychology beyond the usual focus on discipline, emotional control, and trading one's plans to the broader context of sustaining peak performance. Most important, the book aims to nudge traders toward what might be called meta-processes: robust routines for changing our routines and adapting trading to ever-changing market conditions.

It is not enough to find an "edge" in financial markets; as any tech entrepreneur can attest, competitive advantages are perishable commodities. Those who sustain success continually renew themselves, uncovering fresh sources of competitive advantage. That requires processes for assessing and challenging our most basic assumptions and practices. It takes a good trader to create success, a great one to recreate it. Nothing is quite as difficult—and rewarding—as letting go of what once worked, returning to the humble status of student, and arising phoenix-like from performance ashes.

What makes any performance domain worthy is that none of us will ever completely master it. There is always room for improvement in dance or golf; chess players, brewmasters, woodworkers, and racecar teams can always hone their craft. For that reason, performance activities are the consummate psychological crucible, moving us ever closer to self-mastery. This is particularly the case with trading, where the rules of the game continually evolve. What other field demands the utmost of conviction and risk-taking, but also the greatest of flexibility and prudence? In adapting to change, we embrace change, we become change. We cannot rest on individual best practices; we need *best processes* that yield ever-improved practice. There will always be a gap between real and ideal: between who we are and who we can become. If this book can be a resource in bridging your gap, it truly will have fulfilled its aim.

Of course, no performance journey is traveled solo. Life is a team sport and success crucially depends on surrounding yourself with the right teammates. I owe many debts of gratitude to colleagues at Graham Capital, Tudor Investment Corp., Kingstree Trading, and SMB Capital;

the ever-resourceful editorial staff at Wiley; Victor Niederhoffer and the Spec Listers; and Howard Lindzon and the supportive crew at Stock Twits. The book wouldn't be possible without the many talented traders who contributed best practices and inspired the case studies. As in my prior books, the names and identities of the traders in those case studies have been changed to preserve privacy, but I want my debt to the many fine people I work with to be as publicly voiced as possible. The greatest debt, however, is to the family that has offered constant love and support through all the not-so-constant financial markets: Debi, Steve, Laura, Devon, and Macrae; their families; and most of all to my wife, Margie. She, not markets, has been the love of my life, and that has kept me sane through many ups and downs in the business. Finally, to the many readers of the TraderFeed blog a hearty thank-you for your support and all you've taught me. I think you'll find many of those lessons in the pages that follow.

There is a valuable tradition in academic scholarship called the literature review. A literature review is a survey of published research on a given topic, with an eye toward identifying what is known and what remains to be investigated. A good literature review is selective—covering the most important, methodologically sound studies—and it is integrative, highlighting areas of consensus and debate within a research field. Without such efforts, science would generate far more data than understanding. At its best, the literature review is a bridge between observation and explanation. If undertaken properly, it illuminates existing research directions and inspires new ones.

Although the exercise that inspired this book was a performance review and not a literature review, the aim was similar. I identified approximately a dozen of the very best traders I had worked with intimately over a decade of coaching and asked myself what made them tick. On the surface, they were quite different. Some were daytraders in the electronic futures markets; others were portfolio managers in currency and fixed income markets. A few were highly quantitative; others drew on pattern recognition in a purely discretionary manner. Some were outgoing, some introverted; some were highly emotional and passionate about winning and losing; others were relatively calm, cool performers.

When I looked at what these traders did, all I found was variety. When I examined *how* they did what they did, however—the processes underlying their decisions and actions—several common features leaped out at me:

- *Adaptability*. To a person, the best traders were adaptive and flexible. They were sensitive to market environments and altered their trading to fit changing landscapes. Often, they would quickly alter their risk exposure, sensitive to occasions when market action did and did not confirm their expectations. Even more broadly, they adapted to changing market regimes by learning new skills, broadening their trading universe, and reworking their analytics. What made them successful was not merely that they possessed a trading "edge." Rather, they had found ways of continually honing and expanding that edge.

- *Creativity*. The ideal for any trading firm is assembling a group of traders, each of whom delivers superior risk-adjusted returns in a relatively uncorrelated manner. Thanks to the power of diversification, that provides the business with a relatively smooth equity curve and allows it to leverage its capital effectively. Wherever I've seen successful trading firms, I've encountered creative traders: ones who view markets uniquely, find original ways to generate ideas, and express their views in fresh ways that maximize reward relative to risk. Indeed, I would venture to say that I have never known an extraordinarily successful trader who was not extraordinarily original in his or her approach to markets. I refer to such traders as "idea factories," as they develop robust routines for detecting opportunity where others see none.

- *Productivity*. My experience confirms the findings of Dean Keith Simonton's seminal work on greatness: The elite performers generate better ideas because they generate so many ideas. Their hit rate is not necessarily unusually high, but they go to bat so often that they get their share of good pitches and hit their fair share of home runs. Knowing that their strength is processing information and generating ideas—not just holding any particular idea—they are willing to toss aside less promising trades and hold out for truly exemplary ones. This productivity is readily apparent on a day-to-day, week-to-week basis: The greats simply get more done than their colleagues. They organize their time and prioritize their activities so that they are both efficient (get a lot done per unit of time) and effective (get the right things done). How much time do we typically waste as traders, staring unthinkingly at screens, chatting with people who offer little insight, and reading low-priority/information-poor emails and reports? The successful traders invariably are workhorses, not showhorses: They get their hands dirty rooting through data and make active use of well-cultivated information networks. They realize that higher-quality inputs will yield superior outputs.

- *Self-management.* I can think of few vocations that blend risk and uncertainty in as immediate way as trading. In many lines of work, good enough is good enough: Slipups are rarely irreversible or fatal. In financial markets, good enough is the expected, the average; it's not what produces outstanding results. Maintaining focus, optimism, and energy level during periods of drawdown is not easy. Nor is it easy to attend to life's many responsibilities when focused on fast-moving markets. Successful athletes realize that only very high levels of conditioning will allow them to deliver their very best performance. For traders, the conditioning is cognitive as well as emotional. Successful traders I've known work as hard on themselves as on markets. They develop routines for keeping themselves in ideal states for making trading decisions, often by optimizing their lives outside of markets.

Working with traders on a full-time basis, immersed in the daily realities of trading performance, has provided me with a front-row perspective on trading success. My overarching conclusion from years of coaching effort is that what makes traders good are best practices—sound methods for deploying capital and managing risk. What makes traders *great* are best processes: detailed routines that turn best practices into consistent habits. Adaptability, creativity, productivity, and self-management: These aren't just things that the best traders have. *They are what best traders **do**—routinely.*

The most important review you can conduct is not one of the research literature, but of yourself. If you place your best trading under a microscope, you'll initiate your own review and the chances are good that you'll observe how you best adapt to change, innovate, stay productive, and manage yourself. It is difficult for us to appreciate—especially during times of drawdown—that at some times, in some ways, we already are the traders we hope to become. Our task, in markets as in life, is to uncover the practices and processes that enable us to more consistently tap into the best within us.

Very few challenges are as noble or rewarding as fully becoming who you are at your best. Let the journey begin!

Brett Steenbarger

PRELUDE

I'm not sure when I first focused on the fact that time is an event. There are many events that help us define time, from the Earth's daily rotation to the radiation emitted by cesium atoms. We mark time with such events as birthdays and anniversaries; we think of a year in seasons and holidays. Waking up, eating, going to work, coming home, taking vacations—we live life in event time.

Suppose I am an athlete and my energy level is a function of when and how I practice and perform. Sometimes I practice daily; sometimes I take a day off; sometimes I practice very intensively; sometimes less so. If you were to chart my energy level over time, you'd see irregular ups and downs—seemingly no pattern at all. But suppose you defined time in terms of performance events. Suddenly we would have a new chart—a new x-axis—and regularities would become apparent.

It is November 10, 2014. I am in my kitchen, sitting at the center island, accompanied by the youngest of our four rescue cats, Mia Bella. I have just finished overhauling my market charts, removing time from the x-axes and replacing it with an event clock. Examining past markets, I find striking regularities—ones I had never seen before. Soon I will see if those regularities provide actionable insights in real time.

I've had interesting market ideas in the past. This one feels different, however. It feels like opening an animal crate that has been transported from a rural Kentucky high-kill shelter, picking up the soft, gray, purring kitten, and knowing this is the one.

Someone in the crate area watched Mia cling to my shoulder and commented, "She's chosen you." That's the way it is with all great things, whether they be life companions, career callings, or paradigm-shifting ideas: *They choose you.*

But you have to be ready to be selected . . . .

CHAPTER 1

Best Process #1: Adapting to Change

It is not the strongest of the species that survives, nor the most intelligent that survives. It is the one that is the most adaptable to change.

Charles Darwin

■ Emil's Restaurant

Emil is a chef who purchased a restaurant in a prosperous suburb. The restaurant had not been making money for the past few years despite having a broad menu, a friendly owner, and good standing in the community. The young couples that flocked to the suburb because of its superior public education system, convenient shopping, and low crime rate wanted something other than a traditional, sit-down restaurant. They desired a bit of the city life: a lively venue for eating, drinking, meeting friends, and socializing. The old restaurant was just ... too ... old ... and the owner could not keep pace with shifting diner tastes. So he sold the place to Emil.

Emil spoke with the new area residents to learn more about what they wanted in a restaurant. What he heard was that they wanted "fresh": fresh food, a fresh look, fresh music. He asked them to name some of their favorite urban hangouts, and then he visited the establishments. What he found was large bar areas with long tables, so that people could mix and mingle easily and share their "small plates." Few people at those establishments sat down for large entrees and multicourse meals. Rather, it was all about grazing and drinking and mixing with people in an upbeat environment.

Emil recognized that the market had changed. What used to bring in customers no longer was attractive. A growing portion of the dining population desired a social experience, not just a quiet, well-prepared meal. They enjoyed moving around and trying different foods, not sitting and feasting on a single main dish. Creative drinks and lively contemporary sounds were an important part of the experience. The new diners wanted more than the usual background music and traditional beverage selection. They loved upbeat electronic sounds, inventive mixed drinks, craft beers, exotic soft drinks, and a broad selection of unique wines from quality vineyards.

So Emil rebuilt the business. In place of the heavy wooden dining tables and chairs, he purchased modular, colorful seating that could be quickly arranged and rearranged to create a variety of environments, from open bar to sit-down brunch. Gone were the traditional pictures on the walls, replaced by soft, streaming lights that illuminated exotic woods, stone, and glass block. Cutting-edge music videos played on large, hi-def screens, amplified by a high-quality sound system. A fresh website, Twitter feed, and Facebook page alerted diners to the day's upcoming dishes. A photoset of dishes being served was uploaded each day to Instagram and linked to other social media.

Those, however, were not Emil's most radical changes. He decided not to change the old restaurant's menu, but to do away with menus altogether. In place of the traditional fixed menu supplemented with a few "daily specials," Emil committed to making every dish fresh every day, based on ingredients he could source that morning in local markets. If Emil and staff found a superior catch of fresh fish, excellent cuts of dry-aged beef, and several local fruits and herbs, the evening's dishes featured combinations of those ingredients. Each day, he and his kitchen team created an entirely new menu. The slogan beneath the restaurant logo said it all: "A different restaurant every day."

Freed from the constraints of a menu, Emil enabled his customers to order from tablets distributed by the wait staff. Now patrons could read detailed descriptions of each dish and its ingredients, enter their orders electronically, and send orders immediately to the kitchen. The tablets were readily available throughout meals, so that diners could order fresh drinks and even share comments about what they liked best and least. Those comments helped subsequent customers make their choices. Diners especially liked reading about suggestions for pairing dishes and beverages. As the comment base grew, the ordering system became a kind of internal social media site, where dining ideas were crowdsourced and regulars developed reputations for their food and drink reviews.

The greatest power of the ordering system was that it created a database for Emil. Over time, he learned what diners liked and didn't like. He discovered that younger males liked different drink/dish combinations than women in their mid-30s. He learned how couples ordered differently from single patrons; he found that the descriptions and pictures of dishes greatly influenced their popularity. Female customers preferred poultry and fish dishes to ones with red meat; older diners looked for quiet tables and several course meals; customers who ordered the most mixed drinks were also the ones who ordered the most specialty coffee beverages. Gradually, the database helped Emil understand which dishes to emphasize and which to eliminate. He created a different restaurant experience on weekend evenings than weekday afternoons: different food, different layout, and different music. Armed with continuous data from customers, he rapidly adapted to shifting tastes.

And the customers? They loved the up-tempo music, the clean modern lines of the décor, and the "cool" ordering app. The website gained traffic; Twitter followers and Facebook friends exploded: There was a buzz about Emil's restaurant. Were there setbacks? Of course. A customer dropped his tablet and shattered the screen. That led to new protective devices for each "menu." A few inebriated customers wrote inappropriate comments in their reviews, so Emil instituted greater monitoring of entries. Several older customers, befuddled by the newfangled electronic instrument on their table, needed to be coached on how to operate the tablet. That led to simple step-by-step instructions displayed on table tents throughout the restaurant. Each problem led to a fix, and each fix gave Emil an opportunity to show customers he cared.

Best of all, Emil was able to hire a superior kitchen and wait-staff, as people wanted to be part of this cutting-edge venture. He announced sizable bonuses for staff members who generated unique ideas implemented in the restaurant. One waiter suggested that the app could also take people's music requests, so that staff could play diners' favorite tunes during their visits. A junior chef further suggested archiving all the music choices, so that the database included the music selections for customers who completed a profile. Then, when each customer made a dining reservation, his or her favorite tunes were automatically added to the evening's playlist.

What Emil recognized is that adapting to changing markets means being willing to change who you are and what you do. The new restaurant embodied new practices (playing customers' favorite music), but also new processes (electronic ordering informed by crowdsourcing). In redefining dining's social dimensions, Emil created truly fresh experiences for customers and a distinctive "edge" in the marketplace. Thanks to a deep database tracking orders and preferences, he ensured that, in Darwin's terms, he was the "most adaptable to change."

Emil could only accomplish that, however, by embracing change. "A different restaurant every day" became both a challenge and mission. Staying fresh—never static—was the key to success. Instead of structuring the restaurant the way he wanted, Emil let the customers define the experience. His motto wasn't "If you build it, they will come." Rather, he figured out what made people come and built his restaurant around that.

■ The Single Greatest Barrier to Adaptation

By now you have figured out the relevance of Emil's restaurant for trading financial markets. As traders, we have ideas about how to generate returns from markets. Some of those ideas exploit macroeconomic trends or company fundamentals. Others draw their inspiration from technical patterns or carefully tested relationships among predictors and market outcomes. *Rarely, however, do market participants develop explicit processes for adapting to changing markets.* In that respect, we are like chefs who think that if we keep preparing good dishes, customers will forever line our doors. The failure to adapt to shifting markets manifests itself in sadly tone-deaf spectacles: portfolio managers chasing macroeconomic themes in markets dominated by the effects of positioning and sentiment; momentum traders playing for breakouts in low-volatility, rangebound markets; money managers adding to risk on "diversified" portfolios even as correlations and volatilities ramp higher.

In each of these cases, the result is frustration and potential emotional interference with future decision making. *The root cause of the frustration, however, is logical, not psychological:* It is the natural consequence of failing to adapt to a changing world. The restaurant owner who sold to Emil was probably frustrated with the business, but that is not why success eluded him. He was a good owner; he did what made diners happy. Unfortunately, he kept doing it long after a new kind of diner had entered the scene.

To be sure, there are traders with discipline problems and poor impulse control. There are also traders who act out unresolved emotional conflicts in markets, with predictably tragic results. But successful money managers do not suddenly morph into emotional basket cases. When we see mature professionals act out of frustration, ready—like the restaurant owner—to give up the business, there's a high likelihood that this is a failure of evolution, not merely a failure of psyche.

Key Takeaway

Emotional disruptions of trading provide information, often signaling the need to adapt to changing markets.

So why don't bright, successful professionals adapt? Why don't we, like Emil, embrace change and the stimulating challenges of renewal? Too often, the answer is ego: Once we are attached to a given reality, it becomes difficult to embrace another.

The previous restaurant owner *believed* in his menu. He was passionate about his cooking and customer service. And that passionate belief killed his business. He became so attached to—so identified with—his business model that he could not construct an alternative. He didn't *want* to become a different restaurant every day. He wanted customers to flock to the restaurant *he* believed was best.

Therein lies a considerable dilemma. Entrepreneurs need deep, enduring belief in their businesses to weather the arduous startup process. It is that belief that cements a company culture and attracts talent committed to the firm's mission. That same belief, however, can imprison us. It becomes difficult to embrace change when your very heart and soul are wedded to what you are doing. Ironically, the more committed we are to what we do, the more challenging it becomes to make the changes needed to stay ahead. Think of key innovations in the world of technology—rarely have those sprung from the industry giants. The mainframe computer makers were not those who pioneered the personal computer market; the personal computer makers were not those who popularized tablets and smart phones; social media has arisen more from startups than established software firms. Paradoxically, success can harbor the seeds of its own undoing once innovation becomes status quo.

■ ■ ■

A dramatic illustration of the difficulties of adapting to change can be found in a research study conducted in 1945 by Karl Duncker. He posed a problem to subjects in the study, showing them a corkboard wall, a box of tacks, a candle, a table, and a book of matches. The challenge was to use these resources to attach the candle to the wall in such a way that it would not drip on the table when lit. Subjects typically tried a variety of solutions, from trying to tack the candle to the wall to lighting the candle and sticking it to the wall with the drying wax. None of these solutions worked; none guaranteed that the lit candle wouldn't drip on the tabletop. The correct solution was to take the tacks out of the box, put the candle in the box, tack the box onto the wall, and then light the candle. People struggled with the problem, Duncker suggested, because of what he called functional fixedness. They were so accustomed to seeing the box as a container for tacks that they failed to envision its use as a candle holder. They were trapped, it seemed, in their mental sets.

Now here's the interesting part: Subjects facing the exact same candle problem *but initially shown the tacks outside of their box* had a much easier time solving the problem. Once the box was separated from its contents, it was not difficult for the study participants to perceive alternate uses for the box. Instead of seeing it as a container for tacks, they perceived it as an empty box. With a different perceptual frame, subjects were no longer functionally fixed and could shift their mental set and solve the seemingly unsolvable.

In our story of Emil the chef, it's clear that he succeeded, not by improving the old restaurant, but by shifting his mental set and redefining the concept of restaurant. The functionally fixed previous owner might have tried a host of menu and décor changes to no avail. As long as he stuck with the old definition of restaurant, he was bound to thwart the desires of the new generation of diners.

Emotional fixedness fuels functional fixedness. When we identify with a way of trading or a kind of analysis, we not only can't perceive alternatives: *We typically don't want to see them.* Many years ago, I spoke with an equity long/short money manager who was struggling with performance. He viewed himself as a master stock picker based on his ability to identify value that was underpriced by the market. This value orientation made him a contrarian: He liked good companies that were unloved by the Street. The problem was that unloved companies often became more unloved before the market awarded them the expected premium. The stock that was a great buy 20 percent off its highs became a burden to the portfolio once it was 35 percent below its peak. That led to agonizing decisions about selling good companies at bargain prices versus holding losers and risking poor performance and investor redemptions.

I suggested to the manager that his dilemma might be addressed by creating a relatively straightforward money flow filter for the names in his book. I showed him how each transaction in each stock occurred either nearer to the best bid price at the time or the best offer. This execution information, summed over time, could provide a useful indication of the degree to which buyers or sellers were accumulating or distributing their shares with urgency. By waiting to size up positions in his fundamentally strong stocks until they were showing early signs of accumulation, the manager could potentially limit his drawdowns and more effectively leverage his bets.

The manager looked at me in total shock. It was as if I had suggested that he solve his domestic problems by initiating an extramarital affair. "But I'm a stock picker," he explained. "That's what I do best. If I start doing something different, I'll never succeed." For him, stocks traded on fundamentals like boxes hold tacks. He was functionally and emotionally fixed: Any analysis that did not pertain to company fundamentals was suspect. From my perspective, a money flow filter for his risk exposure could have made him a more effective fundamental stock picker, just as the social focus made Emil a better restaurateur. But our manager did not want to track money flows and refine his entry execution; he wanted to outsmart the market and find unrecognized value. In a very important sense, he was looking for self-validation, not profit maximization. And that is a powerful barrier to adaptive change.

■ The Power of Flexible Commitment

Antti Ilmanen's *Expected Returns* text is noteworthy for its conceptual framework. In the book, he breaks markets down into "building blocks" and explains returns in terms of the interplay of these drivers. As an active trader, I look at different building blocks than Ilmanen, but the structural approach is similar. Starting with the vast array of technical indicators in the literature, I identify a small, low-correlated set of potential market drivers and assess which are influencing price action during the most recent, stable market period. Basic to this approach is the notion of *regimes*: What drives price during one period is not what moves markets at other times. When I place a trade, I'm not simply betting that the market will rise or fall: I am also making the key assumption that the stable (stationary) regime that has defined the most recent past will persist into the immediate future.

For example, in the regime for equity indexes that has been dominant during my writing of this chapter, sentiment and positioning have been statistically significant drivers of prospective price action. When equity put/call option ratios have been high and we've seen rises in cross-sector volatility and correlations, we've tended to see bounces in the S&P 500 Index futures. Conversely, low put/call ratios and modest volatility and correlations have led to inferior returns in the index. During other market periods, sentiment and positioning have not been so important to market returns. Factors such as momentum and market breadth have been far more valuable as market predictors. As Ilmanen notes, the drivers of price action change over time. A successful investor finds tools that capture a range of drivers and thereby harvests profits across market regimes.

There are many ways of understanding and assessing market regimes. John Ehlers, who is well known for his MESA work on market cycles, defines the time series of any asset as the result of a linear (trend) component and a cyclical (mean-reverting) component. To the extent that a market is dominated by its linear component, we want to behave as trend-followers. To the extent that a market is dominated by its cyclical component, we want to fade both strength and weakness. Success is not to be found in being either a *momentum* or a *mean-reversion* trader; perennial bulls and bears eventually meet with grief. Rather, the key to trading success lies in flexibility—the ability to adapt one's trading to shifting market environments—just as Emil adapted to the altered dining environment.

An important implication of this line of thought is that, once we define ourselves as one kind of trader, we sow the seeds of our undoing. If we identify ourselves as trend followers, we leave ourselves vulnerable to frustration in low-volatility, rangy markets. If we identify ourselves as faders of market extremes, we open ourselves to getting run over by strong momentum moves. When a market approaches the top or bottom of a range, the strategy that had made money in the cycling environment can now lead to ruin in a breakout mode.

Key Takeaway

The short life cycles of market regimes ensure that successful traders will be the fastest to adapt to changing market conditions.

This, for me as a psychologist, has been one of the greatest surprises working with professional money managers: The majority of traders fail, not because they lack needed psychological resources but because they cannot adapt to what Victor Niederhoffer refers to as "ever-changing cycles." Their frustration is a result of their rigid trading, not the primary cause. No psychological exercises, in and of themselves, will turn business around for the big-box retailer that fails to adapt to online shopping or the gaming company that ignores virtual reality. The discipline of sticking to one's knitting is destined for failure if it is not accompanied by equally rigorous processes that ensure adaptive change.

But how can we be passionately committed to what we're doing in the present and equally committed to leaving it behind as the winds of change begin to swirl?

■ ■ ■

When Chris and Gina came to my office to work on their marriage, they showed few signs of being a dysfunctional couple. They spoke in calm, even tones and did not engage in any of the bickering or defensiveness commonly seen among troubled couples. Nevertheless, they were seriously contemplating a breakup. The theme they came back to time and again was that they had grown apart. It wasn't the presence of any great conflict that led them to think about separating; rather, it was the absence of the bond they had once experienced deeply. As much as anything, they wanted to know: Where had it gone?

"Love doesn't die," the saying goes, "it has to be killed." In the case of Chris and Gina, however, it was difficult to find a murder weapon or even any murderous intent. Both were devoted to their children and household; both held jobs they liked. "We're a great team," Chris explained, "we have good times on vacations and no one could be better with the kids than Gina. But it just seems that something is missing. We don't go out like we used to, we don't do things with friends. We don't have *fun*; there's no spark. It's just not the same as it used to be."

I watched Gina closely as Chris spoke. It seemed she was uncomfortable with what he was saying, but she did not speak. Twice, she turned her head as if in deep thought and looked away from her husband. Finally, curiosity got the better of me and I asked Gina what she was thinking about. She looked a bit embarrassed and explained, "I just remembered that the kids' soccer practice was moved to the weekend." She turned to Chris, "We're going to have to get my car back from the garage.

I'll need it to take the kids tomorrow morning." Chris didn't miss a beat. He excused himself, whipped out his phone, and dialed the repair shop to make sure they didn't close early on Friday.

Like they said, they were a great team. And I had one helluva difficult counseling case.

■ ■ ■

It turns out that one of the most challenging periods for couples occurs when children first leave the home. Why is that? On the surface, the empty nest sounds appealing: ample time to socialize, pursue recreational interests, and travel! For couples who have poured themselves into family life, however, the return to couplehood can be difficult. The shared, daily focus on children is now lost. If there is nothing to replace it, suddenly there's no shared focus. Couples who thrive during such a transition are those who define and embrace new lives for themselves. They retain deep family ties, but now within a broader context of personal and joint social, recreational, and career interests. They sustain prior commitments even as they flexibly adopt new ones.

If you were to look closely, you would see that the most successful couples had already begun aspects of their new lives during their mature parenting years. As the children became older and more self-sufficient, the spouses began doing more things together and individually. They were not threatened by the developmental change in the family. Indeed, they anticipated and embraced it. The successful couples planted the seeds for their future.

The same is true of successful businesses. Firms that thrive nurture a pipeline of new products and services while they are committed to making the most of existing offerings. An automobile manufacturer readies the next generation of electric vehicles while still selling traditional gasoline-powered and hybrid units. A pharmaceutical firm knows that best-selling drugs will eventually go off-patent and conducts the research to find the next blockbusters. A baseball club scouts new talent at the same time it does all it can to maximize its current lineup.

We can only master the future if we embrace the fact that the present is temporary. To paraphrase Ayn Rand, successful people and organizations fight for the future by living in it today. For them, change poses a stimulating challenge, not an onerous ego threat. They pour themselves into their commitments even as they flexibly build fresh ones. That is because they create bridges from the old commitments to the new ones.

The parents' devotion to their children becomes a new devotion to adult children—and, eventually, to *their* families. A company's commitment to automotive excellence remains firm, even as the product line changes from gas-powered engines to hybrid and electric ones. Most people won't abandon a commitment to a cherished A in order to pursue a promising but uncertain B. Create a bridge between A and B, however, and suddenly what felt like discontinuous change is now a natural transition.

Bridges are the key to flexible commitment. Unfortunately, there were no bridges in Chris and Gina's marriage.

■ ■ ■

One of my favorite counseling exercises is to ask people to draw sine waves on a piece of paper, with about a dozen peaks and valleys. I then ask them to list their most positive life experiences at the peaks and their most difficult life experiences at the troughs. The sine waves run from childhood through early adulthood and the present. In a single view, the chart captures the peak and valley experiences of a person's life.

The reason the sine chart is so useful is that people, like markets, are patterned. No one life experience perfectly repeats another, just as no one market precisely replicates past ones. Still there are striking similarities: History, while not repeating, does indeed rhyme. Our lives, no less than any well-crafted novels or symphonies, express themes and motifs.

In the case of couples, we typically have multiple sine charts—and multiple themes. Each partner brings personal themes to a relationship, even as the relationship weaves fresh themes through the lives of the partners. A worthwhile exercise is to ask each member of the couple to fill out a sine chart for the marriage, identifying the high points and low points of the relationship. A comparison of the charts becomes quite instructive: It's possible to see, first hand, the degree to which the couple is on the same wavelength. Each fills out the chart without consulting the other ... then we compare charts.

Of course, good psychologists not only listen for what is said, but also for how it's expressed. You can learn a great deal simply by watching people and observing their postures, facial expressions, gestures, and behaviors. One of my clinical supervisors in graduate school used to ask students to watch a videotaped therapy session with the sound turned off. We then had to describe, as the tape played, what was happening in the session. I was skeptical at first—until the supervisor recounted the essence of one of my taped sessions without listening to a single word!

In the case of the sine charts, I watch to see *how* a person creates the chart. Some people immediately fill out the peaks, others start with valleys. Often, people will spend particularly long periods of time filling out particular periods in their lives—and skip over others. If someone agonizes over identifying a particular peak or valley, there's usually a reason why. An informative variation of the exercise allows each person to vary the frequency and amplitude of the sine waves. It speaks volumes when people draw huge peaks and valleys at certain life junctures, or when they draw multiple peaks or valleys in succession. My own chart drew relatively modest peaks and valleys in childhood; more pronounced ones in college and graduate school; and then a pronounced valley in the early 1980s and an equally significant peak in the mid-1980s; with a return to more moderate peaks and valleys thereafter. No Rorschach test could capture my personality as well as the charting of life-event volatility and direction. Those life-event charts, it turns out, are not so different from market charts.

Watching Gina and Chris fill out the charts told me a great deal about their relationship. Both readily identified peaks and significant valleys in their childhood years, and both identified their courtship and marriage as a significant peak, followed by the big peaks of having children. There were career and health-related ups and downs along the way, but overall their charts were not so different from mine: discrete periods of volatility caused by relationship and career uncertainty followed by the stability of meaningful commitments in both spheres. For them, as for me, crisis led to opportunity: Sometimes we don't bounce higher until we hit bottom.

That, however, was where the similarities ended. After the peaks of having children, Chris and Gina stared at their charts. And they stared. They drew small peaks corresponding to family vacations, job successes, and the accomplishments of their children and small valleys corresponding to financial and job stresses. That was it. What were supposed to be charts of the marriage were anything but. Why? Neither Gina nor Chris could identify any peaks or valleys specific to their recent married lives. They were great as a team, and they did a very efficient job of figuring out when to pick up their car in order to get their kids to the next practice—but that was it. The absence of peaks and valleys had created stability in their lives, and that stability was killing their marriage.

■ ■ ■

Over years of encouraging people to draw the sine-wave charts of their lives, one observation has stood out: peaks and valleys tend to be relatively proportional to one another. Like markets, people go through high- and low-volatility periods—and it's often the high-volatility periods that precede the greatest long-term opportunities. Consider the life histories of many of the Market Wizards interviewed by Jack Schwager: Not a few blew up early in their careers. It took huge valleys to force the self-appraisals and reorganizations that would eventually generate the significant peaks. This was a major conclusion of Thomas Kuhn when he wrote the classic, *The Structure of Scientific Revolutions*: The progress of science is typified by periods of gradual, incremental change within a paradigm, followed by accumulating anomalies (observations and questions the paradigm fails to address), and eventually followed by the upheaval of revolution and paradigm change. At those junctures incremental change yields to qualitative shifts: The science takes an entirely new direction.

A small example of paradigm shift in psychology occurred when the reigning framework of psychoanalysis gave way to more active, directive, briefer forms of intervention. Psychoanalysis was—and remains—an elegant theoretical framework with explanatory power. Freud's core idea was that present-day problems are reenactments of past, unresolved conflicts. The goal of therapy was to reenact those conflicts within the helping relationship, allowing the analyst to provide insight into the *repetition compulsion*. Once patients became aware of their repetitions, they could change those patterns within the therapeutic relationship and, from there, within their other relationships. As you might expect, analysis was a long-term affair, requiring time and effort to achieve insight, wrestle with conflicts within the therapy, and then work through those conflicts in present and past relationships. In the heyday of analysis, it was not unusual for therapy to require multiple sessions per week over a period of years.

Key Takeaway

Change occurs only once the accumulation of problems necessitates the reach for new solutions.

As it happens, people do repeat conflicts and issues throughout their lives—in their marriages and in their trading. What therapists found in their practice, however, were Kuhnian anomalies. Some clients described vexing, long-standing problem patterns and yet managed to change them within a matter of days and weeks—not months and years. Pioneering therapists such as Alexander and French and Milton Erickson began to explore these accelerated change processes and question core tenets of psychoanalysis. What they found was powerful emotional experiences could catalyze relatively rapid change. My life turned around, not because of any grand insight accumulated over years of analysis, but from the single powerful influence of meeting the woman who would become my wife and the children who would form my new family. Anomalies had built to a crisis point in my life, and it was out of the deep emotional recognition of personal, social, and career limitations that I became ready for wholly new commitments.

Once you grasp the Kuhnian dynamic, you can appreciate why sine-wave life charts with few valleys are not necessarily good ones. Mastering the moderate challenges of childhood and adolescence is what gives us the resources to meet the challenges of life's greater valleys. University of North Carolina researcher Angela Duckworth calls this resilience "grit." It's the ability to get off the canvas after being knocked down and still have a shot at winning the fight. Learning to master the small setbacks gives us the tools and confidence to weather the much larger ones. Without experiences of grit to draw on, there is no bridge-building to the future: Change becomes a threat, not a challenge.

And the peaks? Those provide the energy and inspiration that carries us through life's valleys. Often, peaks come from fresh experience: traveling a new career path, giving birth to a child, taking a very special trip. Those new experiences help us see ourselves and our world in novel ways: They open up new possibilities and bring fresh perspectives. One of my recent peak experiences was a trip with Margie to the Alaskan wilderness. It was beautiful beyond words. More than that, however, the trip cemented our desire to see more of the world and to make that a shared experience. In a very important way, a small boat ride to the base of a glacier helped us reorder life's priorities. That is the power of peak experiences.

So what does it mean when, like Chris and Gina, there are few peaks *and* few valleys? Between the ups and downs of life, all that remains is routine. The incident in my office was a perfect example. Chris was trying to capture in words what was missing from the marriage and Gina quickly shifted the topic to a child-centered routine. At other times, it was Chris doing the shifting. On one occasion, when Gina voiced a strong desire to keep the family together, Chris moved uncomfortably in his seat, pulled out his phone, and checked his market position. Gina stopped talking, Chris obtained his quotes, and the topic quickly changed to their mutual concern for the children. Nice, safe terrain—and more of the avoidance of change that was strangling the marriage.

The reality for Gina and Chris was that their children no longer needed to occupy dominant mindshare. Their kids were mature, growing up, and increasingly self-sufficient. Leaving home for college was soon to come. Many of the couple's routines, once glue for the relationship, no longer had a purpose. Without anything to take the place of those routines—without a bridge to the future—the couple foundered. The family had changed and they had not. They had a commitment to each other, but that wasn't enough. They needed a *flexible* commitment.

■ Flexibility and Trading

Ironically, no one should be able to do flexible commitment better than traders. We've all been in situations we're long and suddenly a tape bomb hits the headlines and inspires a bout of selling. What do you do? If the headline is credible and institutions are acting on the news, you very well might hedge your position, lighten it, or get out altogether. You're willing to entertain the possibility that this is a game-changer. The upward trend that you counted on is no longer a certainty. Great traders are not married to the long or the short side. They follow the market's cue—and that requires particular open-mindedness.

If we were to examine the thought process and preparation of those successful traders, we'd see that flexibility is built into their trading plans from the outset. Let's say a trader has built a model of the various fundamental drivers that impact currency prices—from trend/momentum to interest rate differentials to economic surprises—and receives a strong buy signal from his USD model. Our trader initiates long USD positions versus a basket of other currencies and knows that the Federal Reserve is scheduled to finish its meeting and make an announcement in the afternoon. Plan A for the trader is to follow the Fed announcement closely and, if monetary policy is unchanged and language is hawkish as expected, add to the positions on dips in dollar strength. Plan B, however, is to exit the positions and even reverse them should the Fed express unexpected support for monetary ease. At that point, historical odds from the model would take a backseat to the idiosyncratic risk of the present, as a dovish tilt in monetary policy would likely bring in a fresh class of dollar sellers.

So let's say, after moving higher early in the session, the dollar sells off sharply when the Fed notes weakening economic indications and expresses renewed support for a policy of restrained rates. Quickly our trader hits bids and exits the long positions. The dollar sells off sharply and then bounces feebly as stocks stay weak and bonds rally. The intermarket action tells our trader that markets are repricing growth prospects based on the Fed statement. Quickly exiting the positions has given the trader time—and mental clarity—to look for markets slow in repricing, so that what started as a losing day can yet become a winner.

The key to our trader's morning success is not just planning the trade, but *flexibly* planning the trade. It is the active construction and rehearsal of a Plan B that enables the trader to adapt to the unexpected message from the Fed. If the trader had held an unshakable conviction that the dollar had to move higher because of momentum or interest rate movement in his macro model, such flexibility would have been impossible.

But that is flexibility in a single trade. What if we as traders lack flexibility in our basic approach to trading? What if we are like pharmaceutical firms that fail to develop pipelines of new drugs as existing ones approach the end of their patents? *What if our entire careers lack a Plan B?* Caught in trading routines, we—like Gina and Chris—can fail to create our bridges to the future. Like the chef-owner who sold to Emil, we keep cooking the meals we love, until we wake up to the fact that people are no longer coming to the table.

■ ■ ■

The key finding from the sine wave exercise with Chris and Gina was the near-absence of peak experiences in recent years. It wasn't the presence of great negatives but the absence of positives that eroded their marriage. They were so busy climbing the family ladder that they couldn't see they were leaning against the wrong building.

So how does a psychologist help a couple like Chris and Gina? The one thing that *isn't* helpful is focusing on their problems. Both husband and wife already feel as though something is wrong with their marriage. They secretly—and sometimes not so secretly—harbor concerns that something is wrong with them. They know something is broken; more talk of breakage only confirms the negative identity that they have internalized in recent years as a couple. As a rule, by the time people come to a psychologist, they have gotten to the point of experiencing themselves as troubled. Feeling beset with problems and unable to control or change those problems, couples come to counseling in a disempowered state. Spending hour after hour with a therapist, delving into problems, subtly reinforces the notion of "troubled" and often unwittingly contributes to the initial disempowerment.

Empowering people through a focus on strengths is a cardinal tenet of the solution-focused approach to change described in *The Psychology of Trading*. When we are focused on problems and overwhelmed by them, we typically fail to appreciate the fact that there are numerous occasions in which the problems *don't* play out. These exceptions to problem patterns typically hold the kernel of solution: It's what we are doing when problems don't occur that can point the way out.

Key Takeaway

We cannot improve our functioning if we experience ourselves as dysfunctional.

Notice the subtle shift: The troubled person tells the psychologist about overwhelming problems and the psychologist responds by asking about exceptions to those problems—and then by pointing out that the kernel of solution has resided within the person all along! You see, if the solution came from the psychologist, troubled individuals would feel that they have a powerful therapist, not that they are powerful. Solution-focused work succeeds in large part because it reconnects people with their adaptive capacities: the parts of themselves that are not troubled and dysfunctional.

So the last thing we'd want to do with Chris and Gina is spend the majority of our time talking about what has been going wrong. But we don't have peak experiences on the sine-wave chart to serve as exceptions to their problem patterns. Indeed, their very problem—their deadly immersion in routine—is the absence of peak experience. How to proceed?

The answer, as I alluded earlier, is to create a bridge between present and future. What's the one thing holding the couple together? Their love for and commitment to their children. Will they work on their marriage if that would feel like taking time away from the kids? Of course not.

Without a bridge, they remain stuck in the present: They won't trade a known priority for an uncertain one. So we need a way to pursue the future while holding onto present commitments. We are most likely to change if our efforts feel evolutionary, not revolutionary.

I turned the conversation with the couple toward the absence of positives between them and how they thought that the absence affected their children. "What are you role-modeling?" I pointedly asked Gina and Chris. "If the children don't see you having fun, loving each other—being special to each other—what does that teach them about relationships? What kind of relationships would that influence them to seek out?"

I could see that the couple had never contemplated this. I wasn't telling them that they needed to have good times together to be a happy couple. Rather, I suggested that the relationship they had with each other would create a template for their children's relationship expectations. To truly be good parents for their older children, they needed to role model being a good couple. What they would do to enhance and sustain their marriage was one and the same with what they needed to do to role model the next phase of their children's development.

"Of course," I suggested gently, "if you genuinely don't feel positive things for each other, there's no sense creating a pretense for the kids. You'd probably be better off splitting up and finding good relationships that the children could come to appreciate and internalize."

Well, that was the last thing Chris and Gina wanted to hear! They could contemplate being in a marriage that wasn't working, but not working as parents? Never! The bridge was clear: The new definition of being a good parent now included being a good spouse. Their mandate was to pave the way for their children's next phase of development, not blindly repeat the parenting of the past.

So we began looking for those exception situations in which Gina and Chris were already role-modeling good things in their marriage: caring, trust, cooperation, and communication. Clearly there were a number of positives; the conversation picked up. There were no awkward interruptions. It was Gina who hit on the idea of bringing the children to see their grandparents and using the occasion to take an overnight trip as a couple. It would be family time *and* romantic time. Chris loved the idea and the two of them became animated as they planned their overnight excursion. I suggested that the energy they were displaying with each other in my office would not be lost on the children. If parents are excited and in love with each other, the home environment feels exciting and loving. What more could a parent bequeath a child?

This made huge sense for Chris and Gina.

Chris had come from a troubled, alcoholic family.

Gina had been sexually abused as a child.

They found each other and vowed that they would never hurt their children the way they were hurt. They would never take their issues out on their children.

Only when romantic love felt like part of their family commitment could they find a bridge to their future. They weren't willing to change, but they were very open to finding a better way of being who they wanted to be.

No amount of work on problems would have helped Gina and Chris. They needed to find the solution that was there all along.

So it is with many, many traders who find the future leaving them behind. They need to find the bridges that link old commitments to new, energizing directions.

■ The Rebuilding of Maxwell

I mentioned in the foreword that the immediate catalyst for this book was a review of ten of the top traders and portfolio managers I had worked with in the last decade. In a sense, this was my own solution-focused therapy. Performance coaches working with participants in financial markets encounter so much talk of failure, frustration, and shortcoming that it's necessary to occasionally step back and reconnect with all that is possible.

Maxwell was one of the top ten traders I had identified. For years he had been very successful trading intraday patterns in the S&P 500 e-mini (ES) futures market. His frequent refrain was that other traders were "idiots." They chased markets, put their stops at obvious levels, and otherwise replicated behaviors that provided Maxwell with a trading edge. I wouldn't describe Maxwell as particularly intellectual, but he was very intelligent—and unusually shrewd. He was an avid gambler and had an uncanny ability to figure out the other players at the poker table. He seemed to know when others were bluffing, when they were on tilt, and when they held the nuts. While he knew the probabilities attached to various hands, it was his keen perception of his opponents that enabled him to bluff, fold, or go all in.

Maxwell contended that the players in the ES futures were like rookies at the poker table. That's what made them idiots. One of Maxwell's key trading patterns was fading "pukes." When he saw the market breaking key support and traders baling out of their positions, he knew that fear was driving the trade—and that there would soon be an opportunity to take the other side. "The market doesn't reward idiots," Maxwell once explained. By fading the fearful herd, he knew he could make a good living.

When I had the opportunity to watch Maxwell trade live, I realized how he was so consistent in his performance. He sat and sat and sat for good amounts of time, waiting for the market to "set up." During this period, he would observe the flow of volume at various price levels. Watching a depth-of-market screen, he could tell when buyers were coming in or exiting at a particular level. If buyers couldn't take out a prior high or sellers a previous low, he would quickly take the other side. To no small degree, his trading was predicated on figuring out when traders were wrong before they figured it out.

Maxwell loved busy markets: The greater the order flow, the greater the opportunity to find those occasions when bulls and bears were caught in bad positions. Most of his sitting occurred during slow market periods. "There's no one in there," he would shrug. An important part of his edge was not trading when he perceived no advantage in the marketplace.

The bull market ground on, VIX moved steadily lower, and the average daily ranges shrunk. Maxwell found himself with fewer opportunities. To make matters worse, individual traders were becoming less dominant in the market, as daytrading lost its appeal to the public in the aftermath of 2000 and proprietary trading began its descent in the wake of automated market making. With fewer idiots trading, Maxwell's profitability began a slow, steady decline. Gradually he began to wonder if he was the idiot. With larger trading firms increasingly relying on execution algorithms to get best price, prices moved differently than in the past. More than once, he lamented that the old ways of gauging buy and sell levels no longer worked.

Maxwell's risk management was good, so he wasn't losing much money. He also wasn't making much, however.

Not many peaks.

Not many valleys.

The passion ebbing.

Just like Chris and Gina—committed to what worked in the past, unable to find a bridge to the future.

■ ■ ■

You don't just wake up one morning and discover your edge is gone. Rather, as with those Kuhnian paradigms, negative evidence accumulates gradually until it is no longer possible to ignore. The restaurant owner who sold to Emil did not suddenly come to work and find no customers. The erosion occurred over time, during which he did everything possible to boost traffic: Change menu items more frequently, lower prices, run specials, and so on. All of these were changes within the same paradigm, however: They were rearrangements of deck seating on a sinking ship. Incremental changes don't work when qualitative change is necessary. For the restaurant owner, qualitative change was a bridge too far and he sold to Emil.

How many years did Gina and Chris plod forward in a marriage losing its compass before the contradictions accumulated and it was no longer possible to ignore the absence of closeness in the close home they were committed to building? An object in motion, not acted on by any outside force, remains in motion—and people are no different. We are wired to conserve energy: Constant change would be disruptive, exhausting, and inefficient.

It makes sense from a purely evolutionary perspective that what has enabled us to survive would become our default mode, our status quo. Maxwell rationalized the decline in his profitability in many ways: as the result of stress, burnout, high-speed algorithms, and just pure bad luck. Each rationalization helped sustain the status quo. "Don't fix what isn't broken" is common advice. As long as we convince ourselves that we're not broken, we don't have to seek fixes.

Key Takeaway

Routine is necessary for efficiency; breaking routine is necessary for adaptation.

There is another reason, however, why traders don't quickly embrace change in the face of changing markets and opportunities. Even when we possess a distinct and consistent edge in markets, the paths of our profitability can be highly variable. Over the long haul—100 or more trades—an edge tends to be apparent, particularly if one is not engaging in high hit rate/high blowup strategies, such as the naked selling of options. Over the course of any series of, say, 10 or 20 trades, there are random series of winning and losing bets that can play havoc with our psyches.

Last year I wrote a blog post based on the P/L Forecaster that Henry Carstens posted to his Vertical Solutions site. In researching that post, I explored three profitability curves: one with no edge whatsoever (50 percent win rate; average win size equal to average loss size); one with a negative edge (50 percent win rate; average win size 90 percent of average loss size); and one with a positive edge (50 percent win rate; average win size 110 percent of average loss size). Over the course of 100 trades, we could see the edge—or lack of edge—play out. Along the way, however, were surprising ups and downs that were purely random. By running Henry's Forecaster many times, we can see how many ways it's possible to have a constant edge and end up at a relatively constant end point, but with extremely different paths along the way.

Traders very often overinterpret these random ups and downs in the P/L curve. When they have strings of winning trades, they convince themselves that they are seeing markets well and increase their risk taking. When they encounter a series of losing trades, they become concerned about slumps and reduce their risk taking. Those adjustments ultimately cost the trader money. Imagine a baseball player who gauged his performance every 20 or so at-bats. When he gets a large number of hits, he considers himself to have a hot hand and swings even harder at pitches. When he strikes out a number of times, he talks himself into changing his swing to get out of his slump. Both adjustments take the batter out of his game. Ignoring short-term outcomes and focusing on the consistency of the swing is a far more promising approach to batting performance.

So it is for traders. Someone like Maxwell is wise to not overinterpret daily, weekly, or monthly P/L. Rather, he should assess the elements of his trading process, from his generation of trade ideas to his trade execution, and seek to make incremental improvements. When the paradigm is working, the most constructive course of action is to steadily refine the paradigm.

The problem is that, once in a while, 20 trades turn to 40 turn to 60, 80, and 100, and evidence accumulates that the trading paradigm is no longer viable. Even a small edge is apparent after enough instances: That's why it makes sense to keep betting in Vegas when the odds are with you. If you go all in on any single bet, you court risk of ruin: That randomness of the path can take you out of the game. But if you bet moderately with a constant edge, more bets allow the edge to overcome randomness. When randomness overwhelms an edge not just over a dozen or so trades, but over a great number of them, then we have evidence that something has changed. Still, a trader like Maxwell can convince himself that this, too, shall pass.

Tracking your edge is relatively easy when you place several trades per day. What about less active investors and portfolio managers who might limit themselves to several trades per week or month? If trade frequency is low, an entire year of diminished performance could go by and represent nothing more than random bad luck in performance. Imagine, then, the trading firm that allocates more capital to the portfolio manager who has a good year and not to the one who underperforms. Those adjustments, no less than the hot hand/slump-inspired adjustments of individual traders, can drain performance over time.

It's a genuine challenge to track edge and randomness over small sample sizes of trades. If a strategy can be backtested objectively without overfitting historical data, it is possible to generate a reasonable set of performance expectations in the absence of recent, real-time trading. For a purely discretionary strategy, however, the sobering truth is that, over the course of a limited number of trades, we cannot really know whether performance is due to luck or skill. Michael Mauboussin writes convincingly about this challenge in his book, *The Success Equation* (2012), pointing out that our failure to recognize luck makes it difficult to objectively evaluate performance. An overemphasis on recent performance leads traders to place too much significance on recent runs of winning and losing trades, not recognizing the important role that luck plays in those runs. Whenever Maxwell had gotten to the point of trying to make meaningful changes in his approach to markets, he would hit a winning series of trades and convince himself that "the market is coming back." Only after hope was raised and dashed many times did he get to the point of seeking help. By that time, however, like our couple, Maxwell had gotten to the point of questioning whether he could, indeed, go forward.

■ ■ ■

Maxwell was not broken, just as Gina and Chris weren't broken. Like them, he kept doing what worked and stayed confident in his course even after it ceased to take him where he wanted to go. But also like the couple, Maxwell was doing many things well. In avoiding consensus and the herd behavior of traders, he was able to sustain a high level of intellectual and behavioral independence. His ability to detect ebbs and flows in volume helped keep him out of trades going the wrong way, even if it was now far more difficult to anticipate the market's inflection points. In the old days, Maxwell used to be able to point to a chart level and anticipate how the market would behave once it touched that level. Those days, he realized, were long gone. There just weren't enough idiots left in the market to overreact to those chart levels!

One of my favorite solution-focused exercises in such situations is to institute a review of winning trades. Much of the role of a trading coach consists of comforting the afflicted and afflicting the comfortable. When someone is afflicted like Chris and Gina or Maxwell, some comfort in the search for exceptions to problem patterns can be empowering. When traders are in denial, doing ever more of what hasn't worked, some affliction of comfort becomes useful. A review of best trades reminds discouraged traders that they are not wholly dysfunctional. Talents, skills, and experience remain—they just need to be redeployed.

During Maxwell's trade review, we found an unusual number of winning trades held for a short time. He referred to these as *scalp trades*. "I see what's happening in the market and I jump on it," Maxwell explained. It was when he tried to identify longer-term significant price levels and hold positions for hours or days that he was no longer able to make money. From the review, Maxwell and I could clearly see he had retained his reflexes—and his capacity for quickly sizing up markets. It was his thinking about markets and not his instinctive pattern recognition that was off. In scalping mode, he was all instinct—and he made money surprisingly consistently.

Shortly after the review, Maxwell joked with me about an email he had gotten from a guru seeking to charge big bucks for sharing his wave-based trading secrets. He reminded me of my earlier blog post making fun of the "idiot wave" and shook his head at the foolishness of traders who believed such obvious sales hypes. I quickly saw my opening.

"So, Max, if you don't use wave theory, how are you going to figure out where the market will be trading at 3:00 p.m. tomorrow?"

Max laughed and joked that he already had too many crushed crystal balls and was not about to dine on more broken glass.

"But aren't you doing the same thing with your levels that the Elliott guys are doing with their waves?" I challenged. "They're predicting the future and so are you."

Maxwell looked puzzled; he wasn't sure where I was going with this. "Besides," I continued, "you don't need to predict markets to be successful. What the review of your trades told us is that you're plenty good at identifying what the market is doing at the time it's doing it.

Why predict levels for price movement when you can identify what people are doing in real time?"

You could see the wheels in Maxwell's head turn. Predicting an uncertain future was what idiots do. His job was to identify buying and selling pressure, not anticipate it.

Pattern recognition was his bridge to the future.

■ ■ ■

Kahneman, in an excellent research summary, identifies two basic modes of thinking. One is fast; the other is slow. In *Thinking, Fast and Slow* (2011), he explains that fast thinking enables us to respond to challenges in the immediate present. If a car suddenly drifts into our lane, we quickly swerve to avoid an accident. That rapid processing enables us to respond to crisis. If we had to think through every aspect of what was happening on the road, we'd hardly be able to adjust to the flow of traffic—or avoid oncoming vehicles!

The problem with fast thinking is that it is surface thinking. We perceive something, rapidly assess its relevance to us, and quickly respond. In the case of the oncoming car, that's a good thing. In the case where we see an African American man walking toward us on the sidewalk and we quickly cross the street, that same rapid processing allows bias to drive our actions. Indeed, many of the well-known cognitive biases, such as recency bias and the availability heuristic, are the result of fast processing taking control of our decisions and actions.

Slow thinking, on the other hand, is deep thinking. When we think in slow mode, we observe, catalog our observations, analyze what we've observed, and draw conclusions. Such a process is less likely to be swayed by superficial bias, but it consumes a great deal of our cognitive resources. We can drive the car and carry on a conversation while in fast mode. It's unlikely that we could solve a complex mental math problem while remaining fully attentive to road conditions. That's one reason texting and driving so often leads to disaster.

For efficiency's sake, we tend to rely on the efficient fast system except in situations that call for deep reflection. As a result, many of our decisions and actions end up reflecting first impressions, not carefully reasoned conclusions. How many times do we analyze a market, plan a trade, and then do something different in the heat of market action? The problem is not a lack of discipline per se. Rather, our fast thinking brain has hijacked our slow, reasoning mind. Quite literally, Kahneman points out, a different part of the brain controls our fast and slow processing, sometimes taking control at the least opportune occasions.

If we think of two brains—two relatively independent information processing systems—then it isn't a far reach to identify at least two intelligences. We can be smart fast thinkers, smart deep thinkers, sometimes neither, and sometimes both. Think of very talented salespeople or highly experienced air traffic controllers. As a rule, they are not the most intellectual people—not necessarily deep thinkers—but they process information very well, very quickly, and very flexibly. The salesperson reads customers very well and subtly adjusts his or her tone of voice and message to the immediate situation. The air traffic controller doesn't think about each plane, where it's going, who operates it, and so on, but instead quickly processes the many planes coming in and out of a busy airport. This ability to quickly process rapidly changing information enables the controller to make split-second decisions that keep the system functioning efficiently and relatively accident-free.

Key Takeaway

How we think anchors how we trade.

Conversely, we've all known very bright, intellectual people who seem to lack practical sense. They can solve math problems and analyze situations, but then are clueless when it comes to reading the social cues of a dating situation. The engineer could tell you all about the construction and operation of a car engine, but it's the racecar driver who has the smarts to power the vehicle to victory at Indy.

We often refer to trading as if it's a single activity. Trading, however, is like medicine: a broad set of activities and specialties. A psychiatrist is a physician; so is a surgeon, and so is a radiologist. The skills required for each are very different. So it is in financial markets. Market making is very different from global macro portfolio management—and both are quite different from the trading of options volatility.

One of the things that make trading interesting is that it blends fast and slow thinking in myriad ways. At one extreme, we have the daytrader, who performs relatively little deep analysis, but who can excel at real-time pattern recognition. At the other extreme, we have the long-term equity investor who studies companies in depth and constructs complex portfolios that hedge various sources of factor risk in order to profit from the price movements of strong versus weak companies. In between these two are hedge fund managers that combine the deep dives of macroeconomic analysis with the quick processing of market trends and reversals.

My experience is that successful market participants rarely excel in both slow and fast thinking, but they almost always excel in one or the other. If you look at what makes them successful, what you find is that they discover ways to engage markets that leverage either their fast processing or deep thinking skills. In a purely cognitive sense, they play to their strengths. This was certainly true of Maxwell: His scalp trades were the result of considerable fast thinking skill.

Slumps follow when traders respond to market setbacks by switching cognitive modes. The fast thinker begins to overanalyze markets and loses further touch with markets. The deep thinker becomes fearful of loss and acts on short-term price movement. Anxiety and performance pressure take traders out of their cognitive zones—and away from their strengths. So it was for Maxwell. His setbacks began in low-volatility markets that were increasingly dominated by market-making algorithms. He convinced himself that he needed to adapt to these changes by widening his holding periods and trading more strategically than tactically. Instead of following the market tick by tick and gauging order flow, he looked to longer term support and resistance levels on charts and ideas coming from earnings reports, data releases, and recent news. All of these took Maxwell out of his zone: He *was* trying to adapt to change, but doing so by becoming less of who he was at his best. Fortunately, his scalp trades kept his fast thinking skills alive—and his trading account treading water—during this wrenching period of adjustment. Over time, however, his results were becoming more average because he was increasingly relying on his relatively average deeper, analytical skills.

What turned Maxwell around psychologically, however, was that he redefined his emotional commitment to trading. Recall Chris and Gina. What was their prime motive? They wanted to be great parents and provide their children with the kind of upbringing they never had. They could not change their marriage until they reached the recognition that they couldn't be good parents to their maturing children unless they modeled a good marriage. Now their motives were aligned. They practically leaped into enhancing their marriage because they were doing it now for a good cause.

Maxwell's psychological raison d'être was that he was the smart guy who profited from the idiocy of others. Making money for him was an emotional affirmation that he was clever, unique, and distinctive.

When he stopped making money—and especially when he saw market makers profiting at his expense—he began feeling like an idiot. So what did he do? He tried to make himself into a deep thinker, someone who would be smarter than others in a different way. Ironically, he was seeking affirmation by running from his strengths.

What the solution-focused exercise demonstrated was that Maxwell was successful in a number of his trades, but that he was successful by being more tactical, not by becoming a grand strategist. As with Gina and Chris, Maxwell embraced his strengths in spades once he realized that they were the path to his emotional success. A kid from the proverbial wrong side of the tracks, Maxwell had a bit of a chip on his shoulder. He was out to prove himself to be worthy. That emotional priority wasn't going to change. We just needed to align that priority with his best trading. That became much easier when Maxwell was able to see that, in trying to predict markets, he was being one of the idiots he routinely ridiculed. He was no more willing to be an idiot than Gina and Chris were willing to be bad parents.

I won't pretend that the work with Maxwell was easy. The turnaround did not occur overnight. A great deal of work remained to distinguish why some of his tactical trading based on pattern recognition worked some of the times and not at others. It turned out that further investigations of his trading were needed. What I found in breaking down his trades was that he was losing more on the short side than the long side—and this was in markets that had been in longer-term uptrends. Subtly, Maxwell was trying to prove himself by making himself into a contrarian. When he saw that this also was acting like an idiot by swimming against the tide, he became much more open to using simple gauges to stay on the proper side of the market. For example, he defined strong, neutral, and weak markets based on early readings of how the market traded relative to its volume-weighted average price (VWAP), preventing him from fading the very strong and weak markets. By expanding the useful patterns he looked at, he was able to leverage his pattern recognition strengths.

He came to me with problems, but it was his good trading that generated the solutions. Once Maxwell found a way to bridge his fast trading skills with the emotional driver of his trading, meaningful change could occur.

That is the takeaway: *We cannot change if we fail to tap into those emotional drivers.*

■ The Perils of (Over)Confidence

We know how to plan for change in our trades. So why do we rarely get to Plan B in our careers? The cases of Chris and Gina and Maxwell illustrate that our core motivations and commitments can lead us to act in ways that are ultimately self-defeating. Years ago, I worked with a very successful professional who experienced considerable rejection both in childhood and later in a bad romantic relationship. She developed a commitment to self-reliance, determined that she would never be hurt and vulnerable again. As a result, she moved forward rapidly in her career—and she remained lonely, unable to sustain long-term relationships. Her commitment to independence made it difficult to sustain emotional commitments. That couldn't change until she recognized, in her own experience, that she could depend on someone she cared about and still remain independent. A turning point in her therapy occurred when she did not perform a homework exercise I had suggested. It took a while to get her to acknowledge that she was uncomfortable with the exercise and didn't want to go down that path. Instead of exploring her "resistance" to the exercise, I congratulated her on standing her ground and acting on her instincts. We then jointly crafted a different exercise.

What helped spark the change was a relationship experience. She could depend on me—*and* be independent of me. Sometimes change begins in small ways, in a single situation, a single relationship. And many times it begins in ways other than talk.

It takes a while to get to the change point, however. Those anomalies—the consequences of doing the right things and now getting the wrong results—typically have to accumulate before we contemplate doing something different. It took that young lady quite a bit of loneliness before she was willing to reach out to a counselor she could rely on. After all, when our approach to life or trading pays off in the present, we build confidence in what we're doing. That confidence can become overconfidence. We behave as if we've found a permanent life solution, as if we can continue on in our present mode and never get hurt again: never live in a troubled household, never have another losing year. Maxwell wasn't just confident about his trading during his money-making years; he was so confident that he felt no need to analyze his wins and losses or adapt to changing market conditions—until the profits stopped rolling in.

Author Robert Anton Wilson has noted the similarities between those who are totally convinced and those who are totally stupid. He also pointed out that our convictions make us convicts: We become imprisoned by our belief systems. As we saw earlier, a trader with absolute conviction in a statistical model could face quite a loss when the present idiosyncratically deviates from the past. Commitment looks like admirable discipline—until it becomes a straitjacket.

Behavioral finance research finds consistent confirmation and overconfidence biases among investors and traders. A confirmation bias occurs when we selectively process information that supports our views. Overconfidence biases lead us to overestimate the odds of an anticipated trade or market scenario working out. An interesting study of South Korean investors from Park and colleagues looked at their participation on online message boards. As you might expect, their processing of information from message boards reflected confirmation biases: Traders tended to read posts that most agreed with their views. Interestingly, those with greater confirmation bias also displayed greater overconfidence in their ideas, tended to trade more often, and tended to lose more money than did peers with lesser conviction. Scott, Stumpp, and Xu reviewed the literature in 2003 and concluded, "A considerable amount of research suggests that people are overconfident, and that investors in particular are overconfident about their abilities to predict the future" (p. 80). Moreover, they found that such overconfidence biases are present across a variety of markets and countries.

Nor is overconfidence limited to the trading world. In their book, *Decisive* (2013), the Heath brothers echo this conclusion, offering a perceptive quote from Daniel Kahneman: "A remarkable aspect of your mental life is that you are rarely stumped" (2011, p. 2). They suggest a number of strategies for overcoming overconfidence biases, including *multitracking* (entertaining multiple alternatives) and actively considering the opposite sides of our beliefs. The common element among these strategies is cognitive flexibility. Once we are not locked into particular ways of seeing problems—that is, when we are no longer functionally fixed, like the subjects in Dunker's study—we can make better life decisions. *We cannot pursue an alternative future unless we first can envision alternatives.*

It is ironic, then, that so many traders—and even trading coaches—insist that we should trade our convictions and increase risk-taking during times of high conviction. Anyone following that advice is likely to take the most risk when they are most overconfident. And all too often that's exactly what happens: Locked into large positions with über-confidence, even flexible traders become inflexible, punctuating winning periods with outsized episodes of drawdown.

Key Takeaway

If your risk-taking mirrors your level of conviction, you will always be most vulnerable—and least able to adapt to changing markets—when you are most overconfident.

■ ■ ■

Take the case of Joe, a prop firm trader who contacted me following a prolonged period of losing performance. He had been trading stock index futures successfully for several years, but now found that his bread-and-butter trades were not profitable. Specifically, when he left relatively large, resting orders in the book, he found that these were invariably hit, with the market then trading quickly against him. "You can't win," he lamented in our initial talk. "If you don't get filled, you missed the move. If you get filled, you don't want 'em!" It felt to Joe as if someone secretly knew his positions and was pushing the market just beyond his point of tolerance. Of course, someone did know his positions: Market-making algorithms, continually monitoring and modeling the order book, could rapidly detect supply/demand imbalances and exploit them on very short time frames. A large resting order—in Joe's case many hundreds of ES contracts or more—was a sitting duck for sophisticated market makers.

A trading coach Joe had previously contacted had suggested that the problem was that Joe was not differentiating his higher conviction trades from his lower ones. If he were to clearly identify the confidence he had in a particular trade and predicate his level of risk-taking on his conviction, he would avoid lower-probability setups and maximize his performance on the higher-probability ones. It sounded good in theory, but worked poorly for two reasons. First, his increased size in his high confidence views led to even greater visibility and vulnerability in the order book. As a result, when I conducted a historical analysis, I found that his hit rate and overall profitability were lower for his identified high confidence ideas than for his more marginal trades. The second problem was that Joe was most confident when he was on a run. As a result, he would make money on one small trade, then another, then another, and then really size his positions only to have them picked off and wipe out his prior gains. At one point, the coach urged Joe to not lose confidence in his judgment: "You have to be in it to win it!" But it was precisely when Joe was in it that he was losing it.

My analysis showed that when Joe's orders or positions reached a certain percentage of the average one-minute volume trading at that time, the odds of his trades moving against him increased dramatically. During periods of high volume and high liquidity in the book, his trades—even larger ones—were more likely to be profitable. The solution to his problem had nothing to do with conviction—or even psychology. Quite simply, Joe needed to adapt to the new market-making regime and achieve more optimal execution by distributing his orders over time with as little visibility as possible. The change that Joe needed to make was not a psychological one; like Emil, our restaurant entrepreneur, he needed to engage the marketplace in a different manner.

So why is there such an obsession with "conviction" in the trading culture? Very often, the focus on conviction keeps people from pursuing change. After all, why do anything different if you're convinced what you're doing is fine? Imagine a soldier scouting enemy terrain. The odds are good that he will not operate on the premise of conviction. He will move differently through forests and fields; he'll treat every building as a source of potential threat and will remain ever-vigilant for explosive devices. In a changing, dangerous environment, conviction gets you killed. We can only glorify confidence in trading if we cease to view markets as dangerous environments—itself quite an act of overconfidence.

In part, our focus on conviction as a success driver may simply reflect the cognitive consequences of survivorship bias. In any group of traders, the ones who lead the pack in absolute returns will almost certainly be high risk-takers. Now, of course, the cohort of worst-performing traders will also include the high risk-takers. After all, few market participants blow up their books on small bets and low conviction trades. But if we're looking for the successful market wizards, we'll usually identify those who have made the most money and, if we talk to them, we'll generally discover that they went all-in on at least some of their trades. That hindsight perspective easily leads to the assumption that a defining element of trading success is supreme confidence and risk taking.

The problem is that supreme confidence rarely permits supreme flexibility. In previous writings, I've mentioned research pertaining to positive attribution biases. We tend to attribute positive outcomes to ourselves and negative outcomes to situations. So, for example, we're likely to pat ourselves on the back for a good market call when we make money, but complain about rigged markets when we're losing. Similarly, we tend to view ourselves in an unusually favorable light when we compare ourselves with others. A favorite exercise for a medical student class I taught asked the group to evaluate themselves relative to their peers on such adjectives as "caring" and "motivated" using a five-point scale, where 1 = much below average; 3 = average; and 5 = much above average. As you might guess, very few students rated themselves as average or below; consistently, 90 percent of the group deemed themselves to be better than average!

When I've given the exercise to groups of traders, the positive attribution bias has been every bit as clear. Most traders rate themselves as above average in ability, despite results that generally don't support such a view. When asked about the discrepancy between their self-perception and their actual trading performance, they cite their potential, their recent improvement, situational influences hampering performance, and the like. *The problem is that traders who overrate their abilities are not likely to be proactive in recognizing the need to adapt to shifting market conditions.* Joe viewed himself to be a very successful trader and attributed his recent poor performance to a "slump." That led him to seek help with his psyche, though what he needed was a way of adapting to an altered market-making environment. But the same overconfidence bias that can affect single trades can threaten trading careers. *Belief in oneself is necessary for success; flexibility in self-belief is necessary for ongoing success.*

We're now at a point where we can squarely lay out the dilemma: As traders, we operate in a domain typified by frequent, radical change: changes in trends, changes in market volatility, changes in correlations, changes in the strategies of market participants, changes in world events, changes in central bank policies, and changes in macroeconomic conditions. Consumed with the day-to-day focus on markets and need to manage risk, we rarely step back and manage change processes effectively. Like the couple stuck in their routines and restaurant owners struggling to prepare the coming day's dishes, we get by—until the rationale for those routines falls away.

Key Takeaway

Routine is necessary for efficiency; adapting our routines is necessary for effectiveness.

■ Tapping Core Motivations

Suppose you haven't exercised in a while. You find yourself becoming winded when you climb stairs. You don't have the same energy level, and there is a lack of flexibility to your limbs that never used to be there. You know you need to get yourself into shape. How do you begin? How do you sustain an exercise/fitness program, when you barely have enough energy to get through a busy day?

This was the situation I faced not so long ago. You would think that a psychologist who had helped many people make life changes and written numerous books and book chapters pertaining to brief approaches to change would be able to make a straightforward change of lifestyle to lose weight and get in shape. But no: One good intention and one plan after another fell by the wayside. Somehow I managed to do many things for work, markets, and family—but not for my body, *despite knowing quite well that I needed to attend to my physical needs.*

Such situations starkly illustrate that it's not a lack of knowledge or information that keeps us from making changes. All too often, we know precisely what we need to do—and we don't do it! We know we're supposed to hold the trade to our target level, but at the first wiggle against us, we're bailing out. We know we're supposed to exercise, but we stay sedentary behind our screens, drawing on ever-dwindling energy reserves.

A bit of self-disclosure: I can't recall the last time I sat through an entire television show. I attend very few parties and, when I do, I almost always leave early. Sunbathing on a beach? Puttering in the garden? Rare occurrences. Over the years, I've learned sufficient social skills to be friendly in group situations and attend to daily chores and responsibilities. But put me in a downtime situation for more than a short while and my head feels ready to explode. A physician recently asked me about my level of life stress. To her surprise, I responded that I rarely feel stressed. My one source of stress comes from feeling understimulated. If I'm not doing something meaningful, challenging, interesting, or exciting, I feel bored. Boredom feels empty. And, for me, emptiness brings its own kind of stress.

One of my poignant memories is attending a required school party during my middle school years. The students were listening to music, dancing, and talking. I sat at my desk, completely engrossed in a book I wanted to finish, William Shirer's *Rise and Fall of the Third Reich*. To the credit of the teachers, no one bothered me. I probably would have talked with people if they had read the book. But standing around chatting and socializing and leaving the book unread? It never occurred to me.

It's not that I'm antisocial. I enjoy talking with people—indeed, it's the essence of what I do as a psychologist. Talking with people in counseling, however, is different from hanging out with neighbors at the next-door barbecue. Counseling is an instrumental activity, in which people are trying to make life changes. I enjoy those kinds of activities. What could be more exciting that being part of a person's development? Much more difficult for me are activities that seemingly have no grand design. Send me on a vacation where I can encounter a new culture and learn about history, cuisine, and ways of life and I eagerly soak it all in. Stick me on a beach with nothing but sand, sun, and surf and I'm fine for 30 minutes. Then I want to *do* something.

How is this relevant to working out and getting into shape? Intellectually, I knew that I had to attend to my physical needs. I could feel the loss of energy and saw my productivity wane as a consequence. As with Maxwell, those consequences had to accumulate before I faced the need to make changes. Running on a treadmill or doing my reps in the weight room *felt* like boring routine, however, and so I avoided them. My commitment was to productivity and meaningful challenges. Spending time jogging the streets or curling a barbell seemed contrary to that commitment. At a purely emotional level, it felt like routine, promising more boredom than fulfillment.

Now the key question: If you were my psychologist, how would you try to help me? How would you help me tap the motivation to get into shape?

The solution-focused framework that we encountered in the work with Chris and Gina and with Maxwell is particularly relevant here. When you see a problem pattern, look for exceptions to that pattern. What were my exceptions? When did I tolerate and even thrive during routine activity? When did I feel alive and stimulated when performing normal daily tasks or engaging in everyday social interaction?

Scanning the outstanding exceptions to my pattern, I identified a number of occasions in which I performed routines out of a deep sense of caring and connectedness. Every morning I wake up early and, before diving into my work, greet our four cats, pet them, and feed them breakfast. Each cat has her likes and dislikes, and each cat has her particular feeding bowl. I prepare four breakfasts and serve them one at a time to Naomi, Ginger, Mia, and Mali. *That's* a routine I love. The closeness I feel with those purring friends is the best way I can think of to start my day. Similarly, I will spend hours searching through employment ads and reworking resumes if it will aid the job search for one of my children. When we go over resumes or practice interviews, it's not just helping them, which is important; it's also *doing something important together*. Routine doesn't feel like routine when I feel a connection, when I'm making a contribution, or when I perceive a deep purpose to the activity.

Suppose one of my children needed to perform difficult physical therapy as part of their rehabilitation from an injury. I would gladly join in the exercises and make the challenging therapy a shared effort. In such a situation, I would never avoid workouts, because of my deep commitment to my child. It's not that I would have to overcome procrastination. By tapping into a core motivation, I would encounter no emotional resistance whatsoever.

That's it: *core motivation*. It was Maxwell's core motivation to prove himself that led him to put prediction aside and maximize his scalping. It was Gina and Chris's core motivation to provide a great home for their children that sparked them to develop their marriage. *In an important sense, people never change: Instead, they find fresh ways to express the core motivations that define their life themes*. Solution-focused coaching works to the degree that it catalyzes those fresh expressions of who we already are.

Sometimes we find those fresh expressions, not through formal coaching or self-help efforts, but as the result of blind trial and error. One day I opened the door to my exercise area early in the morning, let the cats in, and used my breaks between exercises as part of my bonding time with them. I punctuated each segment of exercise with petting time with my friends. It was fun; I found myself looking forward to getting through the reps so I could have my playtime. After a few days of this, the cats became accustomed to the morning exercise routine. After eating, they now trot over to the basement door, ready for workout time. We've created a positive habit pattern—and, as it turns out, habit creation is one of the most powerful change techniques of all.

■ Why Discipline Doesn't Work

Once you get the idea of core motivation, you can appreciate why the usual ways we try to motivate ourselves fail. We can talk ourselves into New Year's resolutions, but if these don't tap into the core motivations that animate us, we'll inevitably leave them by the wayside. Does anyone really think that reciting affirmations, filling out journals, or any of the usual motivational aids would have gotten me into the exercise room? Rah-rah self-talk would have fallen on deaf ears, but the cats could get me exercising. If I had to share exercise with a rehabilitating child, that would have gotten me pumped for hitting the gym every morning. It took that core motivation of tapping into a cause larger than myself to not only overcome procrastination, but eliminate it altogether.

▌ Key Takeaway ▐

We procrastinate when we try to push a behavior, rather than allow our core motivations to naturally pull us.

Exercise is now a routine part of my morning, in no small part because it has become a routine part of the cats' morning. I no more have to discipline myself to exercise than I have to push myself to shower in the morning or put on clean clothes. The very concept of discipline implies that we are trying to get ourselves to do something. There is a self-division: a part of us that is aligned with a "should" and a part of us that is trying to turn the "should" into a "want." We typically lose that battle, because the "shoulds" don't speak to us; they're not aligned with those core commitments that define the peaks and valleys of our lives' sine waves.

If, however, we can create habit patterns that tap those core motivations, then we swim with our emotional current. Charles Duhigg, in his book, *The Power of Habit*, captures this dynamic effectively. Citing research in cognitive neuroscience, he explains how the parts of the brain that control our habits are not those executive centers that are responsible for our reasoning and planning. Recall Kahneman's distinction between fast and slow thinking. Acting on plans versus acting on habit is the behavioral equivalent of slow and fast modes. Habits enable us to engage in relatively complex behavior while attending to new situations. If it were not for habit, for example, we could never carry on a detailed conversation while driving a car. Habit frees our minds for those slower activities that require our executive capacities: planning, reasoning, and analyzing.

Duhigg illustrates that far more of our lives are dictated by habit than we realize. This makes sense in a purely evolutionary way: The more we automate our behavior, the more we can devote limited resources to challenges at hand. The problem with our traditional efforts to "motivate" behavior is that they call on our executive brains to change our habit brains. A much more promising strategy is to change habits by creating new ones. An alcoholic may not give up drinking buddies at the bar, but may well find a substitution and develop new buddies at A.A. A procrastination habit will not yield to reason, I found, but is easily overcome by a new habit pattern that taps our deepest commitments.

This is why much of trading psychology's emphasis on discipline is misplaced. As of my writing this, I have posted over 4000 entries to the TraderFeed blog. At a rate of one per day, that amounts to writing every single day for over ten years! But I don't write blog posts every day because I'm disciplined. I do so because I have a morning routine that taps a deep desire to meaningfully reach as many people as possible. Once you build the right habits, there is no self-division, no need for disciplining yourself to do the right things.

So how do we build the right habits? Duhigg explains that each habit pattern has a cue—something that triggers the habitual action—and a payoff. If we can find a fresh routine to link cue and payoff, a new habit pattern can be created. A good example would be the smoker who substitutes special chewing gum for cigarettes when the urge to smoke occurs. With repetition, the nicotine gum habit takes the place of the smoking habit. And that opens the door for a non-nicotine gum habit ... a vegetable munching habit ... and so on.

What makes the solution-focus effective is that it taps core life motivations as a source of new routines linking cues and payoffs. A medical student I worked with years ago was very bright and capable but struggled in school. He suffered from a social phobia and felt acutely uncomfortable in social settings. He performed well in the classroom, but froze up when going on hospital rounds with physicians and residents. Relaxation techniques and other stress management methods were to no avail. During his psychiatry rotation, a group of patients approached him about their concern for one of their peers. They were concerned that she might be lapsing into depression and could hurt herself. Most of all, they wanted to make sure the doctors did not release her prematurely. The medical student became concerned for the patient and took it on himself to seek out the resident and attending physician and initiate a case conference. His anxiety was completely gone, replaced by his caring for this vulnerable patient. Once he defined social situations as opportunities to get to know others and help them, he ceased responding with anxiety and instead felt enthusiasm. He didn't improve by battling his nervousness. Rather, he was able to engage others once he allowed a core motivation—helping others—to supplant his social fears. The implications for trading are significant: *We can only adapt to changing markets by finding fresh ways to express the strengths that brought us to markets in the first place.* We commonly hear portfolio managers worry about "style drift." But it is precisely style that must drift if we're to adapt to markets. It is substance—the essence of our core motivations—that must remain intact.

■ The Purpose of Purpose

When our efforts to motivate ourselves fail to tap our core motivations, we in essence push ourselves to become someone we are not. If another person—a boss at work or a neighbor—were to push us to do something we didn't feel was right, we understandably would be resentful. We might superficially comply, but our hearts wouldn't be in it. If we perceive a deeper meaning and purpose behind acts, however, we will labor long hours and deliver superlative efforts in the service of the valuable cause. That sense of purpose has an important psychological purpose: Like a lens, it focuses our energy, allowing us to summon resources that normally remain scattered.

Adam Grant, in his eye-opening book, *Give and Take* (2013), provides compelling evidence that engaging a cause larger than oneself enhances productivity. He cites the example of a call center, where telemarketers faced frequent rejection in their efforts to raise funds. Morale was low, turnover high. One day, the call center routine was interrupted for 10 minutes to make time for a short presentation by a person who had benefited greatly from the funds raised by the calls. In the months following the presentation, measures of call center productivity skyrocketed. Fueled by a sense of inspiration and purpose, the staff looked beyond the daily routine and frequent rejection and poured itself into making more calls with greater urgency.

What is interesting in the call center is that the traditional business incentives, such as bonuses paid for superior performance, were not especially effective in motivating behavior. It was when the staff perceived a greater purpose to their work that they delivered enhanced effort.

Several years ago, I worked at a trading firm that had been very successful and then fell on leaner times. The performance problems were puzzling: Many of the traders who were there during the successful years were still there and markets had not changed so radically as to negate the performance edges of those traders. As I spoke with management, a problem became clear: The firm, run by a new CEO and staff, was now tightly controlled by a small group of people. Management meetings did not include money managers, and the outcomes of those meetings were very rarely communicated to the risk takers. While this was done under the guise of allowing traders to focus on trading, the reality was that it alienated traders from their own organization. This showed up first in subtle ways—referring to the company as "them" rather than "us"—and then in larger ways, as company policies—including risk management rules—were violated. It was not an open revolt; the traders liked the company. It just didn't feel like *their* company. It was a company that employed them. When performance turned down and bonuses dried up, there was little residual loyalty. Several of the best traders and analysts left the firm, hollowing out the talent base. By the time the firm reached out to me, the problem was far gone. A vital, creative organization had become a dispirited one.

What Grant's work has found is that giving is surprisingly correlated with motivation and productivity. Managers who give of themselves build loyalty among employees, which then manifests itself as more positive attitudes and behaviors toward customers. Imagine how the scenario at the trading firm I described would have been different if the company had been run on the premise of servant leadership. Servant leadership is the idea that we most effectively lead others by prioritizing their needs. Think of parenting: Both authoritarian and distant parents generate resentment and rebellion among their children. When parents love, give, and care, children are most likely to want to please them and engage in the right behaviors. The servant leader listens before speaking, includes others in decision making, and takes active steps to ensure that work is satisfying for employees. Had the trading firm been run on those principles, performance challenges would have brought traders together in the service of a greater cause. The money managers would have put their heads together and generated ideas for management—and that could have led to very profitable decisions to deploy resources toward new markets and strategies. None of those things happened, however, because no one on the trading floor believed that the management suite would listen to their ideas. And they were right. Without a grander sense of purpose, the organization lost the very vitality that had built it.

One of the dramatic changes I've seen over the years is the tendency for trading at professional firms to be conducted in teams rather than on a solo basis. In the old days, managers liked to "silo" traders to ensure that they would not fall victim to groupthink and concentrate risk in overlapping positions. With the explosion of information and resources via the online medium, it simply became impractical for individuals to stay on top of everything needed by the business. Team building became an important adaptation, allowing money managers to better conduct timely research, stay on top of fast-breaking developments, and monitor complex portfolios.

With the rise of teams, however, a new motivational dynamic entered the trading floor. The focus was not solely on markets, but also on team functioning. Team members were accountable to one another: Experienced money managers mentored the junior team members and the junior teammates took responsibility for covering areas of the market that were not the specialty of the managers. Each team member had a vested interest in the well-being and performance of the others; after all, if the team didn't make money, no one would be paid at the end of the year! Among the better teams, this created a dynamic opposite to the one I had observed at the fallen trading firm. As the business became tougher, the teams rose to the occasion, spurred by a common cause. During discouraging times, teammates lifted each other up. During periods of progress and good trading, the team celebrated as a unit. Team functioning had given a new—and in some ways larger—purpose to trading. Caring about each other became an important way of caring about the business.

| | Key Takeaway | |

What you will not do out of discipline, you will do out of inspiration.

To be sure, not everyone functions best in a team and not everyone finds their core motivations in participating in team effort. Grant's findings, however, go beyond the "give and take" of reaching out to others; they speak to the power of tapping into any purpose that is larger than oneself. One trader I worked with at a small fund is flat out one of the most creative idea generators I have ever met. Not only did he immerse himself in research daily; his research was almost always out of the box, focusing on unique aspects of markets. During one period when the traders in his shop were highly focused on events in Japan, he was immersed in options data, researching ways of utilizing skew to create asymmetric risk/reward profiles for relative value trades. He did not work in a team and interacting with others provided him with more opportunities for distraction than giving. His joy was discovery and the intellectual challenge of finding hidden edges in markets. I never knew him to suffer discipline issues in trading—not because he recited daily affirmations or made detailed to-do lists, but because his ideas meant so much to him that he would never allow them to be compromised by ill-thought-out decisions.

At one juncture, our creative trader decided to meet with a trading coach at his firm. The coaching lasted for all of two visits. The coach proposed a standardized routine for placing and tracking trades—justified in the name of "process"—missing that the larger part of process for this trader was sustaining the creativity to find ever-new opportunity. The trader realized quickly that standardization would deplete his work environment of oxygen: He needed the freedom to innovate. As long as he was connected to a meaningful purpose, he could keep up with evolving markets. He needed innovation, not regimentation.

■ ■ ■

But—wait!—you might be thinking. If we change by reconstructing our habits, as described by Duhigg, doesn't that mean we *need* routine and standardization? How can we possibly maintain our own quality control if we don't make conscious efforts to consistently do the right things in the right ways?

For the creative trader, the answer to this seeming contradiction was that he had turned discovery into a routine: He cultivated a robust process for innovating. Think back to Emil, the restaurant owner who transformed the business. In continually polling diners, he learned their likes and dislikes and continually fed the information forward into the design of the business and the menu. This turned flexibility into a routine. Emil didn't have to motivate himself to change, because he found the adaptation process intrinsically rewarding. His sense of purpose was aroused by the opportunity to learn about his customers and better address their needs.

One of the most common questions I hear from traders is how to not become overemotional during trading, especially when losing money. Not infrequently, traders will lose money and become frustrated or anxious. Frustration leads to impulsive decision making; anxiety leads to paralysis. Both nudge the trader away from best trading practices. The underlying problem is that losses are viewed as threats. If risk management is poor, losses can be financial threats. If self-management is poor, losses can be threats to confidence and self-esteem.

Imagine a different kind of trader, however, who actively embraces losses. That trader operates under the assumption that every loss happens for a reason. There is something to be learned from every trade outcome—good and bad. The losses can correct our views of markets or prod us to examine how we are trading those markets. Losses have a purpose; they can make us better, if only we can learn their lessons.

Now, of course, the trader who embraces losses will not like losing money, but neither will normal drawdowns pose emotional threats. No trade is a complete loss if it can be a learning experience.

Note, however, an additional benefit to the embracing of loss: It turns trade review into a habit, and that in turn makes adaptation a continuous routine. If we are always identifying what we do right during good trades and what we could improve during bad ones, we now have become process-driven in our change efforts. *Flexibility has become our routine.*

I cannot stress this enough: Over the long run, you cannot succeed as a trader or investor if you do not evolve with markets. But your evolution has to be of the kind that makes you more of who you already are. We evolve by doubling down on core motivations and signature strengths—and finding new contexts for employing what makes us distinctive. Try to change who you are and you will fight yourself all the way and then wonder, amidst the resistance, why you lack discipline. We don't need to push ourselves toward a goal when we're drawn toward our calling. That is the purpose of purpose.

■ Turning Adaptation into a Routine

The challenge of adapting to change occurs on all time scales for traders. Change occurs during the trading day, as volumes rise and fall and trends continue and reverse, and change occurs across entire trading careers. I recently examined what happens to the stock market when a large number of stocks register fresh five-day highs. Until 2013, there was a distinct tendency toward mean reversion: After a large proportion of S&P 500 shares closed at five-day highs, subsequent five-day returns were clearly subnormal. From 2013 forward, such five-day strength tended to bring further strength—there was evidence of momentum. As central banks continued their zero interest rate policies and money sought a home in shares, a fundamental trading pattern changed. Traders who for years had prided themselves on not chasing moves, suddenly found themselves left behind by market rallies.

A simple example of how traders fail to adapt to change can be found in their placement of stop-loss points on trades. Surprisingly often, stops will be placed based on obvious support or resistance levels on a chart or at fixed price levels, determined by such calculations as retracement percentages of moves or Fibonacci levels. Invariably, I find, these methods for setting stops are fertile ground for trading frustration.

One reason for this is that volume changes frequently in markets, reflecting ongoing shifts in market participation. For instance, volume in SPY (the popular exchange-traded fund for the S&P 500 Index) can vary meaningfully from day to day. As of my writing this, the average daily volume in SPY for the past year is a little over 122 million shares, with a standard deviation of almost 43 million shares. Why is this variability important? It turns out that, over that year, the correlation between SPY volume and the average true range for SPY is a whopping .82. That means that over 64 percent of the variability in the day's price movement can be attributed to changes in volume.

When you think about it, that makes sense. The additional participants on higher volume days tend to be directional speculators. Their concerted action is more likely to move markets than the bid/offer participation of market makers. Low volume means that relatively few specs are in the market. As a result, the odds of a big move are reduced. Fixed methods of placing stops fail to adapt to ongoing, real-time shifts in the activity of market specs. If volume rises, the increased volatility will help ensure that stops are hit on random noise. If volume dries up, the lack of volatility will ensure that profit targets are never hit. What an adaptive trader needs is a method for calculating price targets and stop levels appropriate to evolving market conditions. Any uniform method is apt to underperform as market conditions change.

Key Takeaway

It is not enough to be consistent; you must be consistently flexible.

As I've shared on the TraderFeed blog, one way of staying adaptive is to track the most recent median market volatility and calculate the odds of hitting particular upside and downside targets should that median volatility hold for the current day. At frequent intervals during the day, adaptive traders can compare the present session's volume with the median volume *for that same time of day*. If we are busier than in the recent past, we can expect more movement and target more distant objectives.

That also suggests that stops should be wider, and we can take that into account in position sizing. Conversely, if we're trading slower than the recent past, we can be conservative in price targets and set stops accordingly. Key to this approach is a kind of Bayesian reasoning that updates estimates of volume and volatility with each fresh set of market observations. Without such a way of adapting to changing market participation, it's easy to leave profits on the table when trading picks up and fail to take profits in slower markets. That in turn can generate frustration and disrupt subsequent trading.

What is significant in the volatility-based setting of stops is a kind of process noted earlier: *turning flexibility into a routine so that change— adaptability—itself becomes a habit pattern.* This is a very important integration: The trader who adjusts targets and stops for updated estimates of market volatility is both disciplined *and* flexible. For traders, as for Emil the chef, the best processes are ones that embrace flexibility. You can be robustly process-driven *and* flexibly adaptive if you build habit patterns that enable you to identify and adapt to changing conditions.

■ ■ ■

One exercise that I've found useful for traders is having them build a flowchart of their trading process. The chart includes everything from idea generation to trade execution to position management. I don't set parameters: The charts can be as simple or as complex as needed to capture how traders make their decisions.

Two elements stand out quickly once traders complete their process flowcharts. First, some charts are relatively linear: They begin with A, move to B, proceed to C, and so forth, in a relatively straight line. Other flowcharts are filled with loops and if/then contingencies: If the market does X, then I'll do Y. If the market doesn't do X, I'll avoid Y and instead do Z. Very often, the highly branched and looped flowcharts include rules, not only for buying and selling, but for risk management. One trader I recently worked with included in his flowchart a number of branches that led to adding to positions versus taking positions down. He had created a detailed roadmap of both opportunity and risk. He had many more paths to his profitability destination than the trader with a simpler, more linear flowchart, in part because he had made position management an explicit part of his edge.

The second element that stands out in the flowcharts pertains to what lies within the loops and contingencies. For some traders, the branches in the chart pertain to buying, selling, holding, and standing aside. For other traders, the flowchart is not so much a single chart as a set of nested charts. One branch leads to a subchart that pertains to trading longer-term trends; another branch leads to separate decision trees that capture short-term, tactical trading. It's almost as if the trader is saying, under these conditions, I'm this kind of trader; under other conditions, I'm a different trader. A trader I've known for a while has what he calls his "core strategy" for stock index trading. When conditions are not favorable for that strategy, he gauges market conditions for other opportunities in individual stocks. The flowchart that consists of multiple flowcharts potentially captures a variety of ways to win, not just a single strategy that requires the market's cooperation.

Contrast a very simple, linear flowchart of trading with a highly differentiated chart with many nodes and paths. Which chart is most likely to capture the adaptive trader?

Can traders and investors tie themselves into pretzel knots with too much complexity? Absolutely! The short-term, intuitive trader will tend to have a less differentiated flowchart than an equity long–short investor. What would distract the "scalper" from a pattern recognition edge in markets might be an essential due-diligence process for a longer-term investor. I find, however, that even successful short-term participants require a degree of differentiation—flexibility—to their processes, even if it's only to map out how to trade quiet versus busy markets or rangebound versus trending ones. One-size-fits-all would work well in perfectly static markets. When markets shift from being more correlated to less correlated; more volatile to less volatile; more directional to less so, a Procrustean approach to trading inevitably leads to suboptimal results.

Think back to Emil the restaurant innovator. His flowchart would be very detailed, describing the conditions under which he offers particular seating, particular dishes, and so on. His motto, "A Different Restaurant Every Day," neatly summarized his commitment to flexibly meeting the needs of diners. Skilled traders I have worked with have similarly been different traders in different markets. Will they express their views through currency markets or fixed income? Will they hold for a longer-term move or tactically take profits to benefit from market chop? The good traders find multiple ways to win. How different that is from the newbie whose decision making is limited to a few mechanical chart "setups"!

The degree to which a flowchart incorporates branching alternatives and different tactics and strategies reflects the trader's ability to integrate flexible adaptability with robust, repeatable routine. *Problems occur when the market's flexibility is greater than the flexibility embedded in our processes.*

■ ■ ■

Try the flowchart exercise: Start with the ways in which you generate trade ideas and then capture the decisions you make regarding how and when you turn those ideas into trades and how you manage their risk/reward. The flowchart should capture how you prepare for the trading day and how you review your trading. Try to make the chart so detailed that a reader would be able to replicate much of how you trade.

How detailed is your flowchart? How many alternatives for making money does it capture? How well does it structure the times when you *shouldn't* be trading? How well would the process captured in the chart adapt to changes in market conditions?

If your process isn't flexible and adaptive on paper, can we really expect it to provide you with viable alternatives in the heat of battle? A good football team prepares a number of running and passing plays and flexibly draws on those to exploit the defense on the field. Our playbooks need a similar level of flexibility.

■ The Limits of Trader Discipline

If there is a shibboleth more common among trading coaches and traders than the value of taking risk more aggressively based on "conviction," it is the notion that trading success is a function of superior discipline. At one level, this makes sense: If a number of traders make use of a profitable methodology, it will be those that are most faithful in implementing the strategies that will achieve the most consistent returns.

Therein lies the rub, however. As a Despair.com poster wryly observes, consistency only matters if you're not a screwup. Once markets change and traders are now doing the wrong thing—as in the case of Joe—exercising greater discipline in doing the same things only locks in poor returns. Imagine a performance coach exhorting a mobile phone company to be more disciplined in its manufacturing and sales of keyboard-based smartphones just as touch screens and flexible graphical user interfaces become the consumer rage. Discipline is great for doing more of what works. *When the status quo no longer works, however, adaptability becomes the new discipline.*

Consider a different trading example. Years ago, I had found that the morning hours were my most profitable times to daytrade. A breakdown of profitability by hour of the day showed that, after a certain time, I no longer consistently made money. That analysis led me to focus my preparation and trading during my best hours and minimize my market involvement during later, slower periods. More recently, however, I found that my morning trades were not working out as well as they had previously. Despite my best efforts at consistency and discipline, the morning trades were yielding inconsistent returns. That observation—and the frustration of having what seemed to be good trades go bad—led me to carefully examine market behavior as a function of time of day. What I found was that many of the market moves I was anticipating were occurring during European and Asian trading hours, not during the standard US session. By the time I began trading in my time zone, anticipated moves had already occurred and, often, were ready for a natural retracement. Quite simply, liquidity was now distributed differently over time. I attributed this to the increasingly global nature of trade execution among "macro" traders and new intermarket relationships among international assets.

That hypothesis led me to investigate the relative dominance of macro/directional participants in global markets. After several false starts, I made progress by tracking the co-movement of asset classes (the degree to which different markets moved similarly at the same time). I was also able to gauge the directional appetite for stocks by identifying the degree to which above-average volume flows were dominantly lifting offers or hitting bids. Using a simple measure that combined money flows and asset co-movement, I could predicate my entries on how markets were moving, not just on the clock. As it happens, the morning returned as my most profitable time of day—only now the morning began at 3 a.m. EST! Anticipated market moves were occurring with the London opening, not just the New York one.

A narrow focus on discipline would have told me to look harder at my best patterns and trade those with flawless reliability. What I needed, however, was a *different kind of discipline*: one that told me to step back from what I was doing and reassess my market edge. In a very real sense, I had to embrace failure and limitation in order to sustain achievement. It was humility and open-mindedness, not any macho sense of confidence and conviction, which led to the adaptation. From that perspective, my frustration was not a problem: *It was emotional information*, telling me that I was pursuing the wrong path.

Frustration is the mother of adaptation.

Traditional trading psychology has focused on the ways in which emotions can interfere with trading. From that perspective, discipline is a way of minimizing emotions during the trading process. Experiences such as the above, however, illustrate the potential information value of disruptive emotions: *We can experience cognitive and emotional upheaval because we are no longer aligned with markets, just as emotional turmoil can nudge us out of alignment*. Not infrequently, the problem becomes a circular one: Rigid trading during changing markets leads to losses, which leads to frustration, which leads to poorer trading and even wider losses. If you are a skilled trader who has approached markets with consistency in the past and now find yourself beset with frustration, consider the possibility that your challenge is like that of the restaurant chef who sold his business to Emil: The market that made you money is now a different market. In such a case, further efforts at discipline are likely to yield marginal benefits. Discipline will help us climb the ladder of success more steadily, but in itself doesn't ensure that the ladder is propped against the right structure.

49

■ ■ ■

Let's get back to the insight that any market can be modeled as the sum of a trending component and one or more cyclical components. Once we detrend a market time series, it's not too difficult to identify dominant cycles during any stable lookback period. A stable (stationary) period is one that displays consistent behavior. If the period we are investigating includes wildly different market conditions—2008 and 2014 in stocks would be an example—then we are comparing apples and oranges. Before we can identify patterns or rules that the market is following, we need a stable period of analysis. Many times, traders looking for tradable systems overfit nonstationary markets, seeking universal patterns across very different markets. Within a stationary regime, we can identify how much of price action is attributable to a trend; how much can be attributed to cyclical behavior; and how much is unexplained noise.

Oren was an experienced trader who contacted me when he found himself losing money as volatility ground lower. What worried him was that he was losing in both his daytrades and his swing trades. Setups that had worked well for him in the past now left him struggling to stay even. Wisely, he cut back his trading size and avoided doing damage to his account during his slump. Still, as weeks became months, he found himself becoming discouraged, wondering if the market would ever "come back." Each day, he planned his trades in a disciplined manner and each day he credibly followed his plans, only to chop around in his P&L.

I investigated his core market and found a distinct uptrend, accompanied by a dominant cycle of 20 to 30 trading days. The optimal trading strategy was neither one of daytrading nor swing trading. Rather, the strategy best adapted to the market conditions was a core long position, lightening up around monthly highs and adding to positions around monthly lows. Trying to time intraday moves and weekly swings simply left Oren run over by longer-term directional movement. Out of his frustration, he found himself occasionally fighting the market, telling himself, "We're due for a pullback." This left him not only out of step with the market but also fighting the trend. Oren was adaptable, but only to a point. If market moves extended beyond a swing horizon, he could not make the adjustment.

Oren did eventually adapt, but interestingly, he did so by changing markets entirely. He found several commodities markets that moved on his time frame and taught himself basic pattern recognition in those markets. Faced with a mismatch between his skills and interests and the opportunities offered by his market, he retained his core strengths and found a market more suited to his short-term decision making. He knew he couldn't change his core cognitive style, so he identified markets that rewarded his particular skill sets.

■ The Emotionally Intelligent Trader

In my first book, I talked about trading from the couch: reading the nuances of markets as you would read the verbal and nonverbal communications from another person. That requires a degree of emotional intelligence. An important element of emotional intelligence is the ability to put your needs and prejudices aside and remain open to the signals coming to you. In that sense, emotional intelligence *is* a kind of flexibility, the ability to adjust your thought and action to shifting streams of communication.

If you are a therapist, you cannot respond to all your clients the same way. A fragile person in mourning, an alcoholic in denial, an executive seeking a career change—all require very different styles of communication. Parents know this well: One child may respond well to tough love; another may wilt with a single harsh look. Emotional intelligence means that you calibrate your communications to your audience if you want to make an impact. It also means that you have to listen before you speak, so that you can make the right calibration.

We've all had the experience of interacting with someone who talks at us, not with us. With such people, often you can see them formulating what they want to say before you've finished responding. Their need to talk is so strong that it interferes with communication. More attuned to their own needs than they are to you, they are singularly ineffective, whether as salespeople, parents, or romantic partners.

Traders who approach markets in a rigid way are not so different from the self-absorbed person who corners you at the office party. They impose their views on markets, not infrequently pontificating on politics, economics, chart patterns, or esoteric market theories. When markets offer their own communications—breaking out of ranges on increased institutional participation with an expansion of volatility, for example—those fixed traders are so focused on their own views that they fail to listen to the market's message. I've known traders to stay bearish through lengthy bull markets, ignoring clear signs of market strength and focusing instead on the frustrations of "manipulated markets"! Can you imagine a physician who is firmly set in his or her diagnostic preferences and ignores the presenting symptoms of patients? That physician would be open to justified charges of malpractice, as the lack of emotional intelligence would lead to unintelligent—and ultimately negligent—medical practice. Traders do not face malpractice boards; rather, they face the verdict of objective reality through their P/L. Losses are painful, but *they are there for a reason.* Very often, they can help teach us what we need to do to adapt to dynamic markets.

We commonly hear that traders should develop trading styles that fit their personalities. There is wisdom in this observation, as we shall see later in the book when we look at strengths. Indeed, one of Jack Schwager's key observations in the Market Wizards texts was that successful money managers possess different personalities, but all manage to make use of their distinctive characteristics in how they engage markets. Oren, the trader already mentioned, was a good case in point, finding markets that rewarded his information processing skills. Still, like the received wisdom about trading by conviction and the paramount importance of discipline, the notion of trading one's personality has its limitations. As we saw with Oren, sticking to a fixed trading strategy based on the predilections of your personality can be the very embodiment of emotional unintelligence. The restaurant owner who had to sell to Emil "traded his personality": He did what he believed in. Sadly, markets are not there for our validation; they don't care about our personalities or preferences.

Key Takeaway

Just as important as trading your personality is trading the market's.

Successful traders I've known in the commodities and rates worlds have been especially good at adapting their trading to market environments. Sometimes central banks aggressively ease or tighten, creating outright directional opportunities in the fixed income instruments of particular countries. Other times, central bank officials around the world may be on hold, so that patterns of growth and weakness across different countries will end up dictating future action or inaction. At such times, "relative value" trades receiving rates in one country while paying in another can be especially effective. Similarly, going long flat price in crude oil and related commodities can be a great move in periods of Middle East conflict. Trading spreads among products to exploit seasonal and weather tendencies can make sense when distinct macroeconomic trends are not present. How the expert trader pursues opportunity in markets changes with market opportunities. It is the emotional intelligence of reading opportunity sets and sensing changing patterns in markets that enables traders to flexibly adapt their trading styles. When markets become crowded and price action becomes choppy, the style may become shorter-term and opportunistic. When positioning has cleared out and new developments are on the horizon, the trading may become longer-term and more thematic.

Emotional intelligence in a relationship means knowing when to approach and when to back off, when to speak and when to listen. If we were to investigate the daily P&L of an emotionally intelligent trader, we would find occasions of trading actively and occasions of standing back. We would see periods of high-risk taking and periods of caution. All markets are not created equal: Some bring more opportunity, some less. The self-aware trader knows when "it's my market" and goes into opportunity-seeking mode. That same trader knows when "it's not my market" and preserves capital. One trader I worked with years ago traded very cautiously for most of the year, convinced that markets were—and would continue to be—difficult to trade. When political problems came to the European periphery, however, he drastically modified his views and aggressively traded those markets. He made his year in a few trades.

Now, to be sure, none of us is infinitely malleable. None of us can trade all markets in all ways. But neither are markets perfectly static. A worthwhile exercise you can perform is to catalog your best winning periods in the last couple of years and your greatest losing periods. If you study your markets during those times, you will most likely see differences in how those markets traded. A common pattern I've noticed among short-term traders, for instance, is that they'll tend to make money when volatility picks up and give back gains in slow, nonvolatile periods. This is because the short-term traders are often momentum traders: They need markets to follow through on moves in order to make money. An important step toward adaptation for such traders is figuring out how they could have made money during those quieter times. Perhaps they need to widen their holding periods and wait longer for anticipated moves to materialize. Perhaps they need to identify the stocks and asset classes that remain relatively volatile and limit trading to those. Or maybe they can track the relative movements of instruments and fade occasions when those get out of whack in nonvolatile environments. There are many ways to adapt; the psychological key is recognizing the need to adapt. Very often, it's the presence of those losing periods that can focus us on the need for renewal. *The emotionally intelligent trader views losses as teachers, not merely as threats.*

■ ■ ■

Jeff was unusual among traders I've known, because he made emotional intelligence his edge in markets. He developed a routine for identifying the stocks that were opening the day on unusual volume and movement. Many of these were "momo" stocks that had attracted considerable attention from the trading public. Jeff scoured Twitter, StockTwits, and popular trading sites to identify when his names had a strong and emotional public following. He only wanted to trade stocks that had broad public participation. His belief was that the trading public was prone to overreaction, creating profitable opportunities to go the other way. Thus, if traders were short a popular name, Jeff would watch for evidence of buyers coming in to meet sellers and he would quickly join the buying. If he was right—and he often was—the short covering would make his position a winner quickly.

What was unusual about Jeff is that he traded a single strategy, but found many ways to implement it in different market conditions. He traded the long and short side, and every day he was involved with different stocks. When there was good volatility in the market or when it was earnings season, he was more active. Other days, such as slow summer trading sessions, he traded the opens and ended his days early. When his day ended, Jeff never knew what he would be trading the next day and how he'd trade it. He let the emotional trading public give him his opportunities.

Because Jeff's trading process incorporated a high degree of flexibility, he had far more staying power in the prop-trading world than most of his peers. His behavioral edge was not about to go away, as there is consistency to the behavior of herds. When herds were active, so was he; in slow times, he could stand back. Most important of all, Jeff had become a great stock picker. He could scan dozens of stocks across several trading sites and generate a list of names to trade within a relatively short time. He felt no pressure to be long or short; he had no preconceptions of the stocks he should be trading. While other traders—trend followers or breakout traders—struggled during unfriendly market periods, Jeff simply adapted his strategy to market conditions. There were always stocks showing unusual activity, so he went to where the opportunity was greatest.

■ Readiness for Change

So how can we make the trading changes needed to adapt to dynamic market conditions? Let's consider the broader question: How do we make *any* kind of important changes in our lives? Well-known research from James Prochaska, John Norcross, and Carlo DiClemente (1994) found that personal change does not occur all at once. There are many stages to the change process. Initially, there is little awareness of need for change, so we remain comfortable with the status quo. The researchers referred to this as a phase of *precontemplation*. Only once old ways fail us and consequences accumulate is there an active phase of *contemplation* of the need for change. During that contemplation stage, there may be many initial efforts at change and many relapses into old patterns. It is human nature to gravitate to the known and familiar. Eventually, however, consequences become so acute that the desire for change morphs into a *need* for change. That leads to a stage of *preparation*, with initial, incremental steps toward change. Encouraged by the success of those steps, the person finally reaches the point of *action*, during which change becomes an overriding priority. Once those changes occur, the focus turns to *maintenance*: sustaining new, constructive behavior patterns and avoiding a relapse into prior, problematic ways.

If we look through the lens of this transtheoretical model, we can see that most established psychological techniques—and most coaching approaches in general—are aimed at people who are prepared to change and committed to taking action. Traditional helping methods are much less effective for those merely contemplating change. An important conclusion from the work of Prochaska et al. (1994) is that *what is effective in facilitating change for a person in an action stage of readiness is quite different from what is required to spark change for that same person in contemplation mode.* This is a principle poorly appreciated, even by seasoned mentors and coaches. It makes little sense to pursue action techniques when one is not in an action stage of readiness. Instead, if we're contemplating changes in our approaches to markets, efforts should focus on what we need to move from our current level of awareness to a point of committed action.

Key Takeaway

Many coaching and self-coaching failures result from focusing on change rather than readiness for change.

Diets are a great example of this principle: Most of us have contemplated going on a diet and many of us have started a diet—or two, or three, or more! We typically get to the point of actively contemplating change and preparing goals, but fail to sustain the leap from intention to action. Change efforts, as a result, become frustratingly circular: We take initial action, then relapse into old ways, suffer further consequences of stasis, and return to goal-setting and the desire to change. Similarly, it's not unusual for businesses to explore new directions and priorities, only to see those die on the vine as daily pressures dominate manager mindshare. Few of us consciously *choose* stasis—intellectually, we see the need for change and adaptation. As long as status quo is the default option, however, the gravitational pull of relapse becomes difficult to overcome. Focusing on action before cultivating our readiness for action keeps us orbiting the status quo.

So what stands between us and the actions we need to take to make effective changes? Typically, the missing ingredient is *urgency*. I may perceive the need to clean my house, but it is easy to put it off for another day. If I am desperate to sell my house, however, and know that someone has scheduled a second visit to make a possible purchase offer, I suddenly become quite interested in making the place look as good as possible. Spurred by the prospect of making a sale, I will experience no lack of energy for the effort. Urgency is the motive force for many successful change efforts. This is why professionals in the alcohol and drug rehabilitation field observe that people have to hit bottom before they're willing to give up their addictions. It's only when negative consequences have accumulated to the point of real pain that "want to change" turns into "need to change" and excuses lose their appeal.

A while ago, I spoke with traders in US rates markets who were scouring the job market. With global central banks anchoring short-term rates near zero, their traditional sources of market opportunity had dwindled. No longer able to make money in the usual manner by trading front ends, they foundered for a year or two before trying their hands at other markets. Now looking for positions at hedge funds, they found opportunities to be limited. The funds viewed them as beginning macro traders—not as traders with specialized fixed income expertise. Their failure to cultivate fresh sources of competitive advantage while their primary markets were still fertile left them unprepared for tectonic market shifts. By the time urgency had catapulted them to an action phase, their value in the job market had diminished significantly.

This is one of the key challenges traders face: *By the time "want to change" becomes "need to change," it is often too late—because that's after significant losses have been incurred.* Comfort—the antipode of urgency—is enemy of adaptation. After all, why fix what isn't broken? It is a rare trader who can sustain the readiness for change—move from contemplation to action—without incurring the consequences of hitting bottom. As we saw in the restaurant example, those rare traders aren't just ready for change: They love change, they embrace it. They draw immense gratification from the uncovering of new sources of competitive advantage, and so they're in a perpetual state of research and development. It's not mere passion for trading that animates the great ones; it's the passion to master markets combined with the urgency that is born of the recognition that all mastery is fleeting.

■ ■ ■

There is a great deal to be said for "fed up." When we say we're fed up, we have gotten to the point of disgust where we can no longer tolerate a situation. In my early adult years, I stayed in a suboptimal romantic relationship for far too long. I contemplated change for quite a while, and yet I did not make the step to end the situation and begin something new and promising. At one point, however, it struck me that it was precisely when I was in the company of my girlfriend that I was most lonely. It was a feeling of utter emptiness. We were scheduled to get together, but I couldn't get myself to get in the car and meet up. I lay on a porch outside one of the university buildings and stared at the sky for a very long time. From that moment, the relationship was over. I was fed up, not with the other person, but with the sense of being lonely in another person's company. Only when I hit that point of pain was I prepared to make a significant change.

Much later in life—indeed, not so long ago—my lifestyle consisted of getting up at 4 a.m. and working through the evenings on a daily basis. Weekend mornings were also set aside for work, as I kept up with markets and traders, as well as home and family responsibilities. Keeping long hours, I drank copious quantities of coffee to stay awake. I also snacked to keep myself awake, and once in a while I'd pop a couple of those analgesic tablets that consist of aspirin, acetaminophen, and caffeine. Gradually, I put on significant weight. I neglected exercise. My sleep quality deteriorated, as I woke up frequently at night. My work became less efficient, and I compensated by trying to work longer. But working longer meant more eating, more caffeine, and more fatigue through the day.

I finally got to the point where I was sleeping so poorly and was so fatigued during the day that I could not rouse myself to complete even the simplest tasks. Those willpower resources researched by Baumeister and Tierney (2011) were depleted. I simply felt like doing nothing. I was disgusted with the weight I had put on, but most of all frightened by my complete lack of initiative. I didn't feel depressed; I felt depleted—empty of reserves. It was a scary feeling. I knew in a flash that I could not sustain the status quo. I didn't want to ever feel that way again. In short, I was fed up.

That day, I withdrew entirely from caffeine and was rewarded with an epic headache for a couple of days. It didn't matter; at least I felt something! I stopped eating entirely for a day and then gradually reintroduced only the healthiest foods. Almost immediately, I lost some weight. I slept through the night. I regained energy and clarity of mind. My work became more efficient, and my nonwork time was far more enjoyable in an energized state. I began an exercise routine of alternating weightlifting, stretching, and aerobics, which further added to the energy. Someone asked me if I would be able to sustain all those changes. I answered confidently in the affirmative. It was not that the new eating and exercising so motivated me; it was the absolute determination to not ever go back to the de-energized state in which I had found myself.

Fed up creates urgency. We often won't change what we don't like, but we *will* change what disgusts us. A big part of readiness for change consists of a deep emotional connection to consequences. Think about the successful traders interviewed by Jack Schwager in *Market Wizards* (2012). Many experienced early career blowups; they lost just about everything through poor risk management and faulty decision making. It was those traumatic losses that turned many of the traders around. They simply could not tolerate another loss like the one they had undergone. Fueled by "fed up," they moved from contemplation to active change.

■ ■ ■

So what is your level of readiness for change? How prepared would you be if tectonic shifts were to roil your markets? Let's try a short self-assessment, consisting of seven questions. *It's important that you write your responses before moving on in the book*, so please take the time to think about and sketch out your answers—after all, we're talking about your future! A few sentences for each question should be sufficient for the exercise.

Self-Assessment Exercise

- How, specifically, do you expect your market(s) to evolve over the next several years?

- Where, specifically, do you perceive the greatest areas of opportunity in your market(s) over the next several years?

- What, specifically, has been the greatest source of threat to your trading in the past year?

- How would you need to change your trading to keep pace with the shifts in markets, opportunities, and threats noted above?

- What are you doing now, *on a regular basis*, to master the learning curve needed to exploit the opportunities and avoid the threats you foresee?

- What new markets or market information are you examining in detail to help prepare you for the future?

- If you don't have clear, specific answers to the above, with whom do you need to speak and what do you need to research to gain clarity?

Please continue, but only after you've finished your responses to each question.

This was a psychological experiment. Did you continue reading without writing or after merely jotting a few cursory notes? If so, by definition you now know something important about yourself: *You are not ready for change.* You are actively contemplating change—why else would you be reading a chapter on the topic?—but your readiness does not even motivate the simple action of writing. If you felt the need for change *urgently*, you would be willing to write a dissertation if it promised a better future. Without urgency, however, the effort it takes to write is like the effort required in the gym or during a diet: easy to contemplate, difficult to sustain. That's not because we're lazy, not because we have self-defeating complexes hidden in our past, and not because we don't truly wish to improve ourselves. Quite simply, we are operating on a principle that has made sense for us evolutionarily: conservation of energy. If an animal perceives a threat, it mobilizes a flight-or-fight response. If it feels safe, it does not waste energy. Procrastination is the natural result of perceived safety; nonaction is the default mode in the animal kingdom, saving resources for those occasions when survival becomes imperative. Think of a zoo, where threats to survival are almost entirely eliminated. Even the most active and ferocious animals in the wild, placed in utter safety, spend most of their time at rest.

Key Takeaway
Comfort is the enemy of adaptation.

Psychologically, most of us live in zoos. Our basic needs provided, we face few urgent imperatives. But markets are not zoos: There is no enduring safety in ever-changing financial environments. Most traders I've seen exit the profession had contemplated change for years, but never got to the point of tearing down the bars of their psychological cages and taking definitive action.

So what does it mean if you *did* write down your responses in detail? Clearly you have thought about change and are ready to act on perceived need. In taking the action to detail your thinking about the future, you show that you are past the point of contemplation. At the very least, you are in preparation mode—and most likely, you have already undertaken initial change efforts.

The pages to come will address separately the challenges of adapting to change for those in early versus later states of readiness. If you're ready for action, we need to go beyond stoking your sense of urgency. If you're not in urgent mode, no prescriptions for action will be relevant.

So for the moment, let's set aside change and adaptation. Let's first concentrate on how to take the step from contemplation to hands-on preparation. Then, for those of you who wrote out your responses and are in your three-point stances, ready to make changes, we'll explore how to best channel your action efforts.

■ Tapping the Sense of Urgency

In his book, *Leading Change* (2012), John Kotter examines how organizations can make needed changes. Not surprisingly, one of his first recommended steps is "establishing a sense of urgency." After all, organizations can become as complacent and comfortable as individuals—and often for the same reasons. Change threatens the status quo; it invites uncertainty. How many people languish in suboptimal jobs and marriages simply because it's too scary to face the unknown? How many companies cling to what used to make them money long after fresh opportunities have come and gone?

Kotter outlines several strategies for catalyzing urgency within organizations, including creating crises and bombarding people with information about opportunities. In the creating crisis mode, managers go out of their way to collect information about lagging performance and keep the information in front of employees. The idea is to highlight the unpleasant negatives so that employees hit a point of concern (and fed up) that leads them to take action. Crisis turns "I should act," into "I need to act."

Bombarding members of an organization with opportunity-related communications is, in some ways, the opposite strategy. By placing outrageous goals in front of people and showing them what is possible, inspiration can spark steps toward action. We can call the first strategy the fear approach: Nudge people into action by impressing them with the consequences of inaction. A physician who tells a patient what could happen to his heart if he continues to eat in unhealthy ways is using the fear motivator. Conversely, a physician might try to convince the patient that he will have so much more energy and will look so much better if he loses weight. This inspiration strategy relies on capturing the person's imagination and exciting them about the benefits of change.

There is an important respect, however, in which fear and inspiration are not opposite strategies. *Both nudge people out of their comfort zone by changing their emotional states.* The shift from contemplation to preparation and action cannot occur in a status quo mindset. It is necessary to shift the heart in order to shift mind and behavior.

Kotter mentions one effective approach: setting performance targets so high that they cannot be reached through business as usual. If those targets become mandates, they shake people up. Now the greatest risk is not change, but failing to change. If failure is not an option, teams will go to extremes to meet their stretch targets, finding creative alternatives that never could have emerged from status quo thinking and planning. You've probably seen the television show *The Biggest Loser* in which morbidly obese contestants publicly compete to lose the most weight. For years, each of these contestants was unable to lose weight on their own. Now, with coaching, the motivation of competition, and the pressure of public scrutiny, they make Herculean efforts to lose phenomenal amounts of weight. What changed? A fresh set of motivations engaged contestants emotionally and propelled them out of contemplation and into preparation and eventual action.

Think about the extreme training challenges that soldiers endure in order to become part of Special Forces teams. Few people on their own would sustain a regimen of sleeplessness, constant exercise, and harassment from overseers. But once in the program, bonded to peers and inspired to wear the insignia of achievement, the soldiers dig deep and find resources they never knew they had. How can it be that we can be so wedded to inertia and, at the same time, so capable of revolutionary achievements? Without emotional engagement, change simply becomes an object of intellectual contemplation. It is only when we feel the need and desire for change that we become committed—and then anything short of action becomes unacceptable. *Emotional change precedes behavioral change—always.*

■ ■ ■

Parents are very familiar with the challenges of bridging contemplation and action. Children often know what they should do, but other priorities get in the way. When our two youngest children were growing up, it wasn't easy to get them to straighten their rooms, do their schoolwork, and so on. Finally, we hit on the idea of creating "sticker charts." Each time the kids completed their chores for the day, they got a sticker. If they received stickers every single day of the week, they could redeem their filled chart for a "weekend toy."

Now, as it turns out, "weekend toy" was a big deal. It meant that I took Devon and Macrae to a mall and usually out to eat. We would wander the aisles together and they would get to pick out their favorite toy or game. The toy was only part of what made the outing special; it was also quality time for family, where kids were the total focus.

The sticker charts changed the equation for getting chores done. Failure to keep up with responsibilities led to an alert: no sticker, no weekend toy outing. The alert, however, was delivered in a positive way: "I really would like to go out with you this weekend. C'mon, let's make up your bed!" Suddenly an onerous and boring chore turned into an interpersonal bonding. It was easy to make the bed when a fun outing was on the horizon!

But there was an even more subtle motivation: Worse than not getting a sticker was being the only one to not get the sticker. How would Devon feel if Crae earned all his stickers and got to go to the mall while she stayed home? That was not going to happen. With that as a consequence, I couldn't stop her from earning her stickers.

In the parenting example, *what moves the child from contemplation to action is an emotional shift*: The task is redefined so that it engages a core strength and motivation. Had I had poor relationships with the kids, the idea of a weekend outing would have been worthless. I also suspect that merely leaving a toy on the table for each child after the chart was filled would have lost its motivational influence. Eventually, you get so many toys that each subsequent one becomes less valuable. It was turning chores into relationship opportunities and the fun of rummaging through bins and finding the right toy that supplied the energy for changed behavior.

Key Takeaway

Without the energy of emotional buy-in, goals are mere intentions.

Most of us make use of this principle without realizing it. If I have to get through boring and onerous work, I will sometimes strike a deal with Margie: If the work is finished by the end of the afternoon, we'll go out somewhere fun for the evening. That creates an incentive—going out is infinitely appealing compared with much paperwork—but it also taps a second motivation. The goal is now a shared one. Margie looks forward to the evening out and, if there's one thing I don't want to do, it's disappoint her. Left to my own devices, perhaps I'd let work expand to fill the time allotted and crawl through the workload by the end of the day. With this new incentive, however, I'm energized to finish as early as possible.

This works because I am substituting a higher, stronger motivation for a lesser one. Often, when we perceive a need for change and action but don't act, it's because we're tapping into the wrong motivations. By restructuring our approach to the activity, we can move the gearshift from contemplation to vigorous activity. Crisis is a powerful catalyst for emotional change, as I found out when I realized I needed to change my lifestyle. *But we don't need to hit a point of crisis to move us to action. All we need to do is tap into a motivation that moves us already.*

■ See-Feel-Change: The Importance of Optimism

Kotter and Cohen, in their book, *The Heart of Change* (2002), make an important point. They observe our tendency to pursue change through a process of "analyze-think-change." While analysis can help guide a change process, rarely will analyzing and thinking produce the emotional shift needed to move people to a sustainable state of readiness for action. Kotter and Cohen suggest that a more effective change process is "see-feel-change." When we see something that engages us emotionally—inspires us, or perhaps stokes our fear—we feel a sense of urgency and a need to act. Recall the talk given to the call center workers described by Adam Grant (2013). When the workers heard an inspiring story from someone who benefitted from their sales efforts, those efforts picked up materially. A mere process of analyzing and thinking about one's productivity would not have carried the emotional force of that single, short talk.

See-feel-change is crucially important to traders looking to adapt to changing markets. One way to see and feel is to lose so much money failing to adapt that you hit a crisis point and are forced to change or quit altogether. That is not an attractive option. The alternative is to see and feel something so interesting and promising that it inspires you to research, test, and incorporate it into your trading repertoire. Analyze-think is critical to knowing what to incorporate and what to filter out, but before you analyze-think, it's necessary to see-feel. Without that emotional shift of gears that moves you, the odds are good that you won't move. Recall our couple, Gina and Chris. For years, they did not address their waning relationship. Once they shifted gears and focused on the need to role model something positive for their children, they moved directly into action mode.

In their book, *Switch: How to Change Things When Change Is Hard*, Chip and Dan Heath (2011) provide a useful framework for putting see-feel-change into practice. A very important point that they make is that small wins can set the ball rolling for large changes. It is not uncommon for traders to reach out to me only after they have sustained painful losses and/or protracted periods of failing to make money. By that time, they are discouraged and perhaps contemplating leaving the business altogether. That's a difficult place to be, because discouraged people typically can't muster the energy to overhaul themselves and their practices. You may recall from your college psychology classes, Seligman's classic research on learned helplessness. Rats put in cages divided by a low barrier were exposed to an electric shock on the floor of one side of the barrier. It didn't take long for the rats to jump over the barrier and go to the unshocked side. When placed in a different cage where both sides of the barrier were shocked, the rats would jump, get shocked, jump again, get shocked, and eventually give up on jumping, collapsing on the floor and whimpering. Once the collapsed rats were returned to the original cage, what happened? They didn't jump over the barrier. They learned, Seligman suggested, that they were helpless. They learned that they could not change their situation, so they failed to attempt change even when change was easy to achieve.

This situation is not so different from that of the troubled trader. Like the restaurant owner who sold to Emil, traders give up the business when they no longer believe they can avoid the shocks of market setbacks. When Seligman physically moved the helpless rats over the barrier to the unshocked side, they eventually learned to go over on their own. They needed to see—in their own experience—that their actions could make a difference. The small wins described by the Heaths enable a trader to see that success is possible. That recognition brings a new feeling and energy. See-feel-change. "When you engineer early successes," the Heaths observe, "what you're really doing is engineering hope."

Traders who contemplate change but cannot sustain preparation and action typically are caught in analyze-think-change mode, rather than see-feel-change. They think about their problems and lament their problems, but none of that builds hope and optimism. Only seeing the possibility of success in a first-hand way provides the emotional fuel to inspire change. Recall the analyses of successful trading I undertook with Maxwell. Was it the brilliance of those analyses that sparked his change? Of course not. He had been lagging in his performance and my analyses merely showed him that he was, indeed, trading very well at times. The emotional recognition that he was trading well even in his slump roused him to look deeper into the sources of his success and do more of what was already working.

The Heaths point out that this is one of the important strengths of a solution-focused approach to change. As we've seen, if a trader is mired in a drawdown, problem-focused talk—endlessly analyzing and discussing what has been going wrong—yields little inspiration value, even if it does bring intellectual insight. That same trader, shown exceptions to the drawdown, suddenly realizes, "Hold on a minute, maybe I *can* do this. Perhaps my situation isn't as hopeless as it seems." Ken Howard and colleagues have studied the process of psychotherapeutic change: how people make changes when they work with a mental health professional. Their research identified a first step of "remoralization" before there was any "rehabilitation." Prior to any behavior change, there was an emotional shift toward hope and optimism.

My work in brief therapy identified precisely such a change trajectory. Reviewing the major approaches to short-term treatment, I found that a common element was what I called a *translation*—a unique perspective from which people could view themselves and their problems. Psycho-dynamic therapies translate people's problems into patterns grounded in their past; cognitive therapies translate problems into dysfunctional thought patterns, and so on. A curious finding in the psychotherapy outcome literature is that all the major therapies appear to be more effective in generating change than no therapy at all, but none of the therapies appear to be more effective than the others across all people and problems. That has led researchers to propose the idea that perhaps there are common factors accounting for the effectiveness of the therapies. It's not what analysts do differently from behaviorists or family therapists that contributes to change; it's what all the major approaches are doing that makes them work. One of those common factors is that remoralization described by Howard and colleagues: By translating problems into new terms for a person who feels hopeless and helpless, the therapist helps instill the idea that solutions may indeed be possible. This brings a greater sense of optimism and control. It is not so different from Seligman's guiding the helpless rats to the unshocked sides of the cages.

In that sense, any form of coaching, counseling, or therapy is a method of creating see-feel-change. Through the power of a positive relationship, we learn to see ourselves through a different set of eyes. That new seeing creates a new feeling and an emotional shift of gears that moves contemplation to action.

Key Takeaway

To feel differently, you must see differently.

So let's go back to our exercise and the questions you were asked to answer. If you did not write down your responses per the instructions, does it mean you're lazy or disinterested in change? Not at all. It means that the way you are currently seeing your situation is not generating the feeling—the urgency—needed to move to action. It's going to take an emotional shift of gears—either a jolt of fear or a burst of hope—to move you to action.

■ ■ ■

As I've been writing this, my Siamese cat Naomi has been by my side. She uses my computer bag as a bed, so she spends a lazy afternoon in the bag while I type away. Once in a while I pet her or call to her, but she pretty much keeps eyes closed and remains at rest. Suddenly, a fly came buzzing by the kitchen island where we were sitting. Naomi immediately raised her head and watched the fly. She tensed her body, leapt off the island, and pursued the new moving object. She is now sitting behind me, along the window wall, intently watching for the fly. In a moment, she was transformed from slumbering, lazy animal to action-oriented huntress.

Seeing this, my mind goes back to our initial adoption of Naomi as a traumatized kitten. It was a pathetic spectacle when we took delivery of the kitten in a crate. She was cowering at the far corner, literally shaking. We never found out what had happened to her, but we strongly suspected someone had mistreated her. She was intensely afraid of people—anyone.

It became a real problem when we brought Naomi home. She cowered under furniture, scampered into rooms where she could be alone, and did everything she could to keep herself hidden. On those occasions when we could get close, she shook violently. This was more than fear—it was terror.

The first piece of progress came when I went into the bathroom with Naomi and closed the door. There was no place to hide, so she leaped up onto the window sill and slipped behind the curtain. I quietly went over to her and touched her, then retreated. After doing this many times, I was able to get her to the point where she no longer shook. She accepted food from me and that became a way to get her out in the open.

The breakthrough occurred when Naomi was on the bed, enticed by food. I put my hand under the cover and moved it around and—just as with the fly—Naomi's eyes got large. She arched her body and went after my hand. She was so intent on hunting the moving thing under the bedcovers that she forgot to be fearful!

That's when I realized that our newest household member had taught me a valuable lesson about change. When we are in our normal state of mind and body, acting on our normal motivations, nothing changes. When everything is normal, our behavior gravitates to our norm. *If, however, we can substitute a stronger motivation for the one that leaves us passive, procrastinating, or troubled, the fresh energy sparks behavior that previously had been elusive.*

When I worked in a community mental health clinic in upstate New York, I met several veterans of Alcoholics Anonymous who had hit bottom and emerged with a deep religious faith. This was not a gradual, planned process. Rather, it came as a blinding insight, more like a revelation than a reasoned conclusion. So powerful was this feeling of being touched by the Lord that it literally reorganized thoughts, feelings, actions, and priorities. Desires to drink did recur, but now in the context of a far more powerful set of desires and commitments. What broke the cycle of contemplation, initial change, and relapse was a greater motivation that supercharged the desire for sobriety. Like Naomi, who found her way out of fear by engaging the more powerful hunting instinct, these alcoholics overcame addiction with a more profound spiritual attachment.

Now we can see the wisdom behind the Heaths' idea of small wins. The slogan in A.A. is "one day at a time." If you can maintain sobriety for a single day and work your steps to start rebuilding your life, perhaps you can do it for another day, and another. Recall the shift in my exercise routine when I opened the downstairs exercise area to the cats. What had been a solitary activity now tapped into a playful motivation with my four companions. That change started as a small win: a single experience of enjoying interspersing my exercise with my time with the cats. That small win gave motivation to repeat the experience and soon a new habit pattern was born. Small wins are catalysts; they are shots of hope and optimism. Once they spark action, action can become habit—and that is what sustains change.

■ The Dangers of Trader Isolation

Notice a common thread among the see-feel-change strategies: *Most of them involve interacting with someone or something new*. In counseling, it's the relationship with the helping professional that creates the translation that helps a depressed person see, "*Hmmm* ... maybe it's not that I'm a bad person; maybe I've just learned a way of thinking that makes me feel that way." In Naomi's case, it was interacting with me in a way that allowed her to be the huntress and forget her fear of people. Without the fresh interactions, it's all too easy to stay mired in old ways of seeing and feeling. New experiences enable us to experience ourselves in new ways.

One of the themes I've emphasized on the blog is that *everything we do and everyone we interact with is a mirror*: a way to experience ourselves. A profound romantic relationship or deep friendship is powerful in part because it provides us with an affirming experience of self. Over time, immersed in love, we internalize the sense of being lovable. Similarly, troubled relationships present us with negative and distorted self-experiences: Think of the damage done by abusive relationships on children. When we engage in an activity, we perceive ourselves through the mirror of our experience. More mirrors—and better mirrors—create more opportunity to shift emotional gears. That is why travel to a new culture can be so powerful—it's a fresh lens for seeing self and world.

Trading can be a tremendously isolating experience, even on a large trading floor. The majority of the trading day is spent following markets, researching ideas, and reviewing performance. Screen time inevitably exceeds time spent in significant interaction with others.

While social media has opened the door to frequent contact among traders, the majority of interactions are too brief to serve as effective mirrors. Without fresh social interaction and novel activity, traders lack the mirrors that could catalyze see-feel-change. Change requires fresh inputs; people don't move from contemplation to action by mere reflection alone. The isolated trader all too often is the static trader, caught in doing the same things—even when those things stop working.

The potential for trader isolation is a major reason I have emphasized the importance of networking. Networking—meeting up with other traders and "talking shop"—has the potential to turn see-feel-change into a vicarious process. When we see other traders encountering success through their ideas and applications, that mirrors to us what is possible—and can provide a meaningful emotional gear shift. At a recent networking event that I helped organize, a trader described how he was approaching the market, trading a very limited set of tested patterns. To be action-worthy, those patterns had to occur at particular times of day, with a threshold level of market participation (volume). His idea immediately sparked a thought that I could qualify my own market indicators by the context in which they occurred. This ultimately led to a new line of research that I utilize to this day in my trading.

What is psychologically significant is that this interaction during the networking filled me with the motivation to pursue a new idea. Through the experience of the trader, I saw that something was possible in my own trading—*and I couldn't wait to get home to test it out*. There was no dawdling between contemplation and action: Hearing of the trader's success was so energizing that it led directly to action. Had I been isolated, that experience could never have happened.

The beauty of positive mirrors is that they spark change without the need to go through crisis. Fear is a great motivator; hitting bottom can be a most effective catalyst for change. But hitting bottom in trading can mean going broke. The game is over before change can occur. The positive mirrors created by networking with the right people bring change through inspiration, rather than fear. In sharing someone else's small wins, we experience those vicariously as wins for ourselves. That sparks optimism, inspiration, and the drive to make change happen.

Key Takeaway

It is better to move to action through inspiration than desperation.

Indeed, we can think of networking as a group-based solution-focused intervention. Imagine a group of talented traders, each sharing best practices. One person's ideas spark ideas for others, which in turn lead to new directions and fresh possibilities. Each person's small wins contribute to the discussion, which ultimately becomes about winning. This in turn mirrors to each participant the sense of being part of an adaptive, winning group. Networking is a powerful tool for overcoming the limitations of isolation, as each conversation provides a potential see-feel-change experience. By expanding the quantity and quality of our mirrors, we generate an ongoing source of energy for launching ourselves beyond contemplation, into action.

■ Changing the Internal Dialogue

A small win is a small mirror. It reflects a winning image to us. Accumulate enough small wins and that winning image starts to become familiar. We internalize that which we experience repeatedly. That's one of the reasons positive emotional experience is important, per the research of Barbara Frederickson's lab. Positive experience broadens the scope of our thinking, which in turn helps us build new experiences and skills. Broaden and build is not so far from see-feel-change. When we experience small wins, we perceive our ideal self, and that inspires us to new efforts.

Recall Charles Duhigg's insight that change is a function of habit creation. It's simply too exhausting to rally ourselves through motivation every time we need to shift contemplation into action. Much more efficient is the creation of action patterns that activate automatically with the right cues. People I've known who are particularly adaptive have made small wins a habit pattern. They undertake many new challenges and regularly define meaningful, doable goals. They set themselves up for success. Positivity becomes a habit, a lifestyle, making the whole issue of discipline moot.

Suppose, however, negativity becomes our habit pattern. Instead of positioning ourselves for small wins, we set ourselves up for repeated failure. We internalize repeated experience, so over time we internalize a sense of failure. Eventually, like Seligman's rats, we find no escape and collapse in helplessness, unable to control the outcomes that matter most to us. That keeps us frozen in contemplation, unable to sustain action.

How do people get into such a state?

■ ■ ■

Depression is the most dramatic example of circular negativity. As cognitive therapists have emphasized, depressed people process information with negative biases, viewing the world, so to speak, through inverted rose-tinted lenses. Imagine two traders finishing the day with a moderate loss. One sees the opportunity to add to positions at better levels; the other throws his hands in the air and wonders why he trades like an idiot. The latter is a version of depressive thinking, interpreting events with negative self-attributions. Cognitive therapy is effective in part because it helps depressed people think about their thinking. If you can show the depressed person that he would never say to others what he is saying to himself—he wouldn't tell a trading buddy he's trading like an idiot after a losing day—the changed perspective helps shift the way of thinking. It's the equivalent of Seligman taking the helpless rat and plopping him over the barrier to the unshocked side of the cage. If you can talk to yourself the way you've learned to speak to others, perhaps you can break the cycle of interpreting outcomes as small failures.

Depression and its cognitive treatment illustrate the degree to which we create our own realities through our internal dialogues. Many times we fail to move from contemplation to action because our negatively skewed information processing generates more helplessness than empowerment. We don't need to be clinically depressed to fall prey to such negative thinking. Many traders are competitive by nature and become frustrated when they lose money or make poor decisions. That frustration can be channeled externally ("These markets are manipulated!") or internally ("I can't do anything right!"), but in both cases the channeling is not constructive. It doesn't help a person learn from the situation and move forward in a positive fashion. It doesn't naturally lead to small wins. Indeed, by emphasizing a victim mindset—bad things happen to me—such thinking systematically disempowers a trader. If you are the victim of bad luck, bad markets, and bad trading, how can you become the author of your own turnaround story?

One of the habit patterns most important to cultivate as a trader is the ability to lose in a way that gives you energy, rather than robs you of initiative. Of course, losses will be frustrating to a competitive trader, but frustration need not be paralyzing. If you have built a process whereby you routinely look for mistakes and turn them into fuel for self-improvement, you have turned the transition from contemplation into action into a habit. Every mistake is an opportunity—and an obligation—to do something different, something better. Less-than-ideal trading becomes a trigger to work on your ideal self.

Half of the battle is catching yourself in the act of becoming mired in frustrated self-talk. This is why cognitive therapists encourage people to keep journals of their thinking. By writing down what is going through our heads, we can become more objective about the things we tell ourselves. At times, I've also had traders voice their thinking into a recorder and then listen to themselves rant. As a listener, the traders can see that what they are saying is not helpful, which helps halt the process. It is not enough, however, to halt the negative thinking. We need positive habit patterns that shift negative thinking into constructive actions.

■ ■ ■

Larry was a young developing trader working under a senior money manager. At times he felt overwhelmed by his learning curve and worried that he would never meet his mentor's expectations. This was particularly upsetting, because he respected his mentor immensely. No matter how many times the mentor assured Larry that he was progressing well, Larry found himself worrying about whether he would ultimately be good enough to manage money on his own.

Worry is a form of negative thinking different from depression. Depression tends to be backward looking, blaming the self and casting doubt on the future. Worry is forward looking, anticipating that bad things will happen. The depressed person says, "I can't." The worried person says, "I'm afraid to try." A common observation among traders is that worry can lead to problems with "pulling the trigger" on sound trade ideas. More psychologically attuned to potential loss than reward, the worried trader takes the "safe" route and fails to act.

That was the problem bedeviling Larry. He found himself so concerned about losing money that he either traded very small or didn't trade at all—even when he identified his ideas as being sound. It was as if he were two different people: one seeking opportunity in his market research, the other avoiding market loss in his trading. Over time, this created considerable frustration, as he realized he was not living up to his potential. On one especially frustrating occasion, he told me about his well-researched idea to buy the currencies of strong emerging-market countries. He cited positive economic fundamentals in those countries and liked the fact that the positions were "positive carry": because of interest rate differentials, he would get paid to own the positions. When the currencies opened higher the next day, he told himself he would buy a pullback. When they extended their gains, he told himself he would not chase the move and buy at bad levels. When the currencies closed the day sharply higher, he felt completely stupid, failing to act on an idea that he had pitched to others. Nothing is worse, he remarked, than getting calls from others congratulating you on your trade when you never put it on in the first place!

Larry had plenty of ideas for improving his trading and putting on good trades. His problem was that he could not move from idea to action. What inhibited him was his thought process. As long as he saw the threat of losing as greater than the threat of not acting, he remained paralyzed. A turning point for Larry came when we realized that his love of generating ideas was what really motivated him in markets. The trades simply were ways of seeing ideas work out. He loved the process of coming up with market views that escaped others—and he took justifiable pride in his work. At one point I encouraged him to write down in advance, not why he should or shouldn't take the trade, but why he should act on or betray his research. In other words, we reframed his worry pattern as one of self-sabotage. Understandably, he had never thought of holding back on implementing ideas as a betrayal of his life's work, but his reaction to the thought was visceral. He would never want to betray his best work; else, why do it? Through that reframing, he was able to move to action, because he now viewed inaction as a risk far greater than losing money.

Larry's worry problem is especially common with respect to fear of the unknown. There is no guarantee that change will be successful; sometimes familiar troubles feel safer than unfamiliar, unexplored territory. This is where small wins become extremely important. If the change process is ongoing and evolutionary, there need be no fear of revolutionary change. Traders often will try something new in small size and just see how it works over time. Several traders I've worked with have segmented their books into different strategies, with the more experimental strategies taking fewer positions with less risk. It's a way of testing ideas in a nonthreatening way. If the ideas are good, they generate the small wins that can lead to a scaling up of the strategy.

I | Key Takeaway | I

When change is threatening, small changes can inspire further action.

As we will see shortly, however, there is a big difference between making changes and sustaining those changes. Viewing his thought process in a new light helped Larry make a change, but he needed to turn that new view into a habit pattern in order to keep the change going. By writing down the pros and cons of betrayal each day for a number of days, and actively mentally rehearsing how he would feel if he let himself down, Larry was able to internalize the change. He did so, not by becoming a different trader, but by doubling down on what had brought him to trading in the first place. It's back to our experience with Naomi, the traumatized kitten: Find a motivation greater than the motivation powering the problem and change can occur naturally.

■ The Perils of Perfectionism

Depression and the worry of anxiety are two modes that keep people from change. Very often those represent ways of channeling frustration. There is another cognitive pattern, however, that is less recognized as a problem than either of those: perfectionism. As I have noted on the TraderFeed blog, perfectionism masquerades as a virtue. The perfectionist prides himself on being driven and not accepting anything less than the best. He justifies perfectionism as motivation, as if the only alternative were complacency. In reality, however, perfectionism destroys motivation. It is a formidable barrier between contemplation and action.

The stark truth is that perfectionism is driven by insecurity. The motif of the perfectionist is "not good enough." It doesn't matter if you made money today or this week; you left something on the table and could have made more. If you had several winning days and a losing day, it's the losing day that gets the focus—and the frustration. *Over time, the message that your efforts are "not good enough" creates small defeats, the opposite of small wins.* Perfectionism can take winning experiences and turn them into losers. The response I often hear from perfectionists when I offer them positive feedback is, "yes, but." There is always something they could have done better, or something they failed to do.

The easy way to see that perfectionism is destructive is to simply imagine yourself speaking that way to your trading buddies or your own children. If your little girl came home from school with two As and a B, are you really going to launch into her for failing to get all As? What would be the result for your relationship with her? What would be the result for her self-confidence? Repeated experiences that this isn't good enough and that isn't good enough eventually mirror the sense that *you're* not good enough. The measure of so many things in life is whether they give energy or drain it. It's a great filter for the people in your life, the activities you engage in, and the work you perform. Perfectionism drains energy. It does not inspire performance; it turns inspired performance into something "not good enough."

The idea of small wins means that your focus should not be on perfection, but on improvement. This is why the right kind of goal setting is so important. Research from Locke and Latham suggests that goal setting is effective in changing behavior. Their work finds, however, that when goals are too difficult or threatening, they tend to not be effective. Perfectionistic goals, by definition, have strong odds of not being met. Instead of creating wins, they pose the threat of failure. When goals are framed in terms of improvement—challenging and yet doable—they are much more likely to inspire.

I cannot emphasize strongly enough: *We internalize repeated experience.* Our internal dialogues frame our experience. When we frame life events in negative ways, we create drains on our energy that keep us from adapting and growing. Constructive, positive framings are important because they keep us experiencing ourselves in ways that give energy. Perfectionism attempts to push behavior from behind with the threat of failure. Inspiring goals pull behavior from a positive vision of the future.

■ Relapse

As I mentioned earlier, initiating change is only part of the battle. Another part is sustaining change. Prochaska, Norcross, and DiClemente, in their book, *Changing for Good* (1994), stress that relapse is a part of the change process. We rarely make changes in straight lines, where we take new actions and leave past patterns forever. Rather, change is a bit of "two steps forward, one step back." Many of our patterns have been with us for years; they are well-engrained habits. It is easy to fall back into them.

Relapses tend to occur during periods in which we lose mindfulness. Mindfulness is a state in which we are self-aware, as emotionally neutral observers to ourselves. When we are in a mindful state, we don't react to situations; we observe ourselves responding to situations. A good example would be going out to eat when I'm on a diet. I'm aware that there will be many foods available and that people around me will be eating. I prepare myself in advance and decide that I will only eat the healthiest options, and in moderation. That self-awareness enables me to sustain my longer-term intention.

Baumeister and Tierney's research on willpower (2011) suggests that people in general are not good at forgoing short-term temptations and acting in their longer-term self-interest. When people perform an effortful task and then are placed in front of tempting foods and told to not eat them, they are much less likely to resist temptation than people who have not performed the task. This suggests that willpower is a finite resource in the short run. When we expend energy in intentional action over a period of time, our willpower muscles become depleted and it's easy to fall into reactive patterns. This is a very important concept. As Kelly McGonigal points out in her book, *The Willpower Instinct*, "Our brains mistake the promise of reward for a guarantee of happiness, so we chase satisfaction from things that do not deliver" (2012, p. 132).

McGonigal's (2012) distinction between reward and happiness lies at the heart of many relapsed efforts at change. What would make us happy is losing the weight. What feels rewarding is eating from the dessert tray at the party. The problem is that what is rewarding ultimately does not bring us happiness and, indeed, can sabotage our longer-term satisfaction. Most traders know what happens when they get caught up in short-term market action and enter a position they would never contemplate had they engaged in mindful planning. The promise of quick reward from a short-term trade temporarily overwhelms the longer-term happiness of following a sound business plan for one's trading.

One of the psychological factors that depletes our willpower is negativity. When we make ourselves miserable with self-blame and worry, it is much easier to seek solace in immediate reward. Such negative thinking robs us of energy, and that robs us of willpower. Conversely, it is much easier to stick to a diet or a trading plan when we concretely see the benefits coming to us. And, of course, once a new behavior pattern becomes a habit, it no longer takes willpower to sustain it.

How can we overcome negativity and the psychological leaks that drain us of willpower? It turns out that research on mindfulness meditation is quite relevant to the prevention of relapse. Research from Teasdale and colleagues (2000) found that mindfulness-based cognitive therapy was significantly effective in preventing relapse among people with major depressive disorder. Mindfulness practice has also been found to confer health benefits, stress reduction, social connectedness, and improvements in concentration. The reason for this is that mindfulness allows us to become neutral self-observers, rather than caught up in the frustrations of the moment. Consider the difference between the person who says, "I'm a total failure; I can't succeed at anything!" and the person who says, "Now I'm telling myself that I'm a total failure and that I can't succeed at anything." The first person identifies with the negative message. The second person takes a self-observing stance—not just thinking and feeling, but being consciously aware of how they're thinking and feeling.

By quieting the mind and body, perhaps by focusing on deep, regular breathing, meditation places people in a state that is incompatible with emotional arousal. When a stressful event occurs, we respond with fear or frustration and our bodies go into overdrive, preparing us for fight or flight. Part of that overdrive involves the blood flow shifting to the motor centers of the brain and away from the executive centers that facilitate our planning and reasoning. This is why I mentioned in my earlier books that worked-up traders are literally out of their minds. They analyze and plan their trades with the frontal cortex activated and then, in the heat of market action, act out of the fight-or-flight responses of their motor centers. In his excellent book, *The Hour Between Dog and Wolf* (2012), John Coates explains that these shifts are mediated by chemicals within the body, which promote risk taking (testosterone) and reacting to stress (cortisol). As a former trader as well as a neurobiologist and economist, Coates makes a powerful case that many of our actions in the heat of battle are more biologically than logically driven.

Key Takeaway

Our emotional state generally follows our physical state.

Relapse tends to occur during overheated periods, when we are least mindful. It is one thing to maintain sobriety while at A.A. meetings, focused on helping ourselves and our peers. It is something very different to maintain sobriety when we are sad, angry, or anxious. Once willpower drains, we fall back into old patterns—and all too often lack the self-awareness to arrest the process. Prochaska, Norcross, and DiClemente, in *Changing for Good*, cite research that finds 60 to 70 percent of all relapses in drug and alcohol, smoking, and eating behavior are preceded by emotional distress. It is when we are taxed by upsetting situations that we are most likely to lose willpower and mindfulness and act on autopilot.

■ ■ ■

Kevin was a skilled daytrader I worked with early in my career. Most of the time he was workmanlike in identifying buyers and sellers in the depth of market screens. He also displayed unusually good risk management. He could take a loss, step back, figure out what went wrong, and continue trading without becoming caught up in stress reactions. Every so often, however, Kevin would experience large, painful trading losses. At those times, he would trade extra-large size and hold positions that went against him far beyond levels where he would ordinarily stop out. Ironically, when he was trading his normal size, he was diligent and religiously adhered to his stops. It was when he was largest—and hence most vulnerable to outsized drawdowns—that he became stubborn.

At the time I began working with Kevin, he had undergone a painful drawdown. The owner of the trading firm made it clear to Kevin that either this behavior had to stop or else Kevin would be prevented from trading significant size. As Kevin and I talked, it became clear to me that he was not operating with a hidden self-sabotage wish, nor was he impulsive or imprudent as a person. It was at times of maximum confidence that Kevin would trade his largest size. Convinced that he was right in his view, he would allow trades to move far against him before admitting defeat. *It was not the distress of losing money but the euphoria of being on a hot streak and having a promising idea that nudged Kevin out of mindfulness mode.* That was an eye-opener for me: It showed that *any* form of emotional and physiological arousal—not just the emotions of distress—can put us "out of our minds."

I used the emotional thermometer exercise with Kevin, where he had several sheets of paper in front of his trade station each day, printed with a picture of a thermometer. During the morning, midday, and afternoon he had to "take his emotional temperature," indicating how "hot" or "cool" he was. Key to the exercise is that we clearly identified excitement and confidence as "hot" states. The thermometer was a device that helped Kevin become more regularly mindful of how he was feeling. Once he explicitly identified that he was hot, he could take corrective action to cool down.

The simple mindfulness exercise that we performed to help Kevin cool down was a deep, slow breathing with eyes closed. With each breath, he told himself that he was cooling down, becoming more and more chilled. His sole focus was on his breath and the self-suggestion. On his own, Kevin modified the exercise to simply repeat to himself the word "chill" with each inhalation and the word "out" with each exhalation, in the manner of a mantra. This quieted him in mind and body and placed him in a state where he became very sensitive to how he was thinking and feeling. Whenever he started to get excited, he simply closed his eyes for a moment, took a deep breath, and reminded himself to "chill ... out." He found it much easier to act in a desired way when he was in a cognitive, emotional, and physical state that kept him mindful. *Relapse requires mindlessness*; if you are not operating on autopilot, you have the opportunity to steer yourself.

■ Summing Up: Moving from Contemplation to Action

We began with a short exercise to answer questions regarding your approach to adapting your trading to evolving market conditions. One purpose of the questionnaire was to assess your readiness for change. Many readers will have skipped the completion of the questionnaire or only jotted down or mentally noted very general and generic responses. Most traders are aware of the need to keep up with changing markets, but few take purposeful, directed action toward adaptation. By the time the need for change is painfully apparent, much damage can be done to one's psyche and one's trading account.

Two motivations move people from contemplation to action: fear of negative consequences and the inspiration that comes from visioning positive and possible outcomes. If you have been contemplating change for a while but remain in a personal or trading rut, you are operating somewhere in emotional limbo between those emotions: not feeling the fearful imperative of the need to change, and also not feeling the inspiration to move to the next level of your development. Only an emotional shift can nudge you to action; routine trading by following daily routines can never take you out of limbo.

When you have a sound trading approach that is working well, sticking to a disciplined routine makes all the sense in the world. When that approach is no longer working, sticking to that same routine keeps you from adapting. The idea that successful trading must tame our emotions makes sense when we're making decisions in the heat of battle. Less appreciated is that we must *amplify* our emotional experience to move from status quo to a new and positive equilibrium.

When I lost weight and got myself in better physical shape, two emotional shifts made a big difference. Having my cats become part of the downstairs exercise routine, as mentioned earlier, was helpful in developing a fresh habit pattern. I've consistently found that turning an activity from an individual one to a social one creates a fresh emotional experience. As a college sophomore, I was pleased with my academic development but felt I was not as socially well developed—or confident—as I wanted to be. So what did I do? I signed up to serve as the social director for our dormitory hall. Stronger than my social reticence was my desire to not fail in an undertaking where people were counting on me. As I poured myself into organizing parties and reaching out to other halls, I found that I not only enjoyed the social experience, but was pretty good at it. Recall how the traumatized kitten Naomi overcame her terror at the sight of people. Once I played with her by moving my hand under the bedcovers, her hunting instinct took over. She pounced on the hand and joined in the game, forgetting her fear altogether. Tapping into our strongest motivations and values helps us make similar shifts. I might not take action to go to the gym when left to my own devices, but if I make a commitment to a friend doing physical therapy, there's no way I'll fail to show up.

The second force that prompted me to lose the weight and get back into shape was simple, sheer disgust. I stepped on the scale and the needle hovered near 200 pounds. My clothes weren't fitting as well and my energy level was at low ebb. I was drinking too much coffee, eating too much, and working long hours that I used to justify not exercising regularly. When my energy level was drained and I stepped on that scale, change no longer felt like an alternative; it was now an imperative.

At some point, most of us care enough about ourselves that we will not allow negative consequences to accumulate indefinitely. You might not pursue change because you're losing money, but you will embrace change once you're sick of losing money.

■ ■ ■

Years of working in proprietary trading firms, banks, and hedge funds have taught me that there are two types of trader: one who is drawn to trading for negative reasons; the other who is drawn for positive ones. The person who is drawn to trading for negative reasons is looking for an escape. Perhaps it's an escape from working an 8-to-5 routine; perhaps it's an escape from working for someone else; perhaps it's an escape from past failures and shortcomings; perhaps it's an escape from hard work. In all those cases, trading is the playing out of a fantasy—the hope that it will be possible to be maximally successful with minimal effort.

Those drawn to trading for positive reasons find in trading an ideal fit of values, skills, and interests. Trading becomes an expression of their identity—an exercise of their strengths, not an avoidance of their vulnerabilities.

You can tell what kind of trader someone is by how time is spent outside of market hours. The trader with a positive source of motivation has an interest that goes beyond the thrill of putting trades on and making/losing money. The positive source of motivation might be the intellectual curiosity of understanding a global macro picture; the satisfaction of discovering new relationships driving markets; the mind-broadening of sharing ideas within a network of colleagues; or the fulfillment of working on improving one's performance. In each case, the motivation does not fade when markets aren't open or when they are not providing profits. For the trader whose motivations are primarily avoidant and negative, there is little appeal to markets outside of the immediate experience of putting trades on and making money. Because they are looking to markets for self-validation, there is nothing to be gained when markets are closed.

This distinction is crucial, because it once again suggests that an important way to shift from contemplation to action is by tapping into core motivations and generating the emotional shift that they can provide. When my trading has stagnated, nothing works better than taking some time away from screens and going into idea-generation mode. I certainly enjoy being profitable, but what is particularly satisfying is generating a fresh idea that brings profitability. Stepping back from trading and opening my mind to new perspectives recharges the batteries and energizes me to make the changes I need to make in markets out of a desire to make the most out of those new ideas.

Recently I found, however, that even the hunt for new ideas was not getting me past a trading block. I examined my trading and found a pattern. After taking some time away from markets, I would get a big idea, trade it, and make good money. I would then place subsequent trades and lose money. That led to taking time away from trading and generating new big ideas. The cycle got to the point where I found it difficult to rouse myself to stay engaged with markets. That surprised me, because I normally don't find myself demotivated. I spent more time with my research, but that did little to spark my trading interests, also something that was surprising.

It suddenly hit me that what I most loved about markets was not analysis, but the synthesis of all I had analyzed. It was coming up with that big idea. That was what I was good at—not breaking the market down, but compiling information into a coherent scenario. When I was in synthesis mode, I generated overarching ideas and did quite well with them. When I became too granular and attempted to trade patterns in my analysis that were devoid of a bigger picture, I was net unprofitable, but also less engaged. My core motivation was not just the scientific one, but also the creative one: I love looking at a broad range of analyses and then synthesizing them into ideas that bring opportunity.

Key Takeaway

Moving closer to our strengths can provide the emotional shift needed to take action.

That recognition led to a very important change in my trading process. With the help of the Evernote app, I began writing out my market ideas, using the writing to synthesize all I had been observing and researching. The writing was fairly stream-of-consciousness and not intended for any audience. Not only was this enjoyable; it also led to important insights. Connections I would have never perceived simply by thinking in the abstract came to light when I was in writing mode. By shifting myself to an information-processing strength—writing has always been a native mode of thinking—I was able to create a rhythm between idea generation and trading. No trade could go into the book without time for synthesis; all trading had to reflect big ideas. In a relatively short period, I moved from being demotivated to taking significant action.

■ ■ ■

Let's say my underlying motivations for trading came, as Maslow would say, more from deficit needs than the actualization of strengths. Perhaps I had not been successful in life and now needed markets to make me money or validate me as a person. Perhaps I was not getting gratification and excitement in various parts of my life and needed markets to fill the void. In such a situation, once I had gotten into my trading rut, there would have been little to pull me out. Indeed, the pattern of making and losing money might have proven so frustrating to my unmet needs that, instead of revamping my process, I might have gone on tilt and traded out of frustration, creating larger losses and wounding myself further.

Trading can be quite exciting, and it can be quite profitable. Those, however, cannot be your primary motivations for engaging markets.

There will always be low-volatility markets that are not exciting, and there will always be periods of drawdown. Thrills and profits will carry you through the good times, but leave you nothing to draw on during lean periods. When markets change profoundly, the work of rebuilding one's trading is neither exciting nor immediately profitable. The traders I've known who have sustained long-term success have always been driven by something beyond immediate excitement and profitability. Very often, those drivers have reflected core strengths and interests that provide energy, even when markets are not paying out. It is that energy that catalyzes the transition from contemplation to action. We don't operate in limbo and autopilot if we are tapping into our most profound values and capacities.

■ Taking and Sustaining Action: Identifying Opportunity

Let's go back to that earlier questionnaire and review the actions you are pursuing to adapt to new and challenging market conditions. As with any strategic review of a business, the questionnaire is designed to tap into your perceptions of both opportunities and threats in markets. How can you pursue opportunity and avoid threats in the next several years? If you did not answer the questions earlier, please now jot down your best responses:

_____

_____

_____

_____

_____

Self-Assessment Exercise

■ How, specifically, do you expect your markets to evolve over the next several years?

■ Where, specifically, do you perceive the greatest areas of opportunity in your markets over the next several years?

- What, specifically, has been the greatest source of threat to your trading in the past year?

- How would you need to change your trading to keep pace with the shifts in markets, opportunities, and threats noted above?

- What are you doing now, on a regular basis, to master the learning curve needed to exploit the opportunities and avoid the threats you foresee?

- What new markets or market information are you examining in detail to help prepare you for the future?

- If you don't have clear, specific answers to the above, with whom do you need to speak and what do you need to research to gain clarity?

Now that you've answered the self-evaluation questions, let's take a look at those responses and their implications. We'll start with the answers to the first two questions: How do you expect markets to evolve and where do you perceive areas of greatest future market opportunity? If you are like many traders, your responses are more general than detailed, extrapolating the clearest, most recent trends into the future. Perhaps you responded by saying that an increasing proportion of trading would be dominated by computers or that large financial institutions would grow at the expense of smaller ones and individual investors/traders. While those trends may well continue to be the case, they don't represent new information. Today's success stories are those who recognized those developments a decade or more ago, as they were gaining traction—not once they were firmly established.

Strong answers to these questions, on the other hand, elicit an "aha!" response from knowledgeable market participants. A while ago, I observed that a growing share of trades among large, discretionary traders was conducted via execution algorithms. As I spoke with those who used and developed these algos, it became clear that most of these leave distinctive "footprints" in markets. After studying the sequencing of transactions in a trade-by-trade time series, I could identify with a meaningful degree of accuracy whether buyers or sellers were executing with particular urgency at any point in time. Aggregating this information led to promising measures of buying pressure and selling pressure that provided insights not possible when viewing traditional price and volume charts. Those analyses profoundly shaped my view of markets. They provided more than an improvement on my old perspectives; they represented a wholly fresh perspective, not unlike Emil's vision for the restaurant.

Two elements contribute to clear visions of the future: new observations and new information. In the previous example, the new observations came from studying execution algorithms and their transaction patterns. The new information came from transaction-level data. As I commented to a colleague at the time of my study: "Everything of interest is occurring within the one-minute bar." Quite simply, I was seeing markets differently because I was looking at different market data. Emil's adaptation to the future was similar: His study of diners and their favorite restaurants led to new observations. His tablet-based ordering system generated consumer preference data that simply had not existed when ordering was conducted manually, via wait staff and printed menus. If you're looking at the same things in the same way—making similar observations and relying on similar data—the odds are strong that you'll remain mired in status quo views, hampering any efforts at adaptation. *To do new things, you have to be looking at new things*. New observations spawn new questions and those can generate fresh answers.

Imagine executives at companies like Samsung or Hyatt responding to the first two questions in our exercise. The odds are high that they have been studying consumer trends and preferences in smartphones and travel and have a strong sense for how their markets are likely to evolve. They collect data on their customers; they conduct focus groups; they study retail and lifestyle trends. Fresh observations at Samsung may reveal emerging demographic trends that will necessitate a more radical integration of computing and mobility, as phones become part of a *quantified self* revolution. Hyatt's studies may lead to the recognition that aging Baby Boomer customers with discretionary income are gravitating toward convenient, all-in-one destination resorts that provide unique adventures and cultural experiences amidst the usual amenities. Such insights enable the companies to actively pursue the future, even as they succeed in the present. How long would they stay in business if their responses to the first two questions above consisted of a couple of sentences, filled with vague generalizations?

One of the best ways of answering the first two questions is to see what has been working in markets and what has not, including who has been making money and who has not. As I write this, one of the most common assumptions I have heard from traders and investors is that the "financial repression" imposed by central banks—the holding down of interest rates and continued purchase of government debt—will unwind and result in bear markets in bonds and stocks. That may eventually occur, but operating from that framework blinded investors to meaningful returns in segments of the stock and bond markets over many years.

By tracking the returns of who has been making money and who hasn't, it's possible to see what the winners are doing differently from the losers. This, too, is one of the great benefits of networking. Talking with experienced traders reveals their best practices, some of which can be incorporated into your own. Going into discussions with traders with an eye toward reverse-engineering their success is a great way to figure out adaptations that could be useful to your trading.

Key Takeaway

You are most likely to sustain profitability if you study the successes of others.

Sometimes opportunity can be identified by looking at markets in unique ways. For instance, focusing on relative performance—how some stocks, regions of the world, or currencies are performing relative to others—we can generate ideas that would not be apparent if we were to focus solely on outright price. Fresh opportunities can be found in patterns of volatility and among stocks that have little institutional following. At the time of writing this, large capitalization shares are underperforming smaller capitalization ones due to the differential impact of US dollar strength on large exporters versus small domestic firms. Learning to view markets through multiple lenses helps us make key adaptations in our trading, as one theme wanes and another waxes to take its place. As we shall see later in the book, this is a major reason why creativity is essential to adapting to changing markets.

■ ■ ■

Many of us search through markets to see what they're doing. Not as many of us re-search those markets, studying their patterns in a rigorous manner. When I returned to trading following a hiatus occasioned by full-time work at a hedge fund, I found that markets had changed during my years of absence. Many of the short-term patterns that had been reliable no longer proved profitable, particularly short-term patterns of mean reversion in stocks. This led to an extended period of research in which I tracked the cyclical ups and downs of the stock market. What I found was nothing like what I had expected: The cycles were longer in duration than my past trading embraced and were more related to such structural factors as volatility, correlation, and sentiment than any particular fixed durations. In other words, cycles appeared in the market, but were aperiodic: They occurred over varying time frames. Interestingly, however, the cycle phases displayed structural similarities that helped me estimate whether we were in rising, topping, falling, or bottoming phases. Only after seeing this research play out in real time did my trading evolve from shorter term to longer, more variable holding periods. Searching led to researching led to adaptive trading practice.

This is one of the great advantages of research: It can generate fresh insights that open the door to new opportunity. From consumer goods companies to pharmaceutical firms, research and development is an important component of adaptation in business. Before automobiles, smart phones, and menu items are launched, they have been extensively researched and tested on multiple segments of the public. A research pipeline does not guarantee success, but the absence of one almost certainly ensures stagnation.

Another important advantage of research is that it taps into some of those core motivations that not only move us toward change, but help us sustain change processes. For the most part, the aforementioned research led me to put aside the shorter-term trading that used to be my bread and butter and focus on larger ideas grounded in the cycle work. The excitement of seeing new ideas play out has eclipsed any regrets I might have felt about leaving behind my former trading. It is the sense of opportunity that drives any entrepreneur: the desire to bring a vision to life. Once operating in that entrepreneurial spirit, sustaining a change process becomes natural, as the work gives energy.

■ Taking and Sustaining Action: Identifying Threats

It is not enough to identify and act on opportunity; we also must avoid threats to our trading businesses. One trader I worked with was experiencing unusual success trading microcap stocks. He attributed that success to the fact that market-making algorithms were not as dominant in those markets, which permitted a cleaner read of supply and demand. He did very well for a number of months and then, during a risk-off period in equity markets, the microcap market all but dried up. Speculative action in those shares was fine during bull market periods, but was among the first to go when markets traded defensively. Clearly this was a threat to his business, and he needed to supplement his microcap trading with other sources of opportunity.

Sometimes the greatest areas of opportunity also pose the largest threats. The transition from basic cell phones to smart phones opened phenomenal opportunity, but also imperiled the makers of traditional devices. Exchange-traded funds (ETFs) have created great opportunities to trade a variety of stock market sectors and asset classes in cost-effective ways, but these funds have also contributed to increased correlations that have made long/short investing more challenging. One of the trends I'm currently tracking is social investment. Brokerage firms such as Motif Investing allow investors to purchase baskets of stocks and ETFs to express particular market themes and views, all for a single retail commission fee. The themes and portfolios are shared among investors, who develop reputations and followings for their acumen. It's not difficult to see that this trend enables the average investor to operate as a virtual hedge fund, constructing portfolios across multiple regions of the world, asset classes, and themes. This is a tremendous opportunity for the individual investor, but also a challenge to traditional investment advisers. It's not at all clear to me that people will pay high fees to advisers when they can receive credible, crowdsourced guidance or standardized advice from robo-advisers.

The continued rise of social trading and investing promises to increase the interconnectedness we already observe in the trading world. When I first began work with hedge funds, I was surprised to find how connected portfolio managers were with one another, not just within firms but across companies and across continents. It didn't matter whether I was speaking with a money manager in New York, suburban Connecticut, or London: The same research came up in the conversations and the same positions appeared in the portfolios. Many of the best performing traders were those who were most connected, as they were able to get in and out of positions most nimbly, based on their ability to read the investing herd. Traders who were less connected, particularly older traders not involved in social media to any significant degree, found themselves scrambling when positioning extremes led to mass runs for exits. Connectedness provided an opportunity for some money managers, a threat for others. For example, views and positions become so crowded at times that it becomes difficult for trend-following managers to stick with their holdings, as markets move in violent waves of buying and selling. The choppiness of market movement, exacerbated by positioning extremes, plays havoc with stops and sound entry execution, making it difficult to keep drawdowns small while riding longer-term moves.

Yet another market threat in recent times has been the crushing of volatility across assets in the wake of activist central bank policies. For a number of years, traders who relied on momentum and price extension for their trading found that such follow-through was missing. This was particularly threatening for traders who tended to scale into positions. Just as they added to winning trades, the markets reversed and took their P/L negative. Of those traders who adapted successfully, some experimented with different entry execution—entering large and progressively scaling out when trades went their way—and others moved to more volatile assets, where momentum patterns were likely to play out. One trader I know has used VIX as a gauge: When it got below a certain level, he pulled back on his stock index trading and instead looked for setups in individual stocks trading above average volume.

What shifts do you need to make in your own trading process to adapt to market changes that threaten your profitability? Among the possibilities you might contemplate are:

- *New inputs*: Fresh fundamental information; new information about supply and demand in your markets; novel perspectives on related markets, including shifts in market trends and themes

- *New markets to trade*: Markets, market sectors, or stocks that appear to be well-positioned for benefiting from the developments you perceive on the horizon

- *New time frames and times of opportunity*: Longer or shorter holding periods to adapt to shifting market conditions; changes in times of day for finding opportunity and executing trades

- *New strategies*: More relative trading versus directional, outright trading; greater emphasis on trading volatility versus price direction; trading of mean reversion/range/reversal patterns versus momentum/trend/continuation patterns

There is so much you can change—in what you follow and how you trade—that the choice can feel overwhelming. How do you decide where to focus?

■ ■ ■

Many times, the answer can be found in your own trading. This brings us full circle to the solution-focused framework. It is rare that we trade poorly all the time in all respects. Sometimes we make decisions that are more adaptive; other times, we make particularly poor decisions. A careful inventory of where and how you're losing money (and where and how you're making money) will provide you with a particularly useful perspective on threats and opportunities in your trading universe. It was precisely such an inventory that enabled Joe to see that sizing up his positions was responsible for a large proportion of his losses. When he entered a scalp trade in moderate size, he was much more likely to be profitable. That pattern had not been apparent to him before our meetings: He never thought to break out the patterns underlying his successful trades.

Key Takeaway

Many times, you are already making adaptive changes in your trading and not recognizing it.

Yet another money manager had a solid hit rate on his trades and was profitable in most months. Every so often, however, he experienced painful drawdowns that significantly reduced his profitability. More than once, I had the image of the mythical Sisyphus rolling the large stone up the hill only to have it roll back and leave him at the base. When we examined his trading, it became clear that the losses occurred during periods of high market volatility. At those points, correlations among positions increased significantly and what looked like a diversified portfolio no longer behaved as one. Because of those correlations, he was taking much more overall portfolio risk during rising volatility periods than he had realized. By more carefully monitoring volatility trends and adjusting his book to shifts in volatility regimes, he was able to significantly attenuate his losses.

This was a particularly interesting situation because, at the time the money manager engaged me, he assumed that his problems were psychological. From his perspective, there had to be something wrong with his psyche to repeatedly go through cycles of making money and then losing it. In point of fact, however, the problem was more logical than psychological: It was the result of failing to identify and adapt to volatility and correlation shifts in markets. I find this bias to be quite common among traders: Instead of looking for threats in markets and ways of adapting to these, they assume that poor performance necessarily has a psychological origin. This can certainly be the case, but surprisingly often, it is not. Assuming that trading problems are emotional ones prevents us from taking a hard look at our trading and making needed changes. In my experience, it is just as common for poor trading to create emotional upheaval as the reverse, especially among experienced traders.

In the case of my trading adaptation, the inventory of profitable and unprofitable trading revealed that time was a crucial element. The likelihood of losing money was directly proportional to the frequency of my trading. When I took the time to synthesize my market research and formulate overarching scenarios, I was much more likely to participate in meaningful market moves. When I traded patterns setting up in markets, heedless of a larger context, I inevitably lost money. What seemed like random performance was actually quite meaningful once I pulled out successful and unsuccessful trades. In my case, it wasn't so much emotional factors as cognitive ones that impacted my performance. Markets were moving in longer-term cycles and, if I did not adapt to those and place immediate price action into their larger context, I was likely to be chopped up.

■ Where to Look for Fresh Directions

Many times, it is not clear to us how markets are shifting, making it difficult to chart an adaptive path. The final question of the questionnaire assesses this issue: Do you know where to look for tomorrow's answers?

This is where networking with traders can be especially helpful. By networking, I'm talking about actually getting together with traders and talking shop with them, not merely exchanging chat messages online. When you spend time with traders, you find out what they are looking at—and also what leads them to shift their focus. This can help you become more sensitive to important changes in economic data, central bank policies, and geopolitics. I recently met with a group of macro strategists who work at hedge funds and expected a lively discussion of monetary policies around the world. Instead, their discussion focused on oil and commodities and factors that were influencing prices. Their emphasis was on inflation versus disinflation within the United States, not on global economics. That made an impression and helped me become more sensitive to interrelationships among asset classes.

Fresh perspectives can also come from reading research in applied finance. SSRN is a particularly fruitful source of research papers that can be downloaded free of charge. Recently, I read a review of momentum trading strategies that I found via SSRN. The work suggested a unique way of looking at momentum that could apply to my own trading. Often when I read such ideas, I will test them out over varying time periods to see if they yield any meaningful predictive value. Usually there's not too much exciting, but once in a while a fresh relationship will emerge. It was just such testing that led me to examine the relationship between realized and implied volatility among stocks and identify momentum opportunities when implied volatility (the volatility anticipated in options pricing) is high relative to the volatility that has actually been realized.

In a broad sense, there are two sources of edge that enable traders to adapt to changing markets, build their businesses, and rebuild them: informational edges and behavioral edges. Informational edges come from obtaining information not widely shared within the trading and investment world when that information holds predictive value with respect to markets. The trader who has access to satellite data to see weather and crop patterns has an informational edge in the agricultural commodity markets. The trader who can aggregate upticks and downticks among all stocks trading throughout the day has a potential informational edge over traders merely looking at bar charts. Many times, informational edges can come from building a better mousetrap. While others look to advance–decline lines for signs of breadth, I track stocks across all US exchanges and the percentage trading above their moving averages. The latter ends up being a far more sensitive—and informative—measure of breadth than the standard indicator.

The other form of edge is behavioral. Participants in markets behave in ways that are patterned. It is often possible to observe those patterns and identify ways of profiting from them. Sustained market advances frequently follow from violent selloffs: When the majority of the public is bearish and defensive, markets often have their greatest upside potential. Similarly, periods of waning breadth, bullish sentiment, and low volatility among stocks typically lead to subnormal returns. The trader who segments market moves based on time of day exploits behavioral patterns among market participants. Similarly, event traders may count on investors to underreact to earnings or data releases that are well off consensus, leading to profitable short-term trades.

To repeat a theme that is central to this book: The majority of experienced traders do not fail because of lack of discipline or an absence of emotional control. Skilled traders fall by the wayside for the same reason that skilled restaurateurs do—they keep doing what has made them successful until it works no more. Attached to their old ways, they fail to appreciate the opportunities and threats around them. It is not enough to trade today's edge; we must also find tomorrow's. That requires diligence, openness, productivity, and creativity. Can we cultivate those virtues? That is the topic of the second section of this book.

■ ■ ■

Trading Psychology 2.0 is grounded in the ABCD themes: Adapting to changing markets; Building strengths; Cultivating creativity; and Developing best practices and processes. We've just seen that it is not sufficient to develop an edge and assume that it will last indefinitely. Successful traders learn to generate new sources of edge and incorporate those into their businesses. But how can we not only master markets, but re-master them as well? Adaptation requires building the future on the foundation of our current successes. Understanding our strengths—our talents, skills, interests, and sources of excellence—is essential to defining our future. Our goal is to leverage the best within us, so that we can understand and exploit ever-shifting market dynamics.

CHAPTER 2

Best Process #2: Building on Strengths

Do not let your fire go out, spark by irreplaceable spark, in the hopeless swamps of the approximate, the not-quite, the not-yet, the not-at-all. ... The world you desired can be won. It exists, it is real, it is possible, it is yours.

Ayn Rand

■ The Trader in a Slump

Charles had been a successful trader for years. When he came to his new firm, he couldn't have been more excited. He had access to much greater capital and world-class research and analytics. He was surrounded by bright, talented colleagues and enjoyed support services to assist with every facet of his trading. Everything for Charles at his new setting was perfect, except one thing: He could not make money.

Everyone at first attributed Charles's slow start to the transition to a new platform. After all, risk management policies were different, and there was a learning curve associated with new software, new resources, and new colleagues. So no one worried after a few months of tepid results. But a few months became half a year and then stretched to a full year. No one spoke of Charles's transition problems any more. They quietly spoke about his slump.

For his part, Charles was diligent in not losing too much money. He started at his new firm by taking only modest risk and, as he failed to gain traction, he never significantly bumped up his risk taking. So it wasn't that he was deep in a hole. Rather, he slowly bled capital. His hit rate was lower than it had ever been. Sometimes he failed to put on good ideas; other times his ideas were just plain wrong. As he became more risk-sensitive, his hit rate declined further. By waiting for markets to move in his direction before he entered, he missed good portions of moves and exposed himself to normal—but still painful—pullbacks.

What was most perplexing to Charles, however, was that he didn't feel he was doing anything different from what he had done when he was making money at his old setting. His methods for analyzing markets were similar, as were his processes for generating ideas. The new environment wasn't distracting for him. Indeed, he made selective use of the new resources and colleagues specifically so that he would not disrupt his methods all at once. It simply seemed as though a light switch had been thrown the moment he entered the door of his new firm and suddenly he was no longer able to make money.

Slowly, Charles began to doubt himself psychologically. He wondered if, deep inside, he feared success at the new and larger firm. He didn't think he was doing anything to sabotage himself, but a comment from a longtime colleague stuck with him. When Charles described one of his trades, his friend responded, "What are you doing, trading like that? That's not the Charles I know!"

Could it be that Charles had changed and didn't even know it?

That was the question he brought to our first meeting.

■ ■ ■

There is a revolution afoot in the field of psychology, and it goes by the name of *positive psychology*. Positive psychology owes early inspiration to a variety of theorists, from Carl Jung, who studied spirituality and creativity, to Abraham Maslow, whose work on self-actualization was startlingly original for its time. Over time the interest in positive facets of human psychology has become highly research-based. The work of Dean Keith Simonton, Ed Diener, Mihalyi Csikszentmihalyi, Martin Seligman, and many others has turned the trickle of interest into a full-fledged subdiscipline.

So what is positive psychology? At its broadest, it is an attempt to understand positive aspects of human experience: happiness, life contentment, health, relationships, productive work, creativity, spirituality, and much more. The key insight of the positive psychologists is that the positive aspects of our experience are not simply the result of resolved conflicts. Rather, we each possess competencies and capacities that contribute to our life fulfillment. As a result, positive psychologists study health: happy, successful relationships; eminent creative geniuses; and people with high levels of subjective well-being. This in turn has led to a variety of techniques to increase the positive aspects of life. The old paradigm of seeing a psychologist to work out your problems has been turned on its head. Steeped in the research and practice of positivity, the new psychologist can find ways of helping average, normal people achieve supernormal outcomes.

This has opened the door to a radical revisioning of the problems people face. Perhaps we fall short, not because of our deficits, *but because we fail to enact our strengths and draw on our greatest assets.* What if problems are the result of too little positivity, not any excess of negatives? If that is the case, the role of psychology is not so much to help us change, but to help us become more of who we already are when we are most fulfilled in life.

I first glimpsed the implications of positive psychology when I worked as a counselor for medical students and residents at a Syracuse medical school. As one would expect, these were largely bright, motivated students dealing with high performance demands. Fully half of the students I met with were simply trying to cope with the stresses of their work and the impacts of those stresses on their personal lives. One first-year student particularly stood out in my experience. He was very bright, very organized, and very motivated to succeed. His academic record as a college undergraduate was excellent. And yet, relatively early in his first year of medical school, he was struggling with poor grades. Not so different from Charles—a change of setting and a decline in performance.

It turned out that my medical student had been identified with a learning disorder. He could process the spoken word very well, but was almost completely dyslexic. This was not a particular problem in college, as he lived at home and was able to have people read him his text material. He also had access to a very good special education department, who provided him with audio books and learning supports. Once he moved to the medical school, the resources were limited. There were no audio texts for many specialized medical volumes and little access to people who could read the books to him. By the time he came to me, he was very afraid of failing one of his courses and had an important test in just a few days.

I'm not often stumped by people's problems, but this one was challenging. Yes, I could help him beef up available resources, but it wasn't clear to me that this would adequately address the monster reading load of the first two years of medical school. His attitude was constructive— I didn't feel he had any particular psychological problems. Rather, he was in a setting that did not play to his strengths at all. And he was anxious about a do-or-die major exam in an important course.

I couldn't think of anything else to do, so I suggested we spend time together and go over the material aloud. Out came the books and notes— he did have access to a note-taking service—and I proceeded to read the material to him, section by section. To my amazement, he not only listened attentively, but asked very good questions and nailed all of my questions. As soon as I read the notes aloud, he picked up on the material he had heard and, in many instances, finished the ideas for me. At one point it struck me: Just as some people have a photographic memory, this student had a tape recorder memory. Once he heard something, it stuck. He lacked reading ability, but somehow compensated for that with an incredible auditory memory. If he had to read to learn, he was a bad student. If he could process the material aloud, he was an absolutely stellar student. It wasn't so much that he had a disability; he truly was differently abled. He was like my blind calico cat Mali, who can't see, but has developed a freakish sense of smell, touch, and direction and can navigate a multi-floor home.

Key Takeaway

Many performance problems are the result of failing to access performance strengths.

The student ended up passing the test with flying colors and we worked with the school and his parents to hire readers and audio record all lectures. I reached out to the student community to form study groups and was gratified by the eager response. The groups were a very effective way for the students to quiz each other, learn from each other, and process information in fresh ways. He became a significant contributor to his study group and, by the end of his second year, had achieved honors in several courses. Once schoolwork moved to the patient care settings, clinics, and hospital floors, much of the learning was by observing, doing, and discussing and he performed very well.

Once he could access his strengths, he was a success. Without those strengths, he faltered.

And so it was for Charles.

■ ■ ■

By the time I met with Charles, I already had 19 years of experience with medical students and quite a few subsequent years with traders. Over that time, I learned one very important lesson: Cognitive skills are every bit as important to performance as personality traits. People process information in very different ways, as we saw with our medical student. They also differ in their cognitive strengths. Some traders are startlingly intuitive; others are incisively analytical. I've worked with portfolio managers who have unusual abilities to read market patterns and others who have an uncanny ability to sort through information to detect a macro big picture. How we trade is intimately linked to how we think. *And, very often, trading problems are the result of failing to draw on our signature cognitive strengths.*

When Charles came to his new firm, he was hired as a solo money manager. At his previous shop, he had access to an assistant and a group of researchers able to delve into ideas for him. Although Charles was able to perform this research on his own, the absence of team members meant that he was now working in relative isolation. Idea generation had been a team-based activity at his prior setting. Now it was his task alone.

What I came to realize was that this was every bit as disruptive for Charles as the switch to the medical school was for my dyslexic student. Charles was not only outgoing; he was also uncannily good at reading people and knowing when they talked their books and when they held genuine convictions. Like my medical student, Charles was also quite effective in processing information interactively. He benefited from hearing himself talk, and he learned from the responses of others. When he drew on these cognitive strengths, idea generation was an iterative process. Trade ideas unfolded with interaction. In his new setting, he was siloed. There was limited interaction. Without conversations to flesh out ideas and people to read, he no longer had access to the cues that helped him develop his best trade ideas.

As we explored this idea, it became clear that the interpersonal cues of market interactions were an important part of Charles's timing. He was able to read when traders were suffering in positions and about to stop out. He could also pick up on themes that were about to become a growing consensus and enter them early. A friend of mine who was a very good tournament poker player tried to master the online game and eventually gave it up. He explained that his edge was reading the tells around the table. In the online game, those cues were limited and he couldn't find an edge by simply calculating the probabilities of his hands. He was very much like the floor traders who struggled when an increasing share of market making went electronic. The sights and sounds of the pits provided them with important cues about volume and buying/selling interest. Sitting in front of a screen without those cues, they lost their feel for markets.

Charles's skill was as much an ability to read people as markets. He thrived on observing traders and their reactions, and he used his interactions with researchers and assistants to assess their beliefs as well as his own. Without a team, he was like a quarterback lacking running backs or receivers. He could not generate plays on his own. In isolation, he was a mediocre trader, with a so-so feel for markets. Embedded within a dynamic team setting, he gained unusually good insights about market participants and market trends. When we turned our efforts to team building, Charles's enthusiasm returned. Some of the team building involved reaching out to the right people within his new firm. A large step was his hiring of an assistant, who was able to help him develop useful conversations with coverage on the sell-side. With the return to his old cognitive strengths, his performance picked up and he regained his excitement over trading.

■ Why Strengths Are Key to Performance

There is an important lesson in Charles's experience: Not all trading problems are the result of lost discipline or a lack of emotional control. When traders change their settings or strategies, they can stray from the strengths that underpin their success. Similarly, the changes that traders make during slumps can make problems worse by taking them further from their signature strengths.

A common example of this problem is the trader who seeks to change his or her holding period. Sometimes this occurs because of life circumstance: Perhaps it's no longer possible to follow markets as closely as before because of new commitments. Other times, the shift in holding period comes from a desire to harvest returns from longer-term market moves. Very often, the switch of time frame comes at a fearsome cost.

Why is this?

Let's look at the extremes. Take the *scalper*—the trader who trades very short time frames, seconds to minutes. Classic scalpers derive cues from the order book, observing rapid shifts in the depth of market screen that show how demand and supply line up at key price levels. This is the essence of pattern recognition, the ability to make quick reads of rapidly moving markets and act decisively.

Now consider the investor. Investors typically perform in-depth research to help them identify macroeconomic trends and/or compelling valuations. Many investors I've worked with compare their efforts to detective work: Most of their time is spent digging for pieces to a puzzle that they assemble over time. Notice how this is a wholly different set of cognitive skills from pattern recognition: The latter is much more implicit and perceptual; the former is explicit and grounded in extensive analysis and reasoning.

As the short-term trader moves to longer time frames, the quick reads of market patterns become as much as source of distraction as edge. What is signal to the scalper is noise to the investor. Even the short-term position trader, holding positions for hours to a few days, needs to overlook short-term patterns that are the bread-and-butter of the scalper. With the extension of time frame comes a shift in cognitive activity. For the short-term trader, that can mean getting away from the skills of pattern recognition and relying on information processing modalities that are not distinctive strengths.

Conversely, when investors try to narrow their time frames, they speed their thought processes and can short-circuit the explicit reasoning that is their strength. I vividly recall working with a very skilled macro trader at a hedge fund who had achieved a superior track record. She shared her research with me, and it was surprisingly original. At her new firm, risk was managed very tightly. A trader's risk taking could be cut after losses of only several percent of capital. What that meant in practice was that she continued to trade big-picture ideas, but now had to manage her positions on shorter time frames to avoid drawdowns. As market choppiness took her out of her best ideas at horrible price levels, she grew increasingly frustrated. Her unique strength was her ability to research markets and assemble her findings into market themes. When she had to focus on chart patterns, support and resistance levels, and short-term P&L, the trading process became frustrating *because it was no longer intrinsically rewarding.* She was only able to overcome this problem by sizing down her positions, widening her stops, and using options to help her sustain staying power in longer-term views.

Key Takeaway

We are most apt to find fulfillment in the enactment of our strengths.

My work with this portfolio manager taught me an important lesson: Strengths are essential to performance, because they tap us into our deepest motivations. I have long enjoyed basketball. The perpetual movement, the combination of individual effort and teamwork, and the combination of planned plays and improvised moves make basketball fascinating. I find a sport like bowling or track interesting, but have no motivation to play or master either. My skills do not fall in those domains, and I have little feel for the activities. Put me on a basketball court, however, and I'm immediately reading defenses, gauging whether the opponent moves better to the left or right, and looking for opportunities to create turnovers. In one sport, my play would be lackluster and unmotivated. In another, it would stand out.

When traders lose their excitement about markets and their performance weakens, a common problem is that traders change their approaches to markets and lose touch with the strengths that generated their initial success. Frustrated by drawdowns, we try to remake ourselves, when the real challenge is to leverage our best capacities and find a way to apply them to fresh market opportunities.

■ ■ ■

Once we appreciate the importance of strengths to performance, we can see why so many efforts at trader education fall short. Many efforts to train traders focus on very specific approaches to trading, such as chart reading. Students are shown examples of good "setups" and trades and expected to apply them on their own. Alternatively, training efforts may occur at the trading desk, where a trader or portfolio manager takes a junior trader under his or her wing and models good trading practice. All of this can work well if there is a good fit between the strengths of the student trader and the approaches being taught. Very often, however, no such fit is even considered. This results in an unusually high failure rate.

Compare the education of traders with that of medical students. A medical student spends significant time learning the basic science principles underlying medical practice. Work with patients begins with rotations through a variety of clinical services, including such different specialties as internal medicine, radiology, psychiatry, and surgery. During these rotations, students first observe the practice of advanced trainees and mentors and gradually participate in routine tasks necessary for patient care. By the end of the clinical rotations, the medical student has a reasonably good feel for which medical specialties hold appeal and which do not. This is because they develop a keen awareness of which practice areas make greatest use of their strengths and interests. Students with strong interpersonal skills and interests may gravitate to family medicine or psychiatry; those with greater technical performance skills might lean toward surgery or radiology. Those with broad interests will find appeal in primary care; those with focused interests will lean toward sub-specialization. A major part of medical education is discovering one's strengths and passions and applying those to fields that are most likely to draw on those.

Imagine a trading education that grounds students in economic, monetary, and trading fundamentals and then rotates them through currencies, fixed income, equities, options, short-term trading, longer-term investment, relative value and spread trading, quantitative trading, hybrid trading, discretionary trading, market making, and trading within and across various international markets. In such a comprehensive education, the trading student, like the medical student, would learn a great deal about his or her strengths and interests. Those with strong analytical skills might gravitate to quantitative trading, options, or spread trading; those with well-developed intuitive abilities might pursue market making and short-term trading. Some would develop specialized interests in individual markets or asset classes; others would become macro generalists. The success of such an educational effort would be far higher than the abysmal rates typically achieved, because students would have the ability to select the fields most conducive to their success.

Without such structured programs, trading novices are typically left to their own devices in discovering ways to trade successfully. Many run through their capital before ever finding their optimal niche; many give up in frustration before success is achieved. Can you imagine a medical student learning clinical practice through reading and disconnected online courses? Oddly, we expect an equally sparse infrastructure to yield success in highly challenging and competitive financial markets.

To add insult to injury, when developing traders find standard educational offerings to be wholly unsuited to the task of mastering global markets, there is a cadre of "trading coaches" in the wings, ready to convince students that their failures are primarily emotional! If they only stick to the plans and setups they've learned and control their fear and greed, they, too, can achieve the returns of world-class money managers. After all, trading is a mental game; if we master ourselves, we can master markets!

I find it difficult to hide my contempt for such intellectual and moral bankruptcy. Preying off trading's most vulnerable participants, self-proclaimed gurus, mentors, and coaches all too often peddle generic trading principles as education and then pass the blame of failure to students who understandably founder while following wholly untested signals. I was once asked to participate in trading seminars offered by a well-known educational group. When I looked into the program, I found out that the classes were taught by failed traders who now needed to make a living by teaching. The curriculum consisted of technical chart patterns that could be obtained in any primer. There was no evidence whatsoever that the courses led to successful trading among students. Indeed, the lack of success was used as a rationale to entice students to take more courses and obtain further coaching and mentorship.

Trading is a mental game in precisely the same way as chess or surgery. Once one has acquired a solid base of knowledge and skills, mindset is important in delivering consistent, high performance. Teaching a mental game to a beginning chess or medical student and pretending it will lead to world-class professional practice would be rightly viewed as folly. There is nothing more important to your development as a trader than studying multiple markets and trading styles, testing them out on paper, and following your talents, skills, and interests. The best way to win the mental game is to align your play with your greatest strengths. Who you are is a meaningful predictor of how you will trade successfully.

■ Finding Strengths in the Smallest Places

Sometimes all it takes is a small shift to align us with our strengths. Recall how I had problems sustaining a regular exercise program until I opened the door to my basement workout area and let our cats hang out with me. It was typically early in the morning when I went downstairs to exercise, so I was the only one awake in the house. After greeting the cats, replenishing their water, and feeding them, I began my exercise routine—and the cats hung out with the only person who was awake with them. Once the exercise became part of the cats' routine—Naomi and Mia typically would run to the downstairs door after finishing their meals—it became easy to make it part of my own routine. The strengths that brought me to psychology (caring for others) played out with the cats, bolstering my exercise routine. No complicated psychological techniques were necessary to get me to exercise—just opening a door and turning an individual activity into a shared, caring one.

My initial writing of this book proceeded slowly. Many other activities intruded, from trading markets to working with traders and family responsibilities. At one point I decided to change my work setting and write in my den instead of at my usual venues of cafés and grocery-store food courts. Normally, staying at home and writing in the den would expose me to far too many distractions, including those cats! The small change I made, however, was to program my own radio station on Pandora, hook up my portable speakers, and blast a steady stream of favorite music while I wrote. I had learned many years ago that I worked best surrounded with a high degree of stimulation. Most of my studying in college was performed in cafeteria and commons areas, rarely in my dorm room. I knew that if I played the wrong music—the music that does not appeal to me—that it would be a mere irritant and distraction. Electronic music with high beats per minute, however, has always been energizing for me and, oddly, calms me considerably. For example, as I am writing these words, a very loud soundtrack of EBM (electronic body music) is playing in the background with a thumping bass line and driving vocals. The novelty of fresh music tracks from Pandora, all drawn from a style that I enjoy, has kept me alert and engaged. And that keeps me productive in my writing.

A colleague that I greatly respect also listens to music when he works, but it is through headphones and it consists entirely of classical music and relaxing instrumental tracks. His purpose with the music is almost the exact opposite of mine: He is looking to filter out the world; I am seeking outside stimulation. His strength is focus and concentration over sustained periods of time, allowing him to analyze topics in depth. My strength is perusing large amounts of material and pulling together ideas. His work style avoids distraction; mine avoids boredom. In both cases, small changes in the environment can greatly impact our productivity—particularly when those changes draw on our strengths.

We perform best when our environments are aligned with our strengths.

As we saw with the example of Charles, a change of environment can create massive changes in performance. We possess emotional and cognitive strengths that are highly responsive to our environments. By sustaining work environments that facilitate our strengths, we make work more engaging and enjoyable and, not surprisingly, get more accomplished. When Charles hired an assistant, it made a huge difference in his performance—not because the assistant gave him such great trade ideas, but because adding a social element to the environment allowed Charles to access his information processing strengths.

Perhaps no environmental variable is as important to accessing our strengths as our close relationships. I function best in a very stable emotional environment and find any form of drama exceedingly distracting. I can sustain a high degree of intellectual interest and curiosity, but not if I'm emotionally distracted. If I were in an unstable romantic or family relationship, my performance would drop precipitously. Others respond to relationships differently. I can work alone for long periods of time (in the right environment); others need social stimulation and find aloneness to be isolating and noxious. One trader I worked with spent almost all of the trading day in active chat with other traders. I would have found that to wear thin after a few minutes. For him, however, the chat was like my music: stimulating and engaging. He traded best when he was in a socially enhanced environment.

It is difficult to engineer our environments for performance, however, if we aren't aware of the strengths that drive our performance. Too often, we perform in generic environments that fail to bring out our strengths. *We have to know who we are in order to consistently access the best within us.*

■ What Are Your Strengths?

The positive psychology movement has made great strides in understanding the different strengths that comprise personality. Let's take a look at two particularly thorough surveys of personal strengths and see what they might mean for trading.

The first survey comes from Buckingham and Clifton's 2001 book, *Now, Discover Your Strengths*. Grounded in the research of the Gallup organization, Buckingham and Clifton outline 34 strengths that are assessed by their online instrument, known as StrengthsFinder. That test is particularly useful because it identifies clusters of strengths that can be synergistic. Here are the 34 dimensions identified by the authors:

1. *Achiever*—a high level of achievement drive and orientation.
2. *Activator*—a doing orientation and an ability to take decisive action.
3. *Adaptability*—the ability to adjust to new conditions and situations.
4. *Analytical*—the ability to use data and logical reasoning to understand the world.
5. *Arranger*—the ability to manage and coordinate complex situations.
6. *Belief*—a strong system of values that guide decisions and actions.
7. *Command*—the ability to take charge and lead.
8. *Communication*—the ability to translate ideas into written and spoken words.
9. *Competition*—the drive to outperform rivals in performance situations.
10. *Connectedness*—the capacity to feel linked to others and feel part of something larger.
11. *Context*—the ability to understand events by placing them in a wider framework.
12. *Deliberative*—the ability to think ahead and plan actions.
13. *Developer*—the drive to help others realize their potential.
14. *Discipline*—the capacity to guide actions through structured routines.
15. *Empathy*—the ability to see the world through the eyes of others.
16. *Fairness*—the desire to treat others with equality and consideration.
17. *Focus*—the ability to be guided by the efficient pursuit of goals.
18. *Futuristic*—the drive to vision and work toward a desired future state.
19. *Harmony*—the desire to interact with others based on shared perspectives.
20. *Ideation*—the capacity to work with and become excited about ideas.
21. *Inclusiveness*—the drive to broaden social horizons and include others.
22. *Individualization*—the ability to perceive and value the unique qualities of others.
23. *Input*—the desire to collect new things and experiences.
24. *Intellection*—the ability to derive enjoyment from intellectual pursuits.
25. *Learner*—the drive and desire to continuously engage in learning.

26. *Maximizer*—the desire to make the most of one's own assets and those of others.
27. *Positivity*—the ability to see the best in situations and others.
28. *Relator*—the desire to make the most of close friendships and relationships.
29. *Responsibility*—the ability to take ownership for actions and outcomes.
30. *Restorative*—the drive to tackle and solve problems.
31. *Self-Assurance*—the ability to project and act with self-confidence.
32. *Significance*—the belief in the importance of one's efforts.
33. *Strategic*—the ability to select means to reach desired ends.
34. *Woo*—the ability to persuade others.

This is a very broad list. All of us have at least some of all of these qualities, so it can be difficult to identify which might be our signature strengths.

Self-Assessment Exercise

To identify the strengths that most clearly drive our passions and performance, let's try an exercise.

Write down 10 of the most fulfilling and meaningful experiences of your life. These could be work experiences, academic experiences, relationship experiences, or purely individual ones. What is important is that each of these experiences should stand out as ones that were very happy, significant, and successful for you—and that remain peak life experiences for you even now. Some of these experiences may have occurred in childhood or early adulthood; others may be recent. Take time and write out what happened in each experience and what made it positive for you. Don't move on in the chapter until you have written out your top experiences.

Once you've compiled your list, review the 34 strengths above and identify the three strengths that are most relevant to each of the 10 peak experiences. Although more than three might apply to each, do your best to identify the three that are most important to each of the positive experiences. This will give you a list of 30 strengths, though some undoubtedly will be repeated.

Please turn the page, but only after you've finished your responses to each question.

Let's take an example. One of my peak experiences was adopting my two youngest children. These were somewhat complicated private adoptions and required several strengths to reach fruition. The first of these was Arranger, navigating complex practical and legal constraints to make the adoptions happen. The second was Positivity. This manifested itself as an overcoming of numerous obstacles and frustrations and a focusing on the ways in which the children would contribute to our lives and we would contribute toward theirs. The third strength was Responsibility. We realized that we were taking on huge responsibilities in adding to our family and found this to be challenging and meaningful, not overwhelming.

If I think of other peak experiences, certain successes as a therapist stand out: ones in which I was able to make a significant contribution to another person's life. Most of those successes in counseling also involved a degree of Arranger, working through complicated life problems, as well as Positivity and Responsibility. Just the other week, I brought together a group of money managers from various firms to enjoy craft beer and discuss markets and ideas in finance. Once again, we see the themes of Arranger, Positivity, and Responsibility.

Of course, peak experiences can embody quite different strengths. One of my most fulfilling experiences was writing and publishing my first trading book. Key to that achievement was Focus, Ideation, and Significance. I wrote the entire book without a contract in hand, because the sheer elaboration of ideas was important to me and I knew, in my heart, that I had something worthy of publication. Those same qualities of Focus, Ideation, and Significance lie behind my daily writing of the TraderFeed blog since 2006. They also lie behind my passion for teaching and mentorship.

Key Takeaway

Experiences become peak experiences when they uniquely draw on our signature strengths.

As in my examples, you want to look across the 10 peak experiences that you wrote down and observe recurring strengths. If a strength appears in multiple positive life experiences, there is a very good likelihood that it is an important part of you. Across my 10 experiences, the strengths that recur include Positivity, Ideation, Significance, Learner, Intellection, Focus, Responsibility, Communication, and Achiever. Take a look at the strengths that most commonly frame your peak experiences. The odds are good that these are central to who you are at your best.

Now here's the key point: Your trading is most likely to be successful if it draws on the strengths that have supported your most fulfilling and meaningful life experiences. We commonly hear that successful traders possess a passion for markets. That is true, but it does not explain where such passion comes from. Successful traders are passionate about markets, because markets engage the signature strengths that bring passion to their lives.

■ How Strengths Interact to Create Successful Experience

The list of strengths makes it appear as though these exist in isolation. Nothing could be further from the truth. Strengths interact with one another in synergistic ways that make each of us unique. Often, it is the interaction of multiple strengths that define our most important capacities.

For example, the strengths of Ideation, Learner, and Positivity combine to support the writing of this book. They are also central to my coaching of traders. A core aspect of who I am is the desire to learn new things, discover new ideas, and apply those in positive ways to improve people's lives. It is not coincidence that I have adopted children and multiple rescue cats and that I reach out in my coaching to young, developing traders. The strengths of Responsibility and Positivity are central to all of those. Although Ideation is a strength, I could never function as a pure academic. It is the combination of ideas and their application to caring, positive contexts that most excites me. Similarly, what excites me about markets is not just making money, but seeing ideas come to fruition in a challenging, competitive context.

To continue our exercise, take a look at how the strengths you identified for the 10 peak experiences are grouped. Very often, if you see one strength, you'll find others. *When clusters recur, it's a strong indication that these groupings are important to your performance.* Some of the common strength clusters I've observed among traders include:

■ *Deliberative and Discipline*—strengths that involve planning and sticking to plans

- *Adaptability and Learner*—strengths that enable traders to adapt to changing markets

- *Analytic and Strategic*—strengths that make use of research to guide forward action

- *Focus and Activator*—strengths that involve goal setting and following

- *Communication and Relator*—strengths seen among traders working well in teams

Of course, clusters can include three or more strengths. I've known very strong traders who display strengths in Learner, Intellection, Analytic, and Ideation. They are great idea generators and succeed from the depth and breadth of their research. I've also known traders with distinctive strengths in Self-Assurance, Woo, Maximizer, Developer, and Command. They have been very effective team leaders within trading firms. *Note that strengths greatly shape how we approach trading*: The trader with analytic and learning strengths is highly research based; the trader with leadership strengths constructs trading within a team context.

Reflect on how long it took you to identify the strengths for your peak experiences and how easy or difficult the exercise was for you. If you found it very difficult to identify peak experiences and their associated strengths, it may well be the case that you are not well acquainted with your greatest assets. You would be surprised how common this is. When traders go through rocky periods in their performance, they become quite focused on their problems, but not their strengths. This is reflected in many trading journals. Many journals maintained by traders are filled with descriptions of problems and frustrations. Few track strengths and their application to trading. Much of the time, if trading goes well, we don't feel a tremendous need to analyze our performance. It is only when we begin to go off the rails that we reflect on what has gone wrong. As we saw earlier, that tends to keep us problem focused and not solution focused.

It also keeps us out of touch with the essential drivers of our success.

■ ■ ■

Tina was a young developing trader. She was very motivated to learn about markets. She read numerous books and took several online courses. Most of what she read and learned pertained to daytrading. She worked hard at tracking markets on an intraday basis and showed a positive learning curve in simulated trading, so she began trading live.

Her returns were mixed, as she neither lost much money nor made much. Oddly, however, her love for trading seemed to diminish as she actually pursued trading. More than once, she put the trading aside, only to pick it up when her curiosity returned. It was almost as if she were in love with the idea of trading, but not with trading itself. Her mixed responses made little sense to her, and she reached out for help.

When I met with Tina, I found her to be personable and quite curious about markets. She asked many questions about markets and the qualities of successful traders and spent surprisingly little time focusing on her immediate situation. Once I brought the conversation around to her, she spoke at length about her husband and children and the challenges of balancing her day job, her home responsibilities, and her trading interests.

Very often when I first meet someone, I learn as much by how they talk as by what they say. In Tina's case, I found it striking that her pace of speaking and her vocal inflection picked up when she spoke about her family. It was clear that she relished the role of being a wife and mother and worked well with her husband to coordinate the school and extracurricular activities of their two children. Tina was especially proud of her children's grades in school and their success in several sports. When Tina spoke about markets, there was definite interest and curiosity, but none of the excitement that I heard in her voice about her experiences with her children. There was relatively little excitement at all regarding her day job.

As we spoke, it became clear that Tina's strengths were distinctly interpersonal. On the Buckingham and Clifton dimensions, she would have scored quite high in Relator, Empathy, Developer, and Connectedness. She possessed other strengths, but those were some of the ones that accounted for the energy in her voice. Which of those strengths were expressed by her trading?

None.

The problem was that her trading, geared to the day time frame, tended to take her away from the children and family. Her day job was part time and largely took place while the kids were in school. That left early mornings and late afternoons and evenings for trading and preparation. As she spent more time with her trading, she felt more distant from the family activities that gave her joy and she felt more frustrated with the conflict she felt over how to spend her time. Her husband was quite accommodating and encouraged her trading, but Tina just could not derive from trading what she got from being there when her children returned from school.

We will explore the issue of strengths as weaknesses a bit later. What turned Tina's situation around is that she began to dabble with longer-term trading using a variety of options structures. These were relatively low-risk strategies that enabled her to ride positions for weeks, with minimal time needed to hedge or otherwise adjust positions. Much of her research and preparation could be performed during weekends. The lengthened time frame allowed her to be involved in markets, but not at the expense of her other commitments and passions. The reduced pace of trading also gave her time to create a network of developing traders that engaged in mutual mentorship, directly drawing on her strengths.

	Key Takeaway	

Successful trading has to fit into your life, not the reverse.

What Tina's situation teaches us is that *we don't have to have all of our needs met through our trading, but we cannot allow our trading to frustrate our most fundamental needs and strengths*. One of Tina's pitfalls was that she fell for the stereotype that a successful trader has to have such a passion for trading that it becomes an overriding interest. What she ultimately found is that such a passion does not have to take the form of an obsession. By stepping back, trading a longer time frame, and using options to flexibly express views and manage risk, she discovered a sustainable way to pursue markets passionately, while not compromising the strengths and commitments central to her identity.

◼ What Strengths Don't You Possess?

Let's now return to the list of 30 strengths you identified for your 10 peak experiences. Review the Buckingham and Clifton list of strengths above and identify which items you did *not* select as strengths. It turns out that the areas that are not your strengths can be quite important to your success.

Of course, just because a competency is not your strength doesn't make it a weakness. Rather, capacities that are not your strengths can represent areas for personal growth. For example, across my 10 peak experiences, the strengths of Fairness, Harmony, and Inclusiveness are nowhere to be found. I suspect if you asked people who knew me well, they would say that I possess those qualities, but they are not self-defining. Similarly, the strengths of Command and Woo were not part of my list. Can I lead and persuade others? Yes, in certain situations. Those, however, have never been key parts of my self-concept or life successes. In my personal relationships, however, I have tended to seek out people who embrace Fairness, Harmony, and Inclusiveness. Being with others who possess those strengths brings out those qualities in me. Similarly, in my business relationships, I have enjoyed working with colleagues who are strong in Command and Woo. Those qualities effectively complement my own.

When we move too far from our strengths, we can compromise our motivation and that compromises our performance. Trying to make ourselves into someone we are not is a recipe for frustration and failure. For years, I tried convincing myself that I *should* trade in ways similar to others I had observed and admired. It was great in theory, but simply did not fit me and led to dead-ends and losses. Similarly, when I have tried to take on Command and Woo roles, I have not been particularly effective. My heart hasn't been in it. I am very good as a Relator, not as one who would Command.

This desire to emulate others is a particular pitfall for developing traders. Eager to find the success that others enjoy, they approach markets in a manner that might fit the strengths of their mentor, but not their own. One trader I met ran into one problem with discipline after another in markets, though in other areas of life was quite disciplined. It turned out he is quite Deliberative in his cognitive style. Given enough time, he can creatively think of ways to approach most any situation. Trying to trade rapid chart-based setups, however, he felt rushed and frazzled. This led to poor decision making. Coaches exhorted him to do a better job of following the "plays," but it was precisely those setups that were disrupting his performance. When he moved to a longer holding period and more selective criteria for entering and exiting trades, he no longer felt harried and suddenly possessed fine discipline!

Competencies that are not our strengths, however, can be valuable if we work within a team-based environment. This includes both formal and informal teams: groups we might work with inside trading firms and colleagues with whom we collaborate in virtual space. A couple of savvy short-term traders I know subscribe to sophisticated research services to help them gain a bigger picture sense for markets. If they tried to perform such research themselves, it would bog them down and interfere with their normal market preparation. Drawing on the analytical strengths of researchers, however, provides them with perspectives they could never accomplish on their own.

One team I worked with for many years consisted of a portfolio manager who was unusually aggressive and decisive in his trading and his more cautious analyst. His analyst in fact was extremely detail oriented, prudent, and conservative in risk taking. Over time, they developed an effective collaboration, in which the manager benefited from knowing that the analyst's recommendations were well-grounded and researched and the analyst benefited from knowing that his ideas would be expressed forthrightly in the portfolio.

Marriages are not so different. Similarity of values and temperaments but complementarity of strengths can be a formula for lasting marital success. I can think of many happily married couples in which one member of the couple is highly achievement oriented and the other is very interpersonally sensitive and capable. I tend to be idea-oriented and love to develop big-picture plans. Margie is highly responsible and detail oriented. One of us is good at planning vacations; the other is great at getting bills paid on time! By teaming with people whose strengths complement our own, we can expand our horizons without interfering with our own signature capabilities.

As you look over the strengths that are not ones that you identified for your peak experiences, select one or two that you believe could complement your trading. For instance, perhaps you are very strong at generating trading ideas (Ideation and Analytical), but not so strong in managing the positions stemming from those ideas (Discipline and Deliberative). Collaborating with a highly disciplined colleague by sharing ideas and trading plans could be a great way to create synergy. Some of the best collaborations of this nature that I've seen have resulted when a trader with great ideas teams up with a skilled quantitative analyst and programmer. On their own, the quant programmer could never generate insightful trading ideas. Left to his or her own devices, the creative trader could never test ideas and implement them with model-driven consistency. The blend of strengths creates a hybrid trading—neither wholly discretionary nor wholly automated—that incorporates the best of each.

Effective collaborations also come from traders who view markets in complementary ways. For example, one might be unusually talented at discerning macro themes over the medium term. Another is quite sensitive to how markets trade around short-term price levels and can anticipate intraday swings in markets. Together, their teamwork results in superior entry and exit execution of longer-term trades.

There is much to be said for self-acceptance. We are who we are. Our job is to discover our strengths and find the kind of relationships and productive work that embrace and express the best within us. But there is also much to be said for making life—and trading—a team sport, even when you're a solo trader. No one has strengths in all areas relevant for optimal performance. By drawing on the strengths of others, we expand ourselves. By contributing our strengths to others, we cement effective working relationships. Isolation is a recipe for stagnation. If you find the people who bring out your strengths—and who are willing and able to share their own—you can expand yourself, even as you remain grounded in who you are.

■ Can Your Strengths Also Be Weaknesses?

Strengths can derail success if not expressed and fulfilled. Recall Tina, the trader whose family strengths and commitments made it difficult to focus on active trading. When Tina was highly absorbed in the moment-to-moment action of markets, she felt detached from her family life. This, in turn, distracted her and diminished her excitement about trading. Out of the resulting frustration, she made poor decisions that resulted in losses. A casual observer might conclude that Tina lacked emotional control and discipline. Nothing could have been further from the truth, however. What sabotaged her daytrading were her unfulfilled needs and strengths.

Look at it this way: We naturally gravitate to what we do best and what feels best to us. Give me free time and I will gravitate to my lounge chair, a book, and a cat on my lap. I rarely watch TV, visit with neighbors, or chat on the phone. It takes no discipline to get me to read new books or spend time with Ginger or Mia downstairs. If someone wanted me to watch a certain amount of television each day or engage in a number of daily phone chats, that would take concerted effort, and I'd likely experience a fair amount of procrastination. I don't find excuses to avoid books or cats and motivation to enjoy those is not in short supply.

Imagine, however, that the only job I can find is one in which I spend all day on the phone talking with people about television shows. Perhaps it's a job surveying people about the television shows they most enjoy. I would experience little connectedness within the job and would greatly miss intellectual stimulation. Over time, my ardor for the job would diminish. That would show up in my performance: Perhaps I'd make fewer calls per day or fail to ask the right follow-up questions during the surveys. My manager might conclude that I'm an unmotivated worker, but the problem would be more subtle than that. Work that does not tap core strengths cannot tap our deepest motivations and passions. In that setting, my strengths become a weakness, preventing me from fully devoting myself to the demands of the job.

Key Takeaway

Unexpressed, unfulfilled strengths derail performance.

A classic example that I described in earlier writings occurred when I left my full-time work as a psychologist at a medical school and sought to trade full time. I hated it. Sitting all day in front of a screen and focusing solely on markets and trading plans struck me as unbearably sterile. Why? One of my most distinctive strengths is Developer: I love helping others reach their potential. It's why I enjoy teaching, why I love counseling, and why I've adopted children and rescue cats. Being part of the fulfillment of another being is deeply fulfilling to me. Trading solo in my own office gave me none of that.

So what happened? I began to reach out to other traders online and responded to their questions, especially of a psychological nature. I met many interesting traders that way and enjoyed helping them. Too often, however, I spent time in online chat mode helping traders and missed my own trading setups! After failing to make several good trades, I had to stand back and ask myself what in the world was going on. Quite simply, my unmet needs and strengths were intruding on my trading. When the psychologist in me was not fulfilled, I could not find fulfillment in markets. Those Developer strengths help me as a coach, but derailed my full-time trading.

■ ■ ■

One of the greatest challenges for business management is the problem of employee engagement. Suppose you ask workers if they feel psychologically committed to their jobs and if they believe they are making positive contributions to their organizations. How many do you think report a high degree of engagement? How many feel as though they're invested in their work and are making a positive difference?

The Gallup Organization has undertaken this research on a global scale. Across 142 countries, only 13 percent of workers feel engaged in their work; 24 percent report being actively disengaged; and the rest simply say they are "not engaged." In the United States and Canada, 29 percent of workers report being engaged; over 70 percent are either not engaged or are actively disengaged. Given that employee engagement is directly correlated with employee productivity and that actively disengaged employees are least likely to deliver quality work and customer service, this represents a significant challenge for business and other organizations.

There is a very simple reason for this epidemic of disengagement. When employees are hired, they are typically brought in to fill a prescribed slot within the organization. Jobs are not tailored to the strengths of employees; employees are expected to fit into prefabricated job descriptions. People need jobs and, given the choice, most will choose a job that is less than fulfilling over being unemployed. So people fill slots, their strengths go unnoticed and unexpressed, and eventually a measure of alienation sets in.

I recently had the good fortune to visit a company in which all employees were included in periodic company meetings. All were strongly encouraged—and incentivized—to make suggestions to improve the firm. From the lowliest clerk to the most senior manager, everyone had a voice. Moreover, each employee was expected to draw up a plan at the start of the year, outlining goals for personal and professional development. That plan was a central part of employee reviews and the determination of bonuses. Managers were specifically tasked with helping employees hit their goals. The achievement of those goals was formally—and informally—recognized and valued within the company. During my visit, the degree of employee engagement was tangible. The company had no turnover problem whatsoever and was able to recruit top talent, even though salaries were not sky-high.

Compare that situation with the average retail outlet or manufacturing firm. In many companies, employees never hear from senior managers and managers don't know the names of many of the employees. At one trading firm where I worked, there were no programs to develop young talent—on and off the trading floor—and up-and-coming stars were given no formal recognition and no role in management committees and processes. Many of these young people had excellent suggestions for improving the firm, but more often than not, these did not receive a response. Over time, the trading firm lost its best young talent, as employees felt little loyalty to their company. By defining leadership processes in ways that excluded employee strengths, management ensured that they would have a disengaged workforce.

So that raises an interesting question: What is *your* level of engagement as a trader?

■ ■ ■

Dale was an analyst at a trading firm, but his goal was to become an independent money manager. Eager to attract Dale to his team and keep his motivation high, his portfolio manager boss gave him a small trading account. He made it clear that Dale needed to put his analytical work for the "big book" front and center, but also encouraged Dale to trade his small book well, because that could lead to allocations of more capital over time. Dale's boss had discussed the arrangement with me and liked it for two reasons. First, by seeing the positions that Dale put into his own portfolio, he would see clearly Dale's greatest convictions. Second, he liked the idea of teamwork and the possibility that Dale could mature into a co-manager of the team's funds. This structuring of the role, he believed, gave Dale a real incentive to remain loyal to him and the firm.

Several months into the new working relationship, the boss gave me an assessment. Dale's work was excellent. He was attentive to detail work: booking and reconciling trades, keeping in touch with relevant research, pricing options when needed, and sending out alerts when positions were near key price levels. Dale stayed on top of central bank minutes and data releases and updated the team's risk metrics each day. The portfolio manager said he had never worked with such a diligent assistant.

Still, he was frustrated with Dale.

Although Dale had plenty of opportunities to take risk in his small portfolio, he had entered few positions. When he did take a position, it was sized unusually small, even for his modest capital. On several occasions his boss encouraged him to take more risk and Dale agreed, but somehow it never happened.

I was also surprised. I felt Dale had talent and could develop into a successful portfolio manager. He had the mentorship to accomplish this goal, and he was given a clear path to growing his capital and developing a track record. How many young traders would raise heaven and earth for a shot at such an opportunity? Dale recognized this and told me he would put more attention into his trading. I offered to meet with Dale on a weekly basis simply to focus on his trading as a way of expressing my interest and confidence in him. More often than not, however, Dale had to cancel the meetings because he was busy attending to the big book.

It became clear to me that Dale simply was not engaged as a trader. He agreed it was something he should do, but he sounded like my kids paying lip service to eating their veggies. It wasn't in his blood and didn't seem to give him any thrills whatsoever.

So I tried a little experiment.

When I met with Dale, I congratulated him and said that I had been hearing good things about his work. I asked him to step back mentally and review the year to date. What were his greatest successes and what gave him his greatest sense of challenge and accomplishment in his work to date?

Dale responded quickly and enthusiastically. He said that he was contributing to the team portfolio not only by taking care of mechanics, but also by helping to shape the expression of the trade ideas. For example, Dale's boss wanted to be short fixed income in the United States. Dale examined various points on the curve, relationships between the United States and other curves, and the pricing of different instruments. He eventually found a way to express a short view that carried well and had a far better risk/reward profile than a plain-vanilla short position in the futures market. When shorts were squeezed, many managers lost money on the trade, but Dale's team did not lose money. By expressing the view in relative terms and selecting mispriced points on curves, the team saved considerable money.

Dale proceeded to show me another trade that he was working on. Many portfolio managers wanted to be long US stocks, but Dale liked the pricing of options to express the view, particularly given important monetary policy meetings and data releases ahead. He wanted to benefit from a pickup in volatility, as well as an upward move in stocks. My immediate impression was that Dale was playing on a three-dimensional chessboard. He saw an edge in the directional view, but he also saw the edge in volatility. By combining the edges he had a trade superior to the one that 90+ percent of traders would take. I had no doubt that Dale was adding significant performance to the portfolio through his ability to find unique expressions of ideas that enhanced risk-adjusted returns.

I also had the strong sense that Dale's greatest love was research and analytics. The actual trading of positions and worrying about profits and losses did not appeal to him in the least. Dale was also extremely dedicated to his work and loyal to his manager. He liked making money, but most of all liked making a contribution to the larger business. If I had to label Dale's strength, I'd say that he was an excellent servant leader. He showed real leadership in expressing and executing trades, but accomplished this by serving within a team. He did not want the limelight and wasn't motivated by huge paydays. His strengths were his diligence and ability to collaborate effectively.

Dale was not engaged in his trading because it pulled him away from what he most loved doing. His very strengths were weaknesses in the trading context. We naturally engage activities that maximize our values, interests, and abilities. When we see disengagement in trading, it's generally because there is a mismatch either between trading and strengths or between the particular trading approach pursued and those strengths.

Dale eventually put trading aside altogether. He indicated that he was best suited to a role as an analyst and strategist. His manager was entirely supportive, recognizing that he could not find anyone else to replicate Dale's work. Dale wanted neither the limelight nor the pressure of managing capital. He derived joy from developing ideas and seeing them blossom for the team. Focused on what he loved and what he excelled at, he had no problem whatsoever with engagement.

■ ■ ■

So back to the earlier question: What is your level of engagement as a trader? Too often, traders respond to this question with the glib assertion that they, indeed, have a "passion" for trading. Putting aside emotional expressions for moment, however, let's consider your behavioral engagement: *How intensively are you engaged in the concrete tasks associated with trading?* Surprisingly, many of those who most loudly proclaim their passion for trading are relatively disengaged when it comes to quality time spent in trade planning, research, position management, and performance review. As basketball coach Bob Knight once observed, everyone has the will to win, but far fewer have the will to prepare to win.

Key Takeaway

Engagement is what enables us to deliver our peak performances.

In his 2014 book, *Faster, Higher, Stronger,* Mark McClusky details what goes into peak performance in athletics and other performance fields. He stresses that small, continuous improvements in processes lead to large cumulative impacts on performance. The key to such improvement is the constant measurement of outcomes, feedback about what can be improved, and efforts toward improvement: the deliberate practice described by researcher Anders Ericsson (1996). For example, slow-motion filming of a baseball pitcher may reveal that he is not fully transferring his weight from back foot to front foot during his windup and release. By extending his follow through, he is able to improve his velocity, while not losing accuracy. In itself, that's a relatively small change. Imagine, however, that it is followed by similar small but meaningful improvements in strength conditioning, in grip of the ball, and in pitch selection. Over time, the good pitcher becomes a great one. McClusky's point is that elite performers don't just get better; *they get better at getting better.*

Note the level of engagement that is required for such ongoing improvement. *An elite performer spends far more time working on his or her performance than in actually performing.* A weekly basketball or football game may last a couple of hours or so. The preparation for that game extends over many days. The actual time spent in direct Olympic competition is very small compared with the years of training and prep work. If a soccer player was engaged on the field during games but not during practice and training, he would quickly lose his slot to a player immersed in McClusky's continuous improvement process. A trader who enjoys the thrills of victory and challenges of losses while markets are open, but who is not engaged in research, idea generation, risk management, and performance review, is similarly likely to fall behind the trader who embraces all of those processes.

The ratio of time spent preparing for trading and working on improving trading relative to the amount of time spent actually watching screens and trading is a very helpful metric for engagement. By the same reasoning, the amount of time spent working on trading when primary markets are closed is an excellent measure of engagement. Most traders assume that they are competitive because they like making money. Gamblers like making money also, but that doesn't make them elite performers. Truly competitive traders are competitive with themselves: They track their performance religiously and look for ways to continually better themselves. Their engagement is expressed through learning and improvement, not simply through risk taking.

As rare as it is for traders to find trading approaches that express their strengths, it's even rarer for traders to cultivate self-improvement routines that extend those strengths. When our self-improvement activities don't fit with what speaks to us, we lose the power of engagement. That can help keep us static in a fast-changing world.

■ Making Our Strengths Stronger

In the TraderFeed blog, I have emphasized an important performance principle: *Everything in life is use it or lose it.* We either exercise our capacities or they atrophy. If we don't work out, we lose strength and aerobic conditioning. If we don't actively employ and challenge our personality, emotional, and cognitive strengths, they weaken. Strengths don't remain strong unless we routinely exercise them.

The *use it or lose it* principle has many important implications. Here's a worthwhile exercise: Take a look at your weekly schedule and map out your activities each day of the week during morning, afternoon, and evening hours. Over the course of a typical week, how much time are you doing the following?

- Enjoying and cultivating a romantic relationship

- Spending quality time with friends

- Spending quality time with family

- Exposing yourself to new information about markets

- Engaging in quality conversations with trading colleagues

- Relaxing and nurturing yourself

- Enjoying individual interests and recreational activities

- Engaging in spiritual interests and pursuits

- Reviewing and working on your trading performance

- Engaging in significant physical exercise

- Engaging in artistic and cultural interests and activities

- Getting quality sleep

- Engaging in learning for the sake of learning

- Engaging in political, charitable, and/or service activities

- Going out for meaningful entertainment and socializing

Clearly this is but a small list of the possible activities that could populate one's calendar. It's difficult to imagine being able to do all of these in a given week. Inevitably, we end up making choices regarding the things we do and the things that we put aside. For instance, we may spend a good amount of time working on market preparation, but little time socializing and cultivating friendships. We might attend to family and career, but spend relatively little time in exercise and quality sleep. In the ways we spend our time, we inevitably build certain capacities and leave others relatively underdeveloped.

When strengths atrophy with disuse, they can derail performance. A classic example is the trader who is so consumed with his work that he neglects romantic and family relationships. Eventually conflict builds in those relationships. Spouses feel neglected; children act up to get attention. The unfulfilled needs become a distraction and eventually interfere with concentration and work quality. Similarly, neglecting our physical needs for exercise, nutrition, and sleep can rob us of energy over time and lead to diminished work efficiency and effectiveness. Recall my earlier example: Focusing on trading and neglecting the social strengths that brought me to psychology completely disrupted my trading performance. Had I stopped using my interpersonal strengths and began losing them, my trading experience would have gone from bad to worse, trapping me in work that eroded the very strengths essential for my success.

The bottom line is that if there's a strength you want to build, it has to become part of your daily and weekly routines. If it's not in your appointment book, it's not a hard commitment, and it won't become part of you. As we'll see later in the book, a major reason for becoming process-driven is to ensure that we remain grounded in the best practices that capture our strengths.

Please review the activities in your weekly calendar and identify how many of those activities are specifically designed to challenge you and extend your boundaries. Physical exercise may test your limits or could simply maintain the status quo. Similarly, we can maintain friendships and relationships or we can expand those. A vacation can be routine and relaxing, or it can push us to new experiences. Very, very often, we spend so much time in maintenance mode that we fail to truly strengthen our strengths. McClusky's work makes clear that performance improvement comes from finding our limits and systematically moving beyond those. Ericsson's work finds that elite performers, relative to their lesser peers, spend more time on the activities that are difficult for them. In that sense, deliberate practice is not all passionate fun; it often is very hard work. *To the degree that we do not push ourselves, we cannot benefit from the fruits of deliberate practice.* We may stay good at what we do, but we're unlikely to turn *good* into *great*.

Consider the review processes of traders. Trader A keeps a journal each day, notes some of the problems that occurred during the day, and grades his performance. Trader B tracks each trade and how it was generated and managed, what her mood and energy state were during the trading, and how much money was won or lost. Each week, Trader B examines the factors associated with her worst trades and sets concrete goals for the following week to improve the areas where she fell short.

If you ask Traders A and B if they keep a journal, both will say yes. Both no doubt consider themselves to be motivated and hardworking. Only one of them, however, is on a genuine learning curve, reducing vulnerabilities by strengthening strengths. The journal of Trader A is executed in a routine manner, with little boundary-extending effort. It expresses emotions and makes observations, *but never translates those into concrete goals and plans for future action.* Trader B, on the other hand, pushes herself beyond her comfort level. She makes systematic efforts to find areas needing improvement and address those.

What Trader A probably doesn't appreciate is that he is likely to become a victim of use it or lose it. Secure in the knowledge that he is keeping a journal and "sticking to his discipline," he actually builds no incremental trading skills. He is like a department store that never changes its product mix or marketing strategies. The result is not a maintenance of status quo, because—as we saw in the first section of the book—the status quo itself evolves. By failing to improve his repertoire, Trader A will increasingly find himself with a shrinking arsenal of effective methods.

There is a more subtle manifestation of use it or lose it that results when traders fail to strengthen their strengths. The capacity for sustained, directed effort is itself a competency and strength, as we've seen with research on willpower. One of the important factors differentiating peak performers in the military Special Forces from others is the highly developed capacity to sustain performance under unfavorable conditions. As I described in *Enhancing Trader Development*, recruits for Army Rangers, Navy SEALs, and other elite units invariably undergo an unusually rigorous training process, where they are given little sleep, multiple difficult tasks, and plenty of attitude from drillmasters. Even when not deployed, they are expected to maintain high standards of physical conditioning and drilling of skills. If a recruit cannot sustain effort over time, he inevitably drops from the training process. Those that remain build the strength to face adversity and push themselves beyond their comfort level *as a normal mode of daily functioning.*

This latter point is extremely important. Humans, like other animals, have evolved in a manner that enables them to conserve energy. If there is a threat, we go into flight-or-fight mode. If we are safe and secure, we don't waste energy. This conservation of energy is highly adaptive in an environment of scarcity. In an environment in which basic needs are met, our default setting of conservation works against us. Like cats that sleep much of the day when stimulation is not present, we tend to not generate our own stimulation and challenge. What makes elite athletic and military training distinctive is that it moves the default setting of participants. Stasis is the exception, rather than the rule. The peak performer's default is pushing the envelope; effort itself becomes a source of well-being and fulfillment.

Key Takeaway

The failure to train ourselves is itself a negative training.

The *use it or lose it* principle means that we have to become good at pushing the envelope in every area of life that matters to us. Our Trader A who keeps a rote journal and does not use it to systematically challenge and change performance does not move his default setting a bit. He *is* in a training process, but he is training himself to not sustain the level of directed, sustained effort observed by McClusky among elite performers. Deliberate practice requires the capacity to stay deliberate: We cannot strengthen our strengths if comfort is our programmed default.

■ The Excellence Principle

The previous discussion leads us to a very simple, but very important principle of excellence: *We cannot achieve excellence in any field of endeavor unless excellence is built into our daily routines.* In other words, day after day, week after week of OK-to-good performance will never add up to excellence. To achieve excellence in a career, we have to achieve excellence in our individual acts. There can be no excellence in a trading career without individual, excellent trades and a host of excellent trading processes.

Let's revise the earlier exercise. Now review your weekly schedule and identify how many activities you can truly say were performed in a manner that took you beyond your comfort level. If there is nothing in your daily life performed in an extraordinary manner, then you are grounded in the ordinary. We either use our capacity for excellence or, over time, we lose it.

If you doubt this, take a good look at what happens to so many people in retirement. They work for a career, and what is their ultimate reward? To not work! And they don't. They socialize with friends, they putter in the garden, they travel, and they enjoy what they define as a life of comfort. Not surprisingly, many lose physical conditioning and fall prey to aches and pains that they chalk up to old age. Over time, they are less and less able to sustain meaningful efforts, living more like those sleepy cats than as creative, productive human beings.

But that's not the worst of it. *Use it or lose it also means that if we do not exercise our character strengths, those eventually fade.* If we stop engaging in caring activities, we become less caring. If we no longer need to collaborate, we become more cantankerous, less able to sustain cooperation. I recall one retiree who was happy to leave his job and child rearing behind. Now is *my* time, he expressed to me. The kids were out of the home and raising their own families; they could "row their own boats." Severing connections with family and work, he gradually found himself isolated, lonely, and bored—and made up for that by overeating. Health problems followed from his poor eating and lack of exercise. He chose a romantic partner who was equally untethered to career or family and who filled her void with compulsive shopping. Over time, I watched a successful businessman and family man fall into a low-energy morass of self-indulgence. Years of failing to strengthen his strengths left him with a host of weaknesses and vulnerabilities.

To be sure, retirement can be a stimulating and rewarding time of life, but not if it represents a flight from efforts to extend the self. Most of us are naturally forced to extend our boundaries simply from the demands of raising children and building a career. Once those activities are gone, it can be difficult to find substitute arenas for boundary pushing.

This is very relevant to trading because many traders, deep inside, pursue trading as an alternative to the hard work of traditional careers. I recently attended a trading conference where the speaker, a well-known daytrader, exhorted his audience to work on their trading lest they have to settle for 8-to-5 careers. I could only shake my head in disbelief, recalling all the successful traders I worked with who get up in the middle of the night to track markets in Asia and Europe and spend long weekend hours researching markets, reviewing their portfolios, and preparing themselves for the week ahead. No, they didn't have 8-to-5 jobs: Like so many peak performers, *they live their jobs.* Ironically, the speaker projected trading as a comfortable lifestyle where one is not burdened by 40 hours of work per week. Locked into such a mindset, no trader will sustain the efforts to cultivate strengths and adapt to markets over time. The entire idea of developing one's trading when markets are not open is anathema to work-avoidant traders: They've entered trading as an alternative to normal work, not as a source of extraordinary effort and achievement!

Therein lies a most important distinction: Those who pursue trading as a job, those who make trading a career, and those who approach trading as a calling. Our speaker viewed trading merely as a job. Its appeal was that it promised great pay for few hours of work. Most traders at established trading firms do not have such a view. They bring a level of professionalism to their work and recognize that they operate in a demanding performance field. They see money management as a career, grounded in sound risk management and fiduciary responsibility. Very often, they speak of trading as their "business," taking ownership in the success of an ongoing venture.

The trader whose market participation is an expression of ever-strengthening strengths, however, finds more than a career. Trading becomes a calling. It doesn't matter whether markets are open or closed, whether there is more or less risk in the book. Markets become an ongoing source of learning, challenge, and stimulation. When Ed Seykota compared good and great traders by pointing out that the former have talent, but—for the latter—the talent has them, he captured a very important point: *Our strengths frame our callings.* We are most likely to live the excellence principle when our work becomes more than a job and more than a career. We ultimately retire from both of those. Callings are enduring; there is no retirement from that which is intrinsic to us.

What have you undertaken with excellence today? How will you embody excellence tomorrow? How will you truly expand yourself over the next week?

Those are the questions that transform trading from a routine job or career to an all-absorbing calling.

■ Making a Habit of Developing the Right Habits

Recall Charles Duhigg's excellent book, *The Power of Habit* (2012). His thesis is that changes in behavior are not the result of motivation and conscious efforts at self-improvement. Rather, we develop by cultivating the right habits. Successful people are those who have internalized habits that bring success. This provides them with a consistency that could never be achieved if they always had to rely on fragile willpower.

From this perspective, the strengthening of strengths that we see among elite performers is the result of turning effortful, deliberate practice itself into a habit pattern. Habit becomes the scaffold supporting continuous improvements in performance: We progress by turning a new level of development into a habit and status quo and then build on it once it's been internalized. Ericsson observes that our ability to turn effortful performance into automatic behavior is both a boon and an obstacle. When we turn our concentrated efforts to learn to drive a car into automatic behavior, we free ourselves to better attend to the road and conversations with passengers. Once automated, however, skills no longer improve on their own. *To sustain deliberate practice, we have to take what has become automatic and systematically make efforts at improvement.* The elite racecar driver is one who makes successive levels of improving driving automatic, only to disrupt habit and seek yet further levels of performance. When excellence becomes a habit pattern, development takes on a stair-step course: internalizing new levels of performance, turning those into habits, and then extending those habits to rise to still higher levels.

Consider the elite performers in Olympic events. The entire focus of their training is to push for improved performance. Working on oneself itself becomes a dominant habit pattern—it is the norm, not the exception, in the weekly calendar. To sustain the habit of self-improvement, performers have to get to the point where they actively seek out and embrace their shortcomings. Several decades ago, American carmakers were eclipsed by Japanese firms in part because the latter sought out weaknesses in the assembly process. American firms ran assembly lines at a speed designed to minimize errors. Japanese firms accelerated the assembly lines to find out which parts of processes broke first. They then consulted with workers and instituted process improvements. The American assembly process did not evolve over time; the Japanese achieved continuous quality improvement. They had turned excellence into a habit pattern.

Key Takeaway

Elite performers consciously craft their habit patterns.

Many traders operate more like the old US automakers and less like the Japanese upstarts. They seek to avoid losses and drawdowns. When those occur, they are as likely to become defensive as aggressive in ferreting out and learning from mistakes. A while back, I visited a trading firm and spoke with young traders who had experienced a period of difficult performance. Many of those traders prided themselves on stepping back from markets, maintaining their cool, and not trading emotionally. That was all well and good, but what the traders also avoided was any systematic learning and adaptation in the face of their drawdowns. Their goal was to minimize negative emotions, not maximize adaptive learning. To climb the stair-step pattern of performance improvement, they would have had to have actively revisit their difficult trades, identify the mistakes they may have made, and institute corrective efforts to guide their future trading. At a purely emotional level, however, the last thing they wanted to do was revisit their difficulties. In seeking to move on, they unwittingly reinforced a vulnerable status quo.

When Angela Duckworth et al. (2007) studied success, two factors stood out as contributors: (1) grit, the ability to maintain resilience and rebound from setbacks; and (2) self-control, the ability to chart a course of action and stick to it conscientiously. Pushing the envelope in the spirit of use it or lose it means that we embrace setbacks. If we continually challenge ourselves, we'll fall short on occasion. Without emotional resilience, we cannot sustain true deliberate practice. But grit, while necessary for success, was not sufficient in Duckworth's research. To sustain deliberate practice, we must be able to stay deliberate. That is the self-control factor. The elite performer not only weathers setbacks but also doesn't allow them to set them back.

How are they able to do this?

Emilia Lahti has studied a particular strength, called *sisu*, that is grounded in her native Finnish culture. Sisu is more than persistence under duress. Lahti describes it as a kind of second wind that one discovers as the result of extraordinary efforts. Runners, of course, have experienced the second-wind phenomenon. Lahti points out that sisu is itself a capacity that can be cultivated: We can learn to gain more consistent access to resources of energy and focus at times when we begin to feel depleted.

Sisu is a very important concept, because it suggests that willpower is not exactly a battery that we periodically drain. Rather, once the battery is depleted, we have our own internal alternator that can provide a recharge. Those Olympic athletes and Special Forces soldiers who undergo rigorous training really are participating in processes that cultivate sisu. Pushed to their limits again and again, these performers learn to more consistently access their second winds. That access itself becomes gratifying and pleasurable, setting up the essential performance improvement dynamic in which the extension of the self is itself a giver of energy.

■ ■ ■

Oskar is a trader whose performance has led his firm for a while. It wasn't always that way. When Oskar first began, he went through an extended period of negative performance, though he managed his risk quite well. As he began to make money, his conversations with me did not change significantly. He still looked for improvements he could make and ways of working on those improvements. After a particularly strong period of performance, he emailed me and said he wanted to speak by phone at my earliest convenience. My assumption was that he was weighing how much profit he should take and lock in versus let ride in longer-term positions.

But, no.

Oskar knew exactly how he wanted to manage his upside: He sold some of his cash positions and rolled over his options into new strikes with solid risk/reward. What he wanted to discuss was a trade that he had *not* entered. It was an idea in the equities markets that had caused some losses earlier in the year. Although the opportunity recurred recently, he decided to not pursue the trade because of those earlier losses. Had he entered the trade, his recent gains would have been larger.

Oskar didn't like that. He wasn't focused on the money he had made. He wanted to improve his level of resilience so that he wouldn't avoid good ideas simply because they had not panned out previously. *In the midst of making money, his focus was on getting better*. His urgency in working on the issue was every bit as great as if he had been in drawdown.

Oskar differed from his colleagues in that he was not comfortable with comfort. As soon as he experienced a winning period, he became antsy. He started researching other markets and ideas to find new opportunities. He drilled down on his performance to find things to work on. *In a very important sense, he was motivated by self-improvement, not by trading itself.* Markets simply offered him a kind of gymnasium for deliberate practice workouts and accessing *sisu*. Like many successful traders who find a calling in markets, he could have retired on his earnings years ago. It was the appeal of climbing yet taller heights and achieving even higher goals that drove him forward. Having strengths wasn't enough: He needed to continually hone those.

■ A Look at Character Strengths

The research of Buckingham and Clifton is but one scheme for categorizing and identifying strengths. A very different look at strengths comes from the research-based examination of *Character Strengths and Virtues* from Peterson and Seligman (2004). Their "manual of sanity," clearly designed as a counterpart to the DSM classification system of psychiatric disorders, defines six domains of strength:

- Wisdom and knowledge

- Courage

- Humanity

- Justice

- Temperance

- Transcendence

Across the six domains are 24 specific areas of strength that I will briefly summarize next. These are assessed by a test designed by the authors called the Values in Action Inventory of Strengths (VIA-IS). A particular focus of that test is the assessment of strengths that are valued across cultures.

As with the earlier list, let's conduct a short exercise. Out of the 24 areas, label with 1, 2, 3, 4, and 5 the five strengths that are most central to your trading *and then identify the five strengths most central to your closest relationships.* Then we'll take a look at what your patterning of strengths might say about you.

Here are the 24 character strengths outlined by Peterson and Seligman:

Wisdom and Knowledge

- Creativity: Originality, ingenuity

- Curiosity: Novelty-seeking, open to experience

- Open-mindedness: Independence of thought, critical thinking

- Love of learning: Intellectual activity and curiosity

- Perspective: Wisdom, capacity for multifaceted views

Courage

- Bravery: Valor, willingness to undertake risk

- Persistence: Persistence, industriousness

- Integrity: Authenticity, honesty

- Vitality: Energy, enthusiasm

Humanity

- Love: Connectedness, capacity for attachment

- Kindness: Generosity, nurturance

- Social intelligence: Emotional intelligence, interpersonal skill

Justice

- Citizenship: Social responsibility, teamwork

- Fairness: Moral responsibility, consideration for others

- Leadership: Capacity to take initiative, guide others

Temperance

- Forgiveness and mercy: Compassion, empathy

- Humility and modesty: Accuracy of self-perception, ability to acknowledge mistakes

- Prudence: Deliberate, practical

- Self-regulation: Self-controlled, organized

Transcendence

- Appreciation of beauty and excellence—Capacity for awe, wonder

- Gratitude—Thankfulness, appreciation of life

- Hope—Optimism, future-mindedness

- Humor—Playfulness, ability to have fun

- Spirituality—Sense of faith, purpose

From the exercise, you should have two lists of top five strengths: the first for our trading; the second for relationships. Take a look at how those lists compare. How similar are the strengths that lead to your success in trading and those that bring your relationship happiness?

My trading strength list includes the following five qualities: creativity, love of learning, open-mindedness, persistence, and hope. My relationship list, which covers my marriage and family relationships as well as those with people I coach, includes: love, kindness, social intelligence, integrity, and hope. The one overlapping strength is hope, particularly the aspects of optimism and positivity. Otherwise, the trading and relationship strengths are quite different. Trading strengths borrow heavily from the category of Wisdom and Knowledge, focusing on qualities needed to generate original trading ideas. Relationship strengths draw predominantly from the category of Humanity, emphasizing interpersonal sensitivity. To put the distinction most simply, my trading draws on intellectual strengths and my functioning as a psychologist, spouse, and parent draws on interpersonal and emotional strengths.

Had I performed this exercise before I tried my hand at full-time trading, I would have realized the lessons mentioned earlier in the chapter: Immersing myself in work that embraced one side of me but not the other was destined for suboptimal performance. The same is true with respect to my work as a psychologist. While I deeply enjoy being part of another person's life and success, without the challenges of learning and development in a competitive domain, I would quickly tire of the other-centered focus. In other words, what might appear as a multifaceted lifestyle—active involvement in coaching, trading, writing, and family—is actually a blending of core strengths that allows all to be expressed to a meaningful degree.

	Key Takeaway	

A fulfilling lifestyle integrates our different strengths.

Take a look at your lists and see if you can identify a similar integration. Who you are as a trader may differ significantly from who you are as a spouse and friend. This is not necessarily a problem; indeed, the ways in which you blend relationships and market involvement may represent a higher-order synthesis of your signature strengths.

How do we know if we are successfully blending our strengths? The most basic barometer of this integration is the degree of our personal well-being. When we successfully find expression of multiple strengths, the result is a life that brings happiness, satisfaction, and meaning. When the expression of our various strengths is blocked, the result is conflict and frustration.

One trader I knew many years ago was involved in a relationship with a very bright woman who had strong cultural and artistic interests. He found her interesting and stimulating, and she appreciated the curiosity he displayed about politics, economics, and world affairs. Over time, however, conflicts began to take hold. Making money was not high on her list of priorities, and she could not understand his sometimes-obsessive concern with markets and trading performance. He began to resent what he saw as her lack of support. He gradually pulled away from music and theater activities that had been a large part of their dating, but that increasingly encroached on time for trading and research. The schisms grew: He became more involved in Republican politics; she was a Democrat. She spent more time with friends he viewed as "artsy"; he spent more time with friends she saw as "good ol' boys." What started as seeming complementarity devolved into an unhappy relationship that eventually disintegrated. The failure to integrate differing strengths led to relationship weaknesses.

■ Higher-Order Integration of Strengths

Some of life's greatest fulfillment comes from bringing together multiple strengths. The trader in the unhappy relationship was unable to find such an integration. When we integrate strengths, the result often shows up as a creative approach to work and relationships.

As I pointed out in *The Psychology of Trading*, I found my first niche in trading when I recognized the similarity between tracking the flow of conversation between counselor and client and following the flow of market communications. The skilled psychologist looks for patterns of communication and meaning that shed light on the concerns bringing people to therapy. For instance, a young woman might come to counseling to deal with the aftermath of several unhappy relationships. She recounts one example after another of reaching out and giving of herself, only to be taken advantage of by the men in her life. Shortly after, she expresses hope that counseling can help her find gratifying relationships and asks how much I charge for sessions.

How would I respond to her question? What's going through my mind?

What I wouldn't do is quote a fee. That would address the literal question she's asking, but would be tone deaf with respect to the underlying psychological issue. She feels used by men. Now she's pouring out her heart to me, a male. If I quote her a fee that she finds to be high, I set myself up for symbolically reenacting her issues in our working relationship. Had we already forged a solid relationship, such reenactment could be quite useful as an opportunity to handle feelings and needs differently. Given that this is our first meeting, however, the odds are good that, if I come across as "using" her for her money (the fees), this will complicate the forging of a good alliance.

So what I do is put the fee issue back on her. I point out that she knows her budget better than I do, so she should let me know what she can afford. I emphasize that her happiness is important to me, and I'm not going to let fees stand in the way if she is ready for a new relationship life. The odds are very good that she will read my meta-message—I'm more interested in you than in your money—and will respond with a fee that is reasonable and with an eagerness to begin this new and healthy relationship with a man. That is possible because I can link the themes between her presenting issues and her behavior toward me.

When I first became involved in trading, I found myself drawing on this same kind of pattern recognition. Markets were communicating something about rising and falling strength and weakness; my job was to stand back and read those communications. In trading, as in therapy, if I took the communications in a personal way and reacted emotionally, I could not muster the perspective needed to detect and respond to the underlying themes. Many times I would see markets sell off to new lows on increased volume, but notice that quite a few sectors were not participating in the fresh weakness. Very often, those would be the sectors that would lead a rally from the ensuing lows. The ability to step back, read the communications of the market, and respond to the larger picture became my way of integrating my interpersonal strengths as a therapist with my competitive and creative strengths as a trader. This "trading from the couch," as I called it, became my way of importing a seemingly unrelated strength into a fresh performance domain.

Over the years, the most successful traders I've known are those who have taken a distinctive strength and found a way to integrate it into trading practice. I recall one skilled trader who came from a classical music background. His sensitivity to musical sequences and motifs showed up in trading as a keen ability to track recurring sequences in markets and their underlying nuances. Indeed, he often found himself translating market behavior into musical terms, complete with sequences of rising and falling volume, pitch, and cadence. Crescendos in markets, he found, were not so different from those in music and typically resulted in similar resolutions.

Still another talented trader brought to markets a successful career as an amateur athlete. He defined trading as a competitive sport and constructed his own workouts and "game films." For him, trading was the ultimate sport, pitting him against the world's best competition each day. What made him successful were the very strengths he imported from his playing days on the college field.

Other higher-order integrations of strengths result from wedding trading to seemingly opposed areas of interest. For example, I know many traders who possess a strong sense of social responsibility and interest. Their trading is a solo pursuit, but they find meaning in using a portion of their profits to fund socially valuable causes. Other traders actively pursue opportunities to train junior talent, deriving immense fulfillment in mentoring up-and-coming traders. On the surface, social causes and teaching others might look like distractions from markets. For these traders, however, the synthesis of trading with these interpersonal and social commitments provides meaning and motivation above and beyond the daily movements of profits and losses.

Many effective higher-order integrations of strengths have nothing to do with trading, but can benefit trading nonetheless. I have consistently found that travel to unusual destinations is not only intellectually gratifying, but also makes for a powerful shared relationship experience with my wife—and ultimately stimulates creative thinking in markets. Several traders and I have developed a strong interest in craft beers and periodically get together to sample new and unusual brews. The relaxed setting, appreciation of creative beers, and resulting conversations inevitably stimulate fresh ideas that find expression in coaching and trading. Many traders use midday hours for hard workouts in the gym, enjoying bonding time with colleagues, but also stimulating endorphins that carry over into research and trading.

Key Takeaway

The well-being that comes from expressing strengths outside of trading can ultimately fuel improved trading.

One of the most creative blendings of strengths that I've encountered lately has been the integration of spirituality and trading performance. We don't normally think of trading as a particularly spiritual occupation, but many of the traders I've worked with have benefited greatly from meditation, yoga, and other disciplines designed to promote mindfulness. Part of the appeal, of course, is stress reduction, but it often goes well beyond that. These tend to be traders with strengths that Peterson and Seligman would place in the Transcendence category. They long to feel connected to something larger, higher, and significant. The meditation activities develop this aspect of their personalities; the synergy comes from the additional stress reduction and mindfulness benefits.

Imagine a situation in which I, as a coach, suggest to a stressed-out trader that he undertake meditation or yoga. Very often, there will be little follow-through on the suggestion. Why? Because that strength of Transcendence is missing. People will generally not pursue a discipline—even if it promises benefits—if that discipline does not express some area of strength. A classic example of this is dieting and exercise. Time and again, I have seen people benefit from social programs of diet and exercise after failing multiple times to sustain those activities on their own.

This has profound implications for self-improvement. There's an old saying among physicians that pills don't work when they're in the bottle. In other words, the patient has to be compliant in taking medication for the treatment to be effective. Similarly, all the best self-help techniques in the world will be useless to a trader unless they are actively employed. Much of the secret to behavior change amounts to a kind of creativity: adapting self-help methods to our needs, values, and personalities. I recall vividly a student whom I worked with in counseling who suffered from severe test anxiety. Behavioral exercises and cognitive techniques had limited benefit. When I delved further into the student's mindset, he revealed his very deep spiritual faith as an evangelical Christian. We spoke at length about the power of faith, including the power of prayer. That conversation led to a unique idea: bringing his Bible to classes and engaging in a few moments of prayer to start each class. He had been afraid to do anything like that, fearing that this would label him with peers as a "Bible banger." I encouraged him to bang away! "What is stronger," I asked him, "your faith in the Lord or your anxiety?"

It turned out this very simple intervention worked amazingly well. Standard psychological exercises did not speak to the student. By replacing fear of failure with active connectedness through prayer, he was able to place his worries in perspective. Physiologically, prayer may have had a very similar impact as a breathing exercise, focusing concentration and slowing down thought and emotional arousal. One, however, spoke to the student; the other didn't. What often looks like a motivation issue boils down to an issue of alignment with strengths.

■ Revisiting Multiplier Effects in Development

In *Enhancing Trader Performance*, I described some of the research pertaining to multiplier effects in development. The discovery of multiplier effects was the result of efforts to tease apart the effects of heredity versus environment in developmental outcomes. For example, if I have success as a writer, does that primarily come from inborn talents and capacities or is it cultivated through exposure to the right environmental influences?

What the research found is that our native talents (strengths) lead us, from an early age, to prefer certain environments over others. For instance, I displayed signs of a high verbal IQ from an early age. Interestingly, my performance IQ—a measure of visual/spatial ability—was not elevated in the least and in fact was well below normal! Not surprisingly, I did not gravitate to classic boys' activities such as building things and working with my hands. Early in grade school, however, I devoured every book of Greek and Roman mythology that I could get my hands on. I loved stories of the heroes and gods and their exploits. I spent time in the local library and found encouragement from teachers who appreciated my love of reading. My initial talents led me to seek out environments that made the most of my verbal abilities. This created a multiplier effect: The enriched environments that I sought out further honed my talents, so that I was on an exponential growth curve in that area relative to my peers. Mechanical skills, not evident in childhood, played no role in my selecting environments and hence never became part of my development. To this day, I have little mechanical aptitude.

In his 2008 book, *Talent Is Overrated*, Geoff Colvin makes a worthwhile observation. He notes that the multiplier effects derived from talents, chosen environments, and deliberate practice are ultimately driven by intrinsic motivation. This, he points out, helps to explain a seeming contradiction: Deliberate practice is effortful and yet performers immersed in deliberate practice experience a pleasurable sense of being "in the zone." We will explore the flow state in greater detail below, but it is worth noting that operating in the zone may be a function of the intrinsic motivation derived from expressing and exercising one's strengths. We seek environments that cultivate our strengths precisely because those environments offer the deepest gratification and fulfillment.

Most of the research literature on multiplier effects pertains to childhood development. The principle, however, very much applies to personal and professional development: We grow in exponential ways when we place ourselves in environments that draw on our strengths. Just the other day I spoke with a portfolio manager who left his firm after lackluster performance and is now managing his own capital. He had long sought an approach to trading that minimized stresses and maximized his research abilities. He developed an effective partnership with several colleagues and, together, they created their optimal work environment. The partners were experienced, successful professionals who didn't want to be glued to screens all day, but knew how to take advantage of short-term dislocations in markets. All were also creative professionals able to generate fresh trading ideas. Functioning in this enhanced environment, the portfolio manager's performance and professional development skyrocketed. He was happier than before and more successful. He went from a stagnant environment to one that drew on—and multiplied—his strengths.

Many trading environments do not actively hamper learning and development, but also are not so tailored to our needs that they yield multiplier effects. This is a major challenge, particularly at trading firms where all traders are placed in the same environment. Some traders benefit greatly from interaction on the trading floor; others find only noise and distraction in floor banter and discussion. Even the arrangement of screens works well for some traders and not for others. I recall visiting a very successful trader at his house and was surprised to see no screens anywhere. "When I want a quote," he said, "I'll call for one. I don't need to feed the beast." From his perspective, looking at moving markets only tempted him to trade and that was not his edge. His home environment was engineered to minimize such distraction. Had he worked on a trading floor, no such engineering would have been possible: He would have faced "division effects," not multipliers!

The idea that talents lead us to seek out environments that in turn exercise and develop those talents has profound implications. If we rarely operate in the zone, there is a good likelihood that our physical, social, and work environments are not well suited to our capacities. A great example of this is failed marriages. Our romantic interests help shape our social and emotional environments. When relationships thwart rather than draw on our strengths, they create more conflict and frustration than enjoyment. Good romantic relationships bring multiplier effects: Good partners make each other better. It is the same in solid business partnerships and trading teams.

■ ■ ■

Here's a very quick survey: How, specifically, is your trading different today compared with a year or two ago? What changes have you made to your trading style, markets, and processes over the past year?

Why is this important?

If you are on a positive learning curve, benefiting from multiplier effects, you should be growing your trading practices, not just your profitability. Stagnation—trading in the same ways even as markets change—is the surest sign that you are not multiplying your strengths. The intrinsic motivation that accompanies the exercise of strengths ensures that we continually seek out environments and situations that challenge and fulfill us. That ongoing exposure to fresh inputs, challenges, and environments ensures that we will keep learning and growing. If you cannot identify important, positive ways in which your trading has evolved in the past year, either your trading is not playing to your strengths or your trading environments are not optimally exercising those strengths. In a world of use it or lose it, stagnation brings those division effects, not developmental multipliers.

Key Takeaway
Multiplier effects ensure our growth as traders.

One of my favorite solution-focused exercises is to take an inventory of best trades and reverse engineer those. What made us successful in our best trades, and what caused our downfall during our worst trading? The ingredients of success may indeed reveal the factors that could more consistently contribute to the multiplication of our talents. Many times we *are* evolving, but not consistently. For example, a trader recently emailed me and lamented his trading losses. When he examined his trading, he found that he was taking too many trades, trying to trade in too many ways. Some of those were reasonably profitable and others were disastrous. One interesting observation was that he performed much poorer when he had several trades on than when he focused on one trade at a time. Multiple positions were causing him to divide his attention, which in turn took him out of any possible flow state. When he stopped trying to succeed at trading in general and instead focused on the trading that fit his skills, he was far more immersed in markets, more profitable, and more energized from his experience. As I have so often found, his success did not require changing himself, but rather being more of who he already was when he was trading well.

Are there people who simply are not cut out for trading? Absolutely! No field of endeavor can optimally embrace and express the wide variety of human strengths. Someone who finds their greatest meaning and development as an artist, clergy member, biologist, or entrepreneur is very likely to find trading limited in its ability to bring out their greatest strengths. Trading requires an ability to process large amounts of information, often quickly. This simply is not a strength for many people. I've worked with many analysts who have been excellent in researching companies and macroeconomic trends, but who are not good at the rapid processing of incoming information needed for trading. I've also worked with very talented managers in financial firms who are excellent at managing people, but would have no clue how to manage the information flows of money managers.

Too many traders are attracted to markets because of the allure of making money, rather than to the actual work of trading. Those studies of deliberate practice make clear that it is the process of performance and not merely the outcomes that drive successful professionals. The money incentive is the extrinsic motivation of trading. The intrinsic motivation comes from trading processes. Passionate traders love generating ideas, finding expressions of those ideas in markets, and managing the risks and rewards associated with their ideas. Perhaps most of all, they love self-mastery and the process of improvement. Very often, when we see stagnant trading—little growth over the period of a year or two—it's because intrinsic motivations have taken a backseat to extrinsic ones.

■ Subjective Well-Being: The Most Important Emotions in Trading Psychology

We hear a lot about fear and greed, but psychological well-being is undoubtedly the most important emotional experience for trading performance. Positive emotional experience contributes to everything from concentration and memory to creativity and productivity—and even physical health. It is not just the presence of negative emotions but the absence of positivity that can lead to suboptimal performance.

So what is psychological well-being? Research finds four broad dimensions that contribute to the quality of our experience:

1. Happiness—Positive emotions, including pleasure and enjoyment
2. Contentment—A sense of satisfaction with self and life
3. Energy—Enthusiasm and excitement about life
4. Affection—Meaningful connectedness to others

Note that at any given time we can score high on one or two of these dimensions and low in others. For instance, we might be generally happy and content, but because of poor physical health we could be lacking energy. Similarly, we might enjoy a high degree of affection in our friendships and marriage, but remain less than content with our trading progress. It is also common for these four dimensions to rise and fall in response to life events and changes in lifestyle. It's unrealistic to expect a constant high degree of well-being across all situations.

It is when one or more of these dimensions are chronically low that we find disruptions of mood and performance. Disruptions also occur when negative emotional experience, such as anxiety, depression, anger/frustration, and guilt, dominate positive emotions. *Indeed, it is the balance between positive and negative emotional experience that helps to determine the degree to which we can consistently access and draw on our strengths.* It is very difficult to, say, maintain intellectual curiosity and creativity when we lack energy and are swamped with angry, frustrated feelings.

Self-Assessment Exercise

This emotion journal is a very simple exercise that can help you assess your emotional balance. Print seven copies of the list below and, each day for a week, rate your day's experience on the following dimensions by circling one of the choices following each set of emotion adjectives. By the end of the week, you'll have seven sets of ratings. Note that you're not rating your mood every hour or so. Rather, this is your best assessment of your day's emotional experience.

HAPPY, JOYOUS, HAVING FUN:

very infrequent infrequent occasional often very often

CONTENT, SATISFIED, PROUD:

>   very infrequent infrequent occasional often very often

ENTHUSIASTIC, ENERGETIC, EXCITED:

>   very infrequent infrequent occasional often very often

LOVING, CLOSE TO OTHERS, FRIENDLY:

>   very infrequent infrequent occasional often very often

DISCOURAGED, NEGATIVE, DEPRESSED:

>   very infrequent infrequent occasional often very often

WORRIED, ANXIOUS, FEARFUL:

>   very infrequent infrequent occasional often very often

FRUSTRATED, ANGRY, ANNOYED:

>   very infrequent infrequent occasional often very often

SELF-BLAMING, GUILTY, DISGUSTED WITH SELF:

>   very infrequent infrequent occasional often very often

Return to this page every day for a week.

You can see that the first four sets of adjectives capture positive emotional experience (well-being) and the second four sets capture negative experience (distress). At the broadest level of analysis, the exercise assesses if we experience positive emotions more frequently than negative ones. Frequent well-being and infrequent distress is a good recipe for an enjoyable life.

Interestingly, however, many of the successful traders I have known do not necessarily score with a high balance of positive to negative emotions. Indeed, many experience positive *and* negative emotions frequently from week to week. This highlights a very important set of findings in the research literature.

One of the earliest of those findings is that positive and negative emotional experiences are relatively independent of one another. Of course, at any given moment, positive and negative emotion are likely to be negatively correlated, although we occasionally have "mixed feelings" about certain situations. As we widen the time frame, however, the relationship between positive and negative emotion weakens.

Compton and Hoffman, in their 2013 book, *Positive Psychology*, note that unique processes are involved in moving from neutral to negative emotional states versus neutral to positive states. Reducing positive emotionality does not necessarily imply increasing negative emotions, and vice versa. When successful traders experience high levels of both positive and negative emotions, the sources of those are typically quite different. Positive experience comes from the intrinsic enjoyment of generating ideas and seeing them come to life. Negative experience comes from risk management concerns and keen awareness of vulnerabilities within and across positions. I've often joked that many talented traders are "worriers" and "warriors": they take risk, but keep themselves clear of overconfidence biases by continually preparing for adverse outcomes. The blend of positive and negative emotions actually helps them achieve superior risk-adjusted returns.

Key Takeaway

Negative emotional experience can be very useful in managing trading risks.

As you look over the emotion journal you have kept over a week's time, you will no doubt see variation in both positive and negative experiences that illustrates the relative independence of those. Over even longer periods, you might observe considerable differences in emotional balance, as work, relationship, financial, physical, and social situations can change significantly. Take a look at the variability in your ratings of each of the categories across the seven days of the week. That variability itself is meaningful, as it captures the volatility of your emotional experience. One of the core "big five" personality traits is emotional balance versus neuroticism: the degree to which we experience a relative balance of emotions versus a tendency toward negative emotion.

Research with twins and adopted siblings suggests that temperament has a strong genetic basis: Parents who experience a wide range of emotions are most likely to give birth to emotional kids; those who are relatively even-tempered are most likely to have placid babies. The variability of emotional experience is one way our temperaments manifest themselves. Some of us are more wired for emotional highs and lows than others.

The variability of emotional experience manifests itself in two ways. The research of Ed Diener and colleagues (1997; 2009) suggests that it is the frequency of emotional experience and not the intensity that is most responsible for overall well-being (hence the wording of the response options of the emotion journal). A few extreme experiences of happiness or sadness are less crucial to our overall experience than the amount of time we spend in each mode. One form that variability of emotions takes is a waxing and waning of the amount of time that we spend in positive versus negative states. A good example of this would be the trader whose emotional experience is greatly swayed by his or her profits and losses. Periods of positivity would alternate with periods of negativity as performance traces a relatively random path in the short term.

A different form of variability pertains to the amplitude of emotional experience, rather than the frequency. Some people are simply more intense than others. This shows up in their interactions, facial expressions, and moods. I have known many people who have rich emotional lives and are quite engaging and entertaining for that reason. I would have difficulty living with them, however, as the continual ups and downs would destabilize my own balance. I function best without emotional extremes and an overall positive emotional balance. Others, with more emotional temperaments, would find my optimal state stifling, lacking in richness and stimulation. Our temperaments represent emotional strengths and, as such, lead us to seek out compatible environments that provide those multiplier effects.

It's rarely recognized, but our trading styles are as much about our emotional management as our money management.

■ ■ ■

Consider two traders we will call Steady Eddy and Emotional Edgar. Steady Eddy has a generally positive balance of emotions and this doesn't change greatly over time. He doesn't experience big swings in positive or negative emotion. Trades are planned with targets and stops and winning and losing are both part of the game. Steady Eddy also doesn't change his sizing on trades very much. He looks for neither big wins nor losses. Rather, he makes moderate bets with as much consistency as possible and aims to maintain a positively sloped profit/loss curve. He has a few patterns that he trades in a discretionary fashion and deviates little from those. When those patterns are not present, he does not trade.

Emotional Edgar is a highly competitive trader, with a previous background in high school and college athletics. His emotional balance changes from day to day, as he hates losing but loves battling wits with the world's best money managers and computer systems. He stays engaged in markets most of the time, as fast breaking news or data releases can create opportunities for him. Emotional Edgar's greatest skill is recognizing who is in the market and what they are doing at each point in the trading day. One glance at a depth-of-market screen and he can tell you if the market is dominated by market makers or if there is broad participation among directional speculators. It is in the latter markets that he makes most of his money. His favorite trades come when the speculators are offsides and can no longer drive price higher or lower. At those times, Emotional Edgar is out of his chair, fading the herd with large size. During slow markets, he can bleed capital, but when markets get busy and one-sided, he can make significant amounts of money. Those are the trading days he lives for.

In Eddy and Edgar, we have two different traders with two completely different emotional makeups. Eddy's style of trading helps him maintain his emotional balance and keeps him focused on his core trades. Edgar's style of trading helps him maximize energy and optimism when he sees greatest opportunity and profit greatly when other traders are getting hurt. Eddy has a high Sharpe ratio: He achieves superior risk-adjusted returns. Edgar can and does make and lose a good amount at any time, but he achieves superior absolute returns. Each is successful, because each has found a way to trade that maximizes his particular type of well-being.

■ ■ ■

Now let's consider two other traders, whom we will call Research Rachel and Social Sarah. Research Rachel trades from her own office. She reads copious research reports and conducts her own studies by modeling economic data. She maintains a quiet work environment, because she finds she generates her best ideas when she is content and not distracted. Soft music plays in the background, and the office is well decorated, with original art on the walls and scented candles on the desk. During intensive work periods, all calls go to voice mail and the phone is muted. Screens are turned off at those times as well. Rachel is never happier than when she is completely immersed in the investigative process.

By comparison, Social Sarah is a whirlwind. She occupies a seat on the trading floor, but rarely stays in the seat. She walks up and down the aisles, speaking with traders, carrying on conversations by phone, and watching the financial news on the overhead televisions. Social Sarah's great strength is the information network she has cultivated. She routinely speaks with dozens of colleagues per day, gathering information about overseas central banks, latest economic reports, and flows affecting major markets. At times, all of this information comes together and Sarah furiously phones for quotes and market color before placing orders. Her relationships keep her abreast of who is doing what at all times. This tells her when a market is likely to move and when it is likely to reverse.

Key Takeaway
Our work and environment shape the ways in which we will experience well-being.

Once again, we have two very different traders: one who derives well-being through quiet contentment and focus, another who finds well-being through active and energetic social connections. Each creates an environment conducive to her work style and emotional makeup. Both find psychological well-being in trading, but it is a very different well-being. How we blend happiness, contentment, energy, and affection helps to determine how we engage markets.

■ Well-Being and Personality

The examples of Eddie, Edgar, Rachel, and Sarah illustrate the intimate connection between psychological well-being and broader aspects of personality. A wealth of research identifies a "big five" set of traits that comprise personality:

1. *Neuroticism / emotional balance*—The propensity to experience negative emotions versus a more even balance of positive and negative emotions
2. *Extraversion*—Sociability, stimulus-seeking, and an outgoing interest in people
3. *Openness to experience*—Love of variety, novelty, and aesthetic interests

4. *Agreeableness*—Likeability and the ability to get along well with others
5. *Conscientiousness*—The tendency to approach situations in organized, disciplined, and detailed ways

Each of these personality traits can be thought of as a path toward well-being. Social Sarah, for example, displayed standout strengths on the personality dimension of extraversion. Research Rachel, on the other hand, was more introverted, happiest when open to the experiences of idea generation. Steady Eddie was a model of emotional balance and conscientiousness. Edgar took openness to experience and extraversion to an extreme, seeking in markets distinctive opportunities to take significant risk. Our personalities embrace both cognitive and emotional styles, helping to determine how we process information and what we like to do with that information.

Following are a few common constellations of personality traits, emotional characteristics, and cognitive styles that I have observed among successful traders:

- *The conscientious trader*—This is the trader who is highly disciplined, operating by clear, explicit rules and processes. The conscientious trader approaches markets methodically, sometimes by trading systems or by integrating discretionary decision making with backtested signals. The grounding in rules and routines serves to keep the trader focused and relatively free of emotional impulses and biases.

- *The social trader*—Like Social Sarah, the social trader processes information in interpersonal, interactive ways and works in a highly social, collaborative style. The social trader often participates in online chats, conversations on the trading floor, and gatherings after hours. Very often the social trader is highly attuned to what others are doing in markets, providing a potential edge when the herd is about to shift direction.

- *The creative trader*—The creative trader is turned on by ideas and fresh approaches to markets. The high openness to experience manifests itself through an interest in multiple sources of information and curiosity across markets and trading instruments. Trading may even be secondary for the creative trader, as intellectual curiosity is a dominant motivation.

- *The emotionally balanced trader*—Whereas the conscientious trader derives stability through the imposition of routines and rules, the emotionally balanced trader is naturally stable. Like Steady Eddie, the balanced trader stays focused on markets by avoiding the drama associated with high-risk taking and volatile markets. It is not unusual for emotionally balanced traders to construct relatively balanced positions and portfolios, making use of hedges, uncorrelated positions, and options to circumscribe risk.

In a rough sense, the social and creative traders are stimulus-seeking: They seek input and stimulation from other traders or from research and ideas. The conscientious and emotionally balanced traders are stimulus-dampening: They benefit from strategies and states that curb excitement and discouragement. The issue, of course, is not which style is better or worse, but which is better for you.

As we shall see shortly, psychological well-being is a major foundation of trading performance. The well-being we derive from trading, however, varies greatly with our cognitive, emotional, and personality traits and strengths. One of Jack Schwager's strongest findings (2012) across his many Market Wizards interviews was that each Wizard found an approach to trading that fit his or her personality. This is crucially important. Successful traders did not possess a single personality type or a uniform set of traits or strengths. Rather, they possessed distinctive strengths and found ways to express those through their market participation.

■ What Research Teaches Us about Well-Being

A wealth of evidence has accumulated in recent decades to suggest that positive emotional experience is essential to our success. As we saw above, there are logical reasons for this. We're most likely to immerse ourselves in work and experience those multiplier effects in our development if what we're doing brings happiness, satisfaction, energy, and affection. It is not enough to merely control the negative emotions sometimes associated with trading. Our trading needs to provide energy, fulfillment, and joy if it is to bring out the best within us.

So what do we know about well-being? Here are a few key findings:

- *Positive experience is not the opposite of negative experience.* As noted above, positive and negative emotionality are not opposing extremes of a single dimension. Argyle, in his excellent book, *The Psychology of Happiness* (2001), points to research that finds a −0.43 correlation between positivity and negativity. That means that less than 20 percent of the variance in positive emotion is explained by changes in negative emotion and vice versa. Exercises that can help reduce negative emotional experience, such as relaxation techniques to lower stress, do not necessarily bring joy and affection, for example. Similarly, we can find energy and affection in a good relationship and still experience significant stress in our work. This relative independence of positive and negative emotions has important implications for traders, as it suggests that we need to take active and proactive measures to enhance our day-to-day well-being. Simply coping with stress is not sufficient to fuel performance success.

- *Happiness is different from life satisfaction.* Argyle reviews evidence that shows a higher correlation between happiness and life satisfaction among individualist cultures versus collectivist ones. Diener's research group (2009) has found that positive emotion correlates about 0.50 with life satisfaction and negative emotion correlates about −0.50. Clearly, positivity and negativity are connected to satisfaction, but as the researchers point out, the different measures of well-being tap different time frames. Satisfaction represents a broader judgment about our lives; positive experience is more immediate. It's not unusual to be experiencing stress and distress on a particular day or during a given week and still feel satisfied with life overall. One common pitfall for traders is pursuing happiness at the expense of broader satisfaction. I know a number of financially successful traders who are distinctly unhappy in their marriages and families. Their success has brought experiences of happiness, but not necessarily a sense of ongoing life satisfaction.

- *Well-being tends to be stable over time.* As Compton and Hoffman point out (2013), research points to a "set-point" in our well-being. We have an average level of emotional balance that persists over time. Events can lead us to feel more positively or negatively at any particular moment, but we tend to return to our set points. As the authors note, this is consistent with the idea that our positive and negative temperaments have a strong genetic basis. This doesn't mean that we cannot change our well-being status: Research from Diener and colleagues cited by Compton and Hoffman found that, over a 17-year period, roughly a quarter of people surveyed dramatically changed their level of life satisfaction from the first five years to the last five years. From week to week and month to month, however, our set points are unlikely to radically change. This suggests that it is vitally important to understand our own set points—our own unique balances of emotional experience—and work within those. For example, if we know that we are prone to anger, frustration, and negative states, we can build routines that feature frequent time away from screens to decompress and regain emotional balance.

Key Takeaway

To change our well-being set points, we need to cultivate lifestyles that maximize well-being.

- *Well-being varies significantly across cultures.* Compton and Hoffman (2013) cite several studies that find well-being highest in Scandinavia and lowest in certain African countries. They explain that average income is strongly correlated with well-being, particularly when comparing low and moderate incomes. People tend to be happier and more satisfied when they perceive that they are able to meet their basic needs. As Diener and Suh (1997) have found, however, even among higher-income countries, greater wealth has been associated with higher well-being. Interestingly, higher income is less correlated with happiness than with satisfaction. Higher income can enable people to better meet their social and psychological needs, contributing to enhanced life satisfaction. This is very relevant to traders who attempt to make a living from their trading without having other sources of income or security. When losses in trading threaten one's ability to meet basic personal and family needs, the result can be destabilizing for emotional balance and overall satisfaction.

- *Married people tend to be happier and more satisfied than unmarried people.* Affection is a central element of well-being. It is rare that we can sustain happiness, satisfaction, and energy if we are unhappy in our relationships or if we lack closeness with others. Diener and Suh (1997) have found that marriage predicts well-being among both men and women. Compton and Hoffman (2013) also note research that finds a strong association between the quality of romantic relationships and overall satisfaction. I would argue that relationship quality may be even more important for traders than for people in other occupations. Because markets can be so fickle, traders cannot always count on their work for gratification. That is a very different psychological situation than that faced by salaried workers in reasonably secure jobs. Without guaranteed stability in their work, traders benefit greatly from stability at home. An understanding and supportive spouse is a huge contributor to trading success. Conflict with a spouse about trading and its rigors inevitably takes a toll on performance.

- *Physical exercise is associated with elevated well-being.* This is not surprising, given that energy level is one key component of overall well-being. Argyle's review finds that even short periods of exercise lead to positive emotional benefits. These benefits include not only the "high" created by endorphins but also the increased self-mastery and self-image that fitness can bring. This is critical for traders who very often spend inordinate amounts of time sitting in front of a screen. Over time, this can take a toll on energy level and overall productivity.

- *Well-being is good for our physical health.* Argyle cites research that finds that happy people live longer and enjoy better overall health. Interestingly, negative emotion also has a significant correlation with poor health. One particularly eye-opening study cited by Daniel Nettle in his book, *Happiness* (2005), took a look at the autobiographical accounts written by nuns when they took their vows, rating each of the accounts for positive emotional content. The nuns with the highest positivity (top quarter of the group) lived significantly longer than the others: fully 90 percent lived to the age of 85. In contrast, only 34 percent of the lowest positivity group reached that age. It is reasonable to assume that the higher energy level and optimism of well-being help people engage in healthy behaviors, just as wellness contributes to well-being. What is good for our minds appears to be good for our bodies, and vice versa.

What is the takeaway from all this research? The old trading psychology paradigm of invoking discipline, controlling emotions, and coping with stress is shockingly outdated. *Trading Psychology 2.0* links performance to optimal emotional and physical states—many of which depend on how we live our lives outside of trading. Well-being is not simply a function of trading well and making money; it follows from how we cultivate our relationships, how we meet our physical needs, and how we approach our work. If you think of traders as athletes, then an important part of their conditioning consists of exercising well-being. How many of us live a life designed to optimize our positivity? The research suggests that not only is this possible, but it is absolutely vital to maximizing our health and success.

■ How Can We Cultivate Well-Being?

Can people learn to improve their positivity? If our set points were truly fixed in stone and determined by our genetics, this should be impossible. Research by Fordyce (1983), however, suggests that gains in well-being can be achieved through a dedicated training program. This program consisted of 14 components:

1. Keeping active
2. Increasing time spent socializing
3. Improving productivity at work that is meaningful
4. Improving our planning and organization
5. Reducing worrying
6. Lowering expectations to realistic levels
7. Increasing positive, optimistic thinking
8. Orienting oneself to the present rather than focusing on past or future
9. Working on a healthy personality, including liking yourself and supporting yourself
10. Becoming more outgoing and sociable
11. Making efforts to be yourself
12. Reducing negative feelings and problems
13. Cultivating close relationships
14. Making happiness your top priority

The training program developed by Fordyce lasted a college semester and consisted of two conditions: (1) information about the 14 components; and (2) detailed explanations of them, including specific techniques for accomplishing each. In an interesting twist, Fordyce assigned the control group to the first segment of the program only (information). The experimental group received the entire training. Across a variety of well-being measures, the experimental group scored significantly higher than the control group. Although no effort was made to monitor the compliance of the experimental group, a surprising 93 percent of subjects undertook efforts to put the principles into practice; 81 percent of subjects reported increases in happiness as a result of the training; and 86 percent reported positive cognitive and behavioral changes from the training.

Fordyce observed that most of the subjects did not make use of each component of the program. Rather, they selected from the options to address the areas of happiness most relevant to them. All components overall were rated as valuable, but not all were needed to improve well-being. *This suggests that tailored programs can be effective in improving our emotional balance.* It is not necessary to raise well-being in all respects; focused, consistent improvements in how we think and act can make a meaningful difference in our level of positivity.

Key Takeaway

We can train positive emotional experience.

In his 2011 book, *Flourish*, Martin Seligman describes a well-being program that has been the object of dozens of outcome studies. The Penn Resilience Program is taught to schoolchildren and is designed to improve assertiveness, creativity, decision making, relaxation, and a number of positive coping skills. The program has been delivered in many countries, across many different community settings with very different populations. Overall, the program has been found to reduce depression over a two-year follow-up period. It also increased optimism, reduced anxiety and behavioral problems, and improved general well-being. Interestingly, the program also improved the health of children. These benefits were noticed across racial and ethnic lines.

An extension of the Penn Resilience Program was offered to students outside of Philadelphia, with the goal of improving character strengths, relationships, and emotional balance. Half of the students took the positive psychology curriculum; half did not. The program consisted of twenty 80-minute sessions, each of which provided information, taught skills, and structured homework. Teachers were blind as to which students did and did not participate. At the end of the program, the students who went through the training displayed better grades, improved social skills, fewer behavioral problems, and greater curiosity and love of learning.

Seligman observes that greater participation in the program resulted in enhanced gains among the students. Active participation in both the classes and the between-class exercises significantly improved outcomes.

Among the exercises utilized by the program outside Philadelphia was writing down of "three good things" that happen each day for a week. Students were instructed to write about why the good thing happened and how they could make it happen more often in the future. Still another exercise involved finding their greatest strength on the Values in Action test and finding a new way to use the strength over a week's period. The gist of the exercises was to think more about what brings well-being and then actually take steps to do more of what makes us happy.

■ ■ ■

Seligman's work suggests that a powerful approach to improving well-being is to implement a solution-focused framework. Recall that the solution-focused framework assumes that, at times, we act in ways that are consistent with our goals. Our task is not simply to engage in less problem behavior, but to do more of the things that are already succeeding. In a solution-focused variant of Seligman's well-being training program, we would keep a daily log of activities that bring us happiness, satisfaction, energy, and affection. The result would be a catalog of positive behaviors that work specifically for us. For example, we may find that engaging in a strenuous workout brings both satisfaction and energy. Going out to a new restaurant and enjoying the company of our loved one brings happiness and affection. The idea would be to prioritize—each day—an activity that we know brings us some form of well-being. Work responsibilities and daily tasks would have to fit around the chosen well-being activities, rather than rely on bits and pieces of leftover time to devote to our own fulfillment.

What I've found in implementing such a framework is that people are generally afraid to prioritize their well-being because they assume that they will not have time to get work and daily tasks accomplished. This, however, assumes that our energy level and willpower resources are static. What happens instead is that people energized by tapping into their positive emotional experience become more focused on what needs to get done and more efficient in plowing through their routines. The time spent in the well-being activities is more than made up for in increased work productivity. Without happiness and satisfaction, in a state where we're not enjoying energy or affection, we tend to dawdle and daydream; we are easily distracted. That is much less likely to occur when we feel charged with positive emotion.

In *The Power of Full Engagement*, Jim Loehr and Tony Schwartz (2003) identify four sources of energy: physical energy, emotional energy, mental energy, and spiritual energy. They make the valuable point that we tend to focus on time management to get things done, rather than emphasize the quality of the energy that goes into that time. If we are fully engaged each day, tapping into these sources of energy, both the quality and the productivity of our time will expand meaningfully.

Once again, this is where the solution-focused framework can be valuable. A few questions can get us started toward more consistent well-being. Below I outline those questions and the responses I would give right here and now:

- What recent activities have given me greater physical energy?

  - Starting my day with physical exercise energizes my entire day. The exercise has to challenge me, either through vigorous stretching, weight-lifting, or jogging/aerobic training. If I break a sweat and am out of breath, I am more likely to feel vitalized going forward.

  - I also have more energy if I eat light, especially early in the day, and if I strictly limit my coffee intake to one cup in the morning. Any more than that and I tend to get wired—and then suffer a rebound tiredness.

  - I get more energy if I don't sit for long periods working and instead get out of my chair frequently, walk around, get a drink of water, and so on. When I'm too stationary, I find myself feeling stiff, and that feels very low energy.

  - The quality of my sleep also greatly impacts my energy level the next day. If I eat and drink too close to bedtime, I'm likely to wake up during the night, and that disrupted sleep leaves me more tired in the morning. I also am more likely to feel tired and low energy if I fail to get adequate sleep—usually the result of staying up too late. Reading before going to bed is a great relaxer and helps me get to sleep quicker, which in turn leads to better sleep.

  - Engaging in physical activity at the end of the workday recharges my batteries. A brisk walk or vigorous stretching gets the blood pumping and helps energize my evening. If I try going straight from work to home responsibilities and work that is due the next day, I quickly run out of gas.

- What recent activities have given me greater emotional energy?

  - I am most likely to experience the heightened emotional energy of being challenged when I'm tackling a meaningful situation with someone I'm coaching. For example, portfolio managers work with me to plan their years and craft their requests for more capital. I love the challenge of being part of those efforts and contributing to a trader's success.

  - I enjoy shared challenges at home, such as when I help one of my children with a problem at work or help them succeed in a job interview.

  - Many of the activities that generate heightened emotional energy for me include those tied to longer-term goals, such as efforts to lose weight or get a book written. I love setting benchmarks for progress and then hitting those. Succeeding at one small goal gives energy for the next one.

  - Emotional energy also results from doing entirely new things and testing my limits in unfamiliar areas. For example, taking trips to new areas and engaging in new activities, such as a recent wilderness boat trip to Alaska, is stimulating and energizing.

  - I derive emotional energy from trading when I face multiple sources of conflicting information and have to assemble those facts into a meaningful picture. Seeing the clear picture begin to emerge after a long period of confusion and uncertainty is very rewarding.

- What recent activities have given me mental energy?

  - I know that I am operating at a high level of mental energy with optimism and sustained focus when I have laid out my day in advance and am very busy with the work that I like. I like to be busy with work that I schedule and juggle: Being immersed in the flow of the day keeps me at a heightened level of mental energy.

  - I have much better mental energy when I am working in an environment that is stimulating (music, activity around me) but not distracting (people interrupting me). I work best in early mornings in my home environment, because that is when my focus and mental energy tend to be highest, in a setting that I have optimized for low distraction.

- I have a high level of intellectual curiosity and derive a great deal of mental energy from reading books about new topics, discovering new and interesting websites, and engaging in interesting and new market research.

- My mental energy is greatly increased when I set aside a block of time to work on something and can be wholly focused on that activity. If I get a new idea in markets, I like to dedicate a morning or afternoon to fully exploring it. It is very energizing to see a new idea unfold and show promise.

- I get my greatest mental energy from trading when I am not staring at screens over long periods of time, managing and micromanaging positions. Rather, my greatest mental energy in trading comes from seeing opportunities set up and then having a framework for exploiting the opportunities that allow events to unfold over time.

- What recent activities have given me spiritual energy?

  - I am most likely to experience heightened spiritual energy when I feel closely connected to my children and grandchildren. Texting my children during the day and sharing the events of their lives make me feel closer to them. Sharing activities with family members creates a bond that cuts across generations and is inspiring.

  - My time with the cats is another form of spiritual energy resulting from connectedness. It is very common that they will hang out with me when I'm writing, reading, and exercising, and my day always starts with talking to them, petting them, feeding them, and taking care of their litter. Each of the four cats has her own personality that is expressed in a way that touches my heart.

  - A very special form of spiritual energy comes from engaging in shared experiences with Margie. We take day trips together, visit new restaurants, take in interesting shows in the city, travel abroad, and spend time with family. Almost all of our household challenges, from plumbing repairs to planning investments, we tackle together. Problems are less problematic and time is enriched when we approach life as a team.

  - I derive great spiritual energy from being part of social activities with friends and colleagues where there is active sharing of experiences and ideas. I find most parties and social gatherings to be boring and superficial. Gatherings of likeminded friends create a unique bond that is deeply satisfying.

- I enjoy reading books on philosophy, psychology, and religion where the emphasis is on life purpose and meaning. Especially energizing are books with a heroic, positive outlook that have an inspirational value.

- Activities based on values are very spiritually energizing, such as contributing to worthy causes and being part of the growth and development of promising young people, as through mentoring and teaching.

Note that I have generated quite a list. If I am grounded—day to day and week to week—in these activities, there is no way I will fail to live life energized. Loehr and Schwartz emphasize the importance of rituals in sustaining high energy in the four domains. As we've seen with Duhigg's work, habits become part of you and pull you toward the right behaviors. That is much more effective and efficient than hoping that scarce willpower resources will continually come through to push you to do the right things.

Key Takeaway

Happiness is a habit, not a random emotional event befalling us.

My list is a kind of solution-focused menu that I can draw on to energize each day. *Your challenge is to generate your own menu, based on the activities that most provide you with physical, emotional, mental, and spiritual energy.* Pay particular attention to the activities before, after, and during your trading day that energize your performance. These form the basis for the rituals you want to develop as a trader that will maximize the quality of your time as well as its productivity. We are least likely to fall into bad habits and behave impulsively if we are operating at a high level of energy and well-being.

■ Eliminating Drains on Our Energy

Calvin found himself in a trading funk. He had started the year by making money, but then decided to ramp up his risk taking and pursue truly significant returns. Trends that had benefited him went into consolidation and his profitability flattened out as well. He was an experienced money manager, so it was surprising that he responded to the flat P/L period with a high degree of frustration. After all, he had been through many flat periods and drawdowns in the past and largely navigated them without undue emotional wear and tear. Now, however, he found himself trading like a rookie, doubting himself, chasing trades to avoid missing moves, and stopping out of positions on mere noise. I spoke with Calvin's assistant, who confirmed that he was not trading like his usual self. "We plan the trades," Calvin's assistant explained, "and then the next day he's taking them off when we're 25 bps lower. I keep telling him we have to follow our process and he agrees, but then we make the same mistakes all over again."

Nothing had dramatically changed in markets; Calvin's ideas seemed as good as ever. He was simply trading poorly.

When I took an inventory of what was happening in Calvin's life and trading, here were a few of my observations:

- He had been divorced two years earlier, but recent legal problems returned to the surface over issues of child support and visitation due to his ex-wife's relocation.

- The relocation had led to a dropoff in Calvin's visits with his son. He felt acutely guilty about this, but also powerless to rectify the situation in the short run.

- A recent romantic relationship looked as though it was coming to an end. He wasn't sure why, but suspected his long hours were a factor.

- He had put on significant weight in recent months and stopped a prior exercise program. As his trading suffered, he rationalized that he needed to devote more time to research and position management.

- During his limited free time, Calvin prioritized his time with his son and girlfriend. That meant that other friendships were neglected. He also hadn't taken extended time off work in well over a year.

- By the time Calvin came home from work, he felt stressed and exhausted. One glass of wine turned into two and three. Soon he was drinking to excess, further exacerbating his funk.

What was clear to me was that Calvin's trading problems were the result of broader life problems. In just about every facet of life, he was reactive: trying to cope with negative things happening to him. When I reflected on those ingredients of well-being—joy, contentment, energy, and affection—I could see that Calvin was missing all of them. Without a storehouse of positive experience, he literally had become a different trader.

■ ■ ■

Imagine a house with poorly sealed windows in winter. Cold drafts run through the hallways, making the house uncomfortable. The owner, in an attempt to improve the situation, turns the heat higher and higher, but with only limited benefit. When the utility bill arrives, the heating difficulty becomes a money issue. The solution has created a new problem.

Just as a building can leak energy, people experience their own energy drains. As I had mentioned earlier, I like to divide activities and events into two categories: those that give energy and those that drain it. Calvin's "house" was rife with leaks: Just about every area of life was taking energy rather than renewing it, creating a downward spiral. Think about the physical, emotional, mental, and spiritual energy emphasized by Loehr and Schwartz. In every one of those categories, Calvin was expending far more energy than he was generating. Quite literally, he was physically, emotionally, mentally, and spiritually exhausted. He had become the very picture of what we're like without psychological well-being. His wine drinking was a poor attempt to make himself feel better, but in fact only contributed to his energy leakage.

And what else did Calvin do to turn his situation around? He worked harder ... and harder. He woke up earlier, spent more time on research, and tried managing his positions more tightly (to the chagrin of his assistant). All of this was like turning up the heat in the leaky house. Ultimately, it took more of his resources than it gave him. He was working harder, but not smarter. His solution was adding to his problem.

When you have a leaky house, you install insulation. What, however, could insulate Calvin from his downward spiral?

This brings us back to the principle of use it or lose it. If we do not continually renew our energy resources, we don't stay at a steady energy point. Rather, we gradually lose our resources to the many life challenges that require energy. Well-being in that sense is the insulation that protects us from ongoing leaks. The only way we can deal with continual energy drains is through continual energy generation. The balance that matters is whether each day has added to our storehouse or contributed to its depletion. Because we can lose energy from overuse and underuse of our resources, Loehr and Schwartz stress, it is necessary to periodically engage in activities that renew our energy.

Their point is a very important one. Overuse of energy can lead to burnout. Underuse, however, is equally problematic. When our energy stores are underused, they are like batteries that drain. What taps our energy storehouses are the efforts that take us beyond our comfort zones: Routine activities, engaged in routinely, do not energize us. We find fresh vitality in physical, emotional, mental, and spiritual activities that are special. Returning to the list that I generated, note that it's the stretches of time devoted to creative work; the special trips and joint activities; and the vigorous exercise that give energy. If we stay in routine, we fall prey to underuse. Our batteries inevitably drain.

And that drains life, not just trading performance.

■ ■ ■

When you're up to your eyeballs in heating bills, the first thing you do is stop turning up the heat when it's all escaping through the gaps in your windows. And that's what Calvin did. His first step, after meeting with me, was to take a vacation. He stopped trading and went to an amusement park destination with his son for a long weekend. It was quality time and, to Calvin's surprise, his ex-wife approved of his taking time away from work to get closer to his son. When Calvin returned, he had a heart-to-heart talk with his girlfriend over a relaxing dinner and found out that it was his preoccupation with trading and markets that led her to distance from him. She felt that she was a number-two priority, and that hurt.

Toward the end of the trading break, I met with Calvin and his assistant and I asked each of them, independently, to generate a list of what needed to be improved in trading. Not surprisingly, there was strong agreement between the lists. The number-one priority for both of them was the need to get off the desk and away from screens during the day to review ideas and positions and plan actions rather than react to price oscillations. Making that as a team commitment had particular force for Calvin: He liked his assistant and did not want to let him down. Another improvement that they targeted was the setting of very specific rules for entry execution. They were only allowed to add to positions on retracements, and initial entries had to be of a threshold size so that winning trades truly felt like winners. Every trade had a specific target, stop, and size and these could only be changed if the two of them identified specific developments that changed their market views.

Calvin's assistant was energized by being included in the coaching, and Calvin started to feel like he was returning to his old self. Was he doing anything unique or revolutionary? Of course not. By stepping away from markets, focusing on a key value (his relationship with his son), and using the coaching to return to basics, he simply created small wins—and those provided a degree of insulation. His days started providing more energy than they were consuming, particularly when our focus turned to lifestyle and exercise, healthy eating, and replacement of drinking with socializing with friends. In each case, we took the same approach that Calvin had taken with his assistant: developing a "ritual"—a daily routine—that guided his exercise, eating, and social life. I was as much a cheerleader as a coach: Calvin had done all of these things well during much of his career. He was correct: He had gotten away from being himself. His "cure" was not to change, but rediscover, himself.

Key Takeaway

It is not enough to master stress; we must sustain life passion if we're to energize our trading.

What I saw in Calvin is what I see consistently in working with people: When engaged in the wrong activities, there is a downward spiral, and negativity is followed by increased negativity. When activities focus on well-being, the spiral turns upward and energy leads to fresh energy. The energy that Calvin gained through better sleep, weight loss, and exercise stimulated his social life, which in turn kept him positive and energized for markets. As he began making money again, he found himself wanting to keep the momentum going, so he eagerly continued his lifestyle changes. Had our work together been problem-focused—analyzing his past conflicts, tracking his self-defeating behaviors and thoughts—we would have never reinsulated his house. *Calvin had to rediscover his happiness before he could rediscover his trading.*

■ Conscientiousness: The Underappreciated Ingredient of Success

I recently wrote a two-part series of posts for the TraderFeed blog on why conscientiousness is important and how it can be cultivated. Recall that conscientiousness is one of the "big five" personality traits identified in the research literature. A conscientious person is one who is organized, responsible, and hardworking. When we refer to trading in a disciplined fashion, we are talking about approaching markets in a conscientious manner.

A behavioral analysis from Jackson et al. (2010) identified a number of behaviors negatively correlated with conscientiousness (avoid work; impulsivity; antisocial; and laziness) and ones positively correlated (organize, cleanliness, industrious, appearance, punctual, formality, responsibility). The authors found that conscientious people are goal-oriented and self-controlled; they are organized, hardworking, and think before acting.

Because conscientious people are more likely to work hard, avoid acting on impulse, and pursue goals in an organized manner, they tend to achieve better grades in school than less conscientious people. They are also more likely to succeed in their careers. An interesting study from Kohn and Schooler (1982) found that two factors led to occupational success: "ideational flexibility"—open mindedness—and a "self-directed orientation," which is essential to conscientiousness. People who were self-directed versus non–self-directed were less likely to need close supervision in their work and were more likely to engage in higher paying, less physically demanding work. In other words, responsible people tend to be given more responsibility.

The "industriousness" component of conscientiousness reflects persistence. The deliberate practice emphasized by Ericsson as a cardinal process in the genesis of expert performance presumes a high degree of persistence in learning. The conscientious person is particularly likely to seek detailed feedback about performance and use that feedback to make subsequent improvements. Compared with the lazy or distracted person, the conscientious trader is more likely to keep a journal, set goals, and systematically learn from experience. Conscientious traders are also apt to follow risk management rules and avoid impulsive behaviors that often undermine trading.

Recall Calvin's downward spiral, as one life area after another failed to renew his energy and provide psychological well-being. It was fascinating that the loss of well-being took a toll specifically on his rule-following as a trader. In a very important sense, Calvin became less conscientious over time: Diminished energy led to greater impulsivity and poorer decision making. Most of Calvin's assistant's concerns for his boss centered on his loss of discipline. Normally conscientious, Calvin fell into reactive patterns of what he called "rookie trading."

Michael Posner's (2012) cognitive neuroscience research suggests that attention and the executive functioning of the frontal cortex are essential to conscientiousness, with self-regulation as the link. When willpower is high, we are more likely to behave in organized, disciplined ways than when we are at low ebb. To the degree that well-being restores energy and willpower, we would expect to see happiness, satisfaction, energy, and affection contributing to conscientious behavior and success in school and work. We are more likely to be consistent in our pursuit of ends if we derive well-being from the process.

The striking aspect of Calvin's turnaround is that he became more conscientious once he became happier, not the reverse. An understandable coaching approach would have been to focus on Calvin's poor rule governance and encourage him to become more conscientious by completing journals, planning his trading, and so on. This, of course, would have failed: With his leaked energy, Calvin would have simply lacked follow-through on the journals and plans. His first step toward turnaround came not from working on his trading but from taking a break from markets and immersing himself in enjoyable and fulfilling activities with his son. He then followed up with activities that enhanced his connections to his girlfriend and personal friends, all of which contributed to the energy to revamp his eating, drinking, and exercise patterns. Once he was experiencing greater well-being, the increased energy fed increased discipline. No amount of effort to jumpstart discipline would have generated that well-being and energy.

An intriguing conclusion is that we lack discipline and willpower because we live life at a suboptimal energy level. While most of us are not mired in depression and burnout, we also do not experience passionate interest and love for life on a regular basis. Most of daily experience is spent in routine, which is efficient in the short run but de-energizing in the long run. We bring our energy leaks to the trade station, falling short in our trading for many of the same reasons as Calvin. We then try to make ourselves more conscientious by filling out more journals and analyzing more trades, all the while depleting our energy further.

Emotions of greed, fear, and frustration drain us of energy and lower our ability to sustain intention.

A provocative study from Tang and colleagues found that even a short period of integrative mind–body meditation daily resulted in improved attention and emotional self-regulation. It makes sense that mindfulness would promote conscientiousness: We're most likely to sustain our intentions if we remain mindful of them. What the study authors also found was that the daily meditation also led to enhanced emotional well-being and diminished stress. Meditation appears to be training not only for attention, but also for emotional self-control and enhanced emotional balance. By neutralizing sources of our energy leaks, meditation is an important tool in the cultivation of conscientiousness, as control over mind and body facilitates ongoing behavioral self-control.

■ Biofeedback as a Strategy for Enhancing Well-Being

Imagine carrying out meditative activities—slowing the mind and body, focusing attention—while you are hooked up to monitors that track your blood pressure, heart rate, muscle tension, brain waves, and other measures of physiological and cognitive stress. Beeps from the monitors tell you whether you are succeeding at relaxing and focusing or whether you are getting out of the zone. Over time, you learn the kinds of physical and cognitive strategies needed to keep the beeps at zone levels, using the signals to guide your efforts. That is biofeedback: It is meditation and stress management married to deliberate practice.

For years, I have found biofeedback to be a highly useful tool for traders. This is why I emphasized its use in *The Daily Trading Coach*. With a few adaptations, biofeedback can be used to break a variety of negative patterns and instill new, positive ones. Here are a few of the most promising applications:

- *General training of the flow state*—The combination of physical relaxation and intensified concentration is precisely the set of conditions needed to enter the flow state, in which we become pleasurably immersed in what we are doing. If we think of flow as a skill to be developed, rather than a state that simply occurs at random occasions, then *biofeedback can be used as flow training*. Through biofeedback, we learn to tune out distractions and regulate our minds and bodies. A short biofeedback exercise to enter the flow state can be a powerful way to start the trading day—and it makes a very useful break activity when you are finding yourself saturated and losing willpower.

- *Stress management*—Part of the power of biofeedback training is that it teaches us to enter states of mind and body that are incompatible with stress and distress. It is very difficult to sustain the body's flight-or-fight response if we are slowing our minds and bodies down and exercising enhanced self-control. Similarly, slowing down is incompatible with the impulsivity that typically results from negative emotional arousal. A particularly useful exercise is combining guided imagery with biofeedback, so that you are immersing your mind in something relaxing and quieting while keeping your body still and slowing and deepening your breathing. Through vivid imagery, we can create alternate realities and use those to short-circuit stress responses.

- *Exposure methods*—Here we turn up the heat on imagery and vividly imagine situations that have the potential to stress us out. We re-experience those situations and recreate in as much detail as possible how we would like to think and behave. Throughout this visualization of stressful events, we keep our bodies still and our breathing deep and slow. This trains us to remain relaxed and focused—even as we are confronting our most stressful scenarios. Exposure methods are extremely useful for combating performance anxiety and for preparing for anticipated market challenges. Through biofeedback, we get real-time feedback about our state of arousal, so that we can see, firsthand, that we can keep ourselves under control in the most difficult situations.

Although biofeedback is generally employed as an adjunct to stress management programs, it can be particularly useful in training us to cultivate positive emotional experience, as the example of the flow state suggests. In recent years, my biofeedback work has focused on measuring and controlling heart-rate variability (HRV), which is a measure of the normal variation in time between heart beats. As the MacArthur Research Network (1997) notes, HRV tends to decline with age and also decreases when we are under stress. People who report high degrees of anxiety and hostility also display lower HRV. Conversely, the activities typically needed to increase HRV include relaxation, a low state of emotional arousal, and control over breathing. The quickest way to increase HRV, I have found, is to induce a state of high mindfulness, low arousal, and intensified focus. All of these are the very opposite of the frantic, distracted states that can make traders reactive.

What is especially interesting is that sustaining heightened HRV for an extended time period does not lead to a neutral emotional state, but one that is experienced pleasurably. As already noted, it is a kind of flow state in which we tend to feel—not joyful and pumped up—but calm, at peace, and mentally/emotionally unburdened. Recall the components of well-being described earlier: happiness, satisfaction, energy, and affection. Not all positive states are high energy and high happiness. Calm satisfaction and warm affection can be equally positive, though not in as dramatic a fashion. *Biofeedback training that teaches us to sustain high HRV is a kind of well-being training*, very much connected to the earlier mentioned training of self-regulation and conscientiousness.

Imagine Billy, a trader of multiple global assets. He typically wakes up early to check prices in Asia and Europe and then pours over news, research reports, and emails that have accumulated in the in-box. By the time he gets to work, he has actively processed a variety of developments and started to make adjustments to his trading plans and positions. This sequence of processing new developments, assessing their relevance, and tweaking views and positions proceeds throughout the day, enabling Billy to stay on top of fast-breaking developments. It is precisely this kind of fast, adaptive thinking that has contributed to Billy's success across different market cycles.

Billy's work style works, but it is also productive of low HRV. The odds are good that Billy is jumping from development to development more in a rush than in the zone. Bombarded with inputs and needing to react rapidly to those, he has few opportunities for slowing mind and body and focusing attention. His work style is a kind of anti-biofeedback training, teaching him to sustain a state of low HRV. As we've seen from the prior discussions of use it or lose it, Billy is likely losing the ability to operate in the zone. This is likely to leave him vulnerable once markets pick up and the assembly line of information and market moves doubles its pace. When I first began my work with very active daytraders in Chicago, I wondered how consistently profitable traders could once in a while completely go off the rails and lose large amounts of money. As Billy's example illustrates, that vulnerability is created when our approach to our work is not one that builds our self-control and capacity for well-being.

Interestingly, many of those daytraders were not undone by busy markets but by boring ones. Having adapted to a breakneck pace of trading—many averaged 100 trades per day or more—they found it difficult to throttle back during low-volatility periods. Especially at midday hours, there were many occasions in which the total amount of contracts being transacted in the futures products they were trading simply could not accommodate the traders' position sizes. The boredom they experienced sitting back and waiting for greater liquidity was excruciating for them. The well-being they derived from market participation was one of activity and excitement. Indeed, several of them openly described themselves as trading junkies: They realized that they, like some gamblers, got high on high-stakes action.

The successful gambler knows when to fold a hand or not make a big bet. The conscientiousness of the professional gambler is controlling when to play and how much to bet. It is the gambler "on tilt" that makes outsized bets with undersized odds. I found it particularly interesting that slow markets put many of the daytraders on tilt. If they could not get an action fix, they tried desperately to manufacture one. That gave them action and drama—but of a negative sort.

The flipside of use it or lose it is that everything we use trains us. *We become what we consistently do.* That can work very much to our favor, as when we cultivate positive habits, or it can work greatly against us, when we build harmful habits. The hyperactive daytraders literally trained themselves in a way that amplified their excitability and distractibility. They cultivated considerable strengths at reading market patterns over very short time frames, but they also failed to build strengths associated with focused calm and conscientiousness. They were like bodybuilders who became so adept at working their upper bodies that they looked like Mr. Universe, but only from the waist up. When they could not rely on their upper body development, their spindly legs betrayed them.

Key Takeaway

We are trained by our routines.

Biofeedback and meditation can be viewed as tools for building the legs of attention, concentration, patience, mindfulness, and quiet, calm satisfaction. Through repeated biofeedback work, we can become quite good at invoking the zone, but we also train ourselves to function well in that zone. If we cannot generate well-being without drama, we will gravitate toward drama. That, over time, will be hazardous to our emotional health and our trading wealth. Well-being training enables us to extract energy from situations that we cannot control.

■ Using Meditation to Build Positivity

A 2008 study from Barbara Fredrickson and colleagues examined the psychological impact of an eight-week long training program in loving-kindness meditation. This is a distinctive form of meditation in that the meditator deliberately invokes images and feelings of love, contentment, and compassion while maintaining a stance of focused attention, physical calm, and mindfulness. The goal, therefore, is not simply to empty the mind but to fill it with thoughts, images, and feelings of well-being. In that sense, we can think of loving-kindness meditation as a kind of well-being training.

I found this study particularly intriguing because it was precisely such an invocation of positive emotions that I discovered raises HRV during biofeedback sessions. For instance, when traders I worked with attempted to empty their minds, control their breathing, and stay physically still, their HRV readings were not as high as when they actively cultivated positive imagery. One of my favorite images during HRV sessions has been holding one of my cats, stroking her, and feeling her purr against my body. It turns out that this is exactly the kind of imagery invoked by loving-kindness meditation.

A simple way to think of this is that relaxation training takes a car that is revving and stalling in high gear and brings it to lower gears, generating positive torque and movement. Instead of training ourselves to neutralize negative emotion, we can train ourselves to downshift and enter states that bring far better performance from our engines.

As mentioned earlier, Fredrickson's research, summarized in her 2009 book, *Positivity*, suggests that the development of positive emotional experience brings a host of benefits, including increased emotional resilience and improved health and social relationships. Her work finds that, under conditions of well-being, we broaden our minds and build new strengths. This broaden-and-build process suggests that people who experience themselves and life positively will be more likely to develop in constructive ways compared to those who lack well-being.

Fredrickson and Branigan (2005) conducted a clever study in which they showed subjects films that either had positive or negative emotional content. They then had the subjects perform a task of visual attention that identified whether perception was broader and more global or narrower and more local. The subjects given the positive films tended to perceive the figures on the test in global ways: They responded to the bigger picture. Those who viewed the negative films responded more to the narrow, local aspects of the figures. The implication is that, under conditions of positive emotion, we literally broaden our views of the world. In yet another study, Wadlinger and Isaacowitz (2006) found that subjects in a positive emotional state tended to perceive the peripheral areas of a visual field, while those in a negative state attended primarily to the center of the visual field. When we are negatively focused, we tend to operate in tunnel-vision mode. Positivity broadens our view, enabling us to process information that remains hidden to those in more negative states.

Nor are the broadening effects of positivity limited to perception. As Fredrickson notes in a 2013 research review, people who experience high levels of well-being are more behaviorally flexible when confronted with novel situations. They also tend to be more inclusive socially, broadening their favorable views of others—including those different from themselves. Clearly these benefits of well-being have important implications for trading. A broader, more flexible view enables traders to quickly attend to changing market conditions and make adaptive decisions. Traders mired in negativity are more likely to be tunnel-visioned and unable to generate fresh ideas and adaptive responses to rapidly changing circumstances.

This broadening under positive experience also leads to a building of strengths. In *Positivity*, Fredrickson cites research that shows how positive emotional experience helps to "undo" the negative effects of stress. Those with high well-being react physiologically to stress as do other people, but bounce back much quicker. This resilience is an important element in preventing setbacks from turning into slumps. Positivity also helps to build social networks, which in turn help people learn from each other and benefit from fresh interactions and perspectives. In the 2013 review, Fredrickson reports on research that shows how positive emotion leads to broader approaches to coping, which in turn helped to generate future positive emotional experience. These upward spirals of well-being lead to improved functioning, which in turn brings further well-being. This helps people build fresh capacities in ways that could never occur with the downward spirals of negative emotionality.

One of the upward spirals particularly linked to meditation and biofeedback involves vagal tone, a measure of the earlier mentioned heart rate variability (HRV). In a 2010 study, Kok and Fredrickson found that high vagal tone leads to positive social and psychological outcomes, which in turn lead to further improvements in vagal tone. By training ourselves to sustain high states of emotional well-being and vagal tone, we create conditions in which we are likely to respond to situations with heightened flexibility and adaptability and benefit from enhanced levels of social connectedness.

In the loving-kindness meditation study, those who spent the most time with the meditation received the greatest results in terms of increased positive emotion. Most promisingly, when subjects spent significant time with the meditation activity, the positive effects were more likely to persist in subsequent days, even when they did not meditate. Among the strengths built by participation in meditation were mindful attention, self-acceptance, positive social relations, and good health. Evoking positive images and experiences in a state of heightened focus and self-control not only led to further positive emotional experiences, but also positive life outcomes that added to further well-being.

The implications are clear: *You want your trading process to be a well-being building process.*

■ Using Self-Hypnosis to Feed Positivity

A wealth of studies cited by the International Certification Board of Clinical Hypnotherapy concludes that self-hypnosis can be very effective for such problems as weight loss, pain management, and smoking cessation. Hammond's 2010 review of research found that self-hypnosis is a rapid and effective intervention for overcoming anxiety and stress disorders. These findings are important, because they suggest that the emotional and behavioral self-control problems often faced by traders can be addressed through self-hypnosis.

In *The Daily Trading Coach*, I outlined a simple self-hypnosis strategy that I found to be effective in calming emotional arousal, focusing attention, and cementing discipline. The exercise involves taking a seated position with your hands in front of you and palms facing each other. You breathe deeply and slowly and focus all your attention on your hands. Once you feel completely focused, you tell yourself that there are magnets slowly, slowly, slowly pulling your hands together. As your hands get closer and closer, you tell yourself that you are feeling more and more relaxed, more and more focused, and more and more patient and in control. Your gaze never wavers from your hands, which slowly begin to come together as you breathe deeply and slowly and keep telling yourself that, as your hands come together, you are feeling more and more in the zone. When your hands touch, you tell yourself, you will feel wholly absorbed in the present, with a clear, calm focus. (You can give the suggestions in your head, but it's easy to make a recording and use it for the induction.) As you progress with the exercise, you add one more suggestion: My hands are a gateway to the zone. Any time I bring my hands together, I will find myself breathing slowly and returning to the clear, calm focus.

With repetition, I find that traders can become very adept at this exercise. I have been using it for years, with the result that I can typically reach a state of high focus within a minute or two. The beauty of the exercise is its portability. The suggestions are twofold: (1) you will become relaxed and focused when you bring your hands together; and (2) you will become relaxed and focused any time you focus on your hands and bring them together. In other words, you are programming yourself to use a gesture—the bringing together of hands—to achieve a shift in your cognitive, emotional, and physical state. *That shift is one from lower to higher levels of well-being.*

By now, you've no doubt observed common elements among meditation practices, biofeedback exercises, and self-hypnosis routines such as the one above. In each case, you are altering breathing, slowing the body, and focusing attention in order to access a higher level of well-being. Sustained relaxed focus is the common ingredient linking these methods.

My experience with each of these techniques is that minutes per day of consistent practice yields significant benefits that carry on through the day. In the heat of battle, the traders who have practiced these methods daily are much more able to take a few breaths, center themselves, and stay focused on markets than traders who react to the arousal of mind and body and unwittingly wind themselves up. As Fredrickson's work with loving-kindness meditation suggests, we can use these techniques to access a variety of positive states. In the above example, you can use self-hypnosis to achieve a state of calm focus. In a different variation, however, you can stay focused on a single visual point while performing callisthenic exercises, such as pushing your hands together with force or interlocking your fingers and pulling outward with force. As you perform the exercises, you tell yourself that, as you finish each repetition, you are feeling more and more energized, more and more filled with energy and enthusiasm. Once you're feeling invigorated, you then suggest to yourself that any time you focus your attention and perform the exercises, you will bring that energy back, as if you've been connected to a power source. (Once again, prerecorded suggestions can be quite effective.)

It is not unusual, during business meetings or long periods of working or trading, that I bring my hands together slowly and focus my (wandering) attention. Similarly, when I start to feel at low ebb, I will take a break, stand up, walk around, and perform a few callisthenic exercises while keeping my attention focused. In each case, I am relying on self-hypnosis as a training process, entering a desired state whenever I find myself functioning suboptimally.

Key Takeaway

Through training, we can become the masters of our cognitive, emotional, and physical states.

I cannot emphasize this strongly enough: It is not sufficient to train ourselves to reduce negative emotions such as anxiety and frustration. We can learn to access and sustain optimal emotional states, improving the quality of our lives and our work performance. Many techniques associated with biofeedback, meditation, and self-hypnosis can be repeated throughout the day, meaning that we are using repetition to turn positivity into a habit pattern. *We don't have to wait for good things to happen to us in order to sustain well-being.*

■ ■ ■

Nolan was a successful trader, but he had one overwhelming problem: procrastination. It didn't seem to matter what the responsibility was: Nolan would find a way to put it off until the last minute—and sometimes not until a deadline had passed. Nolan's wife despaired of his lateness to social events and putting off of errands. She learned long ago in their marriage that she would have to pay the bills if their credit wasn't going to be ruined. Interestingly, Nolan was always punctual for markets and had no problem coming in early for data releases or fast-moving markets. While trading, he stayed focused on multiple markets and took few breaks. He worked with strict risk limits and never blew up. Fellow traders considered Nolan to be a paragon of discipline. Everywhere else, however, Nolan was all over the place.

Over time, Nolan's procrastination problem began to catch up with him. He knew he should review and track his trading, but other priorities always seemed to get in the way. He started a journal several times, only to let it slip after a few days. When markets became more correlated, he found less benefit in trading multiple markets. Everything seemed to be "risk off" or "risk on." The benefits of diversification, which had long aided his trading, now were diminished. He either made money on all his trades or lost money. The solid risk-adjusted returns that he had enjoyed for a number of years slowly eroded. Nolan realized that he needed to make changes in his trading, but he avoided the very steps needed to adapt.

A careful investigation early in our meetings discovered that Nolan was most likely to procrastinate late in the day and least likely early in the morning. In the morning, he found fewer distractions and usually felt well rested. By the evening—and especially after an active day's trading—he felt drained. The last thing he wanted to do was dive into new efforts. This, it seemed, was a classic willpower issue: He simply lacked the mental resources needed to direct and sustain effort. This was verified by a key observation: Whenever Nolan procrastinated, he felt tired and/or overwhelmed. A common thought was, "Not this, too!" He recognized that, at such time, he felt on overload. It didn't matter whether he was asked to mow the lawn, help with the kids, or read research papers—all of it felt like a burden, particularly after he had worked all day.

Nolan was a classic case of energy leaking through the windows. His problem was not that his work drained him. Rather, his problem was that he lacked any reliable method for renewing his energy. Borrowing from the solution-focused playbook, we examined evenings in which he didn't feel drained. Not so surprisingly, on most of those occasions he had taken a short power nap—about 20 minutes—after coming home from work. That was sufficient to renew some of his focus and drive.

We decided to build on that element of solution. I suggested to Nolan that, since he functioned best during early mornings, we had to create more mornings for him! The way to do that was to have him take a power nap after work, followed by a short but vigorous exercise session. During the session, he would engage in the self-hypnosis exercise mentioned above, suggesting to himself that each repetition was charging him with energy, renewing his willpower. He added a useful suggestion—as he felt more energized, he would perform his repetitions with greater speed and effort and build his energy even further. As a result, his workouts were relatively brief but strenuous, with effort increasing throughout each session.

Having rested and then pumped up, Nolan felt in the early evening very much how he usually felt first thing in the morning. He began to look forward to using this second morning to tackle his most pressing responsibilities. One of his priorities was to teach himself options trading, as he became convinced that this would provide him with some of the diversification benefits that he had been missing in his recent trading. Instead of achieving diversification by trading multiple markets, he began to look at trading volatility as a source of unique returns. What I found particularly fascinating was that, in the more energized mode, Nolan was no longer a procrastinator. He didn't need to change his personality or enter into any kind of deep therapy. Rather, he simply needed a reliable method for recharging his batteries and renewing his cognitive, physical, and emotional well-being.

■ A Workout for Mind and Body

Yoga is a particularly interesting practice in that it combines work on breathing and mindfulness with physical activity, such as stretching. We commonly think of meditation as a seated discipline. What yoga shows us is that we can be highly physically active and calm, controlled, and mindful at the same time. Indeed, most of the poses taught in yoga are designed to evoke particular physical, emotional, and spiritual states, such as self-awareness and gratitude. Through repetition, yoga practitioners learn to associate particular postures with particular states, creating habit patterns of well-being.

For example, many foundational yoga poses involve opening up the body, stretching muscles, and maintaining balance. All require considerable self-control and precision and all are undertaken in a state of mindfulness, typically with controlled breathing. When we are stressed, we tend to breathe in rapid and shallow ways, react to events without mindfulness, narrow our focus of attention, and tense our muscles. Yoga positions create an unstressed state for the body, even as we are physically active. This is important because it trains us to stay controlled under conditions of physiological arousal. Pumping up the body while keeping the mind focused and mindful prepares us for staying in the zone even when we are pumped up during the heat of market action.

I recently outlined in the TraderFeed blog a workout routine for mind and body that blends the benefits of meditation with those of traditional physical workouts. The speed workout that I described involves an initial period of deep breathing, concentrated focus, and seated calm, in which I am mindful of inhalations and exhalations while maintaining an erect posture. With each inhalation, I repeat to myself, "Energy in," and feel my body energizing. With each exhalation, I repeat to myself, "Energy out," and feel myself relax. After a few minutes, I typically feel quite centered and energized.

Then begins the formal workout: I start with 5 to 10 minutes of stretching, starting with hands and arms, moving to back and waist, then legs, and finishing with situps. That is followed by 10 minutes of lifting on a weight machine, with sets chosen to work neck and shoulders, arms and chest, and legs. The final 15 minutes is spent in an aerobic workout on the treadmill, keeping the pace at a target heart rate. The workout follows two sets of rules across all three activities (stretching, lifting, running):

1. *There is minimum rest time between activities.* I move rapidly from one activity to the next. The idea is to create a concentrated workout that results in getting increasingly pumped up over a half-hour's time. By condensing as much exercise benefit into as short a period as possible, I push my limits without overly taxing any single part of the body.
2. *Throughout each activity, I maintain the same centered awareness as I had achieved during the first several minutes.* What this means in practice is that I remain mindful of my breathing and posture and keep my mind focused on the "Energy in, energy out" mantra throughout each activity. The goal is to stay in the zone, even as I am moving quickly from activity to activity and testing my body's limits.

What I have found is that this exercise routine, repeated day after day, creates much of the benefit that I've derived from self-hypnosis. The initial period of breathing, posture, and awareness becomes associated with getting ready for the speed workout routine. The workout routine in turn is associated with staying mindful during periods of physiological arousal. Because the workout is associated with the breathing work, it's not necessary to motivate myself to exercise; because the workout is associated with mindfulness, it's not necessary to motivate myself to set time aside for meditation. The entire activity becomes a sequence of positive habit patterns.

When I first began this routine, I didn't envision all of its benefits. Indeed, I thought of combining work on mind and body simply as a time-saving measure. It was only later that I discovered the greatest benefit of the combined workout routine.

■ ■ ■

The trade was moving away from me as the market headed lower. I found myself tensing up. My mind began to race. I had anticipated a break to the upside, but it wasn't materializing. I looked across different indexes and sectors and tracked the recent upticks and downticks to determine whether this was a broad shift of market participation. Something felt wrong, but I could not put my finger on exactly what it was.

Suddenly, without advance planning, I shifted my position in the chair and sat up straighter. I adopted the seated position that I take just before the speed workout. I began to regulate my breathing and maintained my focus on the market. I was aware that my heart rate had increased and that I felt tense, but I felt more like an observer to my stress than a participant. The market bounced a bit, held, dipped, bounced, held ... the sequence continued for a few minutes. I said out loud, "The buying has dried up." The NYSE TICK could not move above +500 on the bounce; price could not take out its prior high; a key sector barely budged during the bounce in the overall market. Quickly, I exited the long position and flipped to a short. That is unusual for me. Normally, I would exit and then reassess the market. This time, however, the market's behavior seemed quite clear. Within a short time, sellers reentered the market and we moved back to the day's lows, where I covered, taking advantage of what had been a range trade all along.

Key Takeaway

We learn to function in the heat of battle by training under heated conditions.

What made this little sequence special was not the modest profits of the trade but what the process of the trade taught me. It was the first time I could recollect in which the flight-or-fight response to adverse price movement kick-started me into a state of calm focus and sound information processing. *It was all set up by the shift in posture.* I associated the mindfulness with the open posture of chest expanded and sitting very straight. Once I sat in the proper posture, the breathing came naturally and was quickly followed by the calm clarity of being in a more mindful state. Day after day of training myself to stay focused and controlled while my body was pumping up led to an unexpected focus during a pumped-up trading episode. Quite literally and somewhat unexpectedly, I had trained myself to move deeper in the zone as I became more worked up.

The mindful speed workout has become a major psychological tool in my trading arsenal. It is a way of staying energized, and it is a way of building and sustaining well-being. Most of all, however, it achieves a reprogramming: Instead of losing control when we are stressed, it teaches us to become even more controlled when the stuff is hitting the fan.

■ Special Topics in Well-Being: Love

Do you remember when you first fell in love? It's quite the amazing experience. Ordinary experiences become extraordinary when you're immersed in love. My memory for events is not particularly good, yet I can remember vivid details of the New Year's Eve party in which I met my wife-to-be. Some 30 years later, we took a cruise together and I found it extremely gratifying to experience those same feelings. Love encapsulates all of the experiences of well-being: happiness, satisfaction, energy, and affection. It is one of the most concentrated experiences of well-being that we can achieve.

Too often, however, we accept the premise that the magic of love is something that we outgrow. We see couples that are comfortable but not passionately in love and we assume that this is the natural state of things. Similarly, young people often approach their professional lives with dreams and aspirations—they are in love with their work. As time moves on, however, the magic fades, replaced by a daily sequence of business meetings, project deadlines, and office politics. It's a sad reality that, as people age, they become less enthusiastic, less audacious in their goals, less in love with their lives. They aren't necessarily depressed or unhappy. *They simply lack the glow of being in love.*

We think of love in terms of romantic relationships and, as we'll see, that expression of love is particularly important to well-being. In truth, however, we have a relationship with every major facet of our lives. We have a relationship with our jobs; we have a relationship with our bodies; and we have relationships with our friends. We have relationships with our recreational activities, and with our families. Even more broadly, we have a relationship with our physical environment, from our offices at work to our homes. Life can be conceptualized as an interlocking network of relationships. The quality of our lives is greatly impacted by the quality of those relationships.

Imagine, for a minute, your relationship with financial markets. How would you characterize that relationship? Is it an adversarial relationship? A hot-and-cold, confusing relationship? A fulfilling relationship? Many traders talk about markets as if they are battlegrounds and they prepare for combat each day. Other traders, frustrated, talk about markets being dysfunctional and manipulated. How we relate to markets very much impacts our trading experience. If we think of the market as a casino, we will frame one kind of experience. If we treat markets as battlegrounds, our experience will be quite different.

Now imagine what it would be like to be in love with markets: to find in them something unique, special, and valued. A person who is in love with markets will be market-focused even outside of normal trading hours. They are not simply preparing for a day's trading; they are passionately interested in deepening their market experience, learning everything they can about markets. A good romantic relationship makes us feel visible: We are understood and appreciated for who we are. A good relationship with markets makes us visible as well. As we have seen, it brings out our greatest interests and strengths.

As we've observed so often in this chapter, tapping into well-being means that we don't have to continuously rely on motivation to do the right things. When we are in love with markets, we don't have to make ourselves research, observe, and study: Indeed, nothing can keep us away from our passion. When I worked a full-time job at a medical school, I wanted to study markets intensively, but knew I couldn't follow them in real time. Instead, I printed out charts of major markets and indicators on a five-minute basis and collected them every day. Each day required quite a few minutes to download and print out the data, but over time I developed quite an encyclopedia. I could track how markets and indicators behaved at major turning points, how they behaved in trends, and how they acted during range conditions. I could track breakouts and how they occurred, and I began to observe differences between fakeout markets and true breakout ones.

The investigation was fascinating. I conducted my daily downloads and reviews for two full years. During that time, I placed very few trades. It wasn't about the trading. I was in love with markets.

I recall being asked many times how I could stay so motivated to download and study market information each day. The question amused and confused me. It wasn't motivation; it wasn't even a choice. I no more motivated myself to follow markets than I motivate myself to spend time with my wife and children. When you are in love, interaction becomes a source of joy.

To this day, I maintain the downloading. Each day I track a variety of breadth measures, many of which I update on the TraderFeed blog. One data set has been manually updated daily since 2006. Each day I look forward to seeing the new data, much as you might look forward to the next episode in a television series that you enjoy. It was during my printout days that I discovered the NYSE TICK and the value of tracking market sectors. It was during later data explorations that I learned to break the market down into transactions across a wide universe of stocks and separately assess buying and selling pressure. Over time, all that study has given me an unparalleled database. Most important, it has provided an intimacy with the data that can only come from love.

■ ■ ■

Too often, trading comes at the expense of relationships. The ups and downs of performance and the uncertainties of markets take a toll on traders and partners alike. I recall being asked at one trading conference for the secret to success in markets. My answer was simple, "You should always have something in your life that is more important to you than trading."

That is the power of love. When we love markets, but have something more important to us than trading, wins and losses suddenly fall into perspective. Imagine being a passionate trader who was deeply connected to his or her religious faith. The love of markets would be a powerful motivator, but it would pale beside the power of a deeper, religious love. Could you really become too caught up in the ego implications of winning and losing if your main focus is spiritual connectedness?

Similarly, the love of a spouse and family is what keeps me going. If I experienced a debilitating drawdown in my trading, it would hurt and I would be disappointed—*and* I would still have a good and rich life.

Traders who neglect their relationships implicitly put their trading at the top of their emotional priority list. When that happens, self-esteem, mood, and energy level become correlated with P&L. Love provides an important set of emotional buffers: *When we derive energy, affection, happiness, and satisfaction from activities outside of markets, we don't have to overtrade markets to manufacture good feelings.* Many times, the answer to our market problems is cultivating the positives from our nontrading lives.

■ ■ ■

Research studies tell us a great deal about how love contributes to our overall well-being and effective functioning. In her book, *Love 2.0*, Barbara Fredrickson (2013) summarizes fascinating research conducted by neuroscientist Uri Hasson at Princeton University. He had a young woman tell a story while being connected to a brain scanner. He then had various people listen to the story while connected to scanners. What he found was that certain people related to the story more than others. When people related closely to their story, their brain wave patterns mimicked those of the speaker—even though the two of them had not met. Indeed, when there was a closely felt connection between listener and speaker, the brain wave patterns of the listener actually anticipated those of the speaker! This suggests that, when people connect with one another, there is actually a "neuronal coupling": Minds are in sync. Another person's reality becomes ours.

Research summarized by Lopez, Pedrotti, and Snyder, in their overview book, *Positive Psychology* (2015), finds that when partners in long-term romantic relationships are shown pictures of one another, areas of the brain that are associated with bonding and attachment, as well as with rewards associated with goal attainment, become active. When there has been long-term coupling, the mere sight of the loved person becomes a source of well-being that protects against stress and promotes health. Fredrickson notes that the neuropeptide oxytocin, which is associated with bonding, is stimulated by close, loving interactions. Oxytocin helps to moderate stress and facilitates social interactions. When parents and children are in sync with one another, the production of oxytocin occurs on both ends, helping cement loving, trusting bonds. In short, love places us in greater harmony with others, and that harmony helps make us more loving over time.

Key Takeaway

Our connections to others are a powerful buffer to trading stress.

Indeed, research suggests that social attachment overall is related to well-being. Argyle, in his 2001 book, *The Psychology of Happiness*, cites evidence that satisfaction with friends correlates positively and significantly with both happiness and life satisfaction. He similarly notes that a strong social support system is associated with superior physical health, especially when that system brings actual support, not just a venting of problems. As noted earlier, a variety of studies find that being married is associated with higher levels of well-being. Argyle cites evidence that this is true across cultures, resulting in superior mental and physical health among married individuals. In one particularly interesting study, Berkman and Syme (1978) tracked 7000 people over a nine-year period. Among those over the age of 50, 30.8 percent of those with weak social networks had died by the end of the study, compared with 9.6 percent of those with strong networks.

So what does this mean for trading? Three implications stand out:

1. *Building professional networks*—Among the most successful traders I've worked with, the majority have very active and strong networks of peer traders. This network helps them stay on top of market developments and research, but there is an additional benefit: It provides an effective professional social support system. Fellow traders are most likely to understand the day-to-day challenges of markets and assist with problem solving. Many of these networks include not only information sharing, but also mentorship. A strong and active network is a great way to broaden trading horizons while sustaining well-being.

2. *Sustaining strong romantic relationship and family ties*—It is extremely important that traders cultivate consistent sources of happiness, life satisfaction, energy, and affection as a buffer to the ups and downs of market performance. Too often, traders who experience performance challenges double down on their market focus, further immersing themselves in the source of their difficulties. This creates a downward spiral of energy, a loss of optimism, and a greater likelihood that trading setbacks will become outright slumps. When relationship and family ties are strong, risk taking takes on a different complexion. Trading well becomes part of a commitment to loved ones, not just good intentions on one's own part.

3. *Love workouts*—What we're finding out in this chapter is that any source of well-being can be exercised and cultivated as part of creating positive habit patterns. Successful romantic relationships, like any living, growing thing, need tending and care. Focusing on

day-to-day responsibilities and putting romance and quality time together on the back burner is one of those guaranteed energy drains. What do you do each day that evokes and expresses your love for your children? Your romantic partner? Your closest friends? What are you doing to deepen your closest relationships? Broaden your base of support? Recall that *use it or lose it* principle: Love not actively cultivated is well-being forgone.

The idea is to focus not just on the work productivity of your time, but also the emotional quality. Well-being is the fuel that powers you through the marathon race of a career. Cultivating love, friendship, and social support is essential to health and success. The right relationships give energy and make us better—as traders and as people.

■ ■ ■

Now let's focus on a less comfortable topic: the reverse side of building affection and social support.

Shutting people out.

A very skilled trader I worked with several years ago went into a trading drawdown. He felt that his idea generation had waned and his trading of his ideas was less than sharp. He was especially frustrated by two missed trades. Both were ideas that he had researched and put on the back burner because price action was not yet confirming what he was noticing fundamentally. By the time he returned to the ideas, they had already moved without him. It was an uncharacteristic loss of sharpness, and he was highly critical of his performance.

It didn't take long to isolate a major cause of his problems. His firm had hired several new traders, all of whom were young, eager, and talkative. They brought good energy to the trading floor—and they brought nothing but distraction to the trader. He moved to an enclosed office space for the start of each trading day and conducted his research and reviews in quiet, without distraction. When he wanted to interact with other traders, socially and to share ideas, he came upstairs and sought out the contacts he most valued. That simple change of environment led to a major improvement in performance, contributing to the quality of his market preparation time. He was a trader who truly loved markets, and he loved his time observing and studying markets. When that experience was diluted with noisy conversation, his information processing suffered, his performance declined, and he became unhappy with himself.

I tend to be an optimist. I generally can see the good in people and perceive their strengths, even when they most doubt themselves. Still, the saying that a pessimist is an optimist with experience rings true on this topic. There are some people who are noxious. There are some experiences worth filtering out. It makes little sense to build our well-being, only to see it squandered in a suboptimal environment. Shutting out negative influences is an important if uncomfortable step in maximizing our personal and professional experience.

Consider the following examples of filters that are built into my daily life:

- Every community I have lived in for the past 30 years has had common characteristics: strong support for public schools, parks, libraries, and infrastructure; low rates of crime; a sizable professional population; few traffic and congestion problems; and a prosperous downtown/community center. Experiencing high quality of life in my immediate environment greatly contributes to my outlook. The area where I grew up was very middle class—hardly the lap of luxury—but it was a very family-oriented, school-oriented, safe, and well-maintained neighborhood. If I don't experience those qualities in an area, I spend as little time there as possible.

- Over the years, I've found that some people in work settings are more focused on advancement through office politics and others are more focused on the quantity and quality of their work output. The former group is eager to use you when you have something they need, and they are the first to disown you if you become involved in controversy. I spend very little time interacting with the former group and cultivate good relationships with those in the latter group. One of the greatest inspirations for my own work is being around others who are inspired by what they do.

- Ever since starting the TraderFeed blog, I've been active in social media. Most interactions are quite enjoyable. I love meeting people online who are from different parts of the world and who bring fresh perspectives to markets. At times, however, the online interactions are disagreeable. I have been subjected to sarcastic remarks, slurs, and even accusations if my views do not accord with the (usually anonymous) person commenting on the blog or tweeting me. That is when the "block" button becomes useful. I will generally try a civil, constructive response the first time; after that, everything is blocked. Life is too short for becoming the receptacle of others' drama.

- I find most traditional media to be noisy. Television, websites, and online videos often attract eyeballs by engaging in manufactured controversy and hype. A common example is breathless predictions of market crashes from commentators seeking public attention. I avoid most media when I'm trading: Most of the time it feels like an environmental pollutant.

- When you experience a degree of success in markets, you become like a person who has won a lottery: Suddenly you find yourself with people wanting to be your "friends." Some are looking for hot tips; some are looking for jobs; some want you to share secrets of success. These are not stimulating, collegial interactions. They are painfully one-sided—all taking, not giving. This is particularly problematic if you're active in social media. If thousands of people read my blog each week, it only takes 1 percent of that group to consist of "takers" to create real time and energy sinks. (My favorite responders are the people offering opportunities to "partner" with them on some business venture, where I will inevitably be the partner to provide the capital and name recognition.) Without filters, it's easy to become swamped with unfruitful and unfulfilling correspondence.

- Let's face it: Some people have pretty crappy values. I'm referring to people who need wealth to impress other people; who spend more time on possessions than on their own children; who are insecure and threatened by your achievements; and who are more interested in name-dropping than in discussing real ideas or topics. Some of these people inevitably will be in your workplace; others might be in your neighborhood or in your family. Life is too beautiful to be spent in such company; filtering the amount of time spent with obnoxious people is great for the mental ecology.

You can only enjoy an optimal environment if you filter out all that is suboptimal. No junk food in the refrigerator; no tabloid journalism in the news flow; no empty chit-chat social activity; no unnecessary interaction with those caught up in drama or those envying your success; and as little time spent as possible with people and activities that drain energy.

We can proactively create our environments to maximize experiences of well-being.

I know all of this sounds harsh and judgmental. I almost didn't include it in the book. But it's reality. If you aspire to be all that you can be, you cannot be all things to all people and engage equally in all things. Find the people and activities that inspire you and bring out the best in you and filter the rest.

Special Topics in Well-Being: Affinity Groups

Most of us recognize the importance of friendships and romantic relationships to our well-being. Less appreciated is the power of belonging to a community of likeminded people. Affinity groups appear in many forms: around political causes; spiritual education and worship; courses and training programs; recreational activities; and the like. The key to an affinity group is that it brings people together in common cause. Very often, the participants enjoy shared values as well as interests, creating promising bonding experiences and widening our base of social support. Lopez, Pedrotti, and Snyder, in their review of *Positive Psychology* (2015), observe that spirituality is associated with improved emotional and physical health, as well as better marital and family relationships. They also point to evidence that positive emotional experience contributes to increased spirituality as well as the reverse—a classic example of the upward spiral noted by Fredrickson.

Argyle, in *The Psychology of Happiness*, cites research evidence that church attendance is the strongest spiritual predictor of well-being, as those who attend more frequently report higher happiness and life satisfaction than those who do not. He explains that church attendance is, in part, a social activity, bonding people within a group. He observes that church attendance is particularly strongly correlated with having more social ties outside the family and more frequent contact with one's support system. By bringing people together with common beliefs and values, churches become powerful affinity groups that contribute to well-being.

Many affinity groups organize on a more informal basis. A number of traders I am friendly with participate in chat rooms designed to share information about trading opportunities. Generally, they serve a social function as well, providing an outlet when trading is slow or frustrating. Hedge fund portfolio managers and bank sales/traders very often use dinner meetings to connect with colleagues. I recently participated in a conference organized by the Traders4ACause group. The members pay conference fees that benefit designated charities; the conferences serve both educational and social functions. The conference was a particularly good personal and professional outlet, as it brought together traders with similar trading styles and values.

Participating in affinity groups can be challenging for more introverted traders, and yet it can be tremendously valuable. I have found that many traders, including some who don't participate in the usual dinners and social events, share my interest in craft beers. As a result, I've participated in a number of craft beer tasting outings. The focus on the wide variety of beer styles and offerings satisfies curiosity and interest in novelty, and the outings provide a great social forum for sharing experiences and ideas. Many couples are interested in participating in group activities, as it enables them to meet new people and enjoy each other's company in a fresh setting. Indeed, it's not at all common to find couples with young children socializing with each other to generate bonding opportunities for children and adults alike.

Trading can be a lonely activity and, especially for self-employed traders, it can be quite isolating. If years of coaching traders have taught me anything, it's that there are many talented and creative professionals out there. Those are the people who provide inspiration, insight, and genuine camaraderie. Life becomes richer when played as a team sport.

■ Special Topics in Well-Being: Gratitude

In previous writings, I mentioned one of the practices that most hit home for me occurred during my stint as a team manager for our college basketball team. Coaches routinely put signs up in the locker room to highlight lessons from recent practices and games. One sign, however, was on the wall permanently: "Acknowledge the pass that leads to a score." If a player did not point a finger to acknowledge an assist, he quickly came out of the game. There was no *I* in team; you either played within the team concept or you didn't play.

Of course, what the coaches were also teaching was gratitude. Before you point your finger at yourself and boast of your success, you point toward those who helped make your success possible. When we feel gratitude, we focus on and value what we have. We don't mire ourselves in frustration over what we lack.

When I review a trader's journal, one of the first things I look for is the ratio of positive entries to negative ones. Many traders write in journals only when they trade poorly. They vent their frustrations with themselves and with markets. They do not write about their positive performance and they certainly don't acknowledge passes that led to their scores. Their journals are filled with attitude, but not gratitude.

And it turns out that this is a larger problem than traders realize.

■ ■ ■

Gratitude is closely connected to optimism, and optimism is a key component of emotional well-being. When we feel gratitude, we naturally focus on the part of life's cup that is half-full, not the part that is half-empty. When my son got into a car accident and incurred a fair amount of body damage to the vehicle, I knew there was going to be a chunk of money Dad would need to shell out. My reaction, however, was relief: The focus was on the fact that he was OK and no one had sustained injuries. Next to that fact, the bill for the bodywork was a small thing. Gratitude for the positives in the situation put a potential problem into perspective.

In his 2007 book, *Thanks!*, Robert Emmons describes an experiment in which one group of subjects focused on and wrote about daily burdens, while another group wrote about daily blessings. The idea was to emphasize life's negative or positive events. Over the course of the 10-week experiment, the group counting its blessings raised its happiness levels by 25 percent over the group recounting its hassles. The high-gratitude group also exercised more and reported being in better health. Interestingly, the gratitude group reported significantly greater happiness and satisfaction than the hassled group, but negative emotional experience did not differ significantly between the groups. Gratitude appeared to uniquely contribute to positive emotional experience.

Emmons makes an important observation: *Gratitude leads us to become better at retrieving positive information, because it naturally turns our attention to positive aspects of life*. Depression, on the other hand, typically leads us to focus on negative aspects of life and primes us to selectively retrieve negative information. Gratitude also leads us to focus on the positive acts of others, so it is not surprising that Emmons has found evidence that gratitude leads to a strengthening of social bonds. When researcher John Gottman compared happy couples with unhappy ones, he found that the communications of happy couples were skewed 5:1 in favor of positive emotional content. When the ratio was closer to 1:1, the couples were more likely to be unhappy and eventually divorce. Gratitude in a close relationship brings partners together and enhances the well-being of each.

Perfectionism undermines traders not only because it sets up unrealistic expectations and fosters frustration, but also because it sabotages gratitude. The perfectionist, by definition, is focused on what doesn't go well. If a trade was profitable, it could have been held longer for larger gains. If it was exited well, it could have been better if it had been sized up. One trader I worked with routinely wrote in his journal of everything that did not go well (perfectly) in his trading. He was like the subjects in Emmons's study who wrote only of hassles, never of blessings. This trader insisted that satisfaction would make him lazy and complacent. He prided himself on never settling for less than greatness. The net result of his focus, however, was that he never felt gratitude and, in an important sense, he never felt success. His trading experience brought little well-being and this, over time, took a toll on his trading results. Long a successful trader, he found his focus waning, leading to missed trades. This only led to further self-criticism, still less gratitude, and ever lower levels of well-being.

Key Takeaway

When we demand perfection of ourselves, we display ingratitude toward achievements that fall short of perfection.

How often do you feel pride in your accomplishments? Satisfaction in your progress and development? Gratitude for what you've learned from others? How often do you feel blessed in your work, rather than cursed? In solely focusing on where we fall short, we lose access to joy, contentment, and appreciation. Without those positive buffers, we become mired in negativity and our batteries inevitably drain.

■ ■ ■

So how can we foster a greater sense of gratitude through life? Emmons offers 10 gratitude-building practices:

1. *Keep a gratitude journal.* Identifying daily the positives in your life and connecting to them with an attitude of appreciation fosters both happiness and satisfaction.

2. *Remember the bad.* It is much easier to be grateful for our present situation if we remind ourselves how bad things could be. I recall vividly what it was like to be in unhappy and unfulfilling romantic relationships. This makes it easy to appreciate what I have in my marriage.

3. *Ask yourself three questions.* The questions Emmons outlines are from a Buddhist meditation technique in which you focus on: (a) what you have received from others; (b) what you have given to others; and (c) the problems and difficulties you have created for others. The combination of questions naturally leads us to focus on giving and staying grateful for gifts we've received, despite troubles we may have caused others.

4. *Learn prayers of gratitude.* In prayer, we don't ask for favors and rewards. Rather, we give thanks for what we have. Emmons points to evidence that prayer leads to increased goal achievement, but only for people who pray in a mode of gratitude.

5. *Come to your senses.* Use your senses of smell, taste, sight, hearing, and touch to better appreciate the world around you. Feeling the state of your body and tapping into gratitude for your health is a powerful way to turn something we take for granted into a source of ongoing well-being.

6. *Use visual reminders.* Notes around the house can remind you of gratitude. Emmons refers to *accountability partners*: people who help keep you on a grateful path, much as an exercise partner keeps you in the gym.

7. *Make a vow to practice gratitude.* Making a public vow to engage in gratitude is a great way to keep ourselves accountable and turn a good intention into a full-blown commitment.

8. *Watch your language.* The words we use help shape our reality. Words like *fortunate* and *blessed* are common among people who sustain gratitude. On the other hand, it is difficult to sustain gratitude if language is negative.

9. *Go through the motions.* Behaving in more grateful ways leads to increased feelings of gratitude. Sometimes our minds need to catch up to the actions of our bodies!
10. *Think outside the box.* We can be creative and find gratitude in even negative events, such as what we learn from bad trades or virtues that we develop because of dealing with those who hurt us.

Notice the common theme here: We can grow gratitude—and all forms of subjective well-being—through directed practice. Happiness, life satisfaction, energy, affection: These all are the results of habits that we can cultivate. Quite literally, we can train ourselves to live more positive lives, and that training will help us broaden and build our strengths. It's back to use it or lose it: If we are not actively immersing ourselves in sources of joy, contentment, energy, and connectedness to others, then we are at the mercy of random events and their impact on our moods. *To a much higher degree than we commonly realize, we can mold our cognitive, emotional, and physical realities.*

■ Putting It All Together: Trading, Strengths, and Well-Being

How does expanding our positive experience make us better traders? The old trading psychology taught us to control emotions and minimize them in decision making. The new Trading Psychology 2.0 perspective emerging from research in positive psychology is that we operate best when we are suffused with well-being. It is not by accident that the first portion of this book emphasized adapting to changing markets and the second part has focused on strengths and well-being. In a big-picture sense—and as the upcoming material on creativity will demonstrate—we will be best positioned to keep up with markets if we: (1) play to our strengths; and (2) operate as consistently as possible in a state of physical, emotional, and cognitive wellness. Indeed, that is the ultimate upward spiral described by Frederickson's (2009) research: To the degree that we exercise our strengths, we generate well-being; to the extent that we are positively focused, we make maximum use of our strengths. Deliberate practice, at a psychological level, is simply learning that has been supercharged by the interplay between strengths and positivity.

John Ratey, in his book, *A User's Guide to the Brain*, explains how physical exercise strengthens the brain the same way it strengthens the heart: by increasing the number and density of blood vessels. "The more we use it," Ratey explains, "the more we stress it, the better our circulation is, and the more fit that part of the brain becomes" (2001, p. 359). Ratey similarly observes the benefits of mental exercise, pointing to evidence that nuns (a great research group in a controlled environment) who actively perform crossword puzzles and engage in political debate live longer and have a lower incidence of Alzheimer's disease than those who do not stimulate their minds. A great deal of the cognitive decline that we assume is due to aging is actually an artifact of poor mental exercise. Just as our bodies can become deconditioned with the absence of exercise, our minds can lose their sharpness if they are not actively employed.

Ratey observes in his 2013 book, *Spark*, that we are most likely to exploit the plasticity of our brains and expand our cognitive abilities by engaging in unfamiliar activities. In other words, our brains grow when we push them to learn. Through the process of neurogenesis, we gain new brain cells, which facilitate new learning. When active versus passive mice were placed in an experiment where they had to swim and recall an escape route to get out of the water, the mice that had been physically active learned the route much quicker. Sure enough, on dissection, the active rats had grown significantly more brain cells thanks to their exercise.

What our overview of well-being has shown is that any form of exercise—from physical workouts to stretching our emotional capacities—has the potential to rewire us and extend our capacities. In pushing our limits, exercising our strengths, and cultivating fresh experience, we stimulate the brain and enhance our adaptive capabilities. In short, we become better decision makers and traders because we become better brain makers. Ratey, in *Spark*, observes that exercise "optimizes your mind-set to improve alertness, attention, and motivation … [it also] encourages nerve cells to bind to one another, which is the cellular basis for logging in new information" (2013, p. 53). Exercise is the key to becoming better idea generators, traders, and risk managers—not just physical exercise, but the systematic exercise of our cognitive, emotional, social, and physical capacities.

The true meaning of *use it or lose it* is this: *We grow that which we exercise.*

■ ■ ■

Most traders are familiar with the cognitive biases that bedevil traders and others who make decisions under conditions of risk and uncertainty. Among the more challenging biases documented in behavioral finance research are the following:

- *Confirmation bias*—We selectively look for evidence that fits a preexisting view.

- *Bandwagon effects*—We believe in or do something because others believe or do the same.

- *Overconfidence bias*—We overestimate the likelihood of given outcomes and/or our ability to predict outcomes.

- *Endowment effect*—We overvalue what we own, so we demand more to part with something than to initially acquire it.

- *Framing bias*—We are swayed by the way in which information is presented.

- *Illusion of control*—We believe we can affect outcomes that are not in our control.

- *Hindsight bias*— We overestimate our predictive abilities after changing our appraisal of information after outcomes are known.

- *Exposure effects*—We tend to like things because we've been exposed to them.

- *Anchoring/availability biases*—We make decisions, relying too heavily on individual pieces of available information.

- *Recency bias*—We rely too heavily on recent events when anticipating future ones.

- *Bias blind spots*—We are unable to see cognitive biases in ourselves.

In each of these cases, our information processing becomes distorted because we do not weigh evidence impartially and completely. As traders know, our mood states greatly impact our susceptibility to bias, as we become unduly risk-averse or risk-seeking following losses and gains. Interestingly, research from DeVries and colleagues found that decision making in a rule-based task was worse in a happy mood state than in a sadder mood. As the authors explain, " ... the more positive their mood state, the sooner they switched from the dominant (best) to the dominated (worst) gamble" (2012, p. 3). This was because the happy subjects were more likely to be swayed by recent outcomes than by any logical analysis of the rules that ultimately determined outcomes.

Key Takeaway

Improving our frame of mind doesn't necessarily improve our trading.

What this means is that well-being—a positive mind frame—is not enough to make us successful traders. As experienced traders know, it is often when we feel best about our trading that we fall prey to overconfidence biases, confirmation biases, and illusions of control. Without mindfulness, we are just as likely to be swayed by positive emotions as negative ones. It's not an issue of eliminating or controlling emotions, but rather, one of *using our emotional reactions as information*. We become victims of bias blind spots when we lose awareness of factors that can bias us.

So how can we cultivate positivity and yet not be swayed by the potential biasing impact of positive moods?

To answer this, imagine that you have developed a peak performance program for yourself. The program consists of the following:

- Lay out your workdays in advance to make sure you are processing information in ways in which you are strongest.

- Maximize your physical and social environment to create the right blend of freedom from distraction and stimulation.

- Regularly evaluate your positive performance as well as your performance mistakes, build on what you are doing well, and correct your errors.

- Network with colleagues on a planned and regular basis to learn about markets and strategies.

- Organize your days to create time to build your closest relationships.

- Make sure each day that you exercise your capacity to experience joy, satisfaction/gratitude, and connections to others.

- Make sure each day that you exercise physically.

- Make sure each day that you engage in stimulating, challenging mental activity.

- Make sure that each of these activities are conducted in ways to push and extend your limits.

That is a comprehensive program and, no doubt, it would be challenging to implement all of it all of the time. But for the purpose of conducting a thought experiment, imagine undertaking all of the above on a daily basis. What would be the net result?

I think you can see that, over time, you would become very good at organizing your time and using it to build aspects of performance. You would become very aware of your physical and psychological state, and you would become highly attuned to your social relationships. Most important, you would become increasingly intentional in the conduct of your days, using your self-awareness to guide the best ways of utilizing your time.

In other words, the net result of such a peak-performance program would be a tremendous expansion of mindfulness. Every major activity would exercise your self-awareness and your ability to observe yourself comprehensively and accurately. Instead of letting life come to you, you would be actively guiding your life. *Increased mindfulness is the meta-consequence of a comprehensive effort at building strengths and well-being.* You don't just become a better and happier performer; you become a more self-aware and self-directed human being.

What we do to develop ourselves as traders is one and the same with what we do to develop ourselves broadly. Everything we do, wittingly or otherwise, trains us and impacts our performance.

■ ■ ■

We are now halfway through our ABCD sequence. We found that trading success requires Adapting to changing markets and this in turn means that we must Build our strengths. How can we apply our talents and skills to build adaptive trading businesses? That is where we must Cultivate creativity and the ability to find unique sources of edge in financial markets.

CHAPTER 3

Best Process #3: Cultivating Creativity

Creativity is allowing yourself to make mistakes. Art is knowing which ones to keep.

Scott Adams

■ The Trader as Entrepreneur

The old trading psychology emphasized planning your trades and trading your plans. The new trading psychology—*Trading Psychology 2.0*— stresses the changing nature of markets and the need to develop fresh plans for new contingencies. The old psychology placed a premium on controlling emotions. *Trading Psychology 2.0* is about cultivating positive emotional experience through the exercise of signature talents and skills. The ideal trader, according to the old trading psychology, is a disciplined rule follower. The ideal trader V.2.0 is a creative entrepreneur, uncovering and exploiting fresh patterns and rules.

What is an entrepreneur? When we think of famous entrepreneurs, three qualities come to mind: innovation, vision, and leadership:

■ *Innovation*—The successful entrepreneur creates something new. We are accustomed to seeing Starbucks coffeeshops on street corners, but it wasn't so long ago that premium coffee served in dedicated cafés was a unique idea in the United States. Similarly, personal computing and software for the masses was a completely unique phenomenon when Microsoft challenged the world of mainframe computing. Doing something new and doing it better lies at the heart of entrepreneurship.

- *Vision*—A new product or service doesn't just sell itself. It takes vision to turn an idea into a business. When I first encountered the Capella hotel group I was struck by the vision lying at the heart of each property. Ordinary premium hotels emphasized guest service, standardizing everything at a high level, from the check in process to cleanliness. Capella's vision was different. They went out of their way to individualize each person's stay, personalizing the relationship with each guest. The very good hotels offered excellent accommodations. Capella devoted itself to offering special experiences. That vision became a defining theme for the business, motivating and inspiring best efforts.

- *Leadership*—How many times have we seen mission statements in organizations that become little more than sterile documents hanging on walls? New ideas and an energizing vision go nowhere unless they consistently guide the efforts of a business. It's great to talk the talk of mission, but leadership determines whether a business walks the walk. The entrepreneur takes ideas and turns them into realities, communicating ideas and ideals and translating those into strategies that guide day-to-day activities. Think of the success of companies such as Apple and Google. Innovative products with unique design are central to their success, but consider the intricate project management that goes into the *development* of the next smart phone or messaging app. Without leadership, visions would be little more than dreams.

So how does this relate to trading? A trader comes in, turns on a computer, reviews research and news, gauges demand and supply, and places trades to profit from opportunities. Where is the innovation, vision, and leadership?

If markets were perfectly static, then one would only need to figure out an edge that could work across all markets and time periods and remain faithful to that approach. The trader in a static world need be little more than a clerk, executing the same actions in the same way each day. It is the changing nature of the world—and the resulting changes in markets—that ensure that clerk-like trading has a limited shelf-life in the world of finance. Today's markets, dominated by activist central banks, high-speed algorithms, and tight intermarket relationships bear little resemblance to the markets faced by Bernard Baruch or Jesse Livermore. As we saw in the first chapter, success in trading requires active adaptation to change—and that necessitates a high degree of entrepreneurship.

Key Takeaway

The trader's long-term success hinges on entrepreneurial skill.

When traders refer to their work as their business, they express an important truth. Each trader indeed is a business unit, engaging in processes that result in outputs that yield profits. Those outputs are not products or services, but rather ideas and their implementation. In a very real sense, *traders are intellectual entrepreneurs*: They start with a vision of markets, engage in innovative research and development to identify unique opportunities, and then exercise leadership in turning ideas into trades and managing those trades for superior risk-adjusted returns. We are accustomed to thinking of entrepreneurship as an activity that occurs among many people in business organizations. The trader-as-entrepreneur is a self-contained organization filling many roles: researcher, risk manager, planner, business manager, and new product developer. The success of the trading business crucially depends on the trader's ability to coordinate those roles and infuse them with visionary zeal. That is the essence of entrepreneurship.

What qualities do we find among entrepreneurs? Leutner and colleagues (2014) examined the qualities associated with entrepreneurship and developed a test that assessed four key facets: opportunity recognition; opportunity exploitation; innovation; and value creation. The authors described these as Entrepreneurial Proactivity, Entrepreneurial Creativity, Entrepreneurial Opportunism, and Entrepreneurial Vision. Their research suggests that specific personality traits associated with these four domains are more important to entrepreneurial success than broad personality traits such as extraversion or conscientiousness.

Vision, creativity, proactivity, and opportunism: All of those are qualities that we see among traders sustaining career success. Their talent is not just finding good trades, but building businesses that, over time, identify and exploit opportunity. Generating ideas, translating them into trades, and managing those trades to minimize risks and produce profits—those are the business processes that lie at the heart of money management. At its root, trading—like all entrepreneurship—is a creative endeavor.

■ Allen, the Trading Entrepreneur

Allen is a successful portfolio manager. He is successful because he runs a world-class trading business. What's different about Allen's business is that he has only one employee other than himself: a junior analyst named Misha. Allen trades for himself. Having made good money as a hedge fund manager, he retired from that business and now manages his own capital. This gives him the freedom to set his own risk management policies, pursue his own opportunities, and trade as often or as seldom as he likes.

When you speak with Allen, you quickly find out that one of his favorite topics is how markets work. He began his career as a financial adviser and then grabbed a rare opportunity with an equities long/short team as a senior analyst before getting his own capital to manage. A virtual encyclopedia of information about the companies he covers, Allen does all his own research, creating sophisticated models of revenues, profit margins, and earnings to arrive at his own estimates of value. His assistant, Misha, aids with the collection of information, reading of research reports, and maintenance of the databases. Like many long/short managers, Allen looks to buy undervalued companies with solid growth prospects and sell ones that are richly priced and poorly positioned for growth. He views markets as a giant detective story, where the goal is to gather clues and figure things out before others do.

That, however, is where Allen's similarity to other money managers ends. Allen is anything but a pure fundamentalist. He believes that fundamentals only matter once investors act on them. The key to success, from his perspective, is finding those occasions when investors begin to accumulate the undervalued companies and distribute the overvalued ones.

For years, Allen has studied the footprints of investor accumulation and distribution. Having worked with financial advisers for years and then working at a hedge fund, where he learned the long/short business from the ground up, he gained a keen sense for how traders and investors enter and exit positions. Volume is important, he explained when I visited his home office, but it's how volume appears on the tape that is all-important. The big players that ultimately control valuations enter and exit positions in distinctive ways, particularly in advance of earnings releases. Knowing those footprints, Allen maintained, is essential to understanding when value matters for forward price action.

The amount of research that Allen puts into his calculations of accumulation and distribution is nothing short of astounding. He leaves much of the routine company-based research to Misha, freeing himself to track the analyses that tell him when supply and demand shift significantly for his companies. Despite years of success, Allen continually attempts to improve his edge. He contacted me when he found out, through the TraderFeed blog, that I track the daily number of shares outstanding among major ETFs. That, I found, is an excellent sentiment measure, as it captures the actual demand and supply forces for indexes and sectors. What Allen wanted to discuss was whether money flows in and out of various sectors could be useful in tracking changing sector allocations. Ultimately, he explained, he wanted to see if a sentiment-driven long/short sector book, added to his long/short book of individual names, would add alpha to his performance.

Our conversation lasted for quite a while and covered everything from the cognitive biases of investors to using the shares outstanding data to inform long/short sector trades. It was clear that Allen knew his business, but was always looking to expand it. He maintained a vast network of colleagues precisely to engage in the kinds of dialogues he began with me. Every year, he added one or two new approaches to his trading. The core of his business remained the same, but he continually evolved. He insisted that this is the only way he could have maintained profitability over multiple years.

■ ■ ■

Let's step back for a moment and take a look at how Allen actually spends his time. If I were to break down his process, it would consist of several distinct elements:

■ *Reading and researching*—Allen makes a point of tracking everything he can find about his companies, including new and updated analyst reports and recommendations and breaking news. With Misha's assistance, he also follows world events, economic data releases, and fresh earnings reports. He is particularly sensitive to news that could impact stocks that he is following. For example, he became convinced that budget difficulties between Congress and the president would lead to cuts in defense spending that would impact one of his companies. This became one of his reasons for shorting that company. In addition to the companies in the portfolio, Allen maintains a considerable "bullpen" of companies he is thinking of buying or selling contingent on their business performance and/or price and volume action. Not infrequently, his reading and research lead to additions to the bullpen, providing a fresh source of future trades.

- *Updating of databases*—Allen maintains a large database of information about his companies and a separate database that includes data relevant to accumulation and distribution. He spends considerable time updating his models when his companies release earnings reports or when they provide forward guidance. He tracks price and volume patterns for his stocks on both an intraday and end-of-day basis, updating his views on whether shares are finding good demand or experiencing overhanging supply. These calculations are not only performed for the companies in his book but also those in the bullpen. Indeed, it often is because of material updates that companies are taken out of the bullpen and added to the portfolio or taken out of the portfolio and placed on the sideline. The delegation of work to Misha greatly aids Allen's ability to focus on the information most relevant to his portfolio.

- *Interaction with colleagues*—Allen prides himself on being able to identify talent. He selected Misha after a search process turned up a recent graduate with an unusually strong record as a student and as a competitive chess player. Allen liked the fact that Misha taught himself programming and statistics and used his chess background to understand how tactics and strategy inform trading. Every day Allen and Misha spend time away from the desk to review news and company-specific events, summarize accumulation and distribution information from the databases, and prioritize actions that may need to be taken with existing positions and those being considered from the bullpen. In addition, Allen speaks daily to colleagues in his professional network, all of whom have passed his talent sniff-test. Many of them cover companies and sectors that he does not follow, but he finds their views helpful in gauging the general economy. Once in a while, he learns from a colleague a piece of news that could impact one of his own companies. This ongoing set of dialogues helps Allen compensate for the fact that he covers a broad universe with a two-person team.

- *Idea generation*—This is the most amorphous and yet most essential element in Allen's process. He finds it essential to take time out of the office and reflect on everything he has read, tracked, and discussed. Toward that end he maintains an ongoing journal in which he chronicles his thoughts through stream-of-consciousness writing. Every so often, this reflection and writing leads to important insights that help shape his portfolio. For example, he had noticed some growing buying interest among companies in the consumer discretionary sector in recent sessions and also noted a considerable drop in the price of oil. His conversations with a colleague who followed the energy and raw materials sectors convinced him that there were both supply and geopolitical reasons for the decline in crude oil and that the weakness would persist. He believed this would be a boon to US consumers, confirming the buying interest he was detecting in bellwether consumer discretionary stocks. He looked into several of those stocks more deeply and found several that seemed well poised to benefit from increased consumer confidence and liquidity. These positions, paired with shorts in the energy and raw materials sectors, performed quite well. Other times, discussions between Allen and Misha or between Allen and a colleague will uncover a theme that potentially impacts a range of companies. The addition of such themes to the bullpen and book is a key ingredient in keeping the portfolio balanced with independent bets.

- *Risk management and portfolio review*—Every week, Allen and Misha review the portfolio and especially the correlations among the positions. They are particularly sensitive to increases in correlations during risk-off periods in markets, which could greatly reduce the degree of diversification within the book. They also monitor hidden factor risks in the book. For instance, at one point the portfolio was more weighted with midcap longs than shorts, so that, implicitly, the team was long midcaps and short large caps. That was not a bet they wanted to make, and they quickly rebalanced their holdings. Similarly, after sizable runs by stocks within the book, Allen looks at the relative sizing of positions and decides whether the portfolio needs to be rebalanced. One important exercise is putting the book through stress tests every time it is changed. Those stress tests estimate how much would have been lost by the portfolio in past market scenarios. Allen is careful to size positions and the overall portfolio to survive the market conditions and risks identified by the stress tests.

- *Performance review*—Allen keeps a second journal to track his decision making, focusing particularly on decisions that turned out to not be good ones. He is convinced that his greatest mistakes fall into two categories: (1) being too conservative in putting companies into the bullpen and then placing them into the book; and (2) missing themes that end up driving sector and company performance. As a rule, Allen does not overtrade and does not put on marginal trades. His concern is for opportunities that he fails to spot. As a result, he tracks, not just the decisions about buying and selling, but also the decisions to take or forgo opportunities. He also tracks his idea journal to see where he might have done a better job in spotting themes. Recently, he added a section to his note taking to improve his coverage of central bank developments, as he believed these were exerting an unusual impact on demand for particular stocks that he was missing. After reviewing his performance and increasing his central bank coverage, he initiated several long positions with stocks overseas versus shorts in the same industries in the United States. He believed these "QE trades" would add unique performance to his book. Had he not tracked his missed opportunities, he would never have moved in this direction.

What we can see from this process account is that Allen is first and foremost a manager. He manages his time and effort across several facets of the business; he manages his assistant, Misha; he manages his portfolio; and he manages himself and his performance. In a very real sense, he is an idea factory: He takes numerous raw materials (from news, market statistics, conversations), transforms them into products (ideas), and distributes those products (as trades) to earn profits. Like any automobile or pharmaceutical company, he has a research and development process (idea generation), a manufacturing process (trade structuring), and a distribution process (portfolio construction and management).

Key Takeaway

Trading is not just a business but also a business organization.

What makes Allen different as an entrepreneur is that he fills three organizational roles: leader/visionary, manager, and employee. He guides the business and provides its direction. He also manages the various activities that are responsible for generating profits, and he manages himself to ensure peak performance. A trader such as Allen is a self-contained organization. One of the great challenges of his trading is that it requires unusual flexibility to fill these various roles and make sure that they do not interfere with one another.

There is a second challenge for the trader-as-entrepreneur, however. The product cycle for cars or pharmaceuticals typically lasts years, but the cycle for traders is much more rapid. Allen is by no means a daytrader, but he also is not a long-term investor. When his stats no longer identify distinct accumulation for his longs or distribution for his shorts, he reins in his bets. Even when trades remain in the portfolio, the book itself is constantly tweaked to adjust for shifting correlations and factor exposures. If ideas are the product of the trading business, then the entrepreneur-trader creates new products almost continuously. Without creativity—the ability to see old things in new ways—and productivity, Allen could never sustain profitability. When you are an idea factory, creativity is your principal process.

■ The Success of the Trading Entrepreneur

Allen is an entrepreneur in every sense of the term. If we return to the traits identified in the work of Leutner and colleagues, we can identify Allen's entrepreneurial strengths:

- *Entrepreneurial vision*—The portfolio changes frequently, but behind the portfolio is a highly thought-out philosophy of what moves stocks. If an idea does not fit into this framework, it does not fit into the book. The vision, as Allen sees it, is a blending of the best of fundamental and technical thinking, where companies with compelling stories become compelling trades. He often claims that he trades other money managers as much as he trades individual names. If a long is not under accumulation and a short isn't being distributed, he is out of the trade. If the core fundamental rationale for the trade no longer holds up, he will not chase the stock with buyers or sellers. Allen believes that he succeeds by generating many relatively independent bets informed by the melding of business fundamentals and market dynamics. His success hinges on his faithfulness to this basic vision of market opportunity.

- *Entrepreneurial creativity*—As we shall see shortly, creativity depends on a combinatorial process in which familiar inputs are assembled into unique outputs. Crucial to Allen's success is his consistent interaction with talented peers and his ability to step away from trading to find the themes embedded in those conversations. Many times, he will notice a pattern among the stocks undergoing accumulation or distribution. That pattern leads to further research and eventually can generate a number of fresh ideas for the portfolio. By keeping himself fresh with observations and information, he is able to sustain innovation.

- *Entrepreneurial proactivity*—Allen considers himself neither a momentum trader nor a value investor. He does not buy and sell simply because something is moving and he does not put names in the book simply because they are undervalued or overvalued. He seeks to be proactive by identifying the earliest phases when undervalued companies are being accumulated and overvalued ones are being distributed. This proactivity is nicely illustrated by his concept of the bullpen—a reserve of good ideas that have not yet displayed all the characteristics of good additions to the portfolio. Similarly, Allen always tries to add to his arsenal of opportunities, as in the case of looking into the shares outstanding of popular ETFs as a way of gauging relative sector sentiment. Proactivity means that Allen is always developing tomorrow's portfolio, not just managing today's.

- *Entrepreneurial opportunism*—Allen's basic philosophy of investing is an opportunistic one: He looks to jump on board moves that are already beginning in stocks that he already wants to own or sell. Every day he reviews with Misha news, data releases, latest earnings reports, and company news to identify opportunities that can contribute to the bullpen. He also screens for buying and selling activity each day to determine when supply and demand may be shifting significantly. Unlike many long/short investors, Allen does not limit himself to a particular sector, and he does not rigidly limit his net long or short exposure. He believes that his book should reflect the best combination of opportunities that present themselves at the time. This flexibility and opportunism allowed him to be net short during the housing and banking collapse of 2008 and quite long during the central bank–led stock market recovery.

We normally think of leadership in an interpersonal context: one person leading many. In the case of the trading business, leadership primarily takes the form of self-leadership. Perhaps Allen's greatest strength is his ability to draw on a guiding vision to sustain an ongoing process of imaginative innovation and process-driven rigor. *Success for the trader-entrepreneur is so much more than having a plan and trading it: It's having a vision and actualizing it.*

■ ■ ■

Becoming a trader is not just running a business; typically it's developing a startup business. Jessica Livingston's book, *Founders at Work* (2008), interviews a variety of successful startup entrepreneurs. It makes clear that a significant share of the entrepreneur's success is the ability to attract a core group of committed professionals who will work long hours to cover every aspect of the new enterprise. In a mature organization, there are many employees covering very specific roles. In the startup, the founders are responsible for the entire business, from securing funding to building the information infrastructure to hiring and supervising staff to developing relationships with vendors and distributors. The ability to multitask and work long hours in the face of an uncertain future is essential to the success of the startup entrepreneur. Only a deep belief in the core vision of the enterprise can sustain such effort at a high level.

If we look at successful startups, such as those described in the interviews conducted by Livingston, we find an unusual proportion of entrepreneurs are serial entrepreneurs. It's rarely one and done: The successful entrepreneur often has started multiple companies. This makes sense if the research on entrepreneurial personality traits is correct: In an important sense, starting new ventures is in the blood of the entrepreneur. An interesting 2008 study from Gompers and colleagues at Harvard Business School found evidence of performance persistence in entrepreneurship. Entrepreneurs with a track record of success are significantly more likely to succeed than first-time entrepreneurs or those who failed on an initial attempt. There are several reasons for this, ranging from entrepreneurial skill and experience to success begetting success: Suppliers, venture capitalists, and employees are more likely to be drawn to someone who has been successful than someone lacking such a track record. If entrepreneurial traits are indeed associated with entrepreneurial success, then it also makes sense that those with initial success would also be likely to succeed in their subsequent ventures.

This has important implications for would-be traders. A young person looking to emulate the success of a money manager such as Allen might start as a junior analyst and gradually learn the business from the ground up. They would receive an initial allocation from their manager and then seek to grow that over time. Alternatively, they might try to go it on their own, learn everything they can about trading stocks, and set up an account. In such cases, all too often they don't enter trading with the mindset of starting a business. They think more like franchisees than entrepreneurs: They look for an established success formula and seek to copy it faithfully. What they lack is innovation, the creative spark that lies behind the entrepreneurial vision. But without that spark and vision, they don't have the stick-to-it-iveness that is needed to multitask over long hours and manage every facet of the enterprise.

Key Takeaway

Many traders fail because they establish ineffective trading businesses.

If you ask the average trader why the success rate for professional traders is so low, you'll hear about efficient markets and the challenges of overcoming cognitive biases and the emotions associated with risk, reward, and uncertainty. All of those are true, but they miss an important point: Traders who approach markets with the mindset of franchisees, looking to replicate the success formulas of others, lack the entrepreneurial vision, entrepreneurial creativity, entrepreneurial proactivity, and entrepreneurial opportunism associated with successful startups. What's more, the typical beginning money manager or trader often lacks experience in building an organization—developing and running an enterprise—so there is no way they can benefit from a learning curve like the serial entrepreneur.

Imagine trying to start up a different kind of business—a grocery store or an auto repair shop—without having prior business and startup experience. How would you know which licenses and permits to apply for? How would you know enough to select the right location, negotiate the best lease, hire the right staff, and create the right menu of services? How would you know how to divide work responsibilities among staff members and properly supervise their work? How would you keep track of sales and orders, and how would you handle payrolls and taxes? Without prior experience, there is no way you could effectively get a business off the ground. You would lack the requisite experience—and even if you had a general familiarity with business ideas, you would be hard pressed to organize and manage a complex enterprise.

It is no different with trading businesses. Go back to the description of Allen's business and then ask yourself, as a trader, if you have robust processes in place to do the following:

- Define and sustain a vision that informs and guides the opportunities you seek in markets.

- Systematically gather information—news, economic data, fundamental information, market data—in a form that can be readily manipulated and reviewed for decision support.

- Continually generate trading fresh ideas and bullpens of ideas that stay on top of evolving opportunities.

- Build and utilize an effective information network to stay on top of developments in the industry and across your trading universe.

- Monitor your performance and systematically identify and address areas needing improvement.

- Manage all these activities efficiently and effectively on a daily basis.

Think of the traders you know, and the chances are good that many will engage in the above efforts only in piecemeal ways—not in a structured, business-like manner. They experience problems in markets, not simply because they lack discipline or plans but because they are ill-equipped to run a world-class business. They fail as traders because they fail as entrepreneurs.

As we saw in the last chapter, this is most evident among traders who, ironically, are attracted to trading precisely because they don't want to work for someone else and endure the 9-to-5 daily ordeal. Little do they realize that, in starting a trading business, you work very long hours for the man—only you are the man! The extended hours and intensive multitasking found in business startups are typical among successful money managers. The idea that you can learn a few setups, come in for trading hours and make money, and then live a life of leisure when markets are closed is an ideal that appeals to many aspiring traders—and it is precisely the opposite of true entrepreneurial vision. Those traders fail for the same reason that any entrepreneur would fail trying to start a business from scratch on a part-time basis: They are motivated by the prospect of riches without effort, not by the efforts that flow from an inspiring and invigorating vision.

■ Trading and the Crisis of Management

Let's imagine for a moment that each of the roles that you play within a trading business actually represent separate employees. You are the business owner: Your job is to direct and manage these employees. How many employees do you have? Based on our look at Allen's business, at the very least there would be several employees in your enterprise:

- An assistant who stays on top of news/current events, fundamental information relevant to trading (economic data releases, earnings reports, central bank developments), views from colleagues in an information network, and relevant market action (price/volume patterns, behavior of various instruments)

- A researcher who investigates opportunities in markets, tests them out, and develops new ideas based on information gathered

- A trader who structures the ideas developed by the research process into trades with an attractive reward-to-risk relationship and then executes, monitors, and manages those trades

- A risk manager who stays on top of market conditions and the risk exposure within and across positions, and who ensures that the right amount of risk is being taken to achieve the return targets of the business

- A technology manager who ensures that the business has the right data, equipment, software, and other resources, as well as backups for all of those in case of failure

- A coach who reviews personal and trading information and guides learning and peak performance

If these are the members of your team—the employees of your trading business—then your job is to supervise each of them. You need to structure their roles, ensure that they are productive, and coordinate their efforts so that you are staying on top of developing and trading best-of-breed ideas. That is no small task.

If your trading business is just you, however, then you must play all those roles, manage them, coordinate them, and ensure their superior performance. This requires much more than discipline and emotional control: It requires the ability to multitask at a high level and then exercise the consistency of perspective to bring those roles together in a manner that is consonant with the broad vision and aims of your trading business.

If consistent profitability merely follows from faithfully executing our intentions, a good plan and a few psychological exercises should be all you need for a lifetime of success. If, however, trading requires the integration of many roles cutting across domains—from idea generation to research and risk management—*then organizational and self-managerial skills are essential to success.* Most traders have never needed to cultivate the degree of self-management and organization to simultaneously carry out and coordinate multiple complex roles. Little wonder that they become overwhelmed and fail to execute their processes—not because they are unfocused or unmotivated, but because they have not cultivated the entrepreneurial skills needed to generate a winning startup business.

Imagine trying to run a restaurant where you are the only employee. You are the shopper who acquires the ingredients for all the dishes; you're also the chef, the business manager, the server, and the accountant. You market the business, keep the business running each day, plan the menus, and keep up with industry trends. Even if this were humanly possible in a busy restaurant, the cross-section of skills required—and the ability to stay on top of all of them and coordinate them effectively every single day—would be daunting. Because you can cook a good meal doesn't mean that you can succeed running a restaurant business. Because you can place winning trades doesn't mean that you can succeed as the head of your trading business.

Key Takeaway

The successful trading business weaves best practices into best processes.

What has made Allen successful over years of trading is that he has taken a group of best practices—ways of generating ideas, translating them into trades, and executing and managing those trades—and woven them into best processes. Allen has a distinctive process for gathering information from news sources, people, and markets; he also has a distinctive process for thinking about that information in ways that generate ideas and a well-defined process for adding ideas to the portfolio and managing both positions and portfolio. Through his journals, he also has honed detailed processes for tracking his performance both as a researcher/idea generator and as a trader of those ideas. By assembling many actions and roles into concrete, routine processes, Allen takes a set of activities that seem daunting and unmanageable and turns them into a well-oiled business machine. Our next chapter will be entirely devoted to such best practices and processes. They are the guts of the successful startup business.

We often hear about traders needing to "stick to their process." If only it were so easy! Traders don't simply have "a process": They have multiple, intersecting processes. To coordinate actions into a repeatable process is an accomplishment. What makes a trader a true entrepreneur of his or her own business is the ability to coordinate multiple processes in a manner that is consistent with the animating vision of the startup. A trader can have great market insights, but still fail because:

- The actions needed to sustain trading success are not organized as processes and thus appear and disappear randomly, without consistency of performance.

- The processes needed to sustain trading success are not successfully interwoven, so that parts of the business (generating ideas) work well, while other parts (managing risk) founder.

A great business is well-organized. Too often traders fail because they are not organized. They might have good ideas and might place good trades, but they cannot effectively integrate the many roles needed to sustain success across a career. Here's a useful exercise: Create a list of the major roles that you have to play in order to be successful in your trading. Next to each item in the list, write down the specific activities that go into executing each role successfully. These will be the beginning building blocks of your trading business.

Now, to continue your exercise, look at your daily calendar. How many of those building blocks are hardwired into your daily plans?

Real businesses are hardwired. Every facet of the business at a FedEx or UPS is clearly mapped out and synchronized with every other one. Department stores like Walmart or Target execute every day on ordering, stocking, displaying, selling, and maintaining stores. At a Capella hotel, each major process is mapped out and followed to a *T* to ensure quality control, from reservations and room management to housekeeping to food services.

If your daily calendar does not map out everything you need to do to succeed as a trader, then what you need to do to succeed as a trader is left to chance. As we shall see in the next chapter, it is not enough to have best practices. For quality control, they must be woven into best processes.

■ Trading and the Crisis of Creativity

You've no doubt heard the term *groupthink* and seen it at work among traders online and on trading floors. I have a particularly unique view of groupthink because, as a trading coach, I have worked with multiple proprietary trading firms, banks, and hedge funds. Very often—across completely different firms, where traders are not speaking with one another—I hear the same trade ideas, the same trades. A high-volume spike in a popular stock leads to a rush of daytraders. A central bank development leads to a consensus trade in rates or currencies. When there is groupthink, traders do not bring unique ideas and trades to their firms and trading firms do not bring unique returns to investors. In general, I have found that correlations, within trading firms and across them, are shockingly high.

Perhaps it was easier being uncorrelated before the online world placed everyone in touch with everyone. When trading took place via telephone and tickertape, it was quite difficult for traders to know what other traders were doing. Now, with chat and multiple sources of real-time news, everyone draws from the same information base. The result is that positions become crowded far more quickly now than in the past. The demands of making money and keeping losses controlled lead traders and money managers to chase trades that look like trends and then quickly exit those positions when it appears that trends are ending. These herd effects add to choppiness in markets and make risk management challenging.

This seems odd on the surface. Traders and portfolio managers are bright people for the most part. They realize that they need to generate fresh ideas. They also know that if their returns are simply duplicates of those of their colleagues, they give their employers no reason to bump up their trading size and capital. Even rookie traders understand the need for a distinctive "edge" in markets to achieve success. So why do so many traders, recognizing the need to be unique, wind up as part of herds?

Cognitive biases play a role in this, no doubt. If your peers are starting to make money in an idea, it's difficult to feel as though you're the only one missing the trade. Chat rooms can become echo chambers, contributing to massive confirmation biases. There is, however, another and more subtle influence at work that undermines traders' entrepreneurial uniqueness.

■ ■ ■

Eileen is an early career trader at a proprietary trading firm. She was brought into the firm by a friend who served as her mentor at the firm. From him, she learned how to read the order flow in individual stocks and identify promising "plays" where stocks of small companies were trading on abnormally high volume. These were seen as "pump and dump" candidates, so the way to trade them was to let them rise and then short them aggressively when buying had exhausted. A second setup that she learned was the breakout trade. Her mentor explained that the stocks of small companies were far less likely to be influenced by the market making and short-term trading of algorithms. This meant that they moved in smoother, better trending ways. When a stock had been trading in a narrow range and then broke out on increased volume, the idea was to buy the first pullback for a continuation move, as the range trade became a trend one.

In this style of trading, a good amount of the preparation occurs with the help of specialized screening software that tracks pre-market and opening market activity among a broad range of individual names. This requires intensive real-time processing, as any screen might spit out dozens of potential trade candidates. Winnowing those to a few very promising opportunities is a very important part of the trade preparation. For the traders in Eileen's shop, as a result, the day consisted of active screening and filtering, quick trading for scalps, followed by further filtering of names selected for the day, additional screening, and continued short-term trading. It's a style of market involvement that requires not only rapid cognitive processing, but also the ability to sustain relatively high levels of concentration for large portions of the trading day.

The traders on the floor with Eileen were collaborative, shouting out ideas, trades, and important moves in the stocks being followed. Because they used the same screening software—software similar to that used at other proprietary trading firms—they often tracked the same stocks and the same potential trades. Certain traders had reputations as being particularly profitable; many traders emulated the trades of those leaders. Other traders followed accomplished traders online through platforms such as Stock Twits and Twitter. The similar focus on "momo" stocks—those moving with high volume and momentum and those losing their strength—resulted in many social media mentions for those names. When the Ebola virus was front and center in the news, companies making protective equipment and researching vaccines received heavy attention from the traders. The idea was always to follow the hot money, as that is where movement—and opportunity—tends to show up.

It was an exciting environment and Eileen displayed promise in her trading. Several months into her mentorship, however, the traders on the floor began to lose money. A company received a great deal of hype and had risen on strong volume for several days. To all appearances, there was no reason for such an ebullient move. The company had products in development, but was far from coming to market with them. This seemed like a no-brainer short. At the first sign of exhaustion, traders aggressively shorted. The stock moved down and then rebounded strongly. Traders went back to the well again … and again … and again. Each time they sold the stock, it bounced to fresh highs. Eileen saw that her peers were becoming locked in the idea, and she decided to focus on other names. She focused on a larger cap name that had stalled out after a large runup in the euphoria over social media stocks and shorted that aggressively. It, too, stalled and zoomed higher.

Key Takeaway

When markets change, rigid discipline keeps you doing the wrong things.

The trading floor became more frustrated. A number of traders railed about "algos" and the difficulties of making money in rigged markets. No one wanted to miss the shorting opportunity in the hyped stock when it finally broke, so they were reluctant to abandon their idea. Steadily, P&L eroded. To compensate, many traders took relatively marginal trades, hoping to make money elsewhere. Eileen responded with utter confusion. Everything she had learned over several months no longer seemed to work. What was going on?

■ ■ ■

What was going on indeed? How can a successful trading approach suddenly become an absolute loser?

I spoke with Eileen and her mentor and I found two things:

1. *The ideas they were trading were not only popular, but ultra-popular.* Volumes were expanding significantly and, with the rising participation, came increased volatility. We often hear traders' advice to not catch a falling knife. These traders were fading a rising rocket. The sheer volume and volatility of the trades were working against them.

Because they were not looking at trends in volume or volatility, however—just screening for high levels—they did not realize that they were fighting unusually vigorous trends.

2. *Most of the trades they were pursuing were highly correlated to the overall stock market, and particularly to the small-cap and NASDAQ indexes.* Those were both in solid uptrends, seeing considerable buying interest. The rising tide was lifting even the lower quality stocks, so that the traders in Eileen's shop were fighting the current.

In lower-volatility conditions and especially when stocks were not in a trending mode, fading momentum plays once they stalled succeeded very well. Once volumes picked up and the indexes were trending, the same setups were disasters. What looked like stalling out really was pausing in an impulsive move higher.

When they weren't frustrated and railing at the manipulators, the traders attributed their losses to poor discipline. Some of that was true, particularly with the marginal trades that followed the initial losses. The actual cause of the losses, however, was the failure to recognize the shift in the character of the market. The traders were so busy screening, filtering, and trading that they did not stand back and see that market conditions had changed. They operated as if their setups worked all the time in all markets. That implicit assumption led them to focus on trading rather than adapting.

This was not just a P&L crisis for Eileen and her peers; it was a crisis of creativity. Because they were so immersed in generating ideas and trading on very short time frames, they literally had no process in place for research and development. They were like a stagnant manufacturer, churning out bars of soap and consumer products and never developing new ones! Think back to Allen and how he ran his business. Considerable time was spent with knowledgeable colleagues who could discuss and debate views. He also spent a very large amount of time maintaining his database of market activity, tracking changes in markets and testing new ideas. None of that occurred at Eileen's firm. They operated like an assembly line, churning out trades, rather than a business startup generating products and expanding markets.

When I raised this with the traders, they responded—understandably—that they did not have time for research, reading new materials, and generating new, out-of-the-box creative views. Their attitude was, "We get paid for making good trades; not for doing research." An unscrupulous trading coach would have agreed, sold them on the idea of working on their discipline, and collected fees. The reality was that their business model was broken. They were highly disciplined with their style of trading. They simply lacked a creative process for modifying that style to fit different market conditions. They operated like franchisees—repeating a past success formula—rather than like entrepreneurs.

■ Creativity Provides Food for Our Strengths

If there is a single theme to this book, it is that trading success is directly proportional to our ability to harness cognitive and personality strengths and creatively utilize these to adapt to ever-evolving markets. Success lies at the intersection of strengths and creativity. It is the result of employing talents and skills in new ways to exploit fresh opportunities. Without creativity, we become one-trick ponies. Creative inputs and insights feed our strengths.

A recent TraderFeed post drew on research to describe two trading brains: an intellectual brain and a social brain. As the post observed, these represent two spheres of potential strength. Traders with highly developed intellectual skills and talents view markets through data, models, and quantitative relationships. Traders with highly developed social capacities view markets through the perceived intentions and behaviors of market participants. Their trading leans toward the qualitative and discretionary. This is a fundamental distinction: The two kinds of traders process market information in completely different ways.

Trading with intellectual strengths is largely aimed at prediction. Let's say I am a trader of individual equities. I build models of my companies that link such factors as revenues, expenses, profit margins, and the contributions of various product lines to earnings and price–earnings relationships. If I notice that business is booming in a new product line for a company, I update my models and discover that earnings should be much higher than is being projected by a consensus of analysts. The overall market has fallen on geopolitical news, dragging my company down with it. From the perspective of my model, the company is fundamentally undervalued. I want to be long that company, as my historical analyses show that, over time, prices will revert to a particular multiple of realized earnings.

In this example, my trading process is highly analytical. I have identified historical relationships between price and earnings growth/momentum, and I have developed tools that enable me to forecast earnings based on observations of customer visits, average customer order sizes, and so on. My trade is based on a prediction that links where price trades now and where my analysis says it should trade. Creativity enhances this intellectual trading by suggesting new inputs and fresh models. For example, I might step outside the usual predictor set of revenues, expenses, and so forth, and look at seasonal influences on customer behavior. When winters have been milder, consumers have tended to shop more and make more discretionary purchases. By tapping into longer-range weather forecasts, I can include a new variable in my model—milder, average, or more severe winter conditions—and backtest its predictive power. If it contributes uniquely to the accurate estimates of earnings and price movement, it becomes an ongoing part of the model. Creative thinking leads to new candidates for predictors, which in turn give the intellectual trader an edge over those employing purely conventional models.

The trader who draws on social strengths is not primarily concerned with making quantitative predictions, but rather focuses on understanding trader and investor behavior in a qualitative manner. Let's say that a market has tested a downside level three times and each time has bounced from that level. On the third bounce, I notice that volume has tailed off and that the proportion of buyers relative to sellers, as assessed by the ratio of upticks to downticks among stocks, is quite modest. I quickly make two identifications: (1) the low prices are failing to attract the buying interest of longer time frame participants; and (2) if we should break the recent support level that held three times, that will bring in fresh sellers who tried buying those dips. Notice that my hypothesis is a situational one and not general and predictive. Having worked with traders for a long time and knowing how they think, I can anticipate that a downside break of support will accelerate selling among those who are overleveraged and need to stop out of long trades. It will also attract the fresh selling of those playing for a breakout trade. Given the reduced buying on the bounce and the prospect for price extension on a downside break, fading the bounce and leaning against the most recent highs looks like a good trade in terms of risk/reward. My thought process is less about analysis and prediction than about synthesizing the elements of a trading situation and factoring that into my understanding of trader behavior. In a very real sense, as a trader with social strengths, I, like Allen from the earlier example, am trading the tendencies of other market players.

Creativity feeds trading that utilizes social strengths by yielding fresh ways of perceiving and understanding the behavior of market participants.

Let's say I interview many portfolio managers at large hedge funds. I find out that it has been a modest year of performance, with many managers making only a small return on their capital. As the year comes to a close, several positions are crowded, reflecting consensus expectations regarding upcoming central bank decisions. I realize that these managers cannot afford to lose their years during the final weeks of trading and so will be more risk-sensitive than usual. When a data release fails to produce a move that benefits the crowded positions, I realize that the disappointment could easily cascade into a run for exits. I quickly sell the consensus trades and benefit from large managers bailing out as downside stops are hit. The fresh understanding of end-of-year P&L dynamics has led to a unique insight into situational drivers of price in several markets, inspiring profitable trade ideas.

Key Takeaway

The creative process exercises our strengths and thereby extends them.

For the more empirical, quantitative trader, creativity generates new and better data that aid prediction. For the more social, qualitative trader, creativity generates fresh insights and understandings of how market participants are likely to behave. In both cases, creativity feeds the cognitive strengths of the trader.

Of course, in reality, many skilled traders do not operate wholly in intellectual modes or social modes. Some traders possess strengths in both domains that enable them to fuse the quantitative and qualitative aspects of decision making. In the TraderFeed post, I gave the example of the money manager who possessed an unusual level of insight into the Fed. He tracked measures that Fed members use to anchor their decisions, including economic growth, inflation expectations, and asset performance. He also, however, had personal experience with former Fed members and prominent Fed watchers and possessed a nuanced understanding of the thought processes of various Fed members. He read each speech by each Fed member and tracked changes in their language. This social sensitivity enabled him to identify occasions when the central bank was more and less likely to act on the data it tracked. Others, with blunt models, simply assumed that the Fed would hike rates if the numbers hit a particular threshold. The skilled money manager stood out by placing himself in the shoes of the central bank members and identifying how they were likely to view those numbers.

When trading decisions fuse quantitative and qualitative insights, creativity can yield both new data *and* new perspectives on how market participants are likely to respond to data. This occurred to me during the past year when I spoke with a number of bullish and bearish traders about the stock market. The conversations opened my eyes to the fact that buyers and sellers were completely different participants, looking at markets differently, and operating on different time frames. For years, I had used measures such as the NYSE TICK to gauge buying versus selling strength in the stock market. Based on my conversations, however, I decided to go deeper into the data and separate upticks from downticks and treat those as distinct time series. Instead of looking through the unidimensional lens of buying versus selling, I now had a two-dimensional perspective: Any market could feature high buying and high selling; low buying and low selling; high buying and low selling; and low buying and high selling. The combinations of buying and selling activity turned out to be crucially important in anticipating when strength and weakness were ready to continue versus reverse. This led to quantitative models that made predictions of momentum versus mean reversion—and it also informed my qualitative perspective of the relative activity of bear and bull groups in the market. When I saw an unusually weak data release but then saw bearish activity not rise significantly, that became an important piece of insight for how the bulls might later behave.

Think of physical exercise: We develop when we push our limits. As we saw in the last chapter, it is the same with cognitive exercise. We develop our strengths by using them in new, challenging ways. *Creativity exercises our core talents, skills, and interests.* Without fresh inputs yielding fresh ideas and trades, we starve our strengths. And what we don't use, we lose.

■ What Is the Creative Process?

A great deal of research has been conducted on the factors that contribute to creative thought. Sawyer, in his book, *Explaining Creativity*, describes several stages to the creative process:

1. *Preparation*—gathering raw materials and observations; collecting perceptions and ideas

2. *Incubation*—a period between preparation and insight during which there is an elaboration and organization of the raw materials gathered
3. *Insight*—the experience of generating an idea or product that leads to a fresh perception or understanding
4. *Verification*—the process of evaluating the insight and developing it into a new form

Sawyer makes the important point that "Creativity takes place over time, and most of the creativity occurs while doing the work. The medium of the artwork is an essential part of the creative process, and creators often get ideas while working with their materials" (2006, p. 58). In other words, creativity is a process, not an endpoint, and it follows from immersion in one's materials. Without ample preparation, nothing incubates and no fresh insights emerge.

■ ■ ■

The previous discussion of traders with intellectual and social strengths suggests that preparation will differ as a function of trading style. At the risk of oversimplification, I would say that traders prepare for trading by reviewing information, talking with many market participants, or some combination of the two. In the first mode, we look at many charts, review multiple models, and/or run many statistical studies. Each day, for instance, I update spreadsheets that track volatility, correlation, and breadth across multiple indexes and stock market sectors. Often, a pattern will show up in a few sectors of the market that become leading themes for the overall market, as when one segment of the market breaks to fresh highs or lows ahead of others.

In the second mode, we gain an appreciation for market sentiment and positioning by observing and talking with many informed market participants. During the course of those conversations, we learn a great deal about what traders are looking at and what they think is important. We also gain an appreciation for what is not on the radar of those in the market. For instance, a trader I worked with noticed troubling signs of economic weakness in several emerging markets and was surprised that no one was looking at that. The focus was entirely on Europe and the United States and the activities of their respective central banks and economies. The lack of attention to EM convinced the trader that the observed weakness could lead to meaningful trends once there was an attention shift. His ongoing conversations alerted him to unappreciated opportunity, but also helped him identify when emerging markets were gaining more notice, allowing him to add to positions at good levels.

When preparation combines data-driven views and more subjective views of market participants, we sometimes see efforts to quantify and analyze the behavioral tendencies of other traders. A good example comes from the StockTwits site, which provides an ongoing tally of social media mentions of stocks and ETFs. Such social sentiment gauges can be added to more conventional measures of sentiment, such as put/call ratios, to identify bullish and bearish extremes and their reversals. Recall the stock screening from Eileen's trading firm described earlier: Tracking patterns of volume provided useful clues as to waxing and waning interest in stocks, helping traders gauge the likelihood of moves extending or reversing.

As mentioned earlier, preparation benefits from both breadth and depth. We can look at more things, and we can look at fewer things in greater detail. Essential to my understanding of the stock market is a cross-sectional look at breadth. Whenever the market moves, I want to know if the move is occurring across most or all market components or whether the participation is more mixed. Constantly updating my view of various indexes and sectors enables me to see when moves are gaining and losing strength. At other times, however, going into greater depth provides fresh information. One trader I worked with years ago decided to anchor his conversations with market makers by asking them a list of questions each week. This provided a rich array of information, but also led to a deeper appreciation of shifts in views over time. Digging deeper during each conversation—and doing it in a more standardized way—made the interviews far more useful than they had been when conducted informally.

Whether achieved via breadth, depth, or both, preparation is most effective when it stretches our minds. Many traders, for example, review charts prior to the start of the trading day. This, however, can be conducted in a surface, rote manner with little elaboration or it can expand our awareness. The difference is a function of the intensity and activity of our cognitive process. I like to shake up chart reviews, sometimes focusing across asset classes and sometimes focusing within a given asset. That tells me when themes might be occurring across rates, currencies, and equities, but it also tells me when there might be a story specific to a market, such as a flattening of yield curves in one country but not in others. Shaking up the reviews forces me to look at markets in different ways and put effort and thought into the process.

A convention I've found helpful is not finishing a review session with my spreadsheets until I identify at least one worthwhile hypothesis based on recent observations. That constraint forces me to not only review information, but do so in an active, constructive manner.

Key Takeaway

The quality of our preparation shapes the quality of our trading ideas.

In his book, *Creativity*, Csikszentmihalyi (2013) describes the conditions that lead to successful preparation. These include intensity of focus, the exclusion of distractions from consciousness, and the absence of worry about performance. In other words, effective preparation accesses the flow state: It is an immersion in the present. The quality of that immersion directly impacts the likelihood that the preparation will be fruitful. Creativity, Csikszentmihalyi emphasizes, is an *autotelic experience*: It is enjoyable in itself. It is this intrinsic value to the experience that makes it more than a "to-do" box to check at the start of each day. At the end of a trading day, I may feel tired, but I often revive quickly during my spreadsheet review. For me, the review is like a detective story: I want to track the clues and figure out the ending. When preparation is yoked to intellectual curiosity, it fuels idea generation.

■ ■ ■

One of the great mistakes traders make is that they jump straight from preparation to trading. They gather reams of information and then they plunk themselves in front of screens and expect to make optimal use of that information. Unfortunately, creativity doesn't work that way. Once we immerse ourselves broadly and deeply in information, we typically need a period of incubation to make best use of our new raw materials.

Sawyer observes that creative people tend to multitask: They work on multiple projects at one time. "While they're consciously attending to one project," he explains, "the others are incubating. The unconscious mind seems to be able to incubate on many projects at once 'in parallel,' unlike the conscious mind, which can focus on only one thing at a time..." (2012, p. 97). Creativity, from this perspective, is a dual process, consisting of heightened awareness and attentional focus followed by an automatic and nonconscious process that occurs when we loosen cognitive constraints. Many creative professionals find that their best insights come to them during times when they are not explicitly focusing on problems. They might be taking walks, engaging in routine tasks, or working on other matters. During that time, it seems as though a kind of processing occurs implicitly, combining and recombining the information accessed during preparation.

Sawyer summarizes studies demonstrating the incubation effect on creativity. One interesting study asked subjects to solve three difficult crossword puzzles. In one condition, the subjects worked continuously for six minutes on each puzzle. In a second condition, the subjects were interrupted so that they had to work on the puzzles for two sets of three minutes. In a third condition, the subjects were given 18 total minutes of time and allowed to switch freely among the puzzles. In the latter condition, subjects performed significantly better on the puzzles. Switching attention and letting one puzzle incubate while working on another enhanced performance.

What happens during incubation is a matter of some interest and debate among researchers. One theory of spreading activation suggests that cues we process during the incubation period trigger associations that stimulate our processing of information assimilated during the phase of preparation. For example, I might immerse myself in stock market data and track strength and weakness across segments of the market. While out jogging, my mind might drift to other markets and briefly touch on the surprising upward movement of bond prices. I suddenly have the thought that perhaps these are connected: Increased selling of stocks and buying of bonds is part of a "risk-off" defensiveness among investors. That idea leads me to look more deeply into the correlation between those asset classes—and whether it is accompanied by other, similar correlations.

In such a case, the incubation period relaxes the immersive focus on information and allows for a stepping back to see forest for trees. For instance, I might follow the market in real time, tick by tick, and notice the flow of orders in and out of the market, signifying growing buying interest. When I step back from the order flow and take a break from the market, I'm free to think about longer-term considerations and how today's action fits into broader patterns. It is this perceptual shift that helps us take the materials of our preparation and assemble them in new ways.

Zabelina and Robinson conducted a relevant study in which they found that creative individuals display flexibility in their cognitive control. In one cognitive mode (preparation), the creator focuses attention and operates with serial processing, deeply assimilating one piece of information after another. In the other cognitive mode (incubation), the creator operates with defocused attention and parallel processing, pulling information together. In a sense, preparation provides rigorous analysis and incubation achieves broad synthesis. In one mode, we find the puzzle pieces; in the other, we assemble them. That requires unusual flexibility of thought.

When we jump from preparation straightaway to trading, we analyze without synthesizing, leaving ourselves with a jumble of puzzle pieces that don't coalesce into meaningful wholes. This is one way in which working hard can conflict with working smart. The driven trader pushes to analyze, analyze, and then trade and trade. This neglects the stepping away from markets to incubate and generate fresh perspectives. To the compulsive worker, such stepping away feels like laziness. What we know about the creative process, however, suggests strongly that *not working is a key part of the effectiveness of creative work.*

Can we become better as information incubators? Sawyer, in his 2013 book *Zig Zag*, points out that play is a powerful stimulus for processing material we've absorbed. When we play, we relax cognitive control and enter an open-minded mode. As Sawyer notes, it may well be that activities like play and taking walks help us incubate simply by taking our minds off the problems we're trying to solve and allowing us to reprocess information. A fascinating study by Chrysikou and colleagues used a low-level electrical current to stimulate the brain's frontal cortex while subjects participated in a creativity task. The task required them to generate novel uses for familiar tools. When the right hemisphere was stimulated, there was no impact on creativity, but when the left hemisphere was stimulated, creative output rose significantly. It was the suppression of left hemisphere, verbal, logical processes via the current that facilitated creativity. In a sense, the transcranial stimulation enforced an incubation process by suppressing normal analytical thought processes.

The implication is that we can overthink to the point of losing creativity. It is a combination of tight–loose—intensive, immersive analysis and open-minded synthesis—that seems to facilitate the generation of fresh perspectives.

■ ■ ■

Often, the result of incubation is a kind of "aha!" experience in which we experience a moment of insight. Perhaps because we have been in open-minded mode during the incubation period, creative insight feels as though it comes to us; we do not make it happen. One of my favorite weekend morning routines is to listen to music while I review the data from my spreadsheets and think about the week to come. The music is my equivalent of play; it places me in a good mood and keeps me cognitively flexible. While reviewing one of the sheets recently, I noticed that fewer than half of all S&P 500 stocks had closed above their three-day moving averages for five consecutive trading sessions. As soon as I noticed that (interesting: I had entered the data all week long and never noticed that pattern until stepping back and listening to music), I had a very strong intuition that this was meaningful. I quickly conducted a historical query and found 27 occasions in which this pattern had occurred over the past eight years. Twenty of those 27 occasions closed higher two days later, with a sizable average gain. Clearly there was no significant edge in chasing the market's downside after a full week of broad weakness.

That example raises an interesting question: Is my process quantitative or qualitative? Logical or intuitive? I would argue that, at root, the process is a creative, intuitive one, intimately connected to pattern recognition. This can occur with quantitative or qualitative data; the key is assembling old information in new ways. My insight came as the result of a perceptual shift. When I was updating the spreadsheet during the week, I was looking at each day's breadth data separately, in isolation. When I stepped back with the music, I saw the week's period as a whole. I had observed enough sequences of persistent strength or weakness to intuit that the pattern was meaningful.

Key Takeaway

Insight is the result of a perceptual shift.

Michalko, in his book, *Cracking Creativity*, explains that "Creativity takes place in the perceptual phase of thinking ... combining information in novel ways increases your perceptual possibilities to create something original" (2001, pp. 113–114). He uses the example of da Vinci, who took aspects of the most beautiful faces he could find, combined and recombined them, and eventually came up with the Mona Lisa. It is when we combine and recombine that we are most likely to hit on the pattern that feels right. It feels right because we've seen so many similar patterns in the past. Without a database of relevant experiences generated through repeated periods of preparation, the right combinations would never come to us via intuition.

Dean Keith Simonton's account of *Creativity in Science* views the creative process as one that draws on both chance and logic. He cites Einstein, who referred to productive thinking as "combinatorial play," and points out that scientists will entertain many different combinations, most of which will lead nowhere. Over time, however, one or two provide the "aha!" moment of recognition. What makes scientists great, he maintains, is not so much that they constantly arrive at creative ideas, but rather they entertain so many creative combinations that they are more likely to hit on the few that represent genuine fresh insights. From this perspective, the best path to the "aha!" moment is to look at many things in many ways—truly to play with perceptions and ideas. If only 1 percent of our combinations ultimately provide new information, the trader who entertains 1000 combinations will generate more unique, insightful ideas than the one who looks at only a handful of permutations.

The spreadsheets I maintain require at least a full hour of daily updating. There are dozens of sheets, each of which tracks market measures for an extended period of time across many columns of categories. For example, one sheet tracks NYSE stocks that give buy and sell signals for a variety of technical indicators, such as Bollinger bands. I decided to track this when the thought struck me that those indicators were simply ways of capturing momentum and acceleration. If that is the case, it seemed to me, we should see shifts in the breadth of buy and sell signals prior to market turning points. That, indeed, has proven to be a helpful framework, but for reasons a bit different from what I expected. There are different trajectories of momentum across the indicators, allowing for a nuanced reading of shifts in upside and downside participation. These patterns only jumped out at me once I had immersed myself in the data for a while.

A true aha! experience occurred when I was looking at breadth data from the Index Indicators site, tracking the percentages of stocks in given indexes trading above their 3, 5, 10, 20, 50, 100, and 200-day moving averages. I had collected these data for a while when the thought suddenly struck me that the data as a whole can be viewed as a momentum curve. Just as interest rates exist on a curve, with the shape of the curve capturing monetary conditions, momentum at various time frames captures a broad picture of strength and weakness. For example, as I am writing this, we recently saw a very steep momentum curve with very oversold levels at shorter time frames and strong values at longer periods. When that has occurred in the past, it has generally led to a rally, as the curve captures a dip in an uptrend. That is very different from an opposite curve, in which we are overbought on short time frames and well below 50 percent at 100- and 200-day periods. The curve moves every day and, in the movement of the curve, we can perceive strength and weakness from multiple time perspectives. It is not only the shape of the momentum curve, but its movement from day to day, that conveys information.

Sometimes, to achieve the aha! experience, you have to see the world through the eyes of another. Speaking with other traders about markets—or consulting with economists or researchers—can lead to pattern recognition at a broad level. For example, early signs of broad commodity weakness noticed by traders in those markets alerted macro portfolio managers of possible weakness in the currencies of commodity-producing countries. Those patterns in turn helped managers anticipate a global slowdown in economic conditions, which had implications for central bank policies. Many times, it's the addition of a single puzzle piece that enables a trader to see a bigger picture. It's as if a light bulb goes on: Suddenly the world makes sense. Intellectual isolation is one of the great enemies of successful trading. Fresh information, fresh conversations, and novel perspectives—these are the building blocks of creative insight. If you're working on your own, staring at screens, there is a good likelihood that a major challenge for your trading is the loss of perspective that comes from a deficient creative diet.

■ ■ ■

Creativity doesn't stop with the achievement of an insight. Once we generate a new perspective, it's necessary to test it out in the real world and verify its value. Just because an idea strikes us as significant, doesn't automatically make it so. The creative insight, in that sense, is a promising hypothesis. It still remains for us to validate that hypothesis.

Let's return for a moment to the insights that I develop from my spreadsheets of market data. Many times, I will review the data and a pattern will jump out and strike me as significant. For instance, I collect data on moment-to-moment buying and selling in the stock market through the flows of upticks and downticks among shares. I noticed a pattern in which significant upticking led to further strength in stocks, rather than an oversold retracement. Because the data were already arrayed in spreadsheet form, it wasn't difficult to use the sort function of Excel and isolate those past cases in which we had seen unusually high upticking. Sure enough, these were followed by positive upside momentum on average. The verification process provided me with confidence in the idea, and it also helped me understand the variability of outcomes associated with the data. For instance, in the verification process I learned that significant upticking following oversold market conditions had a different set of forward outcomes than upticking in a market that had already displayed ongoing strength. My insight was validated, but the verification process added to my understanding, clarifying the initial insight.

Too often, when traders do achieve creative insights, they don't structure the process of verification, assuming that the insight is valid simply because it feels that way. That is dangerous, given our propensity to cognitive bias and our typical blind spots with respect to our biases. Traders may convince themselves that particular chart patterns have bullish or bearish implications, but are those true creative insights? If the traders have not undergone true immersion in price and volume data and an incubation of their observations, the feeling of directional certainty could be little more than a recency bias, extrapolating future price action from the latest market movement. The verification process helps ensure that our new idea is actually a sound one.

Verification doesn't always take the form of formal backtests. Sometimes it occurs over time, as we gather observations that either fit with our insight or do not. For example, in the case of seeing a larger pattern of global economic vulnerability in weak commodity data, we might monitor the statements of central bank officials to see if they are concerned about economic conditions. We might also monitor economic data releases going forward to see if those fall short of consensus estimates. While additional relevant data don't definitively prove our idea, they can be very useful in giving us the confidence needed to act on the insight. By identifying what we should be noticing if our idea is correct, we can ensure that we are truly validating our idea and not falling prey to confirmation biases.

■ ■ ■

Paulo is one of the most successful portfolio managers I've had the privilege of working with. He has maintained consistent profitability over many years, trading a basic strategy but always refining it.

One of my early observations of Paulo was that he was also one of the most interesting people I knew. He read unusual and very interesting things, traveled to unique destinations, and knew a wide cross-section of fascinating people. Looking back, I've had many conversations with Paulo and I can't think of a single boring one.

What I came to realize is that Paulo had turned creativity into a lifestyle. He approached just about every area of his life with curiosity and only engaged in activities if they offered unique stimulation. His trading never became stale, because he never allowed himself to become stale. Creativity was embedded in his very approach to life, so it was second nature for him to look for fresh directions in markets. His success has been intimately linked to his creativity; markets have become his creative playground.

■ Finding Problems as Part of Finding Answers

Sawyer, in the second edition of *Explaining Creativity* (2012), elaborates eight steps in the creative process:

1. *Find the problem.* Focus attention on a promising question.
2. *Acquire knowledge.* Learn as much as possible about the chosen problem.
3. *Gather related information.* Acquire new information about the problem presented by the environment.
4. *Incubation.* Step away from problem solving to allow for reprocessing of information.
5. *Generate ideas.* Drawing on knowledge and experience to arrive at new ideas.
6. *Combine ideas.* Putting ideas together in ways that lead to insight.
7. *Select ideas.* Evaluating and reviewing ideas.
8. *Externalize ideas.* Implementing ideas and turning them into finished products.

His account makes three valuable points that are not commonly appreciated about creativity:

1. *Creativity only occurs when there has been extensive study and collection of information.* We can only develop new ideas from a deep foundation of existing observations.

2. *Creativity starts with finding promising problems.* Asking the right questions precedes finding novel answers.
3. *After the insight is achieved, there commonly is an extended implementation process, in which the creative idea has to be given form.* For example, a novel idea can lead to a bad trade if it is not expressed and executed in a way that gives a favorable reward to risk.

Traders tend to be practical people, concerned with what to do in markets and when to do it. They naturally look for answers. This orientation can be limiting, as it does not give proper time to question-asking. Many problems in the real world, Sawyer notes, are ill-defined: They are fuzzy and need elaboration. Spending time clarifying the problems we're addressing helps ensure that we can arrive at novel and useful solutions.

Out of my experience in Chicago, in which I saw algorithmic market making replacing traditional activity in the pits, I became convinced that high-frequency data were an essential key to understanding market strength and weakness. This was only conjecture, however. I needed a more detailed and clear look at the high-frequency world to focus on what was most relevant. That led me away from data from depth-of-market displays and toward data from executed trades, as in the Market Delta application. Because I wasn't interested in higher-frequency trading, however, I naturally turned my problem clarification to longer time frames by aggregating the transaction-based data. The problem I wanted to address is whether high-frequency data, accumulated over hours, days, and even weeks, could provide unique insight into forward price action. Before I could arrive at any meaningful insights, I had to formulate a good problem to work on. In no small measure, the promising answers came from asking a promising question.

Sawyer cites a study from Csikszentmihalyi (2013) in which he studied artists with two very different styles of deciding on the subject of their painting. He arrayed a variety of objects for the artists and instructed them to select several, arrange them in any way they desired, and then complete their sketch. One group of artists arrived at their selected objects very quickly. They spent the majority of their time in the sketching process. The second group of artists spent most of their time arranging and rearranging the objects. They started sketches, changed the composition, and then began entirely new sketches. Their final sketch only took a few minutes; instead of polishing their sketch, they concerned themselves primarily with what to sketch.

Csikszentmihalyi then had several art professors rate the sketches for their creativity. The group that spent the most time formulating the subject of their sketches was rated significantly more creative than the group that spent most of their time in sketching. Five years later, a study of the 31 artists in the study found that the group that spent the most time figuring out what to sketch was significantly more likely to have successful art careers than those who spent their time sketching. Investing effort into formulating a good artistic problem paid off in terms of creative output.

Key Takeaway

Experience does not necessarily lead to expertise; we don't necessarily trade better if we trade more.

Traders all too often behave like the artists who quickly grab an idea and then spend their time drawing. They spend the lion's share of effort on placing and managing trades, rather than focusing on what to trade and when. As a result, they are less likely to arrive at creative insights into markets than traders who arrange, rearrange, and rearrange again the information that informs trades. When I think of the traders and money managers I've known personally, a standout impression is that the successful ones operate much more like Csikszentmihalyi's creative artists: They spend more time generating good trading ideas than in actually trading.

Barber, Lee, Liu, and Odean studied the performance of daytraders over a 15-year period and found that only 13 percent of the 360,000 traders studied earned positive returns after fees. When success was measured over a multiyear period, however, only 0.13 percent—less than 1,000 out of 360,000—made money after expenses. Their conclusion was that daytrading success does exist—but is extremely rare. I am convinced that the shockingly low rate of ongoing success among daytraders is a function of their business model: one that rewards trading far more than creative idea generation. Imagine an art institute that taught people to produce one sketch after another without spending time learning composition, color, shading, and various media. A good trade is the outgrowth of a good idea. By ignoring idea generation, we starve the trading process—and the results are predictably dismal.

■ Can We Become More Creative?

The research we've seen so far suggests that creativity is not a mystical talent that one is either born with or without. Rather, creativity occurs at the intersection of focused immersion in a field; deep experience and expertise in that field; and the cognitive flexibility to perceive one's field from different perspectives. I have lived many years with cats and have learned to understand their "communications." One of our cats is particularly finicky with respect to the food she'll eat. After watching her body language across many feedings, I hit on the idea of preparing her food in a "casserole" where a favorite taste (gravy) was layered on top and the most nutritious food was underneath. Sure enough, she becomes eager when she tastes the gravy and proceeds to finish her meal. Had I not lived with her for a considerable time, I could have never hit on the novel feeding approach. If, say, I suddenly had to care for someone's finicky parrot, I would be completely lost for solutions. In one domain, I can be quite creative; in others, I simply lack the experience base.

What this means is that the best way to become more creative is to become more informed. Immersion in more markets and intermarket relationships; immersion in more market-related data; and immersion in more market-related research provide us with more materials for combination and recombination. Creativity among scientific researchers is particularly interesting in this regard: Successful researchers spend considerable time reading published research. This keeps them on top of their field, of course, but it also helps with the identification of worthy problems to solve. Good research opens new questions; juxtaposing research from different areas can lead to promising new studies.

Simonton, in *Creativity in Science*, observes that creative scientists do not simply flit from topic to topic. "Usually permeating most of their work," he explains, "is a core set of themes, issues, perspectives, or metaphors" (2004, p. 80). This means that the creative scientist is both broad and deep. Simonton points to a wealth of research that shows that creative scientists typically run extensive research programs, with many projects proceeding simultaneously. This creates multiple opportunities for unexpected interactions among the projects, allowing one project to fertilize others. If creativity is, at heart, a combinatorial process, searching and re-searching an area more extensively should lead to a greater number of creative outputs.

One trader I worked with recently reviewed his trading results and found that he was much more successful trading pairs—long one stock or ETF and short another—than trading the instruments outright. There were many possible reasons for the difference in results. His pairs trading was more quantitative than his directional trading and was highly structured by rules. His overall risk exposure was less with the pairs trading, enabling him to stick with views longer. Indeed, when he traded pairs, he often added to positions that went against him, as they offered better value. When he traded directionally, he found himself scrambling out of positions that moved against him. After focusing his attention on good pairs trades, he hit on the idea of "pairs of pairs," in which he combined pairs trades that benefited from rising markets and those that benefited from falling ones. Of course, what he had hit on was the value of portfolio construction: limiting overall risk by finding offsetting trades, each with its own edge. His creative insight led to multidimensional thinking; soon, he was identifying trends in interest rates and commodities and entering pairs that benefited from a falling rate environment or downtrends in commodity prices. Like the scientists described by Simonton, he had many trades on in many spaces, each providing useful information that helped him manage his book.

One way in which we can become more creative, reflected in the previous chapter, is to become more grounded in our strengths. E. Paul Torrance, in the book, *The Nature of Creativity*, summarized personality testing data distinguishing creative people and concluded that " ... the essence of the creative person is being in love with what one is doing ... this characteristic makes possible all the other personality characteristics of the creative person: courage, independence of thought and judgment, honesty, perseverance, curiosity, willingness to take risks, and the like" (1988, p. 68). Based on his research, he wrote a seven-point "manifesto" for creative children and titled it "How to Grow Up Creatively Gifted." His key points were:

1. Don't be afraid to "fall in love with" something and pursue it with intensity.
2. Know, understand, practice, and develop your greatest strengths.
3. Learn to free yourself from others' expectations.
4. Free yourself to pursue your own path that makes good use of your gifts.

5. Find great teachers or mentors.
6. Don't waste too much energy trying to be well-rounded; do what you love.
7. Learn to depend on others and their strengths (pp. 68–69).

Key Takeaway

Creativity follows passion.

It is perhaps not surprising that what makes us productive is also what makes us creative. We will only sustain immersion in a field and tolerate ambiguity to arrive at fresh perspectives if that field is intrinsically meaningful to us. Creative people love creating and their creations are driven by a love for what they are creating. I enjoy going to arts-and-crafts fairs as much to speak with artists as to view their works. When I see creative woodworking, jewelry, or painting, I will ask the artist what inspired the piece. Very often that leads to a conversation that reveals the artists' love for their materials. As Torrence observes, the artists did not set out to become creative. Rather, they followed their interests, immersed themselves in their craft, and generated creations from their accumulated experience. They were able to become more creative by becoming more of who they already were.

■ Trading Failure and the Downhill Spiral of Creativity

If the above research is correct, we are most likely to generate fresh insights when we love what we're doing and do what we love. Falling out of love with our work is a great way to lose our creative edge. But how do we fall out of love with something that is our passion? Can we be creative at one point in time and then lose that edge? I would argue that such downhill spirals are more common than is commonly acknowledged.

Early in my academic career I worked with a young professor who was a skilled researcher. He had published an article in a top journal and aspired to achieving tenure at his institution, a top-tier university. Needing a certain number of peer-reviewed publications to meet his tenure criteria, he played it safe and conducted studies in a well-established area of psychology research. His experiments were not path-breaking, but they addressed clear topics in the literature and were designed to be conducted—and published—relatively quickly.

To the professor's chagrin, several of his manuscripts were turned down from the best journals in the field. They were not deemed to be major contributions to the literature. He scrambled to address the shortcomings identified by the peer reviewers and resubmitted the manuscripts to high-quality, but second-tier, journals. One was accepted provisionally; the others were declined. By now, the professor was concerned. Several top graduate students chose to work in other labs, as those professors were finding particular success publishing in the better journals. Without a solid stable of grad students to work with, the professor could not conduct as many studies. He tried publishing a review of existing research in an area of his interest, but this, too, was deemed insufficiently cutting edge.

As the tenure clock ticked on, the professor became discouraged. He complained of the paper chase and the pressures of "publish or perish." Lost enthusiasm meant lost productivity and contributed to an exodus of graduate students from his lab. This created a downhill spiral in which lost productivity led to lost creativity, fewer publications, fewer graduate student assistants, and further lost productivity. He never waited to be denied tenure. Instead, he sought a position at a different university, where teaching was emphasized more than research. He had loved the research game, but the pressure to perform buried an intrinsic interest in extrinsic constraints. Once the focus became publishing papers and not solving scientific problems, he lost touch with what he loved—and that ground his research career to a halt.

I would argue that something very similar occurs to traders. They start their careers excited about what they are doing and quickly find out that it is not enjoyable to lose money and not bring home a paycheck. While intrinsic interest is necessary for trading success, in itself it doesn't pay the bills. Making money becomes the understandable priority. Like the professor, the traders focus on what they believe will bring them the next paycheck—not on what will cultivate mastery or the next distinctive market theme. The situation becomes particularly intolerable when others online or on the trading floor are making money from a widely shared idea that you are not involved in. I have routinely found that traders at prop firms and hedge funds can handle losing money reasonably well when others around them are also struggling with performance. If they are losing money while others are minting coin, however, the situation becomes intolerable. They would rather chase trades that have already moved to be part of the success around them than watch passively while their relative performance goes south.

This dynamic, for the traders as for the professor, occurs because the short-term need to meet performance criteria takes precedence over longer-term professional development. This subverts intrinsic motivation, turns attention away from process, and directs it entirely to outcome. Imagine the dilemma of a painter who needs to sell his or her artwork to make a living and feed a family. Inevitably, the choice of what to draw will become trapped between two priorities: what inspires the painting and what is most likely to sell. Such a divided mind interferes with the very immersion needed to sustain creative output.

In most professional fields, developing students are shielded from real-world rigors until they have achieved an acknowledged level of competence. In medical school, for example, loans typically keep the student afloat during the undergraduate learning process. Once the medical student reaches MD status, the residency position—when the budding physician develops a specialty field—comes with a salary. While no one gets rich as a medical student or resident, neither are they so distracted by the needs of daily income that it interferes with their learning. Similarly, apprentices in various trades are typically paid a base wage, enabling them to focus on gaining the skills that will provide them with a sustainable career. This shielding of the developing professional is essential to the cultivation of expertise and creativity, because it allows the person to pursue his or her passion without the interference of practical life constraints.

The developing trader typically possesses no such shielding. Very few prop firms pay salaries to new traders, and traders learning with their own accounts face real-world constraints from the outset. Faced with the need to earn a quick paycheck, the trader forgoes learning, incubation, and the cultivation of unique expertise and quickly focuses attention on the next idea, the next trade. When that doesn't work out, what sustains enthusiasm and the drive to improve? The trader, like the professor, becomes discouraged and spirals downward in productivity. Common wisdom, as we've seen, will chalk the failure up to a lack of discipline or insufficient effort. *Trading Psychology 2.0*, however, proposes a very different explanation: We can only master markets when we leverage strengths, cultivate expertise, and creatively adapt to market opportunities. Putting the outcome horse before the process cart inevitably subverts performance.

Is there a way to avoid such a downward spiral? In many performance fields, we find that avocation precedes vocation. Musicians, artists, actresses and actors, chess masters, and athletes all typically perform informally and recreationally—often during their schooling years—before ever pursuing their fields professionally. This is yet another way in which skills can develop and experience can accumulate as part of a developmental process. Several traders I have met recently have taken up trading while holding full-time jobs by devoting most of their developmental time researching market patterns and then testing them out on a trading platform that facilitates simulated trading. By exploring and trying out various trading styles and markets while making—and learning from—their mistakes free of financial pressure, they have given themselves time to discover their strengths and utilize those in generating worthwhile trade ideas.

One of these traders became fascinated by the phenomenon of momentum—identifying when strong and weak market action was likely to lead to further strength and weakness—and found signals that combined breadth and volatility to yield momentum trades with an edge. The signals only fired a few times in a month but were quite reliable when they occurred. He is currently involved in finding other such signals, which will enable him to trade very selectively while sustaining a full-time income from his day job. Making trading his hobby is helping him explore it as an eventual career path.

■ The Essence of Creativity: Reframing Problems

Andreasen, in *The Creative Brain* (2006), describes a number of personality characteristics associated with creativity. These include:

- *Openness to experience*: A tolerance for ambiguity and an attraction to novelty

- *Adventuresomeness*: A love of exploration

- *Rebelliousness*: Questioning convention; dislike for external constraints

- *Individualism*: Internally driven

- *Sensitivity*: Awareness of one's own feelings and those of others

- *Playfulness*: Enjoying creation for its own sake

- *Persistence*: Capacity to sustain productivity in the face of setbacks

- *Curiosity*: Driven by an intense desire to know

- *Simplicity*: Single-minded devotion to work

If we think of these as lifestyle and workstyle variables and not merely as all-or-none traits, then it becomes clear how we can build creativity as a set of cognitive and emotional skills. Andreasen cites research that shows how specific regions of the brain develop among professional musicians as the result of their ongoing creative activity. From this perspective, creativity is a form of brain exercise: Novel thinking leads to an increase in creative capacity.

Key Takeaway

Creativity is a set of skills that we can exercise.

In her book, *inGenius*, Seelig (2012) makes the argument that skills related to creative thought can be exercised and developed. Several of the skills she emphasizes involve cultivating imagination, including the reframing of problems. From this perspective, we become restricted in our ability to find answers if we are stuck in our definition and perception of problems. Shifting the frame of problems can lead to fresh perspectives and potential solutions. A great recent example of this occurred when central banks began pursuing very different monetary policies, resulting in negative interest rates in many regions. Many traders were puzzled by the implications of negative rates and slow to respond. Those that viewed the issue from the perspective of corporate money managers and pension funds, however, realized that these entities would have to retreat from the areas with negative rates and plant their capital in areas with positive rates. Reframing the issue from the perspective of those players helped traders take advantage of a historic rise in the US dollar.

Michalko, in *Cracking Creativity*, observes that an important part of reframing problems is altering our perception. Creativity requires that we literally change how we see. He uses the example of Einstein, who formulated problems in as many ways as possible, to arrive at a good solution—not unlike the painters in Csikszentmihalyi's study. "The more times you state a problem in a different way, the more likely it is that your perspective will change and deepen," Michalko notes

(2001, p. 23). Notice how this process of reframing problems draws on many of the personality elements identified above: It is adventuresome, playful, open-minded, curious, and persistent. In pushing ourselves to view markets in multiple ways and ask multiple questions of markets, we increase the odds of arriving at a meaningful answer.

Michalko gives the example of Toyota, which asked its employees to submit ideas regarding the improvement of productivity. Few ideas were forthcoming. When they switched the request and asked about making workers' jobs easier, many productivity-improving ideas were advanced. The simple change of frame opened fresh perspectives. Not long ago, I wanted to buy S&P e-mini futures, anticipating a broad rise in the stock market. I found myself stuck on the entry execution: I wanted to enter at a good level on the day but also be positioned for the market's anticipated rise by the start of the next day. The question, "Where should I execute my order?" led to no solution. I then asked myself a very different question: "Is this a trend day?" My checklist of criteria for trend days unanimously argued against the day being a trend day. That told me we were likely to trade in a range, oscillating around a central average price. Once I identified a candidate for that price, I waited for price action to move below that point in a manner consistent with a range trade and entered my long position there. It saved me several points, but more importantly it replaced confusion with valuable perspective.

One of the less productive questions I encounter asks whether a market is overbought or oversold. The reason it's not productive is that the path of getting to an overbought or oversold level is as important as the level itself. A more useful question is whether the market is getting stronger or weaker over time. If we have been rising and breadth has been expanding—with more stocks making new highs, fewer making new lows, and buying pressure steadily outpacing selling pressure—we are much more likely to see upside (momentum) returns than if we have been rising on weakening breadth and an increase in selling pressure. The process question yields far greater clarity than the question about absolute, static levels.

I similarly noticed that questions as to the strength or weakness of the US dollar were not particularly productive. In a manner similar to stocks, I began to look at the breadth of dollar moves by tracking a large number of dollar crosses. If a move up or down was occurring across most or all crosses, that told me the dollar was trending, increasing the odds of continuation. If the move was predominantly in one or two crosses highly weighted in the dollar index, that suggested more idiosyncratic behavior and a more mixed forward path. Asking a question about dollar trend strength via a diffusion index turned out to be more helpful than asking a question about the dollar index's most recent move.

The reframing of problems can occur when we're working on ourselves, not just when we're dealing with markets. As I noted earlier, most traders' journal entries focus on mistakes and poor trading practices. They address the question, "What did I do wrong today?" That is not a particularly productive problem framing if it does not lead to specific efforts at solution. A more useful framing of a journal entry is the question, "What are three rules I can follow today that would prevent me from making yesterday's mistakes?" As with the Toyota employees, ideas are likely to spring to the surface, as the new question cues what we know about good trading practice.

One daytrader I worked with pushed himself by posing the question, "What do I need to do to become a world-class trader?" He read books and articles and went to numerous trader events to absorb lessons from world-class traders. His question, however, did not lead him in a positive direction. Inevitably, when he lost money, he became frustrated, seemingly falling further behind in his quest for world-class status. One of my first recommendations was that he replace his question about becoming world class with a different question: "What do I need to do this week to become a better trader than I was last week?" By emphasizing improvement, he would stay constructively focused on achievable goals that would steadily move him to his ideal state. Stressing a distant end goal only served to stymie him. He made significant progress, interestingly, when he stopped worrying about "world class."

The reframing of problems is a central change technique in psychotherapy. When a client enters therapy, it's often because he or she is stuck in a particular view of self and world. A common scenario is the person who has been rejected in past relationships and now behaves in a defensive way when meeting new people. That very defensiveness leads to the relationship failures that are most feared. The client approaches situations with the question, "How can I avoid getting hurt again?" This is unhelpful, because it doesn't focus attention on the basics of cultivating a good relationship—getting to know the other person and sharing experiences. By reframing the dating experience as, "How can I have a good time tonight and get to know this person better?" a great deal of pressure is taken from the situation. The focus becomes one of exploring another person, not entering a new and threatening relationship.

The right reframing of a problem—whether in therapy or in trading—can itself lead to an aha! moment. In solution-focused counseling, the reframing involves finding past occasions when we have already found an answer to our dilemma. So, for instance, the person who is afraid of being hurt in a relationship might be asked, "When have you recently felt comfortable meeting someone new?" and "What put your mind at ease on those occasions?" By drawing on an individual's own experience, a seemingly difficult problem is shown to have a personally relevant solution. The trader may be stumped by contemplating whether a particular market is overbought, but then find valuable solutions when asked, "When have you recently traded overbought markets well?" The right reframings are empowering: They facilitate creativity by directing us toward the right problems.

■ The Skills of Creativity: Switching Modalities

Michalko describes a second strategy for enhancing the creativity of our thought processes: making our ideas visible. This can occur in many ways—discussing an idea with a valued colleague; drawing a diagram of the idea; capturing data in a graphic display; and so on. What we know is partially a function of how we know it. By switching modalities, we can unlock associations and stimulate fresh solutions.

A classic example of the value of modality switching comes from students studying for tests. It is common for students to memorize information in a rote fashion, repeating it as it might have been delivered in a lecture or via a textbook. When the instructor tests for the information, the question might be worded in an unfamiliar way or pull for the information from a different angle. For instance, the student might memorize the organs of the digestive system and their anatomical shapes, but then have difficulty with a question that asks which organ would be most impacted by the ingestion of a poison. The student has processed information in terms of structure, whereas the question asks about a digestive process.

Had our student not only memorized the organs but also drawn them as part of a flow diagram to show how they work together; discussed the structure and function of the digestive system with a study partner; and answered sample test questions covering various aspects of the digestive system, there would have been little problem pulling up the information for the test question. Hearing information, speaking information, writing information, drawing information, explaining information—all of these are ways of encoding material for recall and understanding. Multiple means of encoding facilitate recall under a variety of circumstances.

Key Takeaway

Your access to information is only as good as your means of storage.

Traders all too often operate like the student, processing market information in limited ways. Some will even rationalize that the information contained in a bar chart is all that needs to be known to anticipate price action. Lost, of course, is an understanding of intermarket relationships; shifts in correlation and volatility in the broader market; and information that would reveal whether market conditions are strengthening or weakening. I recall sitting with a trader who was tracking stock index trading following a key data release. The headline data were weak and stocks immediately moved lower. The trader immediately announced that we were heading for a big break in prices.

My attention, however, went to the fixed income market, which was already moving toward unchanged on the session, and NASDAQ shares, which still held well above their overnight lows. I also noticed that one of the key numbers from the release was not especially weak. From my perspective, the selling reaction looked more like a fakeout than a sustainable shakeout, but the trader insisted he had price confirmation. Within minutes he was forced to stop out, as those selling the news were trapped by a bout of buying. In viewing market action one-dimensionally, the trader was too easily locked into a limited view.

Imagine, however, if the trader had actually rehearsed a variety of scenarios for the data release in advance, focusing not only on the headline number, but on key components that were of relevance to Fed policy makers. Imagine, further, that the trader reviewed recent market reaction to data releases to distinguish when these led to trending moves and when they were ultimately retraced. Then imagine that the trader formed a game plan based on these scenarios that was written out, discussed with colleagues, and reviewed aloud in the minutes leading up to the release.

You get the point: The trader in the second scenario is not only better prepared; he is also more broadly prepared. By employing a variety of modalities, the trader turns a plan from a bloodless written document to a living guide to action. Such a trader is likely to respond far more flexibly and creatively to an event than the unidimensional trader.

There are many ways a trader can switch modalities to process markets in a multidimensional fashion:

- Track your stock, instrument, relationship, or market across multiple time frames. How does recent action fit into the broader context of price movement?

- Track your stock, instrument, relationship, or market against related ones. Are they moving in unison or separately? Are they moving in sympathy with any known news or market events?

- Outline in writing the rationale for your position; what would give you added confidence in your trade; and what would lead you to exit the position.

- Discuss your trade idea with a knowledgeable colleague and pull for the colleague's information of what would lead to greater and lesser confidence in the idea.

- Talk your trading plan into a recorder and listen to it before the market opens to prepare for a variety of what-if scenarios.

Notice how switching modalities naturally places the trader in an active information-processing role. Instead of responding to market events, the creative trader is anticipating possibilities and planning for those, so that response can be quick and flexible.

Michalko describes mind-mapping as a particularly valuable method for making one's ideas visible. The mind map begins with an idea in a central circle and then adds associations to that idea as connected circles. Each of those circles then generates its own associations, creating a broad network of associated thoughts. If, for example, my central trading idea was an anticipated rise in US interest rates, my associations would include related ideas about central bank policy; economic strength; inflation expectations; price behavior across fixed income markets; relative movements of currencies versus the US dollar; and so on. Each of those associations would be linked to others, such as the statements of central bank officials, recent data releases, and labor market conditions. The entire mind map would encapsulate my thinking about the trade and the market I'm trading. Reviewing the map would make me sensitive to the assumptions I'm making and would alert me to incoming evidence that either supports or undercuts those assumptions.

Equally important, however, is that the act of drawing the map itself serves as a kind of brainstorming, as associative links lead to new, unexpected ones. I might, say, draw circles from the "economic strength" node to "payroll data" and "GDP data," but then note that the strength in the payroll data falls short of what would be expected from the recent GDP strength, leading to the addition of a question mark in one of my nodes. That in turn leads me to scour other data to determine whether the picture of economic strength is consistent or mixed. The mind map is a way of thinking aloud, but it's thinking aloud in a structured fashion that encourages us to elaborate our thoughts. Michalko also notes the value of group mind maps. Suppose you are working as part of a team, or suppose you and a peer trader share a common trade idea. If each of you independently mind maps the idea, the result will likely be a fruitful sharing of related ideas and assumptions that enable each of you to broaden your understanding. By switching from the modality of thinking to that of drawing and visualizing, you encode what you know in a fresh manner, making it more readily available for real-time processing during the heat of market activity.

■ The Skills of Creativity: Increasing the Productivity of Our Thought

Let's return briefly to Dean Keith Simonton's research on creativity, which links the productivity of thought to the generation of creative output. In *Genius, Creativity, and Leadership*, Simonton points to historical evidence that successful creators tend to start their careers early in life, end them late in life, and sustain high productivity throughout. This means that the successful creator is the productive creator. Like Edison, who held over a thousand patents, the creator produces so much that a proportion of productions end up becoming highly influential.

This dynamic informs daily forms of creativity as well: Generating more ideas is the best path to generating good ideas. As Michalko explains, increasing the fluency of thinking contributes to the creative quality of thinking. This is one reason that curiosity is such an important component of creativity. When you hunger to know, you're driven to look at and think about more things. You don't have to discipline yourself into a state of high productivity; the prodigious output of the creator is, as Simonton observes, a function of one's passion for his or her field.

One trader I recently worked with immediately struck me as unusual because he never lacked for trade ideas. He had an unusual knack for looking at a variety of markets and picking out candidates for good trades. His productivity in generating ideas continued even during a relatively quiet summer period. I was curious to figure out what he was doing differently from the other money managers he worked with, many of whom lamented the lack of solid trading opportunities across markets. Here are a few of my observations:

- *The prolific trader looked in many places for trade ideas.* He spoke with more colleagues, read more research papers, and looked at more charts than his peers. He also did not limit himself to any particular asset class. He was just as willing to trade commodities as stocks or high-yield bonds, and just as willing to entertain a relative value trade as a directional one.

- *The prolific trader wasn't afraid to generate bad trade ideas.* If the idea made sense, it went into his book, albeit not necessarily in size. He preferred to have many trades on—particularly if they were consistent with an overarching theme—so that price action could sort out the good trades from the ones not ready to perform. Instead of spending countless hours performing research and refining his ideas, he kept assembling and reassembling his book until he had the trades he wanted. He was very much like Csikszentmihalyi's painters in that regard.

- *The prolific trader operated on a wider time frame than his peers.* He sized positions moderately and set reasonably wide stops and price targets. His ideas, he pointed out, were designed to take advantage of fundamental developments around the world as well as price trends within markets. He stuck with ideas longer than the average money manager, which allowed the number of positions within his portfolio to stay high.

- *The prolific trader loved the hunt for ideas.* He never complained of choppy, slow, or irrational markets. He treated idea generation as a kind of Easter egg hunt, where good ideas were just waiting to be found. He expected himself to generate fresh ideas every week. That outlook energized his productivity.

In Michalko's terms, the trader I worked with was unusually fluent. He came up with not only more ideas than his peers, but better trades. Where other traders might limit themselves to several "high-conviction" trades, my trader put on anything that had a reasonable rationale. If there was a fundamental story and favorable price action, the trade went into the book. That meant that, at any given time, he would have three to five times as many line items in his portfolio as the other traders. When one or two of those trades displayed unusually favorable price action, he became more aggressive in those positions. Other traders were afraid to "chase" the trades once they had moved and never participated. The fluent trader participated meaningfully in unusual trade ideas, not because he was clairvoyant, but because he generated lots of "mutations" and let the natural selection of the market work to his benefit.

Can we make ourselves more productive as thinkers? One straight-forward method described by Michalko is setting a time limit and quota for generating new ideas. He draws on the example of Edison, who set quotas for himself and his assistants: one minor invention every 10 days and a major invention every 6 months. Over time, such productivity generates quite a stable of creations. One of the guidelines I imposed on my blog writing was that I needed to generate a fresh, high-quality post every single day. That forced me to look in novel directions for fresh topics, ultimately leading me to read books, articles, and research papers that I would have otherwise overlooked. Living up to that quota has resulted in a compilation of thousands of posts across a wide range of topics—something I could have never accomplished without the quota as a productivity aid.

Imagine setting quotas for aspects of your own trading process. You might, for instance, require yourself to write down one distinctive idea that came from conversations with other traders each day. As with my blog posts, such a quota would push you to seek out and speak with the highest-quality thinkers available, improving the productivity of your professional interactions. Alternatively, imagine setting a quota for your meetings: Every meeting on your calendar has to result in a write-up of a novel, promising idea. Driven by that mandate, you would naturally cancel your least-productive meetings and participate actively in those that remain.

Daily productivity quotas turn creativity into a habit pattern.

Setting quotas works because we become most productive when productivity becomes a conscious aim. How much time and energy do we waste as traders, staring at screens, following our positions tick by tick, failing to accomplish anything new in terms of the management of those trades or the generation of new ones? If we operate under the constraint to produce a new idea each day, we refocus our attention and efforts, greatly improving the quantity and quality of our output. One of my recent efforts to improve my fluency was to focus on the productivity of my reading time. I found myself skimming news stories and articles on the Web, with few of those truly contributing to my trading. To solve that problem, I selected the Abnormal Returns site as a well-curated source of market-related links and set myself the constraint of generating one good trading idea each day from the articles covered that day. That pushed me to not only consult the site daily, but become adept at filtering the links, so that I focused on the most promising ones. As a result, I became much more efficient as well as effective in feeding my head with high-quality information.

Fluency is most likely to flourish when we are open to experimentation. Seelig offers the example of a startup company that created an app that allowed users to share their locations with one another. The app did not catch on, so the company founders began experimenting with the adding of features until one in particular caught on: the editing and sharing of photos. The site and company were renamed Instagram and it became a phenomenal hit. The creative idea for the company only emerged after running through many unsuccessful iterations. Similarly, traders willing to experiment with ideas and trades are more likely to find the next big trade than those restricting their idea pool at the outset. A senior trader at a firm where I worked many years ago offered a cash bonus to any junior trader who provided him with a sound trade idea that made money. This led to a huge number of ideas crossing the senior trader's desk, many of which were taken as trades. Over time, he learned who came up with the best ideas—and he figured out when those ideas supported his existing views—so that his idea generation expanded exponentially. It was by experimenting with the new ideas and seeing what worked best that the trader was able to craft his own virtual team.

■ The Skills of Creativity: Finding Fresh Combinations

As we've seen, creativity is at heart a combinatorial process, in which we put new things together and assemble old things in new ways. We can effectively hone our creativity by cultivating our combinatorial skills. This means that we work as hard at synthesizing market information as analyzing it.

A key to the creative value of the combinatorial process is that simple elements, when combined, can yield rich interactions. In their book, *Sparks of Genius*, Robert and Michele Root-Bernstein (2001) cite the example of African tribal music. The music has a complex structure, and yet it is never formally taught or even written out. This is because each musician plays a different instrument and produces a different pattern of beats. Although each musician operates in a highly repetitive way, the combination of musicians creates a form of music in which, at any given moment, some musicians are striking notes while others are silent. Highly regimented performance thus leads to complexity and diversity across performers. The combination of performers generates a musical experience that is far richer than the output of any of the individual musicians.

Markets behave much like African musicians. At any given moment, each stock in a market average may be trading higher or lower and on higher or lower volume. There is little complexity to the movement of a single stock. When we step back and listen to the movement of stocks as a whole, patterns emerge that are not evident in the movement of any single share. Suppose I notice that interest rates are moving lower (fixed income prices are rising). One of the first things I'll do is look at the behavior of rates on the short and long ends of the curve, the behavior of currencies, and the behavior of stocks. What I'm trying to determine is whether we are seeing a macro trade—markets trading in a thematic manner based on macroeconomic fundamentals—or a more idiosyncratic one. The participants in macro moves are different from those in idiosyncratic ones, and the implications for near-term follow-through can be quite different. I can only make an educated guess about what is driving markets by listening to them in concert. The information is in the combination of movements across instruments, not in the behavior of any single instrument.

Notice that synthesis is a fundamentally different information processing modality from analysis. If I'm listening to a collective of African musicians, I can focus on the musician playing the percussion instrument and discern the pattern of rhythm, the rise and fall in the intensity of beats, and the subtle variations of sound produced by striking the instrument in different ways and in different places. Analysis is the cognitive equivalent of a microscope—it focuses in on a part of the whole to reveal rich detail.

During synthesis, on the other hand, we are zooming out, not in. We are listening to the sound of the musicians as a whole, appreciating the interplay of tones and rhythms. In the slow start of a performance, its building pace over time, and its calm, quiet conclusion, we might discern the rhythms of a successful game hunt. We discern a meaning in the whole that is more than the sum of its individual parts. That is because the meaning is a function of patterns, and the patterns are a function of the interplay of simple, individual elements. In analysis, we discern depth; in synthesis, we achieve breadth.

Arriving at novel combinations means that, per our earlier discussion of the creative process, we must step back from our immersion in market information—our microscope perspective—and open ourselves to broader patterns across that information. In markets, the novel combinations may be as simple as the relative price movement of one asset versus another, revealing a rotational trade that might be part of a larger pattern.

A while back, for instance, I noticed that consumer staples and utilities shares were starting to outperform consumer discretionary and tech stocks. That is normally part of a defensive market pattern, as sectors that are relatively resistant to downturns in the economy outperform more growth-oriented sectors late in a cycle. By looking across assets, however, I could also see that fixed income was rallying strongly and that we were seeing solid buying interest among high-yield bonds. That, along with dovish comments from global central banks, helped convince me that we were seeing a chase for yield, not merely a defensive repositioning. The combination of markets suggested that becoming defensive on stocks was the wrong play. Rather, it was time to take the offense with respect to stocks offering safe, growing dividends.

Michalko, in *Cracking Creativity*, suggests a simple exercise for improving our ability to utilize combinations and recombinations in facilitating the generation of new ideas. He suggests that we start by gathering all information about a problem, with each factor related to the problem written on a separate card. We then look for connections among the cards, grouping the cards into categories. Our search then turns to connections among the categories, so that we group the groups and arrive at four to six final categories. We label these categories and, on a separate sheet of paper, list them as columns, with the elements of each category beneath each category label. Finally, we cut the paper into vertical strips and lay them side by side, moving them up and down to explore fresh relationships among the components of each category.

An example will make this tool and process clearer. Suppose that the problem I am working on is improving my discipline as a trader. Perhaps I generate trading plans, but am not consistent in acting on those plans. What I then need to brainstorm are all the factors that are associated with my lapses in discipline. Below is a matrix of categories and factors that I might arrive at:

	Mood	*Market*	*Preparation*	*Thought Process*
Factor 1	Anxious, tense	Slow, quiet	Rushed, incomplete	Afraid of loss
Factor 2	Frustrated	Choppy	Too detailed	Need to make $
Factor 3	Bored	Moves w/out me	No reading	Distracted
Factor 4	Eager, excited	Big breakout for me	No conversations	Locked on 1 trade
Factor 5	Confident	Reverses against me	Info overload	Beat up self
Factor 6	Hurried	Range trade	Covered 1 area only	Can't miss move

Based on my review of discipline lapses, we can see that situations associated with failure to act on my trading plans include periods when I am anxious, frustrated, bored, eager, confident, and hurried; when markets are slow, choppy, moving against me, breaking out in my favor; reversing against me; and trading in a range; when my preparation for the day has been rushed, too detailed, without fresh reading, without fresh conversations, overloaded, and limited to one area; and when my thought process has been afraid of loss, pressing to make money, distracted, overly focused on a single trade, self-blaming, and concerned about missing a move. The brainstorming has uncovered many situational factors associated with discipline lapses.

Suppose we now look at various combinations of these factors as potential problem scenarios to work on. For example, I might combine "bored" mood with "choppy" markets; "rushed" preparation; and thoughts of "needing to make money." In such a situation, I would be pressing to find opportunity in a market that is not offering much directional movement and for which I'm not well-prepared. This constellation of factors I might label as "trying too hard to make things happen," leading me to work on techniques to become aware of boredom and pressing so that I can rechannel my efforts. A second combination of factors might be a "confident" mood; market making a "big breakout for me"; "no conversations" as part of my daily preparation; and thoughts "locked on the one trade." This combination of factors I might label as "playing with house money," as I relax my vigilance when I'm profitable. This would lead to an entirely separate set of techniques, in which I use a process-based scorecard to ensure that I am sustaining a broad view even when I am comfortable in the current trade.

In combining different factors, we can improve our awareness of problems that are impacting our trading. Similarly, if our chart captured various factors related to a market theme, we could see how those factors line up to suggest other possible themes or trades. By breaking down facets of a problem and then juxtaposing those facets in different ways, we create new lenses through which we can make sense of the problem.

One of my favorite ways of combining ideas is automatic writing. After reading a number of articles, viewing a large number of charts, or speaking with many knowledgeable traders, I will write my thoughts in stream-of-consciousness fashion. The key to this technique is to refuse to censor your writing: Just let it flow. The grammar may be poor; the thoughts may be disjointed—no matter. You keep writing until nothing new emerges.

Key Takeaway

When we process information via automatic writing or speech, we synthesize what we have analyzed.

Inevitably, the automatic writing triggers new thoughts and ideas, leading from the combination of thoughts to the generation of new ones. I might notice that one article I read focused on economic growth in the United States; another article stressed economic weakness in the European periphery; still another noted the relative weakness of emerging market stocks relative to those of developed markets. As I write, I find myself wondering about the dilemma of the Fed: Will it really want to raise interest rates when interest rate differentials already support unusual US dollar strength? And will US stocks really meet with selling if the Fed remains relatively accommodative? The new musings lead me to pursue fresh writings on the statements of Fed members, as an idea starts to crystallize that is at odds with the market consensus that rate hikes could squelch the rally in stocks.

Recombination can also occur as part of talking aloud. The dashboard on my trading software is organized so that I can see, at a glance, various measures of stock market breadth, as well as price action across key sectors, indexes, and asset classes. Very often I'll notice something out of whack with the broader picture and will make a note to myself aloud. This is my signal to be alert to a possible change in how I'm trading. Just recently, we opened the day session strong in stocks and then buying pressure faded relatively early in the morning. The number of stocks rising on the day (and making new highs on the day) began to fall, even as the S&P 500 Index price remained near its day's high. I commented aloud, "The buyers are leaving this market." I know when I make a comment like that, it is an important observation: It's an intuition that comes from years of following markets. The talking aloud is like automatic writing—it's a way of putting together a range of observations into a fresh synthesis.

■ The Skills of Creativity: Thinking by Analogy

Many times, we can illuminate unfamiliar topics by casting them in terms of what we know well. Analogies draw parallels that bring patterns to life. It would be very difficult for me to describe the musical style of a favorite new band, but if I told you it sounded like two of your favorite groups, you'd immediately have a sense for the style and spirit of the music. When psychologist B.F. Skinner elaborated principles of behavior, he drew on animal learning as an analogy. That helped explain how people could acquire such unusual patterns as phobias. A different analogy inspired Jean Piaget, who saw in stage-like biological development a process that could explain our cognitive development. A good theory is an analogy that is well elaborated, accounting for our current observations and suggesting new ones.

When we employ analogy, it is as if we change the lenses on the glasses we're wearing. Each analogy highlights something distinct in the subject area we're trying to understand. The Root-Bernsteins, in *Sparks of Genius*, observe that analogies are different from similies, in that they do not focus on surface similarities. If I say, "The star looks like a winking eye," that is a simile. It connects a common feature, but does not capture any wider, more fundamental structural relationships. On the other hand, if I create an analogy between the working of the brain and that of a computer, then I have potentially illuminated a wide range of relationships, from the nature of inputting information, to the retention of material in working memory, to the relationship between the organization of inputs and speed of processing those. The distinguishing feature of good analogies is their ability to creatively recast a familiar topic in a new form. The Root-Bernsteins mention Darwin as a prime example. His theory of evolution drew on two analogies: the breeding of plants and animals to produce various qualities and the work of Malthus, who found that population growth is limited by the availability of resources, resulting in the survival of the fittest members of a group.

One trader I worked with recently found himself unusually distracted by life events, including the interpersonal dynamics on his trading floor. This resulted in missing a couple of very profitable trades that he had researched. He was frustrated with himself, and this only further contributed to his distraction. Interestingly, he suffered from chronic pain in his hip—the result of an earlier sports injury. He was too young for hip replacement, so he managed the pain with medication, lifestyle adjustments, and daily meditation. At one point, I referred to his distraction as the result of *psychological pain* and asked how he could manage *that* pain. He quickly responded that he would need to take care of himself—throttle back his lifestyle—and use meditation to ensure that he did not identify with the pain. Indeed, when he took those steps, he found his focus rejuvenated and his attention turned to researching the next set of trading ideas. No deep psychological analysis was needed for him to deal with his problem. The simple analogy, linking his dealing with emotions to his coping with pain, pointed the direction to constructive steps he already knew how to take.

Analogy is one of the most powerful thinking tools available to us. Indeed, to a large extent, the ideas in this book—and the whole of my work with traders—are based on a core analogy.

■ ■ ■

One of my earliest positions as a psychologist was as a student counselor working first at Cornell University and then at a medical school. I had worked previously at a community mental health center and knew very well what psychological disorders looked like. As the only full-time psychologist in the rural county, I saw most of the significant problems in that community. Work on a college campus immediately struck me as quite different. For the most part, the students were not dysfunctional and did not meet formal DSM criteria of psychological disorders. My perception was that they were basically bright, motivated, normal young adults asked to function at a consistently high level under unusual cognitive load. This helped explain why the most common presenting problem at the counseling centers was stress. The problem, as I saw it, was situational overload, not intrinsic mental illness. For that reason, I insisted on being on a first-name basis with the students and referred to our work together as counseling, not therapy. My goal was to normalize the helping process as much as possible, which in turn encouraged students to seek help. They were very willing to access resources to become more successful students, and less likely to speak with someone who treated them as patients.

Particularly noteworthy among the pre-med students at Cornell (who comprised a disproportionate share of my visits in any given week) and the medical students in Syracuse (of whom first- and second-year "basic science" students were the most frequent visitors to counseling) was that they were very successful in their prior schooling, but were now struggling academically. Their stress largely stemmed from the fact that they were having difficulty keeping up with their new workloads. As I examined the nature of their courses and homework, I identified two major challenges: (1) the amount of work they faced was greater than anything they had dealt with in the past; and (2) the type of material that they encountered in their courses was qualitatively different from that of their earlier coursework. Because of these two factors, the students were on almost constant overload and could not keep up with their work.

When I began to study the students who were able to master the workloads successfully, I found that they studied very differently from the overloaded students. They generally studied with partners, dividing the workload and reviewing the material interactively. They also took breaks with others, keeping each other motivated—and awake! The successful students made greater use of charts and diagrams and less use of notes copied word for word from readings and lectures. Finally, the successful students were better than the others at filtering the most important information. This was not a mystical sense; they simply assumed that if a concept appeared both in their texts and in their lecture, it must be important. They also noted when lecturers spent more time on particular topics, assuming that those were the most important things to learn. By prioritizing important material from less important material, working in groups and dividing the material, and capturing the key information in multiple formats, the successful students were more efficient with their learning, but also more effective.

The less successful students were bright enough and sufficiently motivated that they didn't have to employ such methods in their earlier schooling. They were like naturally gifted athletes who could shine on the field without having to work themselves hard during conditioning and practice. When they came to the big leagues, however, everyone was naturally gifted. Conditioning and practice suddenly mattered.

This interested me greatly because it suggested that the stressed-out students were not dealing primarily with psychological issues. Whatever distress they experienced was more the result of their problems than cause—although the distress certainly did not aid the effectiveness or efficiency of their subsequent study efforts. The real problem was that the stressed-out students needed to become better learners: They needed learning skills, not psychotherapy. Fortunately, there were learning skills specialists on the campus only too delighted to collaborate. We conducted groups to teach students the skills of their successful peers and even enlisted a few of those peers to serve as mentors. We used our group teaching sessions to encourage students to form their own groups and benefit from collaboration. The impact on the students' grades and mindsets was significant. Once the students felt a greater degree of mastery and had tools at their disposal to improve their learning, their efforts were energized and they no longer felt overloaded.

Perhaps the most fascinating aspect of this experience was the reaction of my professional colleagues. Quite a few were absolutely disgusted by my "unprofessional" approach to the students I worked with. They insisted that the students suffered from "deeper" emotional issues that I was ignoring. They felt that my emphasis on study skills and learning cheapened the psychological services offered by the school. Many criticized my use of the term "counseling" rather than "therapy." More than once, my first-name basis with the students and willingness to meet with them in informal groups was called "inappropriate." It was surreal: Every bit of my experience told me that what I was doing was helpful—and that was the feedback of the students I worked with—but the feedback I received from a surprising number of colleagues was unusually critical and bitter.

Fast forward to 2003: It was my first experience working with traders on a full-time basis at Kingstree in Chicago, a firm that provided liquidity in electronic futures markets, especially in CME and CBOT products. My own trading experience was not related to market making and was much longer-term than that of the Chicago traders. I was not familiar with reading order flow from depth of market screens and the dynamics of managing simultaneous bids and offers in a book. Most of all, I had no experience with placing hundreds of trades per day. As a result, my immediate impression when I began work was that I was entirely clueless. I needed to listen and observe before I could be of meaningful help.

Fortunately, the traders were quite willing to educate me, and I was able to observe the very best traders as well as those who were struggling. The very successful traders had a clear idea of who was in the market and what they were doing. They were able to track large trades and high volume at particular price levels and respond quickly to the demand and supply at those levels. Very often, they shared those perceptions with close colleagues, benefiting from the pattern recognition of experienced peers. The Market Profile display proved to be quite helpful in capturing their thought process—it was volume transacted at price levels that anchored their perceptions of value and moves away from value. This allowed them to see when higher or lower prices were attracting business, or whether prices away from value were shutting off activity. The less successful traders were much more focused on price alone, treating all higher or lower prices as evidence of trending activity. They did not verbalize who was in the market and what they were doing. As a result, they were frequently confused by market reversals. They also became overwhelmed when volume picked up and prices moved in volatile ways. Unlike the successful traders, they tended to shut down when markets became unusually busy.

That is when the analogy hit me. It was a creative bolt out of the blue that reshaped my career.

I realized that the troubled traders were just like my medical students: bright, motivated young adults facing information overload. They described emotional difficulties, including stress, frustrated trading, and fear of pulling the trigger, but most had no significant mental health histories. When I examined their lives outside of trading, I could not detect ongoing patterns of emotional disruption. Rather, whatever emotional and behavioral problems they faced seemed specific to the trading setting. Those emotional and behavioral problems were significant, but they were the result of more fundamental trading challenges—not merely the cause of poor trading. What the troubled traders needed more than anything else was a way of conceptualizing volume at price action that could help them make sense of why markets were moving in a particular fashion. Like the medical students, they needed to focus on essentials and draw on one another in a constructive fashion. All the psychological interventions in the world would not help them if they could not make sense of order flow and price/volume dynamics.

Key Takeaway

Analogy creates a profound perceptual reorganization. We act in new ways because we see new things.

The analogy completely reshaped my view of trading psychology and my role as a trading psychologist. It took a very unfamiliar domain—the world of electronic market making—and cast it in terms of something I was very familiar with: the learning process under challenging and competitive conditions. The creative element in the analogical reasoning was the perceptual shift created by seeing trading through a cognitive lens, as a learning and information processing challenge, rather than solely as an emotional one.

What made the analogy more than mere simile was that it led to very specific ideas for helping the traders. Instead of focusing on emotional problems and the search for their roots, I took a solution-focused view and tracked the best practices of those who were successful. That led me to identify best practices from the winning trades of losing traders, helping them understand how they were able to utilize their strengths in making sense of the huge amounts of information from moving markets. Having worked for years with students who benefited from dividing and conquering a workload by drawing on each other, I was able to help traders make more effective use of one another in deciphering market activity. Once the troubled traders were able to more effectively track market activity over the time frames relevant to their trading, their problems with emotional disruptions and undisciplined trading declined significantly. As with the medical students, their emotional overload greatly declined once they felt a greater degree of understanding and mastery.

The analogy was cemented for me, however, when I began to hear criticism from peer trading coaches. I was focusing on "surface" aspects of trading, not the deeper emotional roots of traders' problems. One coach, in a public forum, pronounced that my approach to working with traders was less effective than theirs because it did not take into account the insights of Freudian psychology. Real psychologists got at the heart of problems, not the superficial facets of solutions! I had to smile. There is no way to pursue the cutting edge without alienating those wedded to consensus.

Where I see traders most often make use of analogy is in drawing on their trading experience. Many very successful traders I've known have unusually strong episodic memories. One trader I worked with in Chicago was almost a savant in that regard. He and I would be discussing a recent trading day and suddenly he'd say, "It reminded me of that day at the start of the year when we broke the overnight range and those buy programs came in and scooped 'em up." Sure enough, we'd go back to January's trading and there was a day that eerily resembled the recent one in its price and volume behavior. One hedge fund manager I worked with closely approached analogies in a more research-based manner. If he thought the Bank of Japan would ease monetary policy, he'd go back to all similar occasions in the past when there was such an easing and see how the Nikkei traded going forward. His mantra that "history repeats itself" was his way of using past market patterns as analogies for unclear forward price behavior.

If you're an experienced trader, at some point you've traded a market similar to the current one. Focus on the essential, defining aspects of today's market and you'll find historical analogies. History may not repeat in every detail, but—as the saying goes—it will rhyme.

■ Creativity and Lifestyle

It is very difficult to lead a creative life if you are caught in repetitive routines from day to day. There is much to be said for routine, as the reliance on habits frees us up to attend to fresh daily challenges. When life becomes a mere sequence of routines, however, where will we draw inspiration for tackling those daily challenges in new and promising ways?

Over the years, I have found it important to embed elements of creativity in my day-to-day and week-to-week routines. If I'm not reading new things, talking with new people, looking at new things, or investigating new directions, I'm unlikely to sustain the playfulness of mind that helps me think creatively about markets and the traders I work with. Not all the lifestyle elements of creativity are particularly involved. At the moment I'm writing this, for instance, I'm listening to Reila by The Gazette, a talented band from Japan. It is not exactly an upbeat tune, but is emotionally profound and touches me in unique ways. I consistently find that my thinking about markets is more creative when I'm immersing myself in new music and creative music.

Margie and I have begun a tradition of taking weekend trips at least once a month to neighborhoods and towns in the greater NYC area that offer unique outdoor activities, cultural offerings, dining experiences, and shopping. We've found that traveling even an hour or two from where we live can place us in an entirely new world, with things to discover. It is difficult to become stale—in one's work or one's marriage—when sharing fresh experiences on a regular basis. Instead of booking vacations a couple of times per year, we've committed to finding vacation time on a regular basis.

As mentioned earlier with the idea of using quotas to stimulate creativity, the writing of the TraderFeed blog has also become a lifestyle contributor to my idea generation. I require myself to write one post per day, almost always in early morning hours. I cannot move forward with the rest of my day until I have written something worthwhile about markets, psychology, or trading. The exercise forces me to look at new things to stimulate fresh blog entries, leading me to read a variety of authors the way I listen to music. The blog writing also encourages me to collect and analyze fresh market data, in an effort to illuminate market patterns. I subscribe to several databases for that reason, as the new data often lead to new questions and worthwhile investigations.

Too often, the concepts of "discipline" and "process orientation" are used to justify an assembly-line-like uniformity of practice. Some elements of our trading are worth making routine and even automating. *The essential work of trading, however, is finding opportunity—and that is fundamentally a creative activity*. If our lifestyles don't support open-minded, fresh thinking, we will sleepwalk through our routines, missing the unique opportunities around us.

■ Creativity in Groups

Not all traders trade on their own, and even those working independently can generally benefit from collaboration. Sawyer, in *Group Genius*, makes the important point that innovations are typically the result of group interaction, not individual genius. He offers the example of Wilbur and Orville Wright, who developed a highly interactive approach to designing a flying machine. Their notes reveal a high degree of mutual discussion, with solutions to problems emerging from their interactions. "Collaboration drives creativity," Sawyer explains, "because innovation always emerges from a series of sparks—never a single flash of insight" (2007, p. 7). Sawyer's paradigm for group innovation is the improvisation of jazz music groups and comedy troupes. The output from each member becomes an input for the others, stimulating new lines of direction that others then pick up. What makes improvisation distinctive is that the groups are not working toward a defined endpoint. Rather, the creation emerges through the spontaneous interactions of the group members: They, in a real sense, surprise themselves with the output.

In his book, Sawyer identifies seven features of creative collaboration:

1. *Innovation emerges over time.* Creative output is the result of an ongoing process; it's not a single moment of insight.
2. *Successful teams practice deep listening.* Team members are unusually receptive to the inputs of others and thus can be flexible in incorporating those inputs.
3. *Team members build on the ideas of their collaborators.* Creativity results from the adaptations that team members make to the inputs of their colleagues.
4. *Only afterwards does the meaning of each idea become clear.* The final creative product is not pre-planned; it emerges organically from the interactions and adaptations of team members.
5. *Surprising questions emerge.* The interactions within a team frame new questions and challenges, and those shape the creative adaptations that emerge from their interactions.
6. *Innovation is inefficient.* Many creative directions lead to dead-ends and are rapidly abandoned, replaced by more fruitful leads. There is a great deal of trial and error in the process of creation.
7. *Innovation emerges from the bottom up.* For the jazz or comedy group, there is no leader and no prefigured script. Results spring from the inputs and interactions of team members, not from hierarchical dictates from managers or experts.

Key Takeaway

Trading is best played as a team sport.

This is not a familiar perspective for traders. We typically think of trading as an individual activity, in which one person identifies and trades opportunities. Such a view is reinforced by such sources as Jack Schwager's *Market Wizards*: We view success as a function of the individual, missing the group context in which that success occurs. In point of fact, however, a purely individual approach to trading is suboptimal and helps account for the low success rate of individual traders.

■ ■ ■

Let's follow a trader we'll call Mel, as he goes through a typical trading day. Mel trades his own account and trades out of an "arcade" office that gives him access to superior technology, support, and commissions. The office arrangement also enables Mel to interact with other traders, which is helpful as a break from trading. Each trader in the office trades his own account, his own products, and his own style, so only very broad ideas are typically shared. The group has assembled to share overhead, not to work as a team.

Mel starts his day by reading the news, reviewing how markets are trading, and updating his trading plans. He subscribes to a couple of research services and uses information from these to help him keep up with market developments. A momentum trader, Mel screens for stocks trading in ranges and showing an uptick in volume. These are candidates for breakout trades. When he sees breakouts that line up with general market direction, he will lift offers or hit bids and look to ride the momentum. If volume dries up shortly after the breakout, he will quickly take profits. If volume expands on the breakout, he is more likely to ride the trade as a swing position—particularly if the breakout is from a protracted range. As a rule, Mel makes his money in markets that display good volume and volatility, as these moves are most likely to show continuation. Quiet, low-VIX markets are ones in which he can be frequently whipsawed and taken out of trades.

Now let's follow a different trader, Jose, who trades as part of a team. There are four members of the team: the leader, who has a strong background in global macro trading—especially rates and currencies;

a senior trader who trades a wide range of commodity futures; Jose, who trades breakout patterns in stocks and ETFs; and a junior trader, who runs quantitative studies for the other traders and trades the momentum patterns from those studies. As an integrated team, the four traders communicate on a regular basis. Each calls out patterns that show up in his or her area of focus. Thus, the leader may see considerable selling in European assets, led by the periphery, while the senior trader notes particular strength in gold. The studies from the junior trader suggest that put/call sentiment in the stock market has been unusually bullish, which has been associated with near-term weakness. Jose sees stocks hovering just above their overnight lows and sellers hitting bids shortly after an attempted bounce. He synthesizes the inputs from the team members and calls out his own idea: selling stocks for a break to new lows. The other traders follow Jose's trade carefully, as it will help them handicap the odds of a trend day to the downside across markets.

Note that both Mel and Jose are experienced traders with similar trading styles. Mel operates solo and is limited in what he can follow in real time. Jose, on the other hand, is constantly fed updated information across markets, as well as real-time research studies from the junior trader. This not only helps Jose develop confidence in his ideas but sparks the creation of new ideas. The trading team performs a bit like the jazz musicians and improvisational comedians described by Sawyer: They play off one another, arriving at combinations that none had envisioned initially. For example, when the senior trader calls out an idea that cuts across the commodities, Jose has learned that this can be a valuable trigger for trades in commodity-related energy and raw materials ETFs. It also becomes a prod for the group leader to take a fresh look at commodity currencies. Mel may be able to appreciate all of these relationships, but he cannot process all of the information in real time to realize the improvisational creativity of the integrated team.

We've seen that when people are immersed in meaningful activity, drawing on their strengths, they experience a flow state that facilitates both creativity and productivity. Sawyer refers to "group flow" as the immersion of a team in their interactions and mutual processing of information. When there is group flow among the improvisational troupe, the story line emerges organically from the spontaneous interactions of the members. Each cues the others in unexpected ways, and the group feeds off the meaning and momentum created. In the trading team, the group flow is one in which team members spark ideas in one another.

It is, to use Sawyer's phrase, a "problem-finding" creativity, rather than a problem-solving one. The result of the flow is discovery.

Key Takeaway

Creativity breeds adaptivity.

When the trader operates solo, the mindset often narrows, rather than broadens. The focus on the ups and downs of price action and the need to manage risk and keep up with news flows creates a reactive mode of operation. With the narrower focus, the trader cannot process widely; a wealth of data goes unprocessed. This becomes a particular problem when markets change their behavior; instead of processing and flowing with the new information, traders operating in a silo, like Mel, remain stuck in old ways of thinking. A jazz musician can improvise on his or her own, but will find fresh inspiration if playing off the inputs of other skilled musicians.

■ Does Brainstorming Work?

Perhaps the technique most associated with group forms of creativity is brainstorming. Brainstorming is an approach to group interaction in which members are encouraged to contribute ideas openly, without criticism from others. The focus of brainstorming is on complete non-censorship: producing as many ideas as possible—no matter how crazy sounding—and then pulling from them the most promising leads. Sawyer notes that research has not been entirely supportive of brainstorming as an enhancement of creativity. In many cases, having individuals generate ideas on their own and then later assemble as a group is superior to the freewheeling tossing out of ideas within the group. While traditional brainstorming may lead to more ideas, it does not necessarily lead to better ones. Interestingly, studies suggest that groups encouraged to filter ideas and focus on the most promising, creative ones produce more high-quality ideas than groups that toss out ideas in a freewheeling manner. Linker's book, entitled *Disciplined Dreaming*, captures the essence of the findings of this research: Creativity is aided by rule-following as well as by open-mindedness. When the jazz musicians play off one another, it's not anything goes. There is discipline in the use of rhythm, melody, and harmony, even as there are experiments within those.

Sawyer notes several shortcomings of traditional brainstorming, including the blocking of one's own ideas when members need to process the ideas of others and the tendency of groups to cluster their ideas in a limited range of topics. When individuals can brainstorm on their own—the automatic writing described earlier is a good example—they are more able to freely generate a wide range of ideas. Coming together as a group then enables group flow to begin with high-quality inputs. Individual creativity thus feeds the creativity of the group.

Describing the brainstorming that is a "religion" at design firm IDEO, Tom Kelley offers seven secrets for successful brainstorming:

1. *Sharpen the focus.* Brainstorming works best if a problem or topic is well articulated and specific. When the focus is clearer, groups are more likely to generate relevant and useful ideas.
2. *Playful rules.* A deterrent to creativity is introducing criticism and censorship too early in the idea generation process. When participants are encouraged to voice ideas freely and express them creatively—visually, as well as out loud—there is a greater likelihood that they will stimulate the fresh thinking of others.
3. *Number your ideas.* Keeping track of the number of ideas generated—and even setting a goal, such as 100 in an hour—creates a goal for the group that encourages fertile thought.
4. *Build and jump.* Facilitators of the brainstorming process can step back when the group is in flow and jump to a different focus when the flow slows down. Groups develop a momentum to their creative flow that can be nurtured.
5. *The space remembers.* It's important to write down the ideas generated in a visible form, such on paper that covers the walls of the meeting room. This allows ideas to be grouped, tapping into the spatial memory of participants.
6. *Stretch your mental muscles.* Warm-up exercises can spark the activity and creativity of the group. A homework exercise before the session, for example, can provide an opportunity for team members to share perspectives at the very start of the session, making the most of the time allotted.
7. *Get physical.* Moving around the room, mapping ideas, drawing diagrams, and actively using different materials to illustrate a point contribute to the free and spontaneous flow of ideas.

Kelley's overarching point is that successful brainstorms are dynamic. They have a focus and an allotted time limit, but operate freely within those constraints. Brainstorming works because it is work—and because it is fun.

■ ■ ■

I've generally found that traders work best in teams when there is an alignment of personality and cognitive dynamics. This sustains a positive chemistry among the team members and feeds creative collaboration.

Cara joined a trading team covering the commodity markets, with particular emphasis on precious metals and energy products. Cara came from a strong research background and had excellent industry contacts that kept her in touch with demand and supply. She also had a sound knowledge of the futures curves across the products and was as comfortable recommending spread trades as directional ones. This was very helpful in nontrending markets, as Cara could generate spread ideas and volatility-based trades that were not correlated with the positions of the other team members.

The team was friendly and welcomed Cara, but it didn't take long for her to become frustrated. The senior members of the team were very lax about sticking to meeting schedules, preferring to talk informally on the trading floor. This made it difficult for Cara to discuss her research in detail and get thoughtful reactions from her colleagues. Worse still, her write-ups of trade recommendations frequently went unread, as the team members were more interested in the trade than the underlying logic and fundamentals. From the vantage point of creativity, it was a nightmare: Cara felt that she was learning very little from the team interactions. The managers seemed more interested in what was moving/trending than in grasping the broader picture of economic and industry fundamentals. From the vantage point of personality (conscientiousness versus informality) and cognitive style (analytical versus intuitive), there was a poor fit between Cara and the rest of the team. As a result, there was plenty of chatter on the floor, but no brainstorming.

When the team leader elected to take a position at another firm and was able to take team members with him, Cara used the opportunity to stay at her current firm and join a different team. This one consisted of a single portfolio manager and an execution trader/assistant. The portfolio manager traded most of the liquid macro markets, but welcomed Cara's commodity focus as a diversifying influence. The manager was highly analytical himself and spent considerable time off the desk reading research and meeting with experts. He never entered positions unless there was a compelling fundamental thesis backed by price behavior. The assistant had a solid background in technical analysis and kept track of when market behavior was starting to line up with the group's fundamental ideas. Cara loved hearing about macro fundamentals and soon found herself filtering her own ideas based on their fit with broader macroeconomic considerations. For example, she pounded the table on a Brent-WTI spread trade that not only fit the fundamentals of those oil markets, but also expressed relative economic weakness/strength between Europe and the United States. Brainstorming worked for the group because personality and cognitive style were aligned among the members. Being on the same page, with similar work styles, enabled the group to be unusually fertile in its generation of ideas and trades.

Key Takeaway

A team is only as strong as the culture it maintains.

Culture matters. The values and work styles of teams shape their interactions and can either facilitate or frustrate creative efforts. In *Disciplined Dreaming*, Linkner (2011) stresses seven rules of creative cultures:

1. *Fueling passion*—Productive teams have fun and sustain a sense of mutual purpose.
2. *Celebrating ideas*—Creative teams reward productivity with praise and perks.
3. *Fostering autonomy*—Successful teams reward individual initiative and freedom of inquiry.
4. *Encouraging courage*—Teams that work well encourage intellectual risk-taking and open communication of views.
5. *Failing forward*—Creative teams encourage idea generation, even when the ideas don't work out.
6. *Thinking small*—When teams get too large, they tend to operate by consensus rather than by individual, creative initiative. Smaller teams promote interaction and cross-fertilization of ideas.

7. *Maximizing diversity*—Teams are more likely to find fresh combinations of ideas if the members have different backgrounds and experiences and look at markets in unique ways.

My experience is that teams pay far too little attention to culture. They operate from day to day and week to week with little consideration of how they are interacting and whether their interactions are generating maximum value. A classic example is the team meeting. Many times, teams will meet to discuss markets—a good idea in itself. Very often, however, the meeting has no firm agenda and is not preceded by any kind of focused preparation. Members take turns offering their views, very often similar ones to those voiced already. There is little debate and discussion, as few new perspectives are brought to the meeting. In an important sense, such meetings are anti-brainstorming. They generate little novel output, and the teams soon tire of the meetings, as they don't seem productive.

Contrast such meetings with the gatherings of Cara's team. Everyone is expected to bring to each meeting at least one piece of original or published research that is relevant to the portfolio and that has specific implications for trading. Members are encouraged to pick apart the research and highlight valuable points and vulnerable ones. Very often, the discussion will lead the team to seek out additional information to either support or refute the research-based view. The meetings do not conclude until the team has come up with something new and valuable. This encourages each of the team members to bring multiple research pieces to the meeting, so that there will be plenty of raw materials for generating fresh views. Everyone on the team looks forward to the meetings, as it's an opportunity to bring value to the group and participate in an energetic, creative process.

None of this could happen in Cara's team, of course, if the lead portfolio manager was not open to ideas and the free discussion of those. I once sat in on meetings at a trading firm where a very senior manager led the sessions. He made his views on markets known in no uncertain terms and was dismissive—and even belittling—of competing views. His research assistants, who attended the meetings, depended on him for annual bonuses. What incentive did they have to offer new or controversial views? Not surprisingly, the meetings ended up becoming cheerleading sessions for the trade ideas already expressed by the manager. Tremendous reserves of creativity were wasted because the organizational culture of the team did not reward autonomy and intellectual independence.

One strategy I employ when I interview for coaching positions is to find an occasion to voice a nonconsensus, out-of-the-box view about trading, coaching, or markets. For example, one manager told me that traders at his firm were too risk-averse and not taking full advantage of their capital. I suggested that the firm's risk management policies might have something to do with that and that coaching around trade structuring and portfolio construction might be particularly useful in enhancing risk-adjusted returns. That, I indicated, could be an opportunity for a trading coach to collaborate with risk management staff in unique ways to design and implement strategies that effectively utilize capital. The manager was surprised by my idea and quite interested in it. That suggested to me that this was a culture that valued divergent thinking and the forthright sharing of views—an important piece of information in assessing organizational culture.

At a different firm, I once interviewed for a position and spoke with a number of traders and managers. I indicated to a senior manager that there was a morale problem on the trading floor due to the departure of quite a few new hires. The manager's response was swift and defensive, asserting that this was a business where people were paid for what they earned and that if traders couldn't accept that, perhaps they didn't belong at the firm. In point of fact, the morale problem was as much about how traders were let go as the fact that they were terminated, but there was no openness to such a conversation. Not surprisingly, that firm suffered a hemorrhaging of talent in the subsequent year and I was happy that I did not take a position there. One of the best predictors of failing teams and trading firms, I've found, is an authoritarian culture. If innovation and open dialogue are threats to those in power, the organization simply will not innovate—and that signs a long and painful death warrant.

■ Tapping into Group Creativity Even When You Are Independent

So how can traders best make use of brainstorming and the power of group collaboration? It's important to recognize that it is not necessary for traders to be a part of a structured group in order to benefit from the creativity of group flow. Thanks to the online medium, independent traders can link with one another and create virtual teams. This is one of the greatest—and least exploited—areas of opportunity available to individual traders. To be sure, traders do communicate with one another via chat, tweets, and email. Rarely, however, are such interactions structured in such a way as to lead to creative outputs. Rather, the interactions are more social and expressive and less oriented to the generation of fresh ideas.

Several portfolio managers that I have worked with have sustained virtual teams with valued colleagues who trade from different locations. Usually, the initial catalyst for conversations is simply checking in with each other to see what everyone has heard and observed in the most recent day. Topics will vary from the significance of news reports and data releases to the behavior of various markets and the latest research to hit the street. Invariably these conversations are open-ended and freeform; it's a back-and-forth process in which each manager plays off the observations of the other. I generally find that the conversations are not so much about specific trades as general ideas about events and markets. There's an underlying sense that, if we can figure out what's going on in the world, we'll know how to express it in markets. Even when daytraders are calling out stocks that are moving, the focus is on "keep an eye on this" rather than on "buy it at 18." The idea, as we've seen, is to expand bandwidth, not create groupthink with respect to trade ideas.

Essential to the creation of virtual groups is balancing the quality and compatibility of participants with sufficient diversity to create multiple perspectives. Many times, the conversations will not be group based but will be a series of chats with individual colleagues. Each conversation informs the next one, so that there is some of the benefit of groupness, without dealing with the logistical challenges of bringing everyone together at the same time. When I speak with traders, I want to hear perspectives from successful market participants who trade similar markets and time frames as I trade, but who look at things differently from me. Some of my favorite conversations are with daytraders who have a very good feel for the pulse of the market and what is leading the price action of stock indexes. They track multiple stocks on short time frames, which takes more bandwidth than I can devote to markets, given my other work. In turn, I conduct historical studies of price action that are outside the skill sets of many of the daytraders. This helps provide them with a larger picture context to their trading.

Conversations with other traders are not always about markets. Many times, when a trader gets into a slump, he or she will turn to colleagues for advice. Creative brainstorming can aid our thinking about performance, just as it can feed our generation of trade ideas. A trader friend recently approached me about not making money over the past couple of months. He was not losing money, but also was not making much. I relayed a time when I went through something similar when my risk management was so tight that it prevented me from adequately capitalizing on the upside of my ideas. I was successful at not losing money, but I was failing to give myself a fair opportunity to win. That led to a good conversation about his risk-taking and ways of combining risk sensitivity with openness to opportunity. Ultimately, that led him to more flexibly manage his position sizing during the life of trades—an outcome that sprang from our conversation, but that was wholly independent of anything I had shared with him. He took the idea of giving oneself an opportunity to win and used that to ensure that he always allowed some piece of his position to go to a possible, relatively distant target.

Key Takeaway

Traders can be independent without being isolated.

One of the deterrents to creating virtual groups is the desire to keep one's ideas to oneself, lest too many people gain access to one's "secret sauce." To be sure, it is important to protect genuine intellectual property. If you've developed a promising backtested trading system, no one reasonable will expect you to share the code with them. On the other hand, I've known system traders to share signals with one another and brainstorm ideas for future system development. Most discretionary traders don't possess that kind of intellectual property, and the worry about giving away secrets is overdone. A far greater risk is staying locked in one's own head, failing to process all that transpires in markets. One can share observations and think aloud without sharing or copying specific trades. Treating trading as a team sport, even when trading independently, allows creativity to coexist with independence. Many successful independent traders get that way by becoming interdependent.

■ The Single Greatest Barrier to Creativity

As I mentioned earlier, what has struck me most in years of working with traders is the relative absence of unique, independent, critical thought. Traders assume that a research report is accurate, without taking the time to verify observations and conclusions for themselves. Traders accept that a given chart pattern is bullish or bearish without so much as a single backtest. Traders copy each other's trades, fearful of missing opportunities that their peers might capitalize on. The result of all these shortcomings is groupthink, in which the majority of traders share similar views and trades.

Why do so many traders stick to conventional ideas and traditional ways of doing business? At the end of the day, it boils down to fear of failure. When people are afraid of falling flat on their faces, they won't toss out unique ideas or pursue original directions. Creativity requires the generation of many ideas, many of which are destined to fall short. You cannot brainstorm without the majority of your ideas falling flat. That, however, is the point of creativity: You generate so many combinations that, eventually, you focus on the few that hold tremendous promise.

Ed Catmull describes the culture at Pixar in his book, *Creativity, Inc*. A cornerstone of that culture is the embracing of failure. Mistakes are "the inevitable result of doing something new," he asserts (2014, p. 108). His analogy to the creative process is learning to ride a bike. Mistakes and setbacks are a natural part of the learning curve. "Fail early and fail fast" was one of the mottos at Pixar. The idea is to make mistakes readily—and learn from them quickly. If a culture does not value failure, and especially if people are criticized or punished for mistakes, the result is a shutdown of innovation. We stay with what is known when the safety of familiarity seems preferable to the consequences of failure.

The philosophy of fail early and fail fast is particularly apt for traders. It is very common for traders to lose money on about half of their trades. Their profits come from the fact that their winning trades are larger than their losing ones. Once one embraces the fact that roughly half of all trades will lose money, the trading challenge becomes twofold:

1. *Promptly recognize when you're wrong*—A stop-loss level should reflect when your trade idea is wrong; it should not simply reflect a pain threshold. Stopping out of a trade does not reflect a failure; it is a money management success. Getting out of a losing situation is the first step toward finding a winning one. The difference between the profitable trader and the marginal one often boils down to rigorous control of the negative tail of the P&L distribution.

2. *Learn from losing trades*—If you're wrong in a trade, your loss generally can teach you something important. Sometimes the loss will provide a stimulus for questioning your assumptions about the market; sometimes the loss will lead you to reevaluate your trading practices. When losing trades become stimuli for learning, all is not lost. Losing can catalyze creativity when it prods new ways of thinking.

Have your losing trades crippled your trading, or have they made you a better trader? Do you dread loss or embrace it? One of trading's great ironies is that we only become winners once we come to terms with losing—and use losing to fuel creative adaptation.

■ It All Fits Together

Chapter 1 emphasized the importance of adapting to changing markets. Chapter 2 stressed the necessity of leveraging our strengths. The current chapter has focused on creativity and why it is crucial to approach markets in novel ways. While I've found it useful to separate these topics for the purpose of exposition, in reality, they are closely intertwined. We best adapt to changing markets by playing to our strengths, and we are most likely to find creative market adaptations if we're grounded in what we do best. Our performance will be best if we experience consistent emotional well-being: Positive emotional experience both fuels creative adaptation and broadens and builds our strengths.

Key Takeaway

Creativity is the new discipline.

Traditional trading psychology has begun with the premise that, once you find your edge in markets, all you then need to do is sustain the consistency of your trading. That means that discipline and self-control are the essential building blocks of trading success. *Trading Psychology 2.0*, however, starts with the premise that one never possesses a single, unvarying edge in markets. Opportunity sets are always changing; successful traders, like successful entrepreneurs, adapt to dynamic markets. Discipline and self-control are necessary for trading success, but not sufficient. *In crowded, efficient markets, creativity is the new discipline.* We must maximize strengths, not just reduce vulnerabilities, to stay ahead of the pack. That means that it is not enough to possess best practices. We must transform those best practices into best processes. "Process" is more than simply doing the same thing consistently each day; it is doing the right things—the best things—each day. The last chapter will take a look at best practices and how we can weave those into robust adaptive processes.

CHAPTER 4

Best Process #4: Developing and Integrating Best Practices

If one does not know to which port one is sailing, no wind is favorable.

Lucius Annaeus Seneca

■ What Are Best Practices?

Best practices are the cornerstone of quality improvement. We cannot improve the quality of our efforts if we do not keep score and differentiate between what is successful and what is not. That means that every effective practitioner is to some degree a researcher, tracking outcomes and using those outcomes to guide future efforts. Best practices, in that context, are a crystallization of deliberate practice.

Let's imagine a situation in which a chain of restaurants tracks customer comments and satisfaction levels. Over time, certain units produce reliably better ratings than other ones. Several restaurants in the chain achieve absolutely outstanding reviews; a few also receive startlingly poor ones. Jeff, the head of quality control for the company, decides to visit each of the sites as a customer and observe first-hand the factors that might account for the variability in the ratings. He breaks down his own ratings into five categories: (1) ambiance; (2) initial service; (3) service during the meal; (4) quality of the food preparation; and (5) service at the end of the meal. He visits the 10 restaurants in the chain with the highest satisfaction ratings and the 10 with the lowest ratings. Here is a summary of what he found:

- *Ambiance*—By design, the restaurants are laid out similarly with similar materials, color schemes, and space allotted for diners. Still, there were meaningful differences in ambiance between the popular restaurants and the ones that were poorly rated. The well-rated restaurants were kept unusually clean and tidy. Tables were quickly bussed, floors were kept very clean, and tables were rapidly turned over once diners finished their meals. The less popular units were slower to turn tables over. Poor communication between wait staff and floor staff led to situations in which tables could be sitting for a while before being cleaned off. The same communication gaps created situations in which spills and other messes created by customers (particularly ones entering on rainy or snowy days) were not cleaned up quickly. The popular units seemed to have a buzz about them: The sound level was higher and more energetic. The less popular restaurants seemed dull and unexciting. Several factors seemed to account for the differences. The successful restaurants displayed dishes near the entry way and placed the day's specials in a highly visible location. Diners were greeted heartily at the door and welcomed. Music played at a higher volume than at the less popular restaurants and the selection of music was more up-tempo. The restaurant managers circulated among the tables regularly to make sure everything was OK. This led to conversations with the customers, some of which became lively. At the less successful units, managers were so busy keeping up with diners that they spent little time greeting them and circulating. Little thought went into the music selection, and there was little personalization of the dining experience. At the most highly rated restaurant, the manager took it upon himself to order small coloring book and crayon sets to give to the little children of diners. A picture of each member of the restaurant staff was on a poster greeting diners when they entered, and each staff member wore a prominent nametag. Within a few minutes of sitting down, all customers were given a small sample of the soup of the day and thanked for visiting. Interestingly, not only were the satisfaction ratings for this restaurant through the roof, but average tips were significant higher as well.

- *Initial service*—The observations with respect to ambiance highlighted the importance of initial service. The successful restaurants greeted customers more quickly than the unpopular ones, and they were significantly quicker to seat customers and take their orders. Indeed, the single factor most responsible for the differences in ratings, Jeff found, was the time it took for customers to be seated, orders to be taken, and food to be served. The more diners had to wait, the lower were their satisfaction ratings. The successful restaurants made a special attempt to greet customers in a friendly way and make them feel welcomed. Even when diners had to wait for a table, the greeter and manager made sure they were given copies of menus to look at so they wouldn't feel their time was wasted. In one case, where a wait was longer than usual, the manager personally apologized and said he would provide the party with free desserts. At the less well-rated restaurants, there was little extra effort to greet customers and accommodate them. Even after the seating, initial service differences stood out between the highly rated and low rated units. Wait staff provided a very friendly greeting at the top restaurants and made special efforts to explain the daily specials and even make recommendations if customers seemed uncertain of what to order. At the bottom restaurants, wait staff simply took orders and did not otherwise actively engage diners. The very top restaurants made sure that diners got a basket of rolls and water very shortly after seating. The bottom restaurants were not similarly proactive. At several, wait staff had to be asked for water.

- *Service during the meal*—At the restaurants with the lowest satisfaction ratings, wait staff seemed to operate on the principle of "no news is good news." They did not stop by the tables frequently, seemingly tied up with taking orders from other diners. At the highest-rated restaurants, wait staff regularly checked with diners after they had received their dishes to make sure everything was OK. Managers also stopped by during the meals to ask how everything was. Coffee and water were promptly refilled at the top restaurants and diners were asked if they wanted bread baskets refilled. This service was less consistent at the lesser-rated units. Jeff specifically made sure to ask wait staff about the preparation of one of the dishes he ordered, pointing out that he wanted the meat to be more well-done. At the top restaurants, the staff responded immediately to his concern, apologizing and taking steps to rectifying. This was always followed by a visit to the table by the manager, who also apologized and—in one case—offered a free dessert. At the bottom-rated restaurants, it took longer for Jeff to catch the attention of the staff. They fulfilled his request, but there were no follow-up visits from the manager. The service felt less personal to Jeff; the staff seemed less committed to the satisfaction of the diner.

- *Quality of food preparation*—In general, Jeff found food preparation to be acceptable across the restaurants, with one notable exception. Because the food was served quicker at the best-rated units, it tended to be warmer than at the lesser-rated places. In several instances at the lesser-rated restaurants, mistakes were made in the food prep. In one case, a salad was served with blue cheese dressing rather than ranch, as requested. In another case, a cut of meat was notably smaller than called for by specs. The notable exception to food prep quality concerned cooked vegetables. These were invariably overcooked at the lowest-rated restaurants, coming out mushy. At the better-rated units, the restaurants were more properly steamed, coming out with some crunch and better flavor. After the meal, Jeff made a point of visiting with the managers of each restaurant and offering feedback. He asked them to escort him through the kitchen, so that he could witness food preparation first-hand. The top restaurants invariably had better organized kitchens, with stations well organized and staffed. At all the top restaurants, food was stored properly; utensils and plates were properly washed and sanitized; and food prep staff took adequate precautions to avoid contaminating food by frequently washing hands and changing gloves. At over half of the bottom-rated restaurants, food was stored on the backroom floor rather than six inches above the ground on shelves; utensils and plates were not air-dried or adequately sanitized with the three-sink washer; and staff failed to consistently wash hands or change gloves after moving from food to food. Jeff concluded that a major difference between the top and bottom units was attention to detail and consistency of execution.

- *Service at the end of the meal*—At the bottom-rated restaurants, diners were often left sitting at their tables long after they had finished. This rarely happened at the top restaurants. The serving staff at the best units was quick to ask diners if they wanted to see a dessert menu and if they wanted additional drinks. They were also quick to bring the check to guests and collect payment if the diners had finished their meals. At the lower-rated units, the service was slower and more inconsistent. On several occasions, Jeff noticed that guests had to flag down wait staff to get their checks. This did not occur at the highly rated restaurants. When Jeff mentioned this to the managers, he found out that the managers at the top units invariably kept an eye on the dining floor and acknowledged serving staff when they provided prompt friendly service. The managers also kept a close eye on the kitchen to ensure that orders were processed promptly. At the lesser-rated restaurants, managers were busy putting out fires and kept a less consistent eye on the dining floor and the kitchen. They had less time to acknowledge staff for good performance and indeed seemed harried much of the time. At the best restaurants, there was always someone present to thank the diners for coming when they left. This was much spottier at the lower-rated units.

What Jeff realized is that the difference between excellence and mediocrity was not just one thing, but a host of details that added up to a very good dining experience or one that failed to stand out. The restaurants served the same food and worked from the same menu. They were laid out similarly with similar furnishings and decorations. Still, some consistently performed well and some consistently fell short. *It was the execution of each phase of the dining process that differentiated the best from the rest.*

	Key Takeaway	

Best practices are observable, measurable actions that differentiate successful performance from average and poor performance.

Based on his observations, Jeff broke down each of the five areas that had guided his note taking—ambiance, service before the meal, service during the meal, food preparation, and service after the meal—into specific actions that distinguished the best restaurants. These were deemed to be *best practices*. Wherever possible, the best practices were captured in detail and quantified. For example, one best practice was greeting customers within a minute of their arrival. Another best practice for wait staff was introducing oneself, serving diners water, and giving them menus within three minutes of their seating. Yet other best practices for the kitchen operation was air drying all dishes, tools, and utensils rather than using cloths and using thermometers regularly to ensure that food being served was a consistent, appropriate temperature. All of the best practices across the five areas were collated and assembled into a checklist that managers could use to ensure that their restaurants were firing on all cylinders. The idea was to standardize the level of quality found at the top-rated units, so that there would be a consistent level of customer satisfaction throughout the business.

Jeff took another step, however. He realized that there might be factors related to best practices that he did not observe. He thus took the step of sharing his findings—and tentative checklist—with the managers of the top and bottom units. He found a high degree of openness to the review process, as the managers of the best restaurants wanted to sustain their performance and the managers of the lowest-performing ones wanted to improve. What Jeff learned, however, surprised him. The managers of the worst-rated units talked extensively about how difficult it was to hire quality help. This was not a major concern for the managers at the top units. When Jeff probed further, he found out that the worst-performing restaurants were located in areas where many jobs were available for young people. Hourly wages and tips at the restaurant simply did not compete well with jobs offered at local manufacturing plants and upscale retail outlets. At the top-performing units, there was less competition for labor and so it was easier to hire quality candidates. Indeed, when Jeff examined the staff turnover rate at the top and bottom restaurants, he found much more stability at the well-rated units. He also saw that there were fewer disciplinary issues at the high-performing restaurants. Quite simply, the better restaurants were able to recruit and retain better staff.

Suddenly, things made sense to Jeff. At the unpopular restaurants, managers had to put out many fires created by a staff that did not follow rules well and that was not particularly motivated. When staff performed better at the more popular units, the managers could then properly oversee operations and attend to quality. This suggested to Jeff that an additional best practice was needed on the human resources side of the business. Staff salaries had to vary from region to region to ensure that each restaurant was competitive for good employees. This led to further discussions at corporate headquarters to brainstorm ways of making employment at the restaurant more attractive to high-quality candidates. A revised schedule of raises and bonuses; a more liberal vacation policy; and a new process that allowed staff to flexibly shift hours with each other were deemed promising by the managers of the restaurants. The managers also suggested structured training programs in the best practices to emphasize their importance and ensure that everyone knew the basics of providing excellent service. This training program went through several evolutions and eventually became a best practice in itself.

What Jeff learned is that *it is important not only to identify best and worst practices, but also to understand why they are there*. The managers of the top and bottom restaurants were all motivated, but the latter group dealt with more personnel problems and thus could not manage their restaurants as effectively. Details fell by the wayside simply because managers had to deal with problems on a regular basis. Without consulting the managers, Jeff would never have learned about the staffing challenges and would never have been able to pursue constructive human resources initiatives. By asking "why" questions and soliciting multiple perspectives, Jeff was able to go beyond his observations and help create fresh best practices pertaining to hiring and retaining talent.

■ Linking Best Practices into Best Processes

Notice also that it wasn't enough to simply give each restaurant a list of best practices and hope that they followed those. Instead, the list was just the starting point for a structured training program that introduced all employees to the idea of high-quality customer service. The best practices were not taught in isolation, but rather were conveyed as a coordinated set of activities that deliver value. For example, the practices of greeting customers, seating them promptly, and getting them menus and water was all part of a high-quality welcoming process. The proper storage of food, drying of dishes and utensils, and correct use of the three-sink washing unit were part of a high-quality food safety process. In the organization of the training, *the best practices came together to form best processes*. The goal was greater than simply getting staff to perform individual actions. It was to coordinate those actions in such a manner as to create consistent, memorable dining experiences.

Most businesses consist of actions that are coordinated as processes. These processes are then linked in such a way as to create superior products or services. In the case of the restaurants, there was a process for welcoming guests and quickly seating them, getting them menus, and bringing them a bread basket and water. There was a separate process for taking diners' orders, communicating those orders to the kitchen, and then bringing the food to the table when it was ready. Within the kitchen, there were several processes, including proper cleaning and sanitation; food storage and safety; proper preparation of food; and proper maintenance of food freshness and temperature. Note that each process reflects coordinated actions and comes with a list of *dos and don'ts*. These reflect best practices and unacceptable ones. Quality control and peak performance require that each process be executed both efficiently (in a timely manner) and effectively (achieving its desired purpose). Dividing processes into best practices helps ensure that efficiency and effectiveness goals are achieved with regularity.

In many fields, the enemy of quality is variability. A restaurant does not want soup delivered to tables at wildly different temperatures. It also doesn't want radically different greeting experiences for customers coming to eat. Quality control is all about minimizing unwanted variability and standardizing high levels of performance. Consider a manufacturing plant that makes the metal cases for laptop computers. One process might take raw sheets of steel, heat them, and cut them. Another process would mold the heated, cut metal into the tops and bottoms of cases. Still another process would stamp holes in the tops and bottoms to place the metal hinges and to accommodate the keyboards and screens. Each process is divided into separate actions that can be considered best practices, such as the selection of unblemished steel; the maintenance of an ideal heating temperature for the metal; and the amount of time spent in heating before cutting and stamping. Line staff oversee the manufacturing processes to ensure that there is uniformity in following these best practices. Should temperatures vary too much, or should there be variation in the quality of steel employed for the cases, the result would be a poorer construction and dissatisfied customers.

A great example of a process-driven business is package delivery, such as at UPS or FedEx. Sophisticated sorting and handling processes route packages to the most efficient routes and standardized delivery processes ensure that expedited packages can arrive within a short amount of time of being sent. Key to the success of the business is the ability to track each package at each step of the delivery process to ensure that best practices are being followed—and that mistakes in the process can be quickly identified and corrected. Each person involved in the business, from the clerk who takes the package and ensures it is properly sealed and addressed to the sorting and handling staff who help route the packages to their destinations to the delivery staff who efficiently pick up and deliver packages, follows a set of performance expectations (handling X packages per minute, for example) and a set of best practice guidelines (screen all packages by x-ray before sending for delivery; leave packages in dry, protected areas if dropped off). A very sophisticated, complicated business can run very efficiently by dividing performance into processes and then dividing processes into best practices that can be performed with regularity.

When a business is a knowledge business and not a manufacturing one, a process orientation becomes more challenging. A knowledge business, such as a medical office or hospital, delivers a range of coordinated services, where customer needs can be different at different times. The level of standardization that one might experience on an assembly line or at a delivery facility is not possible at, say, a hotel, where different guests will have different needs and individualization of service is itself a best practice. A consulting firm will offer different services to different clients; there may be very little overlap in service delivery from one project to another. Trading, in that sense, is a knowledge business: The reading and trading of markets is more like consulting and less like manufacturing widgets. As markets change, the actions taken one day can be quite different from those taken another day.

Key Takeaway

The greatest business successes are ones that have been process driven.

Despite the differences between knowledge and service businesses and manufacturing ones, the improvement of quality through process control has become a major theme across these enterprises. An excellent example is the delivery of healthcare, which for years was guided by the individual judgment of trained physicians. Outcome research found significant differences in recovery rates from various diseases from one hospital setting to another and from one surgical provider to another. Although physicians received similar training, their decision making incorporated large amounts of subjectivity. There were no systematic efforts to integrate research knowledge and findings into clinical practice.

With the development of the Cochrane Collaboration and a centralized database of outcome research, physicians could—for the first time—look up world-class findings on any particular disease, treatment, or procedure and identify more and less successful alternatives to care. In many cases, these findings were assembled into best practices and these formed the backbone of best processes. Now, it is not unusual to come to a hospital for a procedure and have your treatment guided by research-informed protocols. These govern everything from surgical preparation to the dosing of anesthesia to the sterilization of the operating room to the aftercare nursing procedures. Just as a pilot consults a pre-flight checklist to ensure that a plane is safe to fly—a nice example of best practices melded into a process—physicians make use of protocols as their checklists, ensuring that each patient receives quality care.

As mentioned earlier in the book, the anchoring of process control in best practices has even taken hold in a field as seemingly subjective and knowledge-based as the delivery of psychotherapy services. Outcome research has greatly shaped our understanding of who can benefit from shorter and longer-term therapies; who can benefit from psychiatric medications; and who might be optimally treated with a combination of these services. My intake process when I directed a student counseling service took best practices identified in the research literature and turned them into a triage process that routed students to the most effective and efficient forms of help for their particular issues. This resulted not only in very high satisfaction ratings from the students and high utilization rates for the counseling, but also eliminated the problems associated with students being denied services because of long waiting periods. The actual counseling was individualized, of course, but how services were deployed was grounded in the best practices identified by rigorous outcome studies.

Trading offers particular challenges to the identification of best practices and their linkage in best processes. Three particular challenges stand out:

1. *Lack of differentiation*—In the restaurant example, Jeff could visit high-rated restaurants and low-rated ones. In trading, it is not as simple as comparing successful and unsuccessful traders. The restaurants engaged in the same business, preparing and serving the same meals. Traders, on the other hand, can vary wildly in the markets and strategies they trade. Instead of comparing skilled and less skilled traders, it is most informative to study each trader during successful and unsuccessful periods of time. This is not easy, because there is no equivalent of Jeff to study the trader. Indeed, the trader who seeks to improve quality is also the trader who is engaged in markets. The lack of differentiation makes it challenging to be both performer and performance researcher.

2. *Lack of hard research data*—Traders rarely collect outcome data that would enable them to identify best practices. While most traders have data on profits and losses, most would not know the profitability of particular types of trades; the profitability attributable to particular research practices; the profitability attributable to particular position management practices; etc. Whether it is a package delivery service, a manufacturing plant, a chain of restaurants, or a hospital system,

quality control begins with data collection at each phase of the business process. As we saw in the case of the restaurants, we cannot know what works well and what doesn't if we don't track performance from the moment diners enter the door to the moment they receive their check, pay, and leave. Without such outcome data, traders are essentially in the dark about their successes and failures, much as country physicians were many years ago.

3. *Resistance to constraints*—Many traders are attracted to their work precisely because they have the opportunity to work for themselves and not face the constraints of traditional business environments. They resist the notion of best practices and process control, as these seem to limit their freedom of choice. A similar dynamic appeared among healthcare professionals when best practices first came to service delivery. Experienced professionals felt that they knew best how to deliver services; they didn't want practice dictated by external research and protocols. When I first developed the triage protocols at the student counseling service, I faced pushback from therapists who wanted every client to receive long-term therapy or medications. They believed in the efficacy of their work and rebelled against the constraints of research-grounded practice.

Despite these hurdles, we increasingly see professional traders take a process-oriented view toward trading. Nowhere is this more evident than in quantitative finance, where large portions of trading processes—from signal generation to trade execution—are automated. A perusal of highly successful funds, from Bridgewater, AQR, Millennium Partners, and QuantEdge, finds that these have taken a data-driven, evidence-based approach to money management. They win because they are simply more consistent in their ability to identify and exploit trading edges.

■ Steps Toward Becoming a Process-Driven Trader

We can use the example of Jeff and the restaurants to identify steps that traders need to take to ground their work in best practices that are woven into robust, successful processes. Let's take each step in turn and see how it pertains to trading:

1. *Breaking the business down into processes*—Jeff segmented his data collection into five buckets: ambiance; service before the meal; service during the meal; food preparation; and service after the meal.

Each of these was an element of the dining experience essential to customer satisfaction. Having broken the business down into these categories, he could then observe restaurants in each area and compare what was happening in successful vs. unsuccessful units. In my work with traders, I typically break down trading into five buckets: (a) analyzing markets and market-related data and gathering information and research; (b) synthesizing observations and research into trading ideas; (c) expressing those ideas as trades with superior risk/reward and assembling the trades into portfolios that provide superior risk/reward; (d) managing trades, including the taking of profits and losses and management of risk; and (e) self-management, the activities traders engage in to keep themselves in peak performance condition, cognitively, emotionally, and physically.

2. *Gathering observations throughout the processes*—Here, we can most clearly see the difference between the quality-focused trader and the one who is not process oriented. Most traders consider it an act of supreme discipline to keep a trading journal at the end of a trading day or week, documenting mistakes made, goals set, and so on. As we can see from the foregoing example with the restaurants, *such an end-of-day journal is wholly inadequate for process control purposes.* Jeff made observations at every step of the customer-service process, noting problems and best practices at each juncture. A simple end-of-meal review would have lost meaningful detail regarding changes that needed to be made. Similarly, when a package delivery service observes problems in its system, they can go back to their data collection at each phase of processing, so that they can quickly identify where problems went wrong. A trader's end-of-day or end-of-week journal is unlikely to capture all the best and worst practices involved in researching ideas, formulating ideas, expressing ideas as trades, risk managing positions, and managing oneself. Much more effective would be noting what we are doing and how we are doing it during each portion of the trading process so that we understand the variability in our process and how this might impact our trading outcomes.

Key Takeaway

Every trading process needs its own journal.

---

3. *Correlating trading behaviors at each phase of the trading process with the outcomes of trading decisions*—Obviously, we are interested in correlating our actions as traders with our profitability, but detailed analyses will inevitably go further than this. For example, good trading behaviors could lead to lower absolute profitability but higher risk-adjusted returns, as we take more money out of markets per unit of risk taken. Certain behaviors may not show up directly in profitability, but may enhance profitability by keeping us out of bad trades or preventing us from overtrading. As we've seen, profitability in the short run can result from random runs of good or bad luck; hence, the correlation of trading behaviors with trading outcomes needs to be over a considerable number of trades. It is over time that we will see patterns linking particular trading-related actions with favorable and unfavorable trading returns. Over time, also, we will see correlations among the trading behaviors. For instance, low scores in self-management (failing to sustain adequate sleep, exercise, or diet; presence of family or relationship conflicts) may be associated with low scores in idea generation and risk management. These clusters can be important, as they alert us to patterns in our own, personal processes. A trader, for example, may have a general process of discipline that enhances both trading and non-trading areas of life. That would have meaningful implications for quality control.

4. *Using the correlations of trading behaviors and outcomes to identify best and worst practices*—Over time, in each facet of the trading process, actions jump out that are associated with trading wins and losses. These become candidate best and worst practices. I say "candidate" practices, because until we isolate them and make conscious efforts to maximize and minimize them, we don't know for sure whether these truly are effective ingredients of success. In my own trading, I observed a strong relationship between the amount of time spent formulating the trade idea and the profitability of the trading of that idea. When trades were formulated more informally and quickly, they were much less likely to be successful. *The profitable trades resulted not only from more analysis, but different forms of analysis.* I thus spent considerable time on the winning ideas linking intermarket views and macro perspectives with more technical considerations. The best trades captured analyses that spanned weeks and even months of market action; the unprofitable trades did not emphasize the big picture and resulted in forest being lost for trees. My reviews also found that time spent formulating sound entry execution was

associated with profitable trading: Waiting for weakness to buy and bounces to sell enhanced risk/reward. Some best practice patterns were unexpected ones that never would have emerged from informal journal keeping. For instance, my best trades resulted when patterns among different breadth measures lined up; worst trades occurred when I traded without attention to these patterns. This observation led me to take a harder look across the breadth measures and more carefully structure trade ideas in light of them.

5. *Within each facet of trading, assembling the best practices into coordinated, best processes*—Once you have candidate best practices, you want to turn them into reliable routines. By placing them in a sequence and creating a work process that joins them, we can turn many practices into a single, repeatable process. I mentioned above that the amount of time spent researching the trade and the attention to a variety of breadth measures was associated with profitability in my own trading. That led me to structure the research process, where each day I read material from selected, high-quality sources; update spreadsheets for the intermarket and breadth measures of greatest interest; and then use this information to update my thinking by writing out my thoughts spontaneously. This "chunking" of practices into processes helps us turn effortful actions into habits/routines that we internalize. My research process is very structured and has become a natural part of the day, which allows me to complete it efficiently as well as effectively. Similarly, I captured my entry execution criteria as a checklist, which enables me to get into trades according to best practices simply by following the list. Over time, the criteria have become so familiar through repetition that good execution has become more of an automatic habit than an active decision-making process.

6. *Continue to track profitability as a function of practices and processes*—Here we want to treat profitable and unprofitable periods in markets as Jeff treated the well-rated and poorly rated restaurants. Variability in profitability may alert us to variability in our implementation of practices and processes; it may also alert us to best and worst practices that we had not initially observed. One trader I worked with was highly process driven and disciplined and yet noticed meaningful winning and losing periods in his trading. We kept track of his thought process and trading actions across the winning and losing periods and discovered that he was assuming that trends would continue, which worked well in some time periods and not well in

others. This led us to identify best practices associated with trend evaluation and a modification of his review processes so that he could be more mindful of the possibility of trend reversal. It is the ongoing tracking of practices, processes, and outcomes that led us to achieve the goals described earlier in this book: Adapt to changing markets; stay grounded in our strengths; and sustain creativity in viewing and trading markets.

What these steps mean is the successful trader will spend as much time studying his or her trading as studying markets. Much of what contributes to success in trading is what occurs outside of trading hours.

■ How Many Trading Firms Are Truly Process-Driven?

A hallmark of a process-driven enterprise is that you can easily create a flowchart that shows, in detail, how inputs are transformed into outputs. It would be easy for a corporate head like Jeff to create a chart that tracks the flow of customers through the dining process. Similarly, any good hotel manager could readily diagram the processes by which guests are checked into prepared rooms and served during their stays. The offices of primary care physicians have their check-in processes, initial assessments by nursing and allied healthcare staff, chart reviews, interviews with patients, examinations, and checkout processes. Each facet of the business is managed separately: The restaurant kitchen is managed by a chef; the housekeeping at a hotel is assigned to a dedicated manager; and the office operations of a medical practice fall to a business manager. Each manager ensures that his or her area operates by best practices and processes, but it is the coordination of the various areas that leads to seamless, high-quality performance.

At large money management firms, we can observe a similar differentiation of functions and management. One firm that I worked with years ago featured a single, highly experienced portfolio manager and a number of research analysts covering various equity market sectors. Each research team followed its own processes, including modeling the companies being followed; meeting with management; keeping up with industry statistics and news; tracking market performance; and updating long and short recommendations. Senior strategists supervised junior analysts in the research process and frequent meetings ensured that information was shared within teams. Regular meetings between the portfolio manager and the various senior strategists conveyed updated information and guided trading decisions. A separate team of execution traders kept an eye on markets and stocks and provided color on supply and demand for each of the team's longs and shorts. This team divided responsibilities across sectors so that orders could be filled quickly when needed. A back office and accounting staff kept records of all transactions and managed the borrowing of shares, while a risk management staff kept an eye on the overall portfolio and its ever-changing risk exposures. Communications with investors were coordinated by an investor relations staff, who helped market the fund to high-net-worth individuals and institutional investors. A human resource staff handled payrolls, the administration of employee benefits, hiring, and employee performance review. Dividing the various activities of a fund into functional areas and assigning them separate management ensured that the portfolio manager could focus on the firm's investments without being unduly distracted by daily business needs.

Key Takeaway

Following a routine does not make you process-driven.

Being well-organized, however, is very different from being process-driven and grounded in best practices. Each management unit at the aforementioned firm operated relatively smoothly and followed a set of routines. For instance, the hiring process was well-organized, with a recruitment manager collecting resumes, letters of reference, and track record documents and a team of managers deciding who should be interviewed. The interviews were coordinated by the recruitment manager and the group of recruitment managers met regularly to review documents and write-ups of the interviews to decide whom to invite back for more detailed and serious consideration. This organizational structure was efficient, allowing the fund to look at many promising candidates at any given time and pounce on the best ones.

A deeper look, however, suggested that while efficient, the hiring process was not as effective as it could have been. Fully half of new hires did not last beyond their first two-year stint. A small portion of new hires worked out spectacularly poorly, resulting in disciplinary action and firing before the end of the two-year contract. These hiring failures resulted in considerable lost time and effort for the fund managers. In many ways, they were like the restaurant managers who became so busy putting out fires that they could not properly supervise real-time operations.

The problem, quite simply, was that each management unit had never undertaken a systematic study of best and worst practices. Their processes were routines, but they were not best practice driven toward continuous quality improvement. Just within the hiring process, several shortcomings were evident:

- *While there were job specifications for each position, these were not translated into specific competencies and ways of evaluating those.* As a result, for example, programmers were hired on the basis of their self-reported skill and experience level, without detailed, well-constructed tests of their competencies across various programming languages and tasks. Analysts were hired without detailed review of their past research.

- *Interviews were not standardized.* Different interviewers asked different questions at different times, so that candidates for a given position could not be easily compared. Interviewers seemed to be unusually influenced by the likeability of candidates and did not have a structured method for probing skills and experience.

- *Managers were inconsistent in considering internal talent for positions.* This was especially problematic with junior analysts and managers, who often were not considered for more senior roles. The lack of a clear career track for the junior staff led to a crippling loss of staff morale.

- *Managers did not engage in systematic reviews of hiring decisions that didn't work out.* When a new hire either had to be let go or left of his or her accord, there was no institutional effort to identify what had gone wrong and how the problem might have been flagged during the recruitment process. As a result, there was no learning over time and hiring routines remained static—and flawed.

Clearly this was a problem within the human resources operation, but the same lack of best practices and absence of process improvement affected just about every unit within the fund. A notable exception was the investor relations group, which conducted thorough reviews of all calls on investors. They placed key information in a central database to identify how to best follow up with each potential investor. When an ongoing set of visits did not lead to an allocation to the fund, the review process was designed to identify what went wrong and feed that information forward to subsequent efforts. Most units within the fund, however, operated more like the hiring process and less like the investor relations one. For example, the trade execution staff did not regularly updated performance metrics to demonstrate good versus poor fills on positions and the value of discretionary versus systematic execution. Incredibly, the recommendations of analysts at the firm were not tracked for performance. As a result, there was no objective way of determining which team was generating the best ideas and whether the portfolio manager was taking full advantage of the ideas of the teams.

In short, accountability was in short supply within the firm. From year to year, everyone did their job pretty much the same way they had always done it. If you asked any of the managers whether they—or the company—was process-driven, the answer would have been affirmative. They assumed that, because they operated by routines, they were process-focused. Without a clear identification of best practices and ongoing review of performance, however, there was no continuous quality improvement. It was a good firm with a good portfolio manager. But that was the problem. With the right practices and processes in place, it could have been great.

■ ■ ■

The previous example, in my experience, is far more common than most people realize. We assume that large firms must be run effectively, but that is not necessarily the case. Shockingly, many trading organizations have little way of gauging how well they are operating other than their profitability over time. By the time problems become truly problematic, it is sometimes too late to craft solutions.

One trading firm I came across relatively early in my career had a very strange organizational culture. On one hand, it was a friendly firm and traders and managers got along well. On the other hand, I detected an unusual tension at times and a lack of willingness to identify and address problems. This was a proprietary trading firm, led by a single owner who provided the capital being traded. He was quite hands-on in his management style and was involved in most decisions about hiring, firing, promotions, bonuses, and so on. He struck me as hard working and very loyal to his employees. Indeed, many had worked for him for a number of years. This made it all the more surprising to me that there was tension in the ranks.

What I discovered was a widespread perception that longevity at the firm was perceived as a function of how well one got along with the firm's owner. He had his favorites, and those were singled out for the largest bonuses. Employees who had conflicts with the owner or the favorite managers were downgraded in their reviews and had less opportunity for bonuses and advancement. The key problem was that criticism of any operations within the company was taken as disloyalty. One trader, for example, complained about computer problems that took too long to be fixed and that, on a couple of occasions, had interfered with trading. The IT manager took exception to the criticism and in turn accused the trader of blaming his losses on others. Interestingly, other traders experienced similar computer issues but did not raise their concerns, as the IT manager was a personal friend of the owner.

This dynamic showed up in trader meetings as well. Traders were encouraged to attend the meetings and share views and research. Interestingly, however, the traders inevitably waited for the owner to begin the meetings and voice his views. Only then would the traders feel comfortable voicing their own observations and ideas. Rarely would those contradict those of the owner. A new hire, a skilled quantitative analyst, once spoke up at the meeting with a backtest that dramatically contradicted the owner's trade idea. An awkward silence fell across the room and finally the owner dismissed the analysis as being "overfit." Over time, the owner made less and less use of the analyst, who offered only views supported by data. When it became clear that there was no upward path for the analyst, he jumped to another firm and a position of significant responsibility. When I connected with the analyst a few years later, he was no longer an analyst. He was successfully running money at a larger firm. His loss was a major self-inflicted blow for the trading house—and yet that was never acknowledged or corrected.

The incident, however, enlightened me as to why so many trading houses fail to follow a quality improvement agenda. When there is a commitment to best practices and continuous process improvement, *data become the guide to business decisions*: You go where the data take you. For many business owners and managers, however, there is an unwillingness to cede control to the data; they want to run the businesses that they want to run. This brings us back to the first chapter and the example of Emil's restaurant. The former owner wanted to cook meals and serve them *his* way. He had an idea about quality, and that was his commitment. Emil's revolution was to listen to customers and learn about the dining experiences they desired. He allowed the data to create a different restaurant every day. The former owner didn't want to run a different restaurant. At the prop firm, the owner wanted to be the boss. He wanted to work with the people he liked. A process-driven firm makes data the boss. To be quality-focused, you have to work with those who make you better—and those willing and able to listen to the verdicts of objective reality.

■ ■ ■

Most of the proprietary trading firms I've had experience with are considerably smaller than hedge funds and less richly staffed and funded. That poses its own challenges for a process focus. Many prop firms lack central research resources and have a small number of managers handling a broad range of accounting, risk management, and information technology needs. As a result, traders focus on what is in front of them—technical setups—and often fail to see what is happening in the broader market or across markets. Risk management is handled by simple position sizing heuristics and hiring processes are neither consistent nor validated by tracking of results. Many such prop firms enjoy an informal atmosphere that appeals to daytraders. It is that very informality, however, that stands in the way of rigorous quality improvement.

At one proprietary trading firm where several friends worked, a few large traders dominated the P/L. Each had position size limits to ensure that losses would not get out of hand. Unfortunately, there was little oversight of the overall portfolio of traders, so that at times the large traders entered overlapping or identical positions. At those times, the firm took far more risk than managers realized. It was only a matter of time before this resulted in a steep loss and the dismissal of many traders. Without anyone rigorously overseeing risk and applying best practices, the firm discovered its vulnerability too late.

The problem is that there are more processes that go into good trading than can be adequately managed by small firms. With limited capital and a need to eliminate overhead, the average prop firm is heavy on traders (revenue generators) and light on those supporting the traders. No research resources? Trade selection becomes a matter of scouring stocks for chart patterns. No feedback about success and failure? Learning is left to the spotty collection of impressions in journals. No risk management software or expertise? Risk is left to informal sizing guidelines and loss limits. No research on performance? Hiring is left to subjective impressions of interviewers. In each case, process is dumbed down to fit the limited resources allocated. Can such a firm keep up with changing markets? Does it even know about the specific strengths of each trader so that those can be maximized? Can it make the most of the creativity of its traders and develop fresh sources of opportunity?

Key Takeaway

Success hinges on operating within the span of your quality control.

I would love to pump readers up with the idea that all that's needed for trading success is a passion for trading and hard work. That does not fit reality. If you don't have the resources to run a tight ship, you're going to spring leaks. Many, many trading firms fail to survive for the same reason that other small businesses fail: They simply lack the resources to keep up with the competition. The average family clothing store cannot engage in the advertising/marketing research and inventory management of Target or Walmart; the average neighborhood car dealer cannot structure the kind of quality improvement process that typifies Toyota. Traditional trading psychology has enshrined discipline as a cardinal virtue, but following a limited set of trading rules is not sufficient to build and sustain a dynamic business.

Does that mean that there is no future for smaller trading firms? Not at all. After all, there are many successful small businesses, even among the Apples, Amazons, Walmarts, and General Electrics of the world. Consider the small downtown clothing boutique that caters to a local clientele and specializes in sourcing unique fashions from a variety of regional designers. Unlike the large clothing outlets, the boutique offers highly individualized service, knowledgeable sales staff, and the ability to find cutting-edge tops, skirts, dresses, handbags, and accessories. The owners have cultivated close working relationships with a variety of up-and-coming designers. This means that they are first to market with fresh designs and new products. They cannot achieve the sales volume of a department store, but that is not the game they are playing. They survive—and thrive—by being best of breed within their niche.

I recently visited a small proprietary trading firm where several traders combined their capital and joined forces. Each had a unique trading strategy that had proven successful over time. One was an event trader, trading specific patterns that showed up during rollover periods, ex-dividend dates, and options expiration dates. Another limited his trades to very specific volatility breakout patterns in a small number of futures markets. Still another was a relative value trader and focused on stretched relationships between instruments and assets. None of the owner/traders tried to trade throughout the day across a variety of markets. Their trading was sufficiently selective that each could focus on the business as well as the trading opportunities. This selectivity also enabled each of them to focus on the development of new trading strategies, with the goal of rolling out at least one new strategy per trader per year. By hiring quant consultants from overseas, the group was able to outsource segments of the research and development process and stay focused on running the business. The prop firm principals decided to grow the firm only once it had expanded its strategies. Instead of hiring independent traders, they hired assistants to develop and manage the new strategies. Hiring was based on a rigorous set of criteria, including market experience and knowledge, quantitative skill, and programming experience. New hires were given a clear path to partnership based on their ability to develop profitable niche trading strategies. Like the clothing boutique, the successful prop firm did not try to be all things all the time. It built a business around its distinctive strengths and stayed highly focused on what it did well.

Small succeeds with focus. This is very important.

■ How Can Individual Traders Be Process Driven?

As touched on earlier, one of the greatest misunderstandings traders have about process orientation is that routine is the same as process. I have a morning routine of greeting and feeding my cats, having coffee and a bite to eat, checking markets, exercising, and showering up for the day, but one would be hard pressed to call that a process orientation to work or life. Now suppose I broke down each aspect of my morning routine, varied it, tracked it, and correlated it with my day's psychological state and productivity. Over time, I might learn that more time—and more vigorous time—spent in exercise is associated with higher energy level through the day and greater productivity. I might also find out that a greater amount of time spent with the cats is associated with a higher degree of calm and satisfaction, leading to better trading decisions. Those observations would lead me to refine my morning routine over time, so that it becomes better and better at generating desired personal and professional outcomes. *That* is process orientation.

Filling out a checklist or journal can help us stay more mindful of our states and actions, but does not, in itself, constitute a process orientation. It is only when the assessment of outcomes leads to systematic efforts to change our efforts that we exercise true process and quality control. When most traders state that they follow "a process," what they really mean is that they engage in regular routines. This may help their efficiency, but over time will not enable them to become more effective.

The previous discussion of process control for small trading firms becomes especially relevant when considering the individual trader. The true solo trader acts as business/risk manager, money manager, and trading coach. Researching markets, assembling observations and data into trading ideas, executing and managing trades, and managing one's own performance: All of those functions must be filled by the same person. Not surprisingly, this exceeds the bandwidth of most people. The typical result once again is a dumbing down of process. A simple checklist substitutes for true, systematic process measurement and improvements. A simple screen for technical criteria substitutes for true, tested market research. Casual rules of thumb for position sizing substitute for rigorous methods of risk management. The average individual trader is like the solo person trying to run a restaurant. Unable to buy the foods and supplies, keep the restaurant clean, bus the tables, wash the dishes, prepare the food, and serve the customers, the solo restaurateur finds it impossible to stay in business. The only way to accomplish all those things is to let so many details slide that the loss of quality becomes fatal.

This is not a perspective one typically finds in the trading literature: *Many trading problems—and emotional problems related to trading—are a function of one person needing to do too many things to run a trading business well. It is lack of bandwidth, not lack of desire or effort, that ultimately undermines many independent traders.*

I hear from many solo traders who follow the TraderFeed blog. Most ask thoughtful questions and strike me as diligent in their pursuit of trading profits. The most common problem I hear about is that they are simply too absorbed in markets and trading to monitor and work on their performance. They can handle the tasks of research, trading, and self-management in a sequential fashion, but lack the bandwidth to multitask across these roles. A large part of the problem is that many solo traders are also active traders, so that trading occupies a large proportion of mindshare and energy. With the inevitable loss of concentration and willpower comes a flagging of discipline and a loss of self-awareness, leading to bouts of poor trading. It is the cognitive load of the work, handled by a single individual, which often is the root problem.

What we saw with the proprietary trading firm described above was that a high degree of focus made demands on bandwidth less burdensome and enabled the firm to succeed with relatively modest resources. I have seen this same dynamic at work with successful daytraders and swing traders. One very successful trader I have known for years only trades at certain times of day when certain patterns set up. Another trades through the day but takes a lengthy midday break to exercise, renew concentration, review performance, and make adjustments. An unusually disciplined trader I met through the blog monitors markets through the day, but only trades a few times per month based on the lining up of shorter- and longer-term indicators and time frames. In each case, selectivity enables the individual trader to play to his or her strengths, but also to have the time and energy to track markets, engage in research, monitor performance, and make steady improvements. To use the earlier analogy, the individual chef might not be able to run a restaurant on a solo basis, but could conceivably run a profitable catering business. Spending a day preparing a meal for the evening is very different from preparing different meals for many people all evening.

What this suggests is that *becoming process driven as an individual trader requires an approach to trading that is cognitively and psychologically sustainable.* The individual trading approach must be more like the catering business and less like the all-night diner. This is particularly true for developing traders who work a day job to make ends meet while learning the trading ropes. The approach to trading must fit around the day job and thus cannot occupy full bandwidth throughout the day. Longer timeframe positions or short timeframe positions managed during limited trading hours become mandatory. The key to sustainability is that the trading approach must leave time and energy for thoughtful performance reviews and planned efforts to factor lessons learned into future trading processes and decisions. Without such review and adjustment of efforts, there can be no adaptation to changing markets and no steady improvement in performance.

Key Takeaway

Success requires a process for improving your processes.

So let's wrap up: Trading itself requires a number of coordinated activities, including the analysis of data; the synthesis of information into trading ideas; and the management of trades based on those ideas. While all that is going on, the trader also faces the need for self-management—managing energy, mood, and concentration—and the need for ongoing monitoring of performance, identifying of best practices, and weaving of those best practices into ongoing trading processes. In large trading firms, there are enough managers and technology resources to deploy for trading-related activities that traders can focus more readily on self-management and process improvement. When traders lack those resources, trading must become focused and highly efficient, so that there is sufficient time to attend to the needs of the entire trading business. If the demands of trading don't leave time to run and improve each facet of the trading business, the business model is fatally flawed. Trading must fit into a business plan; one cannot meet business needs ad hoc around one's trading.

■ Conducting a Process Review of Your Trading Business: Twenty Sets of Questions

Becoming more process oriented starts with asking the right questions. Here are 20 sets of questions that can help you review your performance and begin the journey toward identifying best practices and linking them as robust processes.

Information Collection and Analysis:

1. Which market displays on my screens do I routinely use and benefit from? Which ones don't I use? Which ones have not provided benefit? How can I create more streamlined displays that will enable me to efficiently focus on the information that is most relevant and important for my trading? What information is not displayed on my screens that would add value to what I already look at? What ways of displaying the information would be most helpful to me: Charts? Tables? Multiple time frames? Color coded? Set with alerts? How do I typically make use of my screens when I'm trading well? How do I typically make use of my screens when I'm trading poorly?

2. What sources of market-relevant information do I routinely read and benefit from? Which sources don't I make use of? Which sources

have not provided me with benefit? What are sources of market information that other, successful traders are making use of and how could I incorporate those? What market information do I focus on when I'm trading well? What market information do I focus on when I'm trading poorly? Do I find greater benefit reading market material before or after trading sessions? During the week or during weekends? How do I record and track the insights that I've gained from my readings so that I do not forget them? How can I streamline my reading time so that I am wasting a minimum of time?

3. What sources of market-relevant information do I routinely listen to and benefit from, such as newscasts, online videos, and television? Which sources don't I make use of? Which sources have not provided me with benefit? What sources of market information do other, successful traders listen to and how might I make use of those? What market information do I listen to when I'm trading well? When I'm trading poorly? How can I streamline my listening time so that I'm working as efficiently as possible?

4. What sources of market-related conversations do I routinely seek out and benefit from? Which conversations don't contribute materially to my trading? Which conversations have interfered with good trading? What conversations am I having when I am trading well? When I am trading poorly? Whom do I know and respect in markets who could be a valuable source of information and conversations? When have conversations been most helpful to my trading? Before market hours? During market hours? After hours? During weekends? How do I track insights from my market conversations so that I don't forget them?

5. How do I analyze market relevant data that I am examining? How do I establish whether a given set of data is meaningful to trading or not? How do I distinguish significant information from information that reflects mere noise? How do I validate the conclusions of what I hear or read? How do I test patterns that may be present in the data I observe? How do I analyze information when I am trading well? When I am trading poorly? What additional data analysis skills do I observe among other, successful traders that I incorporate into my work?

Synthesizing Information into Ideas:

6. How do I review all of the information that I gather during the day and week? How do I compare information coming from

different sources? How do I review information when I am trading well versus poorly? How do I identify situations where different information leads to the same conclusion? When information leads to contradictory conclusions? Do I conduct my best information reviews by reading? Discussing? Drawing or diagramming? What kinds of reviews lead to the generation of good ideas? What kinds of reviews are not productive? How can I improve the productivity of my reviews?

7. How do I ensure that I review and emphasize information that doesn't fit with my preexisting views? How do I use my review to ask new, difficult questions that require further research? How do I use my review to add to confidence in my ideas?

8. How do I make use of other traders when I'm reviewing information and generating ideas through brainstorming discussions and mutual questioning? How do I look further into ideas I obtain from others to understand them and make them my own? How do I make use of research resources and analyses to dig deeper into initial ideas that I generate?

9. What routines enable me to best step back from analysis and engage in the synthesis of ideas? How do I make use of technology and statistical analysis to aid my generation of ideas? When do I engage in my best idea generation? Start of the day? End of the day? Weekends? How do I make sure I have quality time each day or week to engage in sound idea generation?

10. How do I handle situations when I come up with few ideas? Trade less? Return to the research process? How do I handle situations when I generate more ideas than I can possibly trade? How do I prioritize those ideas and decide which ones to focus on? What are the characteristics of the ideas that have most often made me money? Most often lost me money?

Managing Trades and Risk:

11. How do I best express ideas as trades when I am trading well? Are my best trades expressed in risk-limited ways (hedged, through options) or as outright directional positions? How do I look at different possible trading vehicles for my trade idea to achieve an optimal risk/reward relationship? How do other, successful traders express their ideas as trades when their views are similar to mine? Do I express my ideas through multiple trades in multiple markets or in concentrated form in just one or two markets?

12. How do I select trades that fit well into a portfolio and balance my risks? How do I track the correlations among my positions and adjust my risk exposure when correlations rise? How do I track market volatility and the volatility of my positions and adjust my risk exposure when volatility rises? How much risk do I typically take when I am trading well? When I am trading poorly?

13. How do I make use of stop-loss levels to reduce my risk exposure for each position? How do I ensure that stops are not placed too close to the market? How do I adjust stop levels when the position has moved in my favor? How do I adjust stop levels when market volatility significantly increases or decreases? How do I calculate a stop-loss level for my overall portfolio to reduce my total risk exposure?

14. How do I size my positions to keep potential losses manageable but also to ensure that gains will be meaningful? How do I add to positions or take them off during the course of a trade, and how much profitability is added by my adjustments to position sizing? How do I track and manage my overall portfolio sizing and risk taking to ensure that worst-case losses across positions will be manageable? How do I size positions and portfolios to ensure that expectable series of losing trades will not lead to risk of ruin? How does my profitability vary as a function of position sizing? Do I truly get paid when I take more risk?

15. How do I set profit targets for my trades that are realistic and that ensure that I have a favorable reward-to-risk level? How do I adjust profit targets for market volatility? How do I manage positions as they get closer to targets? Do I tend to place targets too close (so that markets often run further) or too distant? How do I set targets when I trade well and when I trade poorly? How do other, skilled traders I know take profits in their trades and how could I learn from them?

Self-Management:

16. How do I organize my time before, during, and after trading to maximize my trading performance? How do I use pre-market, post-market, and weekend time when I am trading well versus poorly? How do other, successful traders I know organize their time? How do I use breaks in the trading day when I am trading well and poorly?

17. How do I manage my lifestyle when I am trading well? When I am trading poorly? How much sleep do I get; how well do I eat; what kind of exercise do I perform; what kinds of social activities do I engage in; what kinds of intellectual and spiritual activities do I pursue when I am performing at my best? At my worst?

18. How do I generate emotional well-being when I am performing at my best versus worst? What do I do on a regular basis to generate experiences of happiness, satisfaction, energy, and affection? Which activities most give me energy and contribute to positive trading performance? Which activities rob me of energy and detract from performance?

19. How do I manage the emotions involved in trading when I am trading well? When I am trading poorly? Which actions enable me to avoid frustration, discouragement, overexcitement, overconfidence, and complacency when I am trading? Which actions contribute to negative emotional experience when I am trading: anger/frustration, depression, guilt, and anxiety/worry? How do I stay mindful of my emotional state when I am trading well? How do I handle emotional situations when I identify them in real time?

20. How do I use my observations of my thoughts, emotions, and behavior to improve my performance as a trader? How do I review my performance, personally and professionally, to make sure I learn from what I do well and poorly? How do I set goals to keep me on a path of improvement? How do successful traders I know work on their self-improvement?

Per the earlier discussion, this set of 20 questions should lead you to identify best and worst practices in each area of trading and provide you with raw materials for establishing and reconfiguring trading processes. Please note that it is not necessary—or desirable—to focus on all potential best practices at one time. Rather, you could use the above review to identify the single improvement to each area of your trading—information collection, idea generation, trade management, and self-management—that would make the greatest positive difference in your trading. Once you turn those best practices into ongoing routines, you are then ready to tackle the next set of process improvements. *You don't want to tackle new practices until you fully assimilate the ones you initially target.* The idea is to stay within your bandwidth and set yourself up for success. Fewer goals that you work on intensively are better than a large number of goals that only receive half efforts.

Your efforts at performance improvement should yield positive emotional experience, not frustration.

Realize also that performance rises and falls simply as a function of random variability of markets, so that it takes a while to determine whether a given process improvement is indeed bearing fruit. All too often traders attempt improvements, don't see immediate results, and become discouraged, abandoning subsequent efforts. In some areas, you will notice results rather quickly, such as steps you might take to improve your emotional outlook or energy level. In other areas, such as improving your research process, it may take months to determine whether your idea generation is contributing to better trading performance. One hazard of attempting multiple process improvements at one time is that it can become difficult to determine which improvements truly led to enhanced performance. If you have been profitable but find plenty of room for improvement, you want to make sure that you don't abandon what you're doing well in the search for doing things better. A targeted, steady approach to change, focusing on highest yield areas for improvement, is most likely to meet with success.

A Few Observations on Process Improvement

Pulling together a number of strands from the book to this point, I'd like to offer a few perspectives on process improvement and trading success:

- *What is the vision?* Earlier we looked at trading as an entrepreneurial enterprise. Like any startup, a trading business needs not only funding and clear plans, but an animating vision. For the startup business, the vision is often to capture a unique opportunity in a unique way and fill a need in a way that brings growth and economic success. I'm not sure I perceive a vision behind the trading of many market participants. Too often, the focus is on figuring out the next trade and getting through the current day and week. Success for businesses begins with a clear vision of strengths, opportunities, and mission. What do you do superlatively well in your trading, and what is your source of advantage in the marketplace? What are you trying to build as a business? Where do you want to be five years from now? It's great to make steady improvements, but ideally those improvements should be directed toward a set of longer-term goals. So often, it's the power of the vision that gets entrepreneurs through the long hours of the startup process.

- *What skills do you need to learn?* Just this morning, I worked for a few hours on an improved set of measures for price momentum and volatility. The goal was to create a momentum measure that was sensitive to multiple time frames and a volatility measure that incorporated both realized and implied volatility. Without basic database, statistics, and spreadsheet skills, I would have never been able to conduct the investigation. The idea that discretionary trading makes no use of numbers, statistics, or inferential reasoning is madness. In most fields—from medicine to engineering—the judgments of professionals emerge from careful observation and measurement. If all you have is a chart and a few canned indicators, you are missing much of what drives markets. *In many cases, process improvements require skill upgrades.* The successful trader is willing to acquire the skills needed to identify and exploit market opportunity. The unsuccessful trader expects markets to accommodate his or her skill sets. Acquiring better data, better software for displaying and manipulating data, better skills for analyzing data, better methods for generating ideas, better tools for managing risk—all contribute to a learning curve that can make you better over time.

- *Where does trading fit into your life?*—If you're an average teacher or short-order cook, you can make a living. If you are an average trader, you lose money and go out of business. This is an important facet of what differentiates performance domains from other vocational fields. The average gymnast, baseball player, or chess player does not make a living from his or her activities. Most actors or artists do not support themselves through their work. In performance fields, economic success is a function of elite performance: Many are called, few actually selected for success. Much of *Trading Psychology 2.0* has dealt with trading as a true performance domain, where constant improvement and peak performance become norms. What this means is that, for the vast majority of readers and traders, markets will not provide economic security. That doesn't mean you can't be profitable, and it doesn't mean that developing yourself as a trader is a waste of time. Throughout my career, trading has provided a supplemental income, not my primary living. I enjoy the challenge of trading and believe that developing myself as a trader has contributed to my general self-development. I have ensured, however, that trading fits into my life and not vice versa. A clear perspective on where trading stands in your life will help you define success in realistic terms. Fantasies are not business plans; eyes on the stars and feet on the ground is a great formula for the pursuit of success in any business.

- *Enjoy the journey*—You will never sell the top tick or buy the bottom one with consistency. There will always be opportunities missed, profits that reverse, and losses that extend. There will always be traders who "catch the move" that you miss and there will always be people who trade larger accounts and make more money than you. Too many traders implicitly define movement as opportunity and then castigate themselves for "leaving money on the table." Perfectionism is a great formula for frustration and discouragement. As a performance professional, you want to focus on one goal: getting better. The best yardstick for your goals is whether they inspire, energize, and guide your development, or whether they lead to frustration and disappointment. When you focus on self-improvement, you place yourself in control of your development and ensure that goals are challenging, stimulating, and achievable. If trading is not a source of well-being, it will not be a source of success.

- *Stay honest with yourself*—Right here, right now, with respect to your trading, give yourself a report card. How would you grade yourself in your ability to adapt to different market conditions? Your understanding of the specific strengths that contribute to your success and your organization of your trading around those skills? Your creative ability to generate fresh ideas—and fresh sources of market edge? Your identification of your best practices and development of processes that keep you grounded in those processes? An honest, self-appraisal has to precede meaningful efforts at change. You may believe yourself to be a promising trader, but are you running a promising trading business? If someone else were running the trading business that you're currently running, would you become an investor in that company?

Key Takeaway

The greatest challenge traders face is remaking themselves when they've been successful in the past.

Traditional trading psychology has been all about taming the emotional forces that can lead to poor trading decisions and actions. Its focus was primarily on reducing cognitive and emotional negatives in trading, so that traders could consistently exploit their edge in markets. *Trading Psychology 2.0* starts with the understanding that sources of edge in markets are always changing. Success is not assured by simply reducing psychological negatives; we must leverage our strengths and best practices to ensure that we evolve as markets evolve. In the remainder of this chapter, we will examine an array of best practices—some related to psychology, some to trading, some contributed by TraderFeed readers, some based on my coaching experience—that will help you kick-start your growth from Trader 1.0 to Trader 2.0.

■ Fifty-Seven Best Practices for Trading Success

The philosopher Brand Blanshard once observed that most people "live like raisins in a cake of custom." If we do things the consensus way, the odds are quite high that we'll do them in suboptimal fashion. What is customary is usually not what is best aligned with our talents, skills, and interests. Living in a cake of custom may be comfortable, but it is not a formula for personal or professional distinction.

I have found that some of my best practices were inspired by others and then adapted to best fit me and my trading. In the spirit of offering raw material for your own inspiration and adaptation, here are 57 best practices. A number of these best practices are ones that I have observed among successful traders. Still others are ones that I have developed to aid my own trading. A large number come from readers of the TraderFeed blog in response to a call that I placed late in 2014. Not all the practices will speak to you or your ways of trading, but even if you find value in a handful of the ideas, those can catalyze changes across multiple areas of your performance.

Best Practice #1: Tracking a Basket of Stocks to Anticipate Market Moves and Themes

If we're trading a stock-market-sector ETF or a broad market index, it's natural to track charts of what we're trading. We look for trends, ranges, breakout moves, areas of high and low volume, and the like. Many times, however, what the broad market is setting up to do in the future is telegraphed by what leading stocks are doing right now. A classic example occurred in 2007, as financial shares led the market weakness that fully manifested in 2008. One of the reasons I like tracking new highs and lows on a one-month and three-month basis is to identify the shares that are showing strength in a weak market and weakness in a strong market. Any individual stock can buck the overall market due to idiosyncratic factors. When we see a number of shares moving contrary to the broad averages, however, very often it's a tell worthy of attention. For example, when the capitalization weighted Dow and S&P averages make a new high, but a large proportion of individual stocks stay in a range, it's often worth questioning the seeming breakout.

For a number of years, I've tracked a basket of stocks highly weighted within the large-cap indexes as a way of gauging the breadth of market strength or weakness. In my current basket, I have 10 stocks that I follow in each of nine sectors, plus 10 sector and specialty index ETFs. Here is the current basket:

- *Consumer discretionary*—(XLY)—CMCSA, DIS, HD, AMZN, MCD, TWX, FOXA, NKE, LOW, SBUX
- *Consumer staples*—(XLP)—PG, KO, WMT, PM, CVS, MO, PEP, WBA, COST, CL
- *Financials*—(XLF)—BRK.B, WFC, JPM, BAC, C, AXP, USB, AIG, GS, MET
- *Technology*—(XLK)—AAPL, MSFT, VZ, T, FB, GOOG, INTC, IBM, ORCL, TWTR
- *Industrials*—(XLI)—GE, UNP, MMM, UTX, BA, HON, UPS, CAT, DHR, LMT
- *Materials*—(XLB)—DD, MON, DOW, PX, LYB, PPG, ECL, APD, FCX, IP
- *Energy*—(XLE)—XOM, CVX, SLB, KMI, COP, EOG, OXY, PXD, APC, WMB
- *Utilities*—(XLU)—DUK, NEE, D, SO, EXC, AEP, SRE, PCG, PPL, EIX
- *Health care*—(XLV)—JNJ, PFE, MRK, GILD, AMGN, ABBV, BMY, UNH, CELG, BIIB

- *Specialty sector and index*—IYR (real estate), KRE (regional banks), SMH (semiconductors), XME (mining), IJR (small caps), MDY (midcaps), QQQ (NASDAQ 100), IWC (microcaps), IWM (Russell 2000), XHB (homebuilders)

For the most part, the stocks in each group account for more than half the total weighting in the respective sector ETF. Any broad move in a sector—or any broad stock market move—will include these shares as a result. To achieve a broader view of the market, the last group of sector and index ETFs looks at small- and medium-cap shares as well as specialty sectors.

There are many ways of using the basket to diagnose the broader market, some of which I will outline as separate best practices. My initial screen is simply looking through charts in rapid succession and seeing how many of the shares make fresh highs or lows; how many hold above prior support or below prior resistance; how many close near daily highs or lows; and so on. When the broad market is topping out, for example, it is common to see a number of shares within one or more sectors fail to make fresh highs even as stocks in other sectors continue higher. Noting such divergences not only provides an alert for a near-term market top but also highlights the shares that might be most vulnerable in any pullback.

Another value of the stock basket is tracking stocks and sectors trading with unusual volume relative to their peers. Very often, high volume will be an alert that institutional investors are either acquiring or distributing shares, suggesting that particular sectors are gaining or losing favor. When this occurs across sectors, it can be a useful alert for a broader trending move in the market.

The takeaway here is that we can learn a great deal about the broad stock market from the bottom up—by looking at the behavior of constituent shares. Tracking the stocks that are most highly weighted in sector and index averages can provide useful alerts for what is occurring beneath the surface of those averages.

Best Practice #2: Tracking Volatility and Correlations among Sectors

This is really a formalization of the first best practice, but with a more specific application. A bit of background will help explain why it is helpful to track realized volatility and correlations across a basket of stocks, such as the one outlined above. Consider the market as moving in cycles, where there is no fixed cycle duration or amplitude. In other words, cycles will vary in their length and degree of their rise and fall, but generally posses a common structure. An examination across multiple cycles finds that stocks typically make a bottom on increased correlation among stocks and increased volume and volatility. When the broad averages bounce from a bottom area, it typically is with a continuation of enhanced volume and volatility. During this vigorous up phase of the rise, most shares will participate in the strength and we will see momentum effects: strength leading to continued strength. At some point we reach a momentum peak, with a large proportion of shares making fresh new price highs on solid buying volume. From there, we begin to see distribution among weaker stocks and sectors, even as overall averages can drift higher. During this topping phase, volume and volatility tend to be more restrained and correlations decrease, as sectors begin to move their own ways. Eventually the topping process results in failure of a critical mass of shares to sustain the rise, leading to increased selling and an increase in volume, volatility, and correlation.

Key Takeaway

Looking at the parts of the market can tell us a great deal about the whole.

I track the realized volatility for each of the sectors in my basket in an Excel workbook. I also compute the correlation of each sector with every other sector and compute a running average. Typically, I'll track both volatility and correlation over moving 20-day periods. This provides a useful heads-up for topping markets (falling volatility and correlation) and bottoming ones (stretched volatility and correlation). Backtests of high and low correlation and volatility values are informative: Returns at high levels of correlation and volatility have been significantly more positive than at low levels.

In general, correlation tells us when markets are moving in unison (behaving as a stock market) and when they are moving idiosyncratically (behaving as a market of stocks). Strong trends typically feature strong correlations; range markets frequently occur with more restrained correlations. Volatility is highly correlated with volume and helps us see when large market participants are active in the market. On average, a move with high correlation and volatility has more juice—and more likelihood of continuation—than one with lower values of each. This is a fertile area for testing relationships and developing quant rules for guiding discretionary trading.

Can correlation be of use to the day trader who does not trade multiday cycles? In an informal way, I believe this can be the case. In my quote platform, I have the names of the stocks in my basket and track how they are trading during the day *from the market open*. The symbols are color-coded: They are green if the stock is trading above its market open and red if it's trading below its open. A quick tell for a trend day is that the vast majority of shares will trade above or below their market open. A mixed set of red and green symbols is more characteristic of a mixed—and range-bound—market. The count of red and green gives a rough sense for correlation on the day time frame.

How about volatility? Because volume and volatility are so well correlated, looking at how today's volume compares with that of recent days provides a useful clue as to the relative participation of large traders in the market. It takes a healthy degree of participation from large, directional players to sustain a market move: Volume can be useful in differentiating moves that will extend (higher volatility) versus those more likely to die out and reverse (lower volatility). This is especially helpful in gauging moves to fresh price highs or lows and especially out of prior price ranges.

In general, knowing what average volume has been at each time of day helps us identify when today's market is attracting or cutting off business. When we see that one sector is attracting unusually high volume relative to other sectors, this can act as a useful heads-up on a rotational trade. The short-term trader needs movement to profit: Going where the volume is can put volatility on your side. *Ideally, you want to identify opportunities in which both direction and volatility will move in your favor.* The failure to track volume/volatility during the unfolding of a trade is responsible for much poor trade management, as it becomes easy to overstay one's welcome in shrinking volatility markets and exit prematurely when volatility is expanding.

Best Practice #3: Tracking Price Action, Volatility, and Correlation Across Asset Classes

Many traders only follow the market they are currently trading. In some cases, they only follow the individual stock they are trading.

Unsurprisingly, they get run over when larger market developments swamp the demand and supply for what they are trading. I recall sitting with a daytrader who was having performance difficulty. The market was opening and he talked out his trade ideas. He was especially keen on selling a particular stock, as he saw indications of selling pressure in its order book. Meanwhile, I was looking at the behavior of overseas stock markets, commodities, and fixed income markets and was noticing a general risk-on tendency. I pointed this out to the trader, who remained adamant that his stock was seeing selling pressure. It did indeed move down a bit at the open before reversing sharply and trading higher, stopping him out. He read the order flow just fine; it was just that the order flow was eventually swamped by ETF-driven demand, as his stock was a key constituent of several ETFs and sector funds. Without tracking his stock's correlation to the broader market, he was vulnerable to the move against him.

The same dynamic occurs when a trader watches only the stock market and fails to observe what is happening in other equity markets and across other asset classes. Large money managers trade macroeconomic themes that cut across multiple regions of the world, asset classes, and instruments. Many times a theme will be most apparent in the trading of one or two markets, but not in the market you may be focused on. For example, as of this writing, central banks have been quite activist with monetary policy, buying bonds and adding liquidity to their economies. This impact has tended to show up first in the trading of currencies and only over time in terms of equities. Understanding moves in rates and currency markets has been extremely helpful for stock market traders, as those moves highlight an important driver of price. Similarly, global economic weakness may show up first in emerging markets or in a particular region of Europe and only later spread to other economies. It is very helpful to see when global markets are rising or falling together and when they are out of sync. Weakness abroad is often a harbinger of domestic weakness.

Tracking multiple asset classes is also useful in identifying when large, macro traders are dominating markets. This is important because many of those traders are directional and, as a group, can move markets significantly. Recently, a data release showed unexpected weakness in the US economy. The response of many markets was swift: Stocks sold off, the US dollar weakened, bonds rallied, and gold rose. This pattern of market reaction suggested that macro traders were repricing markets to account for the new information. That in turn was a useful tell for a trending day trade. Markets can move idiosyncratically, as when stocks rise on good earnings news, or markets can move thematically, as when stocks have risen with other assets in response to central bank action. It is the thematic behavior of markets that leads to some of the best trend trades.

On my quote board, I like to see market action across different regions of the world and I like to see prices from a variety of fixed income instruments, commodities, stock indexes, and currencies. If the US dollar is up versus the euro currency, I want to look at other dollar crosses to see if there is general dollar strength or euro weakness. If stocks are up in Europe and Asia, I want to see how the bullishness carries over to the US open. Configuring your quote board to see many markets and many parts of the world at one glance enables you to detect those situations in which markets are in sync, sending an important thematic story. Conversely, seeing some markets move and others refuse to budge can be an early sign of money rotating from some markets to others with greater perceived opportunity. Like a football quarterback, you want to see the whole field, not just the receiver you intend to receive your pass.

Best Practice #4: Tracking Real-Time Buying and Selling Pressure with TICK

The NYSE TICK ($TICK) is a tool I find invaluable for both short-term trading and longer-term position trading. How the indicator is used, however, needs to differ for traders of shorter and longer time frames.

First, however, a quick review: The NYSE TICK looks at stocks in the NYSE Composite Index each second of the trading day and determines whether each stock is trading on an uptick or on a downtick. The sum of all upticks minus downticks is the reading for TICK for that second. For my own intraday trading, which is not high frequency, I track NYSE TICK in real time when executing a trade and on a one- and five-minute basis for my analysis. What the TICK tells us is whether buyers or sellers are more aggressive at any point in time. If buyers are eager to enter the market, they will lift offers and cause upticking. Conversely, if sellers dominate and act with urgency, they will hit bids and cause downticking. Values of NYSE TICK near zero show no particular dominance of buyers or sellers and are common in quiet markets. Trending moves often get underway with very high or low TICK readings. Seeing such extreme buying or selling as prices move to new highs or lows can be very helpful in gauging the degree of interest and participation behind the moves.

Very high or low TICK readings are meaningful for another reason. When TICK hits +800 or more or −800 or less, it means that a large proportion of shares are not only upticking or downticking, but upticking or downticking *at the same time*. This is very important. When stocks move in the same direction at the same time, it means that they are being bought or sold in large baskets. This can only happen if large, institutional participants are leaning one way or another; individual traders and small trading firms cannot sustain such basket activity. For this reason, high or low TICK values provide a useful footprint for the activity of large market participants.

When we see a very large number of very high TICK values and not many low values, an upside trend day is likely underway, and vice versa. When we don't see many high or low values, on the other hand, it is more likely that we're seeing a low-volatility, range-bound market. It is not unusual to see both very high and very low TICK readings as markets make important lows and rise from those lows. Indeed, it is the wholesale dumping of stocks that attracts longer-time-frame participants seeking value, creating the situation in which very low TICK readings are followed by very high ones—a common pattern at important market lows.

I also find NYSE TICK to be quite useful for tracking the trending behavior of the market. By adding each minute's TICK reading to a cumulative total, we can see if buyers or sellers are dominating over time. During a trend day, TICK will spend most of its time above or below zero, which means that the cumulative TICK will move steadily higher or lower. Range markets will show restrained TICK action fairly evenly distributed around the zero level, creating a relatively flat cumulative TICK line. In my longer-term position trading, the cumulative TICK is quite useful in tracking buying and selling interest from day to day. It is not at all unusual for the cumulative TICK to top ahead of price during market cycles and for individual TICK readings to bottom ahead of price. If you construct a short-term momentum indicator of the cumulative TICK (x-day change), you'll also notice a tendency for the momentum measure to top and bottom ahead of price during intermediate market cycles.

Key Takeaway

Aggregating high-frequency data can shed light on longer time frames.

The most common way to track upticking and downticking is NYSE TICK ($TICK), but other measures of upticking and downticking are useful. One that I follow regularly is upticking and downticking across all stocks listed on US exchanges. The e-Signal platform uses the symbol $TICK.US-ST for this very broad measure of ticking. Because it includes all stocks, not just those listed on the NYSE, it is sensitive to the behavior of smaller shares and those listed on NASDAQ. It is not particularly unusual to observe divergences between the NYSE and US versions of TICK. These generally reflect the relative strength of larger versus smaller capitalization shares and can provide an indication of when it could be useful to express stock market views in the Russell 2000 Index, for example, versus the S&P 500 Index. $TICK.NQ-ST reflects the upticks and downticks specific to the stocks in the NASDAQ 100 Index and again can provide useful information when it diverges from the NYSE TICK. When all the TICK measures are consistently staying above or below zero, we generally have a strong indication of a trending market. Often I will glance at a one-minute or five-minute chart of TICK measures on the day time frame and look for shifts in the distribution of values. These shifts can be a great tell for intraday shifts in supply and demand and can provide useful entry and exit points for trades.

Best Practice #5: Using the Dow TICK ($TICKI) to Track Program Trading

The cumulative upticks and downticks for the general market are very useful in detecting the breadth of market strength and weakness. The upticks and downticks for the Dow 30 stocks, however, form a very different distribution. Because the Dow 30 stocks are important constituents of many market indexes, they are actively traded and uptick and downtick rapidly. In any given minute, we can swing from values of +18 to −16, as a majority of Dow shares undergo first buying and then selling. The Dow TICK ($TICKI) is more volatile than other TICK measures precisely because the Dow shares trade many times each minute.

There are several valuable uses for the $TICKI. The first is to use it as a gauge of buying and selling interest specific to large-cap shares. Tracking the cumulative $TICKI across multiple days and tracking whether $TICKI prints more positive values than negative ones during the trading day helps to identify trending moves. Too, there are occasions in which $TICKI paints one picture but other $TICK measures may point differently.

For example, we recently had a situation in which $TICKI was unusually weak over a number of days, but the cumulative NYSE TICK made fresh highs during that period. That told me that selling pressure was limited to large caps and that there was broad underlying strength across the entire market. Recognizing this helped me not overreact to the short-term price weakness in the capitalization-weighted stock indexes.

As with the other TICK measures, I pay particular attention to extreme values of $TICKI. Values above +18 or below −18 gain my immediate attention, as they indicate that a majority of Dow shares are upticking or downticking at the same time. This, as we've seen, typically occurs because of program trading—basket executions of orders among large market participants. An easy way to sell stocks is to dump the most liquid shares, either directly or indirectly by selling index futures products or by selling ETFs. Either can lead the liquid names to uptick or downtick at once. When we see a high degree of upticking or downticking during a given market period, it tells us that large market players are actively buying or selling. I then turn to the other TICK measures to examine whether this is occurring across the entire market or primarily among the large caps. We recently saw a market period in which stocks were weak and bounced higher. The $TICKI readings on the bounce were strong, but the NYSE TICK never exceeded +500. This told me that much of the bounce was short covering among the large caps and not an initiation of fresh buying across the broad universe of shares. That information was useful in fading the bounce and riding the next leg of the downmove lower.

Finally, I will often use readings in $TICKI to help with the execution of my orders. I will generally sell on $TICKI strength that fails to generate new price highs (showing me that buyers cannot move the market higher), and I will buy on $TICKI weakness that fails to bring fresh price lows (indicating that sellers cannot move the market lower). By waiting for the buyers or sellers to show their hand through the upticking and downticking of liquid stocks, I can often get a better price for my entry. Each improvement to execution may not seem like a great deal of money, but over the course of a year, this can add up to a meaningful return for active traders.

Best Practice #6: Tracking Market Cycles Using Stock Market Breadth and Intermarket Correlations

As I've indicated earlier, an organizing principle for my trading is the notion of cycles in stock market prices. Many presentations of cycles make the assumption that these are fixed in duration or follow a fixed scheme, such as wave patterns. I have spent years on the cycles issue and can report that I have found no such reliable regularity. Yes, one can always construct schemes in retrospect and identify alternate counts to explain away contradictions, but I have not found these ideas to be useful in anticipating forward price movement. Cycles do exist in market prices, but these are aperiodic. That is, they vary in duration and amplitude.

At first blush, this doesn't sound particularly helpful. What cycles lack in time-based regularity, however, they make up for in structural similarity. The typical stock market cycle starts at a price low, which typically follows a period of high volume/volatility and correlation. At these lows, we typically see broad selling, with the NYSE TICK hitting extreme negative numbers and then dropping to higher lows on further weakness. At some point, the selling activity, as reflected among the various uptick/downtick measures, fails to generate fresh price lows, and that is often a good indication that sellers have been exhausted.

This leads to the next phase of the market cycle in which volatility and correlation remain high and buyers from longer timeframes jump in to take advantage of the retreat of the sellers. This creates very high upticking readings among the various measures and leads to upside price momentum: Strength is followed by further strength. During the rise from market lows, most stocks participate in the strength and the number of shares making fresh new lows dwindles rapidly. This can be a frustrating period for traders, as they may have missed the price bottom and don't feel comfortable chasing the subsequent market strength. This is a mistake, however, as the rise from important lows does tend to show follow-through. Waiting for the next pullback often entails missing a good portion of the market upmove.

An analytical routine that I have found to be particularly useful separates upticks and downticks into distinct distributions. The way I do this is to take five-minute values for $TICK and one-minute values for $TICKI and treat the high values for the period as "upticks" and the low values as "downticks." I then keep a rolling one-day total of the uptick values and downtick values. This helps me differentiate the activity of buyers and sellers in the stock market. It is very common for "buying pressure"—the cumulative sum of upticks—to fall as markets top out, even as "selling pressure" increases. When buying or selling pressure are on the upswing, up or down moves tend to show follow-through; waning buying or selling pressure generally precede reversal. Per the discussion in the prior best practice, particularly valuable are situations in which we see very strong or weak buying and selling pressure from $TICKI, but not from $TICK. This suggests that the buying or selling activity is limited to large caps and is not extending to the broad market—a nice heads-up that breadth is not confirming what we're seeing in the price movement of large-cap indexes. Such divergences, I've found, frequently occur near cycle turning points.

Key Takeaway

Cycles possess different frequencies and amplitudes, but similar structures.

Cycles change because something among the drivers of price has changed. This can be due to macroeconomic factors, changes in monetary policy, or geopolitical developments. When these broad fundamental drivers shift, we typically observe changes in the behavior of various asset classes. At the time I'm writing this, for example, we're seeing signs of strength in the US economy, which is leading traders to price in a greater probability of Fed hiking. This in turn is helping the US dollar stay strong (anticipated rate differentials favoring the US currency), but has led to a selling of fixed income (anticipating higher rates) and a selling of stocks (anticipating the withdrawal of monetary stimulus). These are meaningful shifts among asset classes and serve as a nice heads-up for the possibility of cycle change in stocks. By keeping tabs on central bank actions, economic releases, company earnings, and the relative movements of rates, currencies, commodities, and equities—as well as the relative movement of those asset classes across countries—we can anticipate broad thematic cyclical changes. Very often, one sector or asset class will lead those changes, providing us with important clues for eventual broad market change. In 2000 and 2007, the relative weakness in technology and financial stocks, respectively, led eventual broad market declines. In 2003 and 2009, the easing of monetary conditions by the Fed helped propel stocks higher. At those market lows, fewer stocks made fresh 52-week lows than months earlier, as an upward shift in breadth anticipated the eventual market rallies.

Even when you trade just one asset class and instrument, using breadth and intermarket correlations to gain thematic perspective and anticipate cyclical shifts in the market is extremely useful in anticipating changes in market direction and volatility.

Best Practice #7: Sizing Positions for Sound Risk Control

One of the most common mistakes I see traders make is sizing positions based on the need and desire for profit, but not for their ultimate risk tolerance. So let's say that a trader is bullish and buys X contracts of the ES futures. X is chosen because of the desire to make a certain amount of money in the trade, but may not reflect how the trader would respond to the position being stopped out. A good example would be buying thousands of shares of a stock and then seeing it gap lower on an earnings warning. The sizing of the position does not take into account the tail, gap risk and leads to a potentially debilitating loss. Another example would be allowing a short-term trade to turn into a longer-term position rather than stopping out at a pre-chosen level. Once the holding period is increased, the variability of returns increases as well. This leaves the trader vulnerable to an unplanned, large loss.

One of the sillier examples of mis-sizing positions occurred when I spoke with a trader who was long the S&P index and decided to diversify his holdings by adding a long NASDAQ position. Of course, the two indexes are highly correlated and become particularly highly correlated during risk-off periods. When stocks sold off, both positions were hit and losses were twice as large as the trader anticipated. A more excusable form of the same mistake occurs when traders own positions in two different asset classes and assume that they are diversified. Simple historical investigation could uncover the waxing and waning of correlations among the asset classes, but often those investigations are not conducted. As a result, an unexpected market event can lead to a sharp move across markets and a convergence of correlation. This can lead to outsized losses.

We may reassure ourselves that a truly adverse event will only occur one in 20 times, but if we're trading actively, making dozens of trades in a month or quarter, that adverse event is guaranteed to happen. Sizing needs to ensure survival in a worst-case scenario, not just meet needs and desires for profits at the moment. If I am holding an S&P futures position overnight, I need to look at worst-case scenarios of overnight moves for the current volatility regime. Those scenarios might be for a 1 percent adverse excursion. That could be debilitating if I hold a highly levered position.

Of course we want to avoid debilitating losses because it takes a while to recoup them. A drawdown of 10 percent requires an 11 percent return on remaining capital to return to breakeven. A drawdown of 25 percent requires a 33 percent return on remaining capital to break even. If we lose half our money, we have to double the remaining capital just to get back to where we started. Making sure that losses are planned and known ensures that we can live with drawdown and have plenty of dry ammunition for coming back.

We also want to avoid debilitating losses because of their psychological impact. It is very easy for a large, unplanned loss to lead to subsequent bad trading. For example, after a stiff loss, many traders will undersize the next good opportunity or miss it altogether. Conversely, some traders, frustrated by their loss, try too hard to make the money back, overtrade, and extend their losses. If our goal is to stay in a zone of calm focus, exposing ourselves to unplanned, large losses will likely throw us from the saddle. Large losses naturally focus our attention on P&L—and that takes our focus away from markets.

A related problem occurs when traders attempt to compensate for large position sizes with overly tight stops. This fails to take into account the underlying volatility of the market, resulting in positions being frequently stopped out on mere noise. The trader who seeks a huge reward-to-risk level in a trade likely is often making this mistake. A simple historical examination would reveal the likelihood of hitting a given downside level for any given entry point. Assuming a timing expertise that even the greatest pros do not have, the trader who seeks outsized reward relative to risk doesn't realize that a 5:1 level is not attractive if the odds of being stopped out prior to reaching the target are 8:1!

I sometimes encounter the opposite problem: placing targets and stops very far from the point of entry to extend the holding period of the trade. If the parameters are placed too far relative to the anticipated holding period, it's easy to wind up with situations in which positions move your way initially, only to subsequently reverse. This is because, at the chosen holding period, you are overestimating market volatility. The wider stops and targets do allow you to stay in a trade, but still must reflect the underlying odds of sustaining the desired directional move. Occasionally I see a trader reduce position size and extend holding times in order to ride a trend. Without a well-defined holding period and stop level, however, the position can still incur meaningful losses over the extended time frame. Traders often forget that extending time frame is equivalent to expanding position sizing. Holding a long-term position with X contracts can be much riskier than holding a shorter position with a multiple of X contracts. A best practice in trading is conducting historically grounded stress tests so that you know how far your market could move against you in your chosen holding period and for foreseeable levels of market volatility. "Above all else, do no harm," is a motto that works for traders as well as physicians.

Best Practice #8: Managing Opportunity as Well as Risk

Let's face it: even when the odds are in your favor, you can lose on a given occasion. You should aggressively bet a poker hand with three kings, but you could always lose if the other play has a full house. That is why it is imprudent to go all in on any single trade. A superior edge in markets can be completely undone by a single catastrophic loss. As long as our ability to anticipate the future is imperfect, we cannot afford to incur a risk of ruin on any particular occasion. A probabilistic edge will work for you over time but at any time can lead to strings of losing trades that, sized too large, can ruin our accounts.

Many traders understand this and realize the need to stay in the game, but make the opposite mistake. In diligently managing risk, they do a poor job of managing opportunity. In other words, they undersize their bets and fail to capitalize on their advantage in the marketplace. This is a problem because, as we saw earlier in the book, no edge lasts forever in markets. It is precisely because every edge has a limited shelf life that we need to capitalize on each one while we can. *The mismanagement of opportunity can be as detrimental to the long-term success of a trader as the mismanagement of risk.*

An exception to this principle would be the new, developing trader. As readers of *Enhancing Trader Performance* know, I am an enthusiastic advocate of simulation trading as a learning tool. Trading with real prices but in simulation mode allows developing traders to test out new strategies and learn from mistakes while preserving capital. While "paper trading" does not simulate the emotional pressures of trading actual capital, it is precisely for that reason that it's a useful step in the learning process. If one cannot follow a strategy and make money from it in simulation mode, profits surely will not follow during the rigors of actual trading. Conversely, once one has made their rookie mistakes in paper trading and now can sustain profitability, moving from simulation to small positions in actual trading is a natural step forward. Leaping from simulation to significant risk-taking is often a bridge too far for developing traders. It makes sense to get one's feet wet gradually in trading actual capital, which means consciously undersizing positions. For quite a while after I had worked out my trading strategies in simulated trading, I traded very small positions in SPY just to acclimate to winning and losing. Those positions grew in size as I found my stride, and eventually I moved to trading the ES futures and using greater leverage. During my developmental phase, I was not looking to maximize my returns but rather to minimize shocks to my trading and give myself time to develop consistency and confidence.

Once the developing trader has moved to a point of competence, however, the proper sizing of positions to exploit one's edge becomes important. One of the most common mistakes traders make early in their development is to overinterpret winning and losing periods in the market and trade larger after winning trades and reduce size after losing ones. The problem with that, of course, is that many strings of winning and losing trades occur simply by chance and do not necessarily reflect bad trading or the erosion of one's longer-term edge in markets. By trading too large after winning periods and too small after losing ones, traders systematically underperform relative to their potential.

Key Takeaway

We need strategies to manage opportunity as well as risk.

The most common reason for failing to act on opportunity, however, is the equation of losing trading with bad trading. It is understandable that traders feel good after making money and not so good after losses. Because trading is a probabilistic game, however, losses are inevitable in trading; they are not necessarily indications of failure. If traders experience losses as failures, it will only be natural to attempt to avoid failure by limiting risk taking. This may limit realized losses, but it also truncates success. A valuable best practice is to mentally rehearse scenarios of being stopped out and undergoing planned losses. If we're uncomfortable with those scenarios, we know that our emotions are not aligned with our trading plan. Without that alignment, we're likely to front run our stops and targets and further erode our trading edge.

A sure way to know if we're failing to manage opportunity is to engage in a different visualization. Imagine that, with your trading size, the market immediately moves in your favor and hits your target. Will you be pleased with your winning trade, or will you feel unfulfilled, because you were sized too small? In that latter scenario, the trader is trapped in a lose-lose mindset: unhappy if the trade loses, but not happy if it wins. Risk management and opportunity management are psychological aspects of trading as well as financial ones. We never want to encounter losses that debilitate us, and we never want to size positions so small that we eliminate a sense of achievement.

Best Practice #9: Dissecting Your Winning and Losing Trades

As mentioned above, losing trades can occur purely randomly. A news item can hit the tape just after you entered a position and you will be stopped out on the resulting noisy trading. It's frustrating, but it's not necessarily an indication that you did anything wrong. In fact, the losing trade qualifies as a good trade if the odds were in your favor and you managed the risk/reward equation well. We are not accustomed to thinking of losing trades as good trades, but that is because we tend to focus on outcome rather than process. A winning trade can be a bad one if it was placed impulsively with excessive risk. It worked on that particular occasion, but was a complete failure from a process perspective.

What you want to ask after both winning and losing trades is whether these were good trades or bad ones. Did you follow your own best practices, or did you fall short? When you dissect a winning or losing trade, you are using the trade as a learning tool. If you did something well in generating the idea, sizing the position, and managing the trade, that becomes a positive takeaway that you want to highlight for future trading. If you did something wrong in these areas, that becomes a takeaway as well. Dissecting your trades enables you to root out precisely what you did right and wrong from a process perspective so that you can feed that information forward into goals for your subsequent trading. If you lost money but traded well, dissecting the positive practices will help you not overreact to the lost capital. If you made money but traded poorly, the trading review will enable you to catch your mistakes before they cost you a chunk of capital.

One of my practices is to make my base case that, if I lose money in a trade, I've made a mistake. I review each aspect of the trade, from how I came up with the idea to how I managed the position, to identify any possible errors I may have made. Very often, that review process generates valuable insights. For example, one losing trade recently resulted from my becoming so focused on short-term cycles that I missed a much larger market picture. That picture would have been clear to me had I properly reviewed all relevant asset classes prior to entering the position. Looking back on the trade, I realized that I became so enamored with the market's short-term picture that I rushed the trade and failed to engage in proper due diligence regarding the longer time frame. I corrected that by requiring myself to fill out a pre-trade checklist before entering another position. That checklist captured everything that needed to line up for me to place my capital at risk. I was not allowed to take risk until I could justify the opportunity in terms of the checklist.

Dissecting winning and losing trades can help us identify patterns in our trading. Those patterns in turn can feed our best practices as well as our efforts at performance improvement. A while ago, I reviewed a series of trades over a period of months and found a somewhat surprising pattern. When I placed a trade soon after a winning trade, it was likely to be a losing trade. When I placed a trade after stepping away from markets following a losing trade, it was likely to be a winning trade. Indeed, the best predictor of whether a trade was a winner or loser was the amount of time intervening since the prior trade. More frequent trading led to losses; more selective trading achieved the best results.

The reason for this was that my best trades capitalized on an extensive research process. When significant time occurred between trades, it was because I had utilized that time to thoroughly review my market indicators, develop a sense for the structure of the cycle we were in, and backtest patterns I was seeing in the market. It was when I had a strong understanding of what the market was doing that I was able to place my best trades. On other occasions, when I relied more on a feel for the market than my research process, I did not have that strong understanding and was more likely to miss something that should have been obvious. Dissecting my winning and losing trades helped me realize that my greatest edge in markets occurred when my head was aligned with my gut: I felt something was happening but also understood what was happening and why. My greatest risk-adjusted returns came from having the patience to wait for that alignment.

Dissecting winning and losing trades can also teach us something about the markets. One exercise that traders I work with find useful is to break down winning and losing trades by a variety of categories, including the instruments traded. Very often traders will find that they were making money in several markets, but consistently losing money in others. Upon review, they realized that they had a clearer understanding of what was going on in some markets over others. This in turn led them to rethink the opportunity sets afforded by markets and adjust their trading accordingly. Sometimes the dissection of winners and losers also reveals correlations in markets and trades that we did not expect to be correlated. This can be important, as correlation breakdowns can signal changes of market regime.

The general best practice is to make sure we are spending time studying our trading, not just studying markets. We want to become learning machines so that we are ever evolving, benefiting from what we do right as well as from what we do wrong.

Best Practice #10: Collecting Trading Metrics

When a baseball coach wants to understand a player's performance, he will turn to sabermetrics. What is the player's batting average against left- versus right-handed pitchers? Fastball throwers versus breaking ball pitchers? When batters are in scoring position? During day versus night games? How often does he strike out? How often does he strike out in clutch situations? How often does he hit for extra bases? Knowing nuances of performance is essential when you're deciding to send one pitcher into a game versus another, or when you're sending one batter to pinch hit rather than another.

In a well-known example, Ted Williams tracked his batting average as a function of the location of pitches relative to the strike zone. Certain locations represented sweet spots, where he had a very high likelihood of getting a hit. Other locations were far less promising. Tracking his performance helped him understand which pitches to swing at and which to avoid. His metrics enabled him to more consistently function in his sweet spots.

Key Takeaway

You can't improve it if you don't measure it.

Metrics are key tools in understanding our performance. Our memories can deceive us: We can think we perform well in situations when in fact we are biased by a few instances that stand out in memory. Metrics provide an objective view of performance. They tell us as traders where our sweet spots lie and where they do not.

For example, I routinely find that some traders trade well in more volatile environments than less volatile ones; some traders perform admirably in trending conditions and get chopped up in ranges; and some traders make their money at certain times of the trading day and lose it at other times. As with Ted Williams, knowing your metrics can help you determine when you should swing and when you should hold back, and when you should take a good swing and when you should not go for the fences. In poker, professional players understand odds and the likelihood of winning with a given hand. Each day and week, markets deliver us hands. We cannot control the cards we get, but we can control whether and how much we bet.

What metrics should a trader collect? Here are a few that I find helpful as general best practices:

- *Performance as a function of instrument and asset class*—This can tell us the markets and stocks we trade best, and it can also highlight where the greatest opportunities lie for our styles of trading.

- *Performance as a function of market condition*—Uptrend, downtrend, range—Very often, traders function best in certain market environments. As noted above, volatility is often an important mediator of performance.

- *Performance as a function of time frame*—When traders hold positions for varying time frames, it's not unusual to observe strengths and weaknesses in performance. For instance, a trader might be quite good at spotting entry points and making money on short-term moves, but lose any edge when holding positions longer.

- *Performance as a function of trading activity*—Some days and weeks, a trader may establish a large number of positions. Other days and weeks find more selectivity among opportunities. If overtrading is an issue, the number of trades taken can correlate inversely with profitability, highlighting the importance of prioritizing opportunities per the Ted Williams example.

- *Performance as a function of position sizing and risk taking*—The greatest risk taking should be reserved for the best opportunities, but this isn't always the case. Traders sometimes are more nimble and see markets more objectively when their vision is not clouded by performance pressure. Knowing the risk levels that correspond to your best trading helps you find a different kind of sweet spot.

- *Performance as a function of setup*—Entries are often predicated on particular patterns occurring in markets, such as breakout patterns or moving average crosses. Tracking performance as a function of the entry setup can help us refine our trade execution. Similarly, tracking how positions performed following our exits can provide us with useful information about the success of our position management.

- *Performance as a function of recent profitability*—I know many traders who trade very well in a hole—when they have lost money—but who then lose discipline after they have gone on a winning streak. Breaking down your future profitability as a function of P&L can tell you whether recent wins or losses might be biasing your trading decisions.

It's a powerful combination when dissecting winning and losing trades is blended with metrics-based reviews of performance. The goal is to use performance data to help you identify strengths and weaknesses, become better and more consistent in exploiting strengths, and learn ways to improve or avoid weaknesses. Metrics, employed properly, are great tools for mindfulness. When we know our sweet spots, we can be more self-aware about the bets we make.

Best Practice #11: Collecting Personal Metrics

Trading metrics are but one side of the performance equation. Equally important are our personal metrics—how our trading performance varies as a function of our personal performance. Tracking personal metrics requires that we collect a range of information about those personal factors that are most connected to our trading successes and weaknesses. Some of the more important personal metrics follow:

- *Emotional status*—How does our trading performance (profitability, risk management, decision making) vary as a function of our emotional states? Keeping track of key emotional variables (frustration/calm; confidence/fear; unhappy/happy) and seeing how those vary with gauges of performance can provide information about the emotional factors that contribute to and detract from performance.

- *Physical state*—In our physical state we can be energized or depleted, rested or fatigued, comfortable or in discomfort, healthy or sick, hungry or filled, toned or out-of-shape, keyed-up or relaxed. Very often our physical state sets the stage for our cognitive performance, as we make different decisions and maintain different levels of concentration when we are in a positive versus negative physical state. Tracking our physical states and knowing their impact on our performance can help us stay mindful of occasions when flight-or-fight responses can undermine our best market preparation.

- *Cognitive state*—Are we focused or distracted, optimistic or pessimistic, open-minded or closed, clear or fuzzy, prepared or unprepared, positive or negative? How we think impacts how we feel and act. By tracking our mind states and correlating those with various aspects of performance, we can become sensitive to situations in which we are more and less attuned to markets and their patterns.

- *Preparation*—It's not unusual for our performance to vary with our preparation routines. How do we perform when we've engaged in longer versus shorter market review, more or less research, greater or lesser physical exercise, more or less sleep, better or worse eating? Our lifestyles can greatly impact our physical, emotional, and cognitive states, setting us up for success or failure.

Out of our personal observations, we should be able to define personal as well as trading best practices. Like any athlete that needs to sustain peak performance, we need to be in shape in all respects to maximize our functioning in the heat of competition. Tracking our work habits, our personal choices, and our physical, emotional, and cognitive states can provide us with a rich database from which we can understand what makes us successful.

Best Practice #12: Staying in Love with Markets

If you've traded for any length of time, you know that trading can be frustrating, difficult, confusing, and overwhelming at times. I have worked with many successful portfolio managers and traders who still go through periods of loss, flat performance, uncertainty, and doubt. All of these have the potential to undermine motivation, concentration, and future decision making. Once we begin to dwell on setbacks, they can become slumps.

The single best predictor of trading failure, I've found, occurs when the psychological negatives of trading begin to outweigh the positives. Traders typically come to markets stimulated by the competitive challenge, the problem-solving, the opportunity to work independently, the fast-paced decision making, the intellectual curiosity, and the possibility of seeing one's work turn into meaningful success. It's not at all unusual for traders to start their career infatuated with markets, spending much of their time observing trading, tracking ideas, and experimenting with trades based on their ideas. It is that sense of being in love with markets that gets traders through the challenges of their often-extended learning curves.

At some point, the frustrations of trading can begin to exceed the positives. This sometimes occurs because of the inability to make money. Sometimes it occurs simply because the ups and downs of performance become emotionally exhausting. Once that occurs, it is no longer so easy to sustain concentration and work ethic. I recall one trader who gradually lost enthusiasm for trading during a prolonged challenging period of performance and instead spent his time on the trading floor talking with other traders. He found a variety of reasons for not taking risk and eventually quit to pursue a different career field. As soon as the negatives of trading began to overcome the positives that brought him to markets, it became very difficult to sustain a learning curve.

A best practice is staying closely connected to the factors that initially brought you to trading. Trading outcomes may not always be gratifying, but it is essential to derive gratification from our work. If we cannot count on winning outcomes, we must focus on what wins for us in terms of trading process. I have experienced many setbacks and frustrations with trading at various times, but have always maintained an active research program to find fresh sources of edge in markets. Even when markets are closed, I enjoy the research process and stay positively focused on opportunity. The love of learning exceeds any temporary frustrations I might experience with losing positions. If I do not actively nurture that learning, however, trading loses much of its appeal for me—and my performance suffers as a result.

In this sense, our relationship with trading is not so different from our romantic relationships. We often start a romantic relationship in love, filled with the wonders of the other person. Over time, however, daily demands and routines can blunt our passion and frustrations can eclipse connectedness. Struggling to meet work demands, the needs of children, and ongoing household chores, a couple can fall out of love simply by not nurturing the experiences that brought them together in the first place. Similarly, traders who spend all their time trading and watching markets can lose contact with what initially interested them in markets. Trading becomes more about making money than loving one's work, killing the passionate motivation needed to sustain a high level of performance.

A plan for peak performance requires a plan for frequent well-being.

The best practice is to clearly identify what brings fun, excitement, and interest in trading and ensure that these activities are a planned part of a daily routine. Every day in work should bring some degree of fulfillment, even if it is the satisfaction of learning something important from a poor trading performance. How you structure your time greatly impacts your daily experience, and that plays a large role in shaping your cognitive, emotional, and physical states. Building time each day for activities that are satisfying and enjoyable ensures that, even in times of slump, you remain highly engaged in markets, moving yourself forward with learning and development.

Best Practice #13: Creating Emotional Diversification

We know the benefits of diversification for portfolios. Owning assets that can appreciate in ways that are not highly correlated smoothes our profit curves, enabling us to invest more with lower risk. When our trading and investment eggs are in one basket, we become vulnerable when that basket becomes unstable. Stocks have been a great investment over a period of decades, but holding them through violent bear market periods would have been quite difficult. By diversifying into fixed income and defensive assets (a combination of long and short positions, for example), we allow ourselves to participate in trends in less wrenching ways.

As much as we may stay in love with markets per the previous best practice, there will be times when markets do not provide us with much in the way of returns or satisfaction. Even as our careers trend over time, we can enter into our own challenging bear market periods. A best practice is to make sure your emotional portfolio is diversified and that you actively pursue sources of well-being in your life outside of markets. That emotional portfolio includes investments you make in romantic relationships and friendships, as well as activities that you find individually satisfying. When each day and week includes activities that give you energy and contribute to happiness, satisfaction, energy, and relationships, it is difficult to become too mired in psychological trading slumps. The trader who can feel grateful for friends, family, and personal interests has a balance to trading stress that keeps mood and performance at high levels.

The goal of this best practice is to ensure that self-esteem and energy level do not wax and wane with profits and losses. When the self-esteem eggs are in many baskets, no one area of setback is overly threatening. This makes it much easier to weather adversity and hang in there to learn from it. A great way to ensure such diversification is by scheduling regular time for the nontrading activities that bring affection, energy, happiness, and life satisfaction. Creating well-being time outside of markets keeps you functioning at a high level, so that stress will never become debilitating distress.

A common mistake traders make is to respond to difficulties in markets by working harder, spending more time on trading, and hoping that sheer effort will arrest their drawdowns. To be sure, focused effort to learn from setbacks is absolutely essential to our development. If, however, we double down on activities that are not providing us with positives, we can quickly become overwhelmed. It is when markets provide their least rewards that we want to be harvesting rewards from other areas of life. That means that we work smarter, not harder, when we go into drawdown. We want to ensure that drawdowns of capital don't become psychological drawdowns. Emotional diversification allows us to ride the ups and downs of market participation without damage to our psyches.

Best Practice #14: Creating Workouts for Our Strengths

Earlier, we saw that our strengths do not exist in a vacuum. The principle of *use it or lose it* means that we either build our strengths or allow them to atrophy. What I have termed "therapy for the mentally well" in my *Forbes* blog is really a concerted push to develop the positives in our lives, rather than minimize negatives. Traditional psychology has focused on mental illnesses, conflicts, and problems—and, indeed, has made significant strides in helping people overcome a variety of obstacles, from drug and alcohol abuse to emotional disorders to adjustment problems that crop up in relationships and careers. No amount of therapy directed at problems, however, can—in itself—build the strengths that we need for elite performance in highly challenging career fields. A positive therapy is one that starts with strengths and the activities that exercise—and expand—them. If the traditional psychologist has functioned as a "shrink," the positively focused psychologist is an expander: one who seeks to help us tap into our core competencies.

On the *Forbes* blog, I introduced the idea of life as a gymnasium, with stations and equipment for every one of our strengths. Imagine getting a workout of our capacity to love, our ability to focus, our creativity, our mental toughness, and our spirituality. Such a workout, just like those in a weight room, would push us beyond our comfort zones, requiring us to exercise our strengths muscles. Such a therapy for the mentally well would not be a talk therapy at all. Rather, it would be an approach to life—a commitment to make each day an opportunity to grow some of our capacities. This could take the form of specific exercise sessions, in which we use methods such as meditation to enhance our emotional control and clarity. It could also become a way to approach our daily activities, such as structuring our time with loved ones to extend closeness and connection. Imagine if, every day, we extended ourselves in just one way that helped us function more positively and productively. The cumulative impact of such workouts would move us far closer to our ideals at work, in relationships, and in our emotional and physical health.

What might some of those workouts look like? Here are a few examples:

- *Each month choose an unfamiliar reading that introduces us to new topics that challenge our understandings of the world.* For instance, we might read a work of Buddhist philosophy or a biography of someone who is unusually accomplished. At the end of each reading, we have to identify several takeaways that we can employ in our work or personal life.

- *Each month, select an overnight trip to an unfamiliar area that you and your spouse would like to learn about.* Plan the activities together, with a particular eye toward structuring stimulating shared experiences.

- *Take a course at a local institution of higher education that is completely outside your area of expertise.* Take the course with a partner or close friend to share the learning and then make practical use of what you've learned. A good example might be a cooking course or a course in creative writing.

- *Begin a new workout routine at a gym with a personal trainer, exercising parts of the body and functions that have been neglected to date.* For instance, start a program of yoga and flexibility if your typical exercise has focused on running or weights.

- *Learn a new language with your children and then plan a trip to a culture that speaks that language.* Let your child teach you and become a partner in planning the trip.

Notice how each of these activities pushes us outside our comfort zones, taking us out of routine and requiring us to learn and do new things. By making those activities shared ones, we can also deepen relationships and experience others in fresh ways. If each activity is a mirror, we select fresh mirrors that enable us to see and develop new aspects of ourselves. It is difficult to stagnate if we are continually enriching our lives.

Best Practice #15: Enhancing Our Creativity

We've seen that finding and sticking to an edge in financial markets is not enough to ensure career success in trading. Because markets are ever-changing, we must be able to adapt to them and continually find fresh sources of edge. That places a premium on creativity and the ability to view markets in new, promising ways. Creativity helps us see new aspects of markets and also enables us to see old things anew. I had long used technical indicators such as Bollinger bands and the Commodity Channel Index to look at the strength and weakness of particular stocks or indexes I was trading. When I noticed that the Stock Charts website tracked all stocks giving buy and sell signals for each of the major indicators, I realized that this information could be used as a proxy of market health. This led to observations of discrepancies among the measures and the recognition that each indicator was capturing a different facet of market strength. Moreover, I found that the time series of buy and sell signals were surprisingly modestly correlated across indicators. This led to my testing trading models that treated buy signals and sell signals as independent variables, some of which turned out to be unusually promising. It was looking at old indicators in new ways that opened entire new directions.

Key Takeaway

Creativity is something we do; it is not a fixed trait.

Creativity is not something we either have or don't have. It is an approach to our work and the information we encounter. We can conduct a business meeting in a creative or routine fashion; we can look at market indicators in consensus or novel ways. Creativity requires an open, inquiring mind; it is a powerful counterbalance to confirmation bias. In the biased mindset, we are imposing our views on markets. In the creative mindset, we are accessing new information and assembling information in new ways to allow views to come to us. For that reason, creativity is closely aligned with intuition. Creative insights often begin as intuitive hunches, as we sense patterns among the pieces of information that we assemble.

How can we more consistently generate creative insights into markets? Here are a few ways to implement a best practice in creativity:

- *Generate new conversations.* Talk with market participants who are talented, but different from you. Find out what they are seeing in markets and share with them your work. Start with the assumption that they are right in their views and you are right in yours. What would that say about the world? Where might you find trades that profit from such a scenario?

- *Track consensus thought.* Follow sentiment measures and trader sentiment on chats and social media. Start with the assumption that the herd will need to exit their crowded trades. What would you look for in such a scenario? How could you profit from such a run for exits?

- *Read new material.* Track blogs, other social media posts, and written research from people with solid reputations whom you have not followed in the past. Read their work with an open mind and see which conclusions strike a chord for you. There are many things we know but don't know that we know—the information is implicitly encoded. Many times new material will resonate with us because it crystallizes what we already know implicitly.

- *Engage in brainwriting and braintalking.* Once you've reviewed your research, spoken with others, and read the works of others, jot down your thoughts in stream-of-consciousness fashion. Such brainwriting is yet another way to make implicit knowledge explicit. Brainwriting can also help you integrate perspectives from multiple sources. You can accomplish the same thing through braintalking: speaking your ideas into a recorder in a stream-of-consciousness fashion. It is useful to then take a break and read or listen to what you have processed. Often, you will read or hear what you've generated with a different perspective, allowing you to pick out gems of insight. Brainwriting and braintalking are very effective ways of listening to ourselves.

- *Follow different markets and time frames.* As noted earlier, the longer-term movement of assets relative to one another typically reflects macroeconomic themes that set up broad trends in the markets you trade. By reviewing charts of different asset classes and instruments and by tracking strength and weakness across countries, we can identify both themes and shifts among themes. It is when we detect those thematic shifts that major opportunities can present themselves. An interesting integration of methods is to brainwrite or braintalk multiple markets and then read/listen to overlaps among your thoughts. We often sense and feel thematic shifts before they actually manifest themselves as trends.

Per the earlier discussion, creativity requires immersion in new information (or old information viewed in new ways), followed by an incubation period of playing with that information, generating new combinations and recombinations. An important ingredient in successful creative thinking is problem finding: starting with a problem worth solving. Unclear market developments can provide worthwhile problems. When we are confused—when solid analyses lead to different conclusions—we often have a problem that can become the focus of creative processing. Staying creative is a great way of staying interested in markets and feeding our intellectual curiosity. As we have seen, finding sources of fulfillment in difficult markets can make the difference between encountering a setback and sustaining a slump.

Best Practice #16: Tracking and Intercepting Negative Self-Talk

We maintain a continuous stream of self-talk, processing the world through an ongoing internal conversation. How we talk to ourselves frames how we respond to situations. In that sense, our self-talk becomes a kind of lens through which we view ourselves, others, and the world around us. If I tell myself that everyone is selfish and out to get something of value from me, I will naturally respond to others with guardedness and suspicion. That in turn will influence how I come across to others and shape the success of my social interactions. If my internal dialogue is all about manipulated markets and unfair algorithms dominating price action, I will respond to even normal reversals in my positions with frustration and anger.

Key Takeaway
Self-talk is destiny.

There are many damaging forms of self-talk. These include:

- *Perfectionism*—Here we look back on our actions in markets—often with hindsight bias—and tell ourselves that we "should have" done things differently. This reinforces not only feelings of regret, but also self-blame. Over time, the sense of constantly falling short erodes self-confidence.

- *Negativity*—Sometimes we become so discouraged that we just assume that bad things are around the corner. Self-talk becomes defeatist, in essence sending the message that nothing we do really matters. Such negative, helpless, hopeless talk keeps us from acting on opportunity and reinforces depression.

- *Catastrophizing*—When we view normal adverse outcomes as unacceptable, we can generate significant performance anxiety. Catastrophizing occurs when we generate very threatening and usually unrealistic worst-case scenarios. "What if the market reverses and wipes out my profit?" might be a reasonable scenario to consider, but if it is entertained with a sense of threat and panic, it is part of catastrophizing. A great deal of flight-or-fight-based stress is generated by catastrophic thinking.

- *Blaming*—Sometimes we deal with the frustration of negative outcomes by deflecting responsibility and blaming external agents. We might blame those manipulators of markets, unfair central banks, faulty software, misleading research, environmental distractions, and so on. Such blame keeps us in a state of anger and fight/flight, and the arousal often interferes with subsequent trades. Sustaining a blaming stance also implicitly keeps us in a victim mindset, eroding our confidence.

- *Overconfidence*—Negative self-talk most often interferes with sound trading, but sometimes self-talk can become exuberant and derail our sober processing of market information. When we've gone on a run or score a large winning trade, we can tell ourselves that we've turned the corner, figured things out, and see things well. In such a mode, we can project future profits and become attached to making the big score. This can lead to imprudent risk management and sloppy trading.

- *Comparison*—The most important comparisons we can make in assessing ourselves as traders are internal ones: how we stand relative to the past. That tells us whether we are learning and developing. Often, however, we can become immersed in self-talk that compares us with others. This can lead to particular frustration when others are making money and we are not. By focusing on others, we take ourselves out of our game and can put on trades simply because it's what others are doing. This reinforces a lack of confidence in one's own judgment and can lead to particular frustration when following the herd gets us stampeded on any rush to exits.

As a rule, we cannot change our self-talk unless we are aware of our self-talk. Keeping a cognitive journal and tracking our thinking during the trading day can become a great way to recognize negative and overconfident self-talk when it occurs. In a cognitive journal, we can also identify situations that trigger the self-talk and take a hard look at whether that self-talk is constructive or destructive. The journal thus acts as a tool to build our mindful self-awareness, and it serves as a practical device for interrupting patterns of destructive self-talk. Most self-talk that interferes with good trading is part of a habit pattern and does not represent our true appraisals of situations—those that we would render if we were focused and reflective. Becoming aware of our self-talk and interrupting patterns helps us break negative cognitive habits and replace automatic thinking with focused reflection. This enables us to avoid reactive trading patterns and sustain our best thinking during trading.

Best Practice #17: Training Ourselves to Stay Calm and Focused

Many of our worst trading practices are triggered as part of flight-or-fight reactions to stressful events. Our physiological arousal stimulates cognitive and emotional arousal, which then precipitates reactive—and often suboptimal—action patterns. Seeing a market move against us can trigger fear, frustration, and regret, all of which arouse our bodies to a state of action—precisely when we need to be focused on good decision making. How many times do we react physically and emotionally to adverse movement in a trade, only to exit on panic and abandon our positions at the very worst time? It's not so unusual to find that a trader's exits on losses actually represent profitable entries. *We become part of the herd when we are caught up in the fight-or-flight reactions of the herd.*

When I first began experimenting with biofeedback—real-time measures of physiological arousal—during trading, I noticed something very interesting. When the biofeedback readings were "in the zone," showing a high degree of calm focus, traders were generally clear about what markets were doing and had a clear plan in mind for managing their positions. Those readings left the zone before traders consciously recognized that anything was amiss in their trades. By the time they clearly saw that the trade was going against them, they were thoroughly out of the zone, displaying very high levels of arousal. Several talented traders, however, displayed a very different pattern. When positions moved against them, they made conscious efforts to calm and focus themselves. They failed to show the same levels of arousal as the less experienced, less talented traders. This fit very well with research from Andrew Lo and Dmitriy Repin (2002), who found that experienced traders responded to market situations with less emotional arousal than inexperienced traders.

In such situations, we respond to what we interpret as threats. The veteran trader has a deep database of experience and knows that adverse price movement can be expected during the life of a trade. It is not a threat. The rookie trader, lacking such perspective, is more likely to react to every move to new highs or lows. This makes it difficult for less experienced traders to stick with the research and plans that inspired their positions to begin with.

A best practice is to use deep breathing and physical relaxation to intercept physiological arousal when problematic situations occur. As soon as we are aware that we are entering a fight-or-flight mode—heart rate speeding up, muscle tension increasing, sweating—we make conscious efforts to slow and deepen our breathing. This has the effect of reducing our body's overall arousal and helps keep us focused. Deep breathing exercises performed as practice before trading can be especially useful in this respect. Spending several minutes each morning focusing on relaxing images, closing your eyes, and deepening your breathing provides useful training in self-control. Then, when markets begin to move against us, we can simply summon the images that we had been rehearsing, take a few deep breaths, and keep ourselves centered. We are unlikely to panic and make rash decisions if we are physically calm and cognitively focused.

As mentioned earlier, biofeedback can be a very useful tool for training in self-control. Heart rate variability feedback helps us identify when we are—and are not—in the zone, making our training efforts more efficient. The goal is to be able to enter a calm, focused mode on demand, so that we control our bodies, rather than have them control us. The combination of physical self-control and use of cognitive journaling can be very powerful in achieving emotional mastery during trading.

Best Practice #18: Sustaining Cognitive Focus

An early use of biofeedback was to improve attention span among children who experience attention deficits. It turns out that many biofeedback measures, such as heart rate variability, do not simply measure relaxation. If we are relaxed but not focused, we do not enter the zone. It is when we sustain both concentration and a relaxed state that we are most likely to experience a state of flow. For that reason, biofeedback can be a highly effective tool for sustaining our focus during trading.

The research mentioned earlier in the book regarding willpower finds that our ability to sustain goal-directed action is limited. We become fatigued after lengthy periods of cognitive effort, and during those periods of fatigue we are most likely to act on impulse. This is a particular problem for traders who follow markets intensively through the day. It is only a matter of time before we become fatigued and less able to act on careful planning.

A best practice is to build our cognitive muscles by training ourselves to sustain focus for longer and longer periods. One way to accomplish that is to use biofeedback not just to enter the zone, but to sustain increasing time in the zone. I've used a software program from Heart Math that accompanies their em-Wave unit in which the user has to keep a balloon in the air for an extended period of time. When the user is more in the zone, the balloon rises. When the user falls out of the zone, the balloon falls. The goal is to prevent the balloon from hitting the ground. It's an engaging app for children and adults alike and teaches us to sustain concentration.

A nice modification of the exercise is to keep the balloon in the air while imagining frustrating market scenarios, such as having markets move against us or being stopped out of trades. The idea is to stay in the zone even when we face challenging situations. This is a version of the exposure therapy I describe in *The Daily Trading Coach*, with the added benefit of building our cognitive muscles.

Key Takeaway

Our focus and concentration define the limits of our consistent peak performance.

Many times traders assume that they lose emotional control because they lack discipline or because they harbor deep, unresolved conflicts.

As we've seen in the previous chapters, that often is not the case. What they lack is the ability to sustain cognitive focus over extended periods of time. Trading is an unusual activity in that respect. Most work allows for reasonably frequent breaks and shifts of focus. The active trader can be glued to screens for hours at a time, making multiple decisions while facing risk and uncertainty. Few activities prepare us for the cognitive focus needed to function effectively under those conditions. It is when we are cognitively fatigued that we are most vulnerable to cognitive biases and poor trading decisions. *Many times the answer to the challenge is not to seek therapy or coaching, but to build our focus muscles.* With increased willpower, we can weather the most unexpected and challenging market conditions.

Best Practice #19: Integrating Coaching and Mentorship

As someone who has coached traders on a full-time basis for over a decade, I have a rather good sense for the promise and limitations of coaching. Those limitations can be significant. It is far from clear to me that coaching, by itself, is the answer to many problems experienced in financial markets. The reason for this is that no amount of coaching, in and of itself, can provide traders with an edge in markets. Less experienced traders often assume their problems are emotional when in fact they are trading purely random patterns. This is particularly true for traders who rely on patterns taught to them by others and canned patterns from trading software. Rarely have those patterns been validated in any systematic way, and rarely have traders worked with them extensively to make them their own. I've met many traders who seemingly lack discipline, veering from their trading plans after having taken losses. The reason for their lack of discipline is that they don't trust their plans; indeed, they sense that they don't truly possess an edge in markets. *All the work in the world on discipline won't be of help if the plans you're hoping to stick to lack an objective positive expected return.*

It is for that reason that I typically do not pursue coaching with developing traders. My general experience is that what they need is teaching and mentorship, not just psychological assistance. To be sure, exercises such as those outlined above—ones to help traders stay focused and mindful of self-talk—can be quite useful to developing traders. If, however, those traders are not trading with an edge in markets, they are going to experience loss and frustration regardless of the psychological techniques they employ. What is particularly useful as a best practice is integrating coaching and mentorship into a holistic developmental process.

A simple analogy makes the point. A developing tennis player needs work on their ground game, backhand, net strategy, and serve, for example. The tennis coach is a teacher, focusing first and foremost on drills, feedback on performance, and work on fundamentals. In the course of that work, efforts will be made to address psychological factors, but this is done on the court, in the context of competition and practice, and not in a consulting room with a psychologist. Taking the developing player off the court and talking about emotional factors that affect performance would be singularly ineffective. The successful tennis coach addresses psychology on the court in the heat of action. There is no division between mentorship (teaching skills) and coaching (teaching psychological strategies); those are seamlessly integrated.

There are many experienced traders who enjoy teaching and conduct mentorship programs as part of their businesses. Some of these are mentors who contributed best practices that you'll be reading shortly. This can be a highly effective mechanism for learning as it allows developing traders to learn from the direct example of a teacher; receive feedback on their trading; and receive coaching for psychological aspects of trading performance. The value and impact of role modeling in a high-quality mentorship program cannot be overstated. When you look at successful training programs—from the development of master plumbers to the training of physicians—mentorship through apprenticeship is a key component of the learning. Through the mechanism of apprenticeship, one receives teaching and coaching, much like the developing tennis player.

Can such integration of coaching and mentorship occur outside of formal training programs? The tennis analogy highlights one option that can be of great value to developing traders: engaging trading partners in efforts to improve performance. Such peer coaching can leverage traders' learning and address both skill and psychological aspects of trading performance. I have observed very useful interactions among traders on a trading floor when problems emerge. Such informal coaching, delivered by experienced traders who have won a high degree of trust, can be quite useful in helping traders deal with challenging situations. Each trader becomes both teacher and student, sharing in learning and skill development. Such mutual learning can also occur online among independent traders, as traders find compatible buddies and create valuable professional networks.

For experienced, successful traders the ideal integration of coaching and teaching can be a coaching relationship in which the coach helps the trader learn from himself/herself. The coach has a unique perspective on the strengths and vulnerabilities of the trader and can help the trader develop a model of his/her success that becomes a guide to future performance. This is where the best practices framework can be particularly powerful. The strengths-oriented coach helps traders identify and extend their best practices, so that mentorship is always integrated with the coaching. Instead of learning from another trader, however, the trader is learning from his or her own performances. Think of chess coaches, football coaches, voice coaches—all are intimately involved in teaching and skill development. By bringing together coaching and mentorship, traders can accelerate their learning curves and benefit from the perspectives of those who have been there and done that.

Best Practice #20: Joining a Team, Building a Team

We've seen that markets are sufficiently complex and interwoven that it is impossible for any single trader to stay on top of them while attending to news, economic developments, and data releases. Over the years, I've seen a distinct trend in which trading and portfolio management occurs within team contexts. This helps traders stay on top of fast-changing markets and still benefit from the deep dives of research.

A common model for team building is that junior members of the team bring research skills and knowledge, quantitative experience, and programming background to the team. This helps to organize the efforts of portfolio managers and traders, and it contributes research ideas that would otherwise go unnoticed. One equity long/short team that I have worked with consists of specialists in various subsectors who contribute their expertise to the portfolio manager. This allows the manager to focus on the overall portfolio and developments within the companies he closely follows, while still receiving ideas about other parts of the industry from team members. Particularly valuable for this team are the regular group meetings in which all share their ideas and research and discuss trends within their spaces. This frequently leads to insights into areas of business that become trading themes for the portfolio.

The beauty of the team model is that the junior members benefit the senior manager by contributing research and ideas and the senior manager benefits the junior members by providing mentorship and guidance. It's a great way for developing traders to learn the business from the ground up, as role modeling is embedded in daily interactions and team meetings. Very often, once the junior members develop a solid level of success with their research and generation of ideas, they receive small allocations of capital from their manager so that they can work on their own trading and portfolio management skills. They thus develop as independent professionals even as they remain contributing team members.

Key Takeaway

The right teamwork multiplies strengths.

Assembling or joining a team brings other benefits as well. Team members keep each other focused on markets and support one another when trading becomes difficult. Team members also share their trading experiences, so that they learn from each other. As the members of a team develop new skills and areas of expertise, they bring greater learning to the group and development becomes exponential.

As mentioned earlier, creating virtual teams—groups of traders who share ideas and experiences online and who conduct their trading independently—can be a powerful way to remain a solo trader and still benefit from affiliating with others. Social media is a powerful tool for identifying potential team members, as you can quickly discern who generates good ideas, who approaches markets in a manner compatible with your trading, and who shares a personality and work style that would make collaboration fun and productive. Trading blogs, Stock Twits, and Twitter are excellent platforms for identifying potential partners. I know many independent traders who maintain chats throughout the trading day and benefit from running ideas by trusted colleagues. It's a great way to stay actively engaged in markets and benefit from the experience of others. The key is finding compatible participants: ones who truly provide insight, who benefit from your input, and who are as committed to sharing as you are. Without such compatibility, teamwork can easily devolve into distraction.

Imagine a situation in which four experienced, savvy traders conduct weekly online meetings to share market research, review performance, and mentor each other. Each participant would receive many times more ideas and guidance than if he or she operated in isolation. Teamwork is a best practice because it can leverage the best practices of multiple participants. As each team member stimulates every other one, the team as a whole becomes more than the sum of its parts. That is a powerful engine for learning and development.

Best Practice #21: Building Inspiration into Your Daily Routine

Here's a quick question: How much of your time during an average day is spent in a state of inspiration? If you're like most people, you probably spend so much time getting things done and living daily routines that little time is left over for those special activities that are inspiring. Yes, we enjoy our work and, yes, we enjoy and love family and friends. But do we experience inspiration? Do our activities truly uplift us?

As I mentioned earlier, I experienced a version of this challenge when writing this book. Generating the ideas for the text was exciting, but the routine of actually writing the pages became a chore—particularly after long days at work. That changed when I moved my work area to my den, attached high-quality speakers to my laptop, and did the rest of my writing from my office—accompanied by my favorite music. Something about music grabs my interest, but also inspires. I can be in a state of fatigue and discouragement and the right music will turn the mood and energy around, almost as if I've been plugged into an electric socket. Pandora has been a major boon in that regard, as it's enabled me to program my own virtual radio station, filled with the sounds that keep me going.

Music is only one source of inspiration, however. There are many ways to tap into the things that bring us joy, excitement, challenge, and meaning. With four cats in the home that we have rescued, there is always at least one of them wanting to play or cuddle. Pets are special, and perhaps even more so when you've had a hand in rescuing them and bringing them into a better life. They are so appreciative and giving of affection that it is impossible to not feel warmth and happiness in their presence—much as I've felt those things with my own children when they were young. The research literature in positive psychology suggests that many of the tender emotions, such as gratitude, appreciation, and tenderness, contribute significantly to mood, relationships, and health. It is impossible to feel discouraged and frustrated when you're cued in to the things in life that you appreciate and that you're grateful for.

What are some other powerful sources of inspiration?

- *Travel*—seeing new places and new cultures; experiencing the history of new areas; meeting new people and seeing the world through their eyes

- *Religion*—tapping into deep sources of faith and meaning; sharing spiritual experiences with others

- *Art and the performing arts*—experiencing the artistic vision of a creator; connecting with the meanings of plays, dance, movies, paintings, and other art forms

- *Social activity*—spending time with people we love and admire; meeting new people and learning from them

- *Physical activity*—turning routine exercise workouts into goal-oriented development, tracking our progress, and appreciating our growth

- *Romantic activity*—creating special moments at home and away by focusing on each other and sharing special experiences

- *Reading*—reading about people, topics, and stories that we find uplifting and energizing

The best practice is to build these activities into your daily and weekly routines, so that you experience inspiration on an ongoing basis. We have seen in this book how it is important to balance the activities in life that require energy with those that give energy if we are to be at our cognitive, emotional, and performance best. Making inspiration a daily habit keeps our batteries charged, energizing our work—and beyond.

Best Practice #22: Going with the Market Flow and Day Structure

One of the most common mistakes I see short-term traders make is focusing on short-term setups and then getting run over by larger trending moves. Understanding what markets are doing over longer time frames is extremely useful for putting short-term movement into perspective. Ideally, we want to have trend and momentum at our back. At the very least, we don't want to be fighting the market tide.

The most basic determination I want to make longer term and shorter term is whether the market is trending or moving within a range—and whether the market is gaining or losing strength. As we look from day to day, several indicators are useful in gauging strength:

- *New highs/new lows*—A rising market should expand new highs; a falling market should expand new lows. When we see new highs fail to expand on a day where the overall index prices are higher and vice versa, we want to be sensitive to the possibilities of reversal, as the broad list of shares is failing to participate in the movement of the index. It's important to note that divergences set markets up for reversal but do not necessarily immediately lead to reversal. For a rising market, a drop in new highs is not the same as an expansion of new lows, and vice versa. It's when we see significant numbers of stocks moving counter to market averages—often led by unusually weak or strong sectors—that reversals from trending mode to range mode are most common. Conversely, when we see a breakout in the number of stocks making new highs or lows after a period of consolidation, this can be an important indication of a transition from a range mode to a trending one.

- *NYSE TICK*—As mentioned in the earlier best practice, the net number of upticks versus downticks among NYSE shares is a sensitive measure of buying and selling pressure across the broad list of stocks. Keeping a running total of upticks minus downticks, like an advance–decline line, provides a simple and useful measure of growing and waning strength. The slope of the cumulative TICK line is particularly valuable in that regard, as flattening and steepening reveal shifts in sentiment among institutional participants—those who contribute most to the broad upticking and downticking of shares.

- *Sector behavior*—A quick and useful way of gauging market strength is to identify the number of sectors participating in a given move. A solid trending market will move the great majority of stock sectors. As noted above, when sector ETFs buck a move in the broad indexes, that divergence is often noteworthy. Range markets tend to be markets that feature sector rotation, so when we see some sectors strong and some weak, it's a good sign that market participants are reallocating their capital, not putting fresh capital to work in pursuit of trends.

Once the market day opens, we want to handicap the odds that the unfolding day is going to be a trend versus range day. Gauging day structure—the shape of the current market day—is essential to sound trade execution. If we see a trend day, we will want to be a buyer or seller early in the session and ride the directional movement. Buying early strength or selling early weakness is not necessarily a bad strategy. Conversely, if we detect a range day, we want to be fading both strength and weakness and not chasing either.

Key Takeaway

Understanding day structure sets up good trades for the short-term trader and sets up good execution for the longer-term trader.

What are some of the indications of a trend day? Several are particularly valuable in the stock market:

1. If you look at the number of stocks advancing versus declining for the day session ($ADD on e-Signal), you'll see early extreme numbers that persist through the day. The uptrend day typically starts with many more stocks advancing than declining relative to their prior closes. The downtrend day displays the reverse. When we see relatively balanced advancing and declining issues on the day, we're much more likely to be in a range, rotational environment. I also like to track the number of stocks on my watchlist that are rising or falling relative to their opening prices. The list will show all green (prices above open) on uptrend days; red (prices below open) on downtrend days; and mixed for range/rotational days.

2. If you look at the NYSE TICK as it unfolds over the session, you'll see many very strong values (+800 and over) early in the session for uptrend days and few if any weak values (−800 and below). The reverse will be true for downtrend days. When we see few extremes for the TICK, that moderation often clues us into a slow, rangy market.

3. If you look at the percentage of stocks trading above their volume-weighted average prices (VWAPs) for the day ($PCTABOVEVWAP .NY-ST on e-Signal), you'll see the number persistently above 50 percent on uptrend days, below 50 percent on downtrend days, and mixed (hovering near 50 percent) on range days. Similarly, if you look at the number of stocks making fresh new highs for the day session ($ATHI.NY-ST on e-Signal) and the number of stocks registering

fresh lows for the day session (\$ATLO.NY-ST), you'll see extremes on trend days and balanced numbers for range/rotational days.

4. When we see strong or weak days turn moderate on the above measures, that moderation often indicates a trend market losing strength and going into consolidation. When moderation in the indicators turns into more extreme readings, we often are seeing consolidation breaking out into a directional move.

The best practice is recognizing context: the market action surrounding the time period in which you are considering placing orders. Day structure and multiday structure tell us a great deal about whether buyers or sellers are dominant—or whether their influence is relatively balanced. The same setup can have very different outcomes depending on broader market context. Even when you're trading individual stocks, it helps to know if the market tide is running with you, against you, or is not running at all.

Best Practice #23: Reading in Parallel to Increase Creativity

If you were to walk into my home office while I was writing a book, you'd see at least 10 books on the floor, bookmarked and in various stages of being read. On the window seat next to those books are typically dozens of reference books for background on related topics. When I read something interesting in one book, I go to the other texts to see what they have to say on the topic. This in turn leads to consultation with yet other books, until I have a multifaceted view of the topic. At other occasions, I'm not writing a book, so there are fewer books tossed about the office, but there are always several. We might call this reading in parallel: scouring a single topic across many books at one time, rather than reading a single book from cover to cover. When researching, I typically work from the actual print books rather than the electronic versions. It is easier to bookmark the texts and read them side by side if they are sitting side by side.

When reading in parallel, you may never finish a book from start to finish. A useful process is to quickly scan the books and find an anchor text: one that seems unusually well researched and well written. The anchor text guides the selection of topics. You read about the topics you find most interesting and relevant in the anchor text and then move to the other books to examine their coverage of the topics. This creates a virtual conversation among the authors, as we view the topics through each of their lenses.

When you no longer encounter new and interesting material on a topic of interest, it's time to move to the next topic. The reading never is boring for that reason. Once you lose interest, you take a short break and switch topics, usually returning to the anchor book. The most interesting and relevant ideas that you encounter can be bookmarked and written down. Evernote is a great tool for saving and cataloging those notes.

The inventor Thomas Edison filed over 1000 patents during his career. He held himself to a discipline in which he and his assistants were required to generate one minor invention every 10 days and one major invention every 6 months. By churning out more inventions, he raised the odds of achieving at least a few significant inventions. Similarly, by reading material from a number of books in a dedicated time period each day, we expose ourselves to more ideas—and then have more ideas to draw on in generating our own. Parallel reading is a best practice, because it's an efficient and effective way to develop a deep understanding of particular topics.

Having worked this way for years, I've become unusually good at skimming books, identifying their main ideas, and deciding if they are worth reading in detail. The same process applies to research papers or online articles on a particular topic. This efficiency means that you can cover more high-quality material than the average person. You also become better over time at identifying high-quality material, so that you provide yourself with a far superior intellectual diet.

Reading a book is like having an expert visit your home for a conversation. Reading in parallel is like inviting a group of experts to your home and participating in their conversation. The acid test for reading in parallel is whether you come away from the exercise with perspectives that are contained in none of the individual texts. That is when reading becomes a truly creative exercise. Parallel reading provides you with multiple angles on a topic and a richer array of information. This enables us to synthesize new views, as we integrate what we read and emerge with fresh perspectives.

Best Practice #24: Developing Rules for Managing Your Risk

This best practice is offered by TraderFeed reader Vlad, who is a discretionary trader of forex, gold, and DAX. He sets a maximum loss limit per day (1.0 percent); week (2.5 percent); and month (10 percent) for his trading. He explains, "That has removed a great deal of the stress from trading, knowing that no one trade or series of trades can bring me down."

The best practice here is risk management: limiting the losses possible for any single trade, idea, or time period. As a psychologist, I've found that the prevention of deep drawdowns is worth many pounds of comeback cure. Losses that set the portfolio back also set us back and tend to impair subsequent trading. If we have three good ideas and lose a great deal of money on the first one, the odds are good that we'll trade the next two smaller and/or more nervously. Trading all three ideas with well-defined risk/reward almost certainly will optimize returns over time.

Readers trading for hedge funds, where capital is levered, will almost certainly set different percentages from Vlad. A loss of 10 percent in a month would be wholly unacceptable at most places where I have worked. Personally, I would not want three months of hitting my downside level to place me in a situation where I had to make over 40 percent on the remaining capital just to break even. Vlad's basic concept of setting loss limits for trading is quite sound. What we need to do is define the level of risk-taking that allows us to survive inevitable periods of poor trading and getting markets wrong.

Look at it this way: If you have a hit rate of 50 percent, then you will have 25 percent odds of two consecutive losing trades; 12.5 percent odds of three consecutive losing trades; 6.25 percent odds of four consecutive losing trades; and a little over 3 percent odds of five consecutive losing trades. If you place 50 trades in a year, guess what? You will almost certainly encounter strings of four and five consecutive losers. *You need to be able to survive that risk of ruin.* If you allow yourself to lose 10 percent of your initial capital on each trade, you will likely get to the point where you need to double your remaining money just to break even. If you allow yourself to lose no more than 1 percent of capital on each trade, any expectable run of losing trades is unlikely to impair your account—or your psyche.

Key Takeaway

We can't win the game if we can't stay in the game.

One of the practices that has served me well over the years is to enter longer-term trades with a fraction of my maximum position size. I've found that, when I'm wrong in a trade, I'm usually wrong early in that trade. Keeping my risk exposure modest initially enables me to lose less money if I'm stopped out quickly, and it allows me to add to my position if my scenario unfolds as planned. If I'm sized maximally, moves against me become a threat. If I'm sized more moderately, moves against my position can offer further opportunity. That's a great place to be psychologically. In a position trade, I never want to be sized so large that I can't take normal and expectable heat against my position.

Finally, loss prevention in trading is greatly aided by diversification. If you have two or more trading systems or methods that each have positive expected returns and are relatively uncorrelated in their return streams, you can create a situation where the expectable series of losing trades for any one method is buffered by the returns from the others. Diversification can also occur in the larger picture of our money management. My trading capital is but a fraction of our family's total investment capital. We have many fixed-income and other yielding investments, for example, that throw off a reasonable return each year. If I were to have a losing trading year, we would still harvest income from our larger portfolio.

Vlad's point is an important one: *Risk management is the best psychological management*. It is very difficult to keep our heads in the game if markets are handing our heads to us with adverse moves. Playing good defense sets us up for taking full advantage of offensive opportunities. Hard rules that govern the risk we allot to each trade, each trade idea, each period of time, and each portfolio help us turn good risk management into a positive habit pattern. No trade idea is so good that it is worth gambling our future. It's been said many times, but it remains sound wisdom: You can't win the game if you don't stay in the game. A great exercise is to network with traders who have sustained longevity in the business and find out how they manage risk and reward and the rules they implement. This can provide you with meaningful guidance for your own trading business.

Best Practice #25: Keeping Yourself in Peak Condition

Our next best practice in trading comes from Enis Taner (@EnisTaner) and captures the idea of keeping yourself in peak condition in all areas of life. Enis explains, "I've found that it is crucial that I am physically, emotionally, mentally, and spiritually healthy if I am to take on the challenges of trading professionally." Here's how Enis breaks it down:

- *Physical:* 30–45 minutes of high intensity exercise, 5–6 times per week.

- *Emotional:* Making it a habit to meet friends and/or family for social gatherings on a regular basis (not less than three times per week). "Good conversation is one of the best methods I've found to reduce mental stress," he observes.

- *Mental:* "I try to practice trading techniques on multiple time frames. Some weeks I will spend my learning time on reading financial statements and conference call transcripts with a focus toward long-term investments. Other weeks, I will test out correlations of short-term technical indicators."

- *Spiritual:* "I spend five minutes each morning on new things for which to be grateful. I've also found helping others, especially young people, with positive thinking and life mentorship overall to be fruitful for my own spiritual well-being."

The key idea here is that it's not enough to reduce stress in order to be a peak performer in markets. Just as an athlete must be in superb aerobic and strength condition with continuous skill practice and work on mental sharpness, the successful trader draws on reserves from all areas of life. It's not difficult to see how Enis's routines could be captured in a checklist, keeping him aligned with personal best practices. Creating our own peak performance processes ensures that we sustain the energy and positivity to weather the normal ups and downs of trading.

Where traders and others typically fall short is by prioritizing their workloads and leaving time for peak conditioning to leftover moments during the day and week. By the time we hit those leftover moments, we generally lack the energy to be pushing our envelopes physically, emotionally, and cognitively. A distinct best practice is to prioritize our conditioning and make our workloads fit into that. If the quality of our efforts follows from the quality of the states we're in, then it makes sense to keep ourselves in top running condition. That enables us to get more done in less time.

Racecar teams realize that it is impossible to win without quick and effective pit stops. If the car isn't maintained properly, it will be at risk of failing before the race is finished. The time we take for developing ourselves, as Enis points out, is our maintenance time. It is what enables us to fire on all cylinders throughout the competitive trading race.

Best Practice #26: Using Meditation to Improve Decision Making

One of the most common challenges for traders is sustaining a focus and state of mind that enables them to make sound decisions in the heat of market action. The emotions of the moment can lead to a fear of missing out (FOMO) and chasing poor opportunities. They can also lead to a fear of loss and premature exiting of positions. It is easy to become overconfident following wins and lacking in confidence after losses. Once our states of mind and body shift, we can lose access to the thinking and planning that lead to our best trading.

So how can we sustain an even mind frame? A valuable best trading practice comes from John Hope-Robinson (@johnhr), who describes meditation as an effective tool in conquering a fundamental trading flaw. John writes:

> We traders can be an insecure lot. We would rather at times be seen as a mysterious genius than just a successful trader. This need, born from a false sense of reality, can lead us to confuse intuition with "into wishing."
>
> We only need a system with a small winning edge to be a successful trader as long as we follow the rules of the system. Herein lies The Flaw. So many traders are just not *patient* enough to wait. The fear of doing nothing can be so terrifying that we feel a need to act to stop the fear and gain instant relief from it. This is the core issue.
>
> Through meditation we can learn to be OK during the necessary times where we need to do nothing but wait. We learn to achieve a clarity and calmness which can allay this perceived need to act. Meditation could well be the best investment a trader may ever make!

John rightly points to three key benefits of meditation:

1. *Enhanced self-control*—Meditation promotes calm, and it promotes focused concentration. Both enhance our cognitive and behavioral control, so that we can become mindful observers of our emotional patterns rather than victims of those. The first step in changing our patterns is becoming aware of them and not identifying with them.

2. *Enhanced access to intuition*—It is when we are still that we have greatest access to what we may know, but not know that we know. Very often, experienced traders possess a keen gut feel for markets, but that feel is drowned by flight-or-fight responses to market action. Meditation promotes a stillness that enables us to listen to ourselves.

3. *Enhanced well-being*—We cannot trade well if we are dominated by fear: the fear of missing moves, the fear of losing money, the fear of being wrong, and the fear of inaction. Research suggests that meditation can lead to enhanced personal satisfaction and subjective well-being, which allow us to act from a position of emotional strength.

There is one other powerful benefit to meditation that makes it a best trading practice: It requires that we sustain cognitive focus at the same time that we keep ourselves still. This is a kind of exercise for our "focusing muscles," training us over time to build our powers of concentration. In that sense, we can think of meditation as a kind of willpower training. The stronger our focusing muscles, the more able we are to withstand the emotional and physiological arousal of experiencing risk, reward, and uncertainty.

Key Takeaway
Meditation is training for mind and spirit.

A corollary of this best practice is that some of the best preparation time for trading occurs away from trading screens. Using meditation as a midday break—as well as a morning preparation for the day—helps us step back from markets and approach them with a fresh perspective. Removing ourselves from markets can be a powerful way of removing ourselves from the reactive trading of markets.

Best Practice #27: Reprogramming Our Minds Through Visualization

If we take a look at angry or fearful people, we notice something interesting: They tend to dwell on scenarios that reinforce their anger or fear. Angry people play movies in their head of confrontation and revenge. Fearful people fill their minds with scenarios of danger. In both cases, they unwittingly program their minds with the very emotions that trouble them. Changing their minds requires a kind of reprogramming, replacing negative scenarios with more realistic and constructive ones.

A valuable best practice is using imagery and visualization to change our thoughts, feelings, and actions as traders. Imagery can be a powerful method for reprogramming our minds and reframing challenging trading situations. TraderFeed reader David Spengler offers this best practice from his own trading:

> In German, the phrase "to jump into cold water" refers to a situation that is new and unknown and therefore risky. Before entering a trade, I am visualizing exactly that situation to overcome fear and procrastination. I close my eyes for a few seconds and imagine it is summer. The sky is blue, it is very hot, and I am sweating. I am standing by a pool. Then I jump into the water headfirst. It is a shock, but only for a second. Then it feels unbelievably good, as I sense every cell in my body and the blood pulses through my veins, my heart pumping fast.
>
> This image reminds me that jumping into the cold water/taking risk can actually feel good. More technically speaking, I reframe the situation. Since I have made it a habit imagining this scene, problems executing my trading systems have been greatly diminished.

Notice here how a situation that could be experienced as unpleasant (risk taking) is transformed into something that is refreshing (diving into cold water on a hot day). By making the visualization habitual, the exercise becomes a kind of self-hypnotic suggestion. David uses the exercise to enter trades, but a very similar exercise could be used to reframe taking losses—or any other challenging situations in markets.

I have found that visualization can also be used very effectively prior to the start of the trading day as a way to mentally rehearse trading plans. By walking ourselves through various scenarios via imagery, we can mentally prepare ourselves to take the right actions. What makes David's technique especially effective is that the imagery *emotionally* reframes the trading situation. If we were to prepare ourselves at the start of the day by imagining ourselves stopping out of losing trades, learning from the experience, and refreshing ourselves for the next opportunities, the act of stopping out would become far less onerous.

Replacing negative self-talk with positive imagery is a great way to retrain our thought processes and channel our efforts constructively. When negative thinking becomes habitual, it means that we need to stand back from our thinking and take the role of programmer of our minds. The emotional preparation to act may be as important as the trading plan itself: We can train ourselves to think and respond in ways that bring success rather than stress and distress.

Best Practice #28: Conducting Regular Trading Reviews

Deliberate practice is a process in which we continually evaluate performance and use those evaluations to make targeted efforts at improvement. Research from Anders Ericsson (1996) suggests that deliberate practice is essential in developing performance expertise. Turning routine trading into structured deliberate practice requires that we actively review our trading, assess what we could have done better, and use that information to make hands-on corrections in our subsequent performance. The assessment of our trading comes from TraderFeed reader Norbert Beckstrom as a best practice and consists of a daily review of trading performance. The power of such a review comes from the fact that it can anchor a process of continuous learning and performance improvement. Here are the questions Norbert puts to himself after a day's trading:

1. Did I put on high-probability (A+) trades that I wouldn't be easily scared out of?
2. Did I trade to win or did I trade not to lose?
3. Did I have enough size in my conviction trades?
4. Did I break any of my rules? Why?
5. Was I mindful of what I was doing?
6. How many of today's trades would I make again under the same circumstances?
7. How many of my trades did I bail on before the stop or profit target? How did that work out?
8. How many of my trades today were placed out of fear of missing a move?
9. How many trades did I miss today because I wasn't paying attention or was working on something else?
10. How many doubles were there that I didn't have an edge for?
11. How do I feel about my trading at the end of the day?
12. What can I do to improve these answers?

Norbert adds that if he conducts this review in the morning before the markets open rather than in the evening at the end of the trading day, the answers are more likely to be fresh in his mind and he's more likely to avoid making trading mistakes. In that sense, his review process is a mindfulness process. Clearly identifying where he could improve his trading helps him work on those improvements in subsequent trading.

Norbert's review is geared to a discretionary day trader. Traders with different trading styles and traders working on different trading issues will likely have very different review lists. My review, for example, is much more about markets and less about making emotional errors. Because my trades are based on backtested rules and relationships, my first hypothesis is that a losing trade means I may well have missed something important and idiosyncratic in the market. This prods me toward further market analysis. Should the trading loss result from not following my rules, that would prod me toward further self-analysis. The review is thus helpful in encouraging us to take fresh looks at markets and at ourselves as traders of those markets.

Ultimately, the most important question is Norbert's final one. Answering the questions is only useful to future performance if the answers anchor specific plans and actions toward improvement. Review is necessary for deliberate practice, but not sufficient. It is what we *do* with the answers to our review questions that determines whether our experience turns into learning and development. First we do, then we review, then we redo based on what we've learned. Every trade is practice; every review pushes us to make tangible improvements in what we do. Trading experience we don't review is lost experience—and that might be the riskiest loss of all.

Best Practice #29: Using Chart Review to Feed Our Creativity

One of the themes of this book has been that creativity is the new trading discipline. Success in markets is not so much a function of rigidly adhering to a single, unchanging edge as continually finding fresh sources of edge in ever-changing markets. But how do we develop fresh trading ideas and sources of edge?

Author and blogger Ivaylo Ivanov (@ivanhoff) offers a best practice that can feed our creativity. Here's what he suggests:

> Studying your own past trades is a must, but it provides a
> limited perspective of opportunity cost—it only helps to

analyze the trades you took; it tells you nothing about the trades you did not take. One of the most practical habits that has helped me as a trader is going through the daily charts of the best performing stocks on a daily, monthly, quarterly, and six-month time frame. Here are some of the benefits of this daily exercise:

- It has substantially improved my setup recognition skills.

- It has given me ideas for new ways to approach the market.

- It provides an unbiased view of what is currently working in the market, which industries are under accumulation. Recognizing industry momentum is of utmost importance for swing traders as it helps to focus on setups that don't only have higher probability to break out or break down, but are also likely to deliver bigger gains.

- The mere going through the screens provides me with a constant flow of great anticipation swing setups—stocks that are setting up for a potential breakout.

Readers will recognize this as a structured exercise in pattern recognition. In his book, *The Five Secrets to Highly Profitable Swing Trading* (2014), Ivaylo outlines his "perfect setup" for swing trades. His best practice described above additionally enables him to learn new setups. It also enables him to identify sectors that are most likely to yield good setup candidates. Indeed, the patterns that emerge from such review could lend themselves to backtesting and possible systematic inputs into discretionary trading.

Key Takeaway

Pattern recognition is a core trading skill that can be cultivated through immersive experience.

I also suspect that Ivaylo's best practice helps him identify market themes early—for instance, the breakdown in energy stocks in the wake of oil weakness or the rise in utility shares resulting from declining global rates. It's not such a leap to go from his exercise to a review of patterns across global markets to identify the macro themes that might be attracting the interest of institutional investors.

Finally, the chart review is a best practice because it combats confirmation bias. We may think that the market is strong or weak, but a thorough review of individual stocks will actually show us strength, weakness, and consolidation. By allowing markets to tell us their stories, we're most likely to capture emerging patterns rather than impose our own.

Best Practice #30: Training Ourselves to Accept Uncertainty

Success in trading requires the ability to act decisively in the midst of uncertainty. Even when a trader possesses a durable edge in markets, the random variation around that edge ensures a meaningful proportion of losing trades. Risk management begins with the acknowledgment that there is much about the future that we don't know and that, at any given moment, we could very well be wrong.

A relevant best practice, submitted by Jonathan Frank, a 20-year-old college student and trader, is the conscious acceptance of uncertainty. Jonathan writes:

> The market goes up and down (crazy, I know) and I have been a successful trader because I know that s**t happens that you cannot always prepare for, as happens in life. You live, you learn, and you move forward. Once you become okay with this uncertainty, you are ready to hit that buy button. Until then, you might want to start searching for another Albert Einstein to come up with the perfect theory and prediction of the future.
>
> I assess market uncertainty by educating myself on consumer outlooks, job reports, and international events that have direct and indirect effects on the US markets. I then decide if we are in a state of composure or panic.... Market uncertainty is like the weather in that there will always be people speculating about whether stocks are going to go up or down in the future, but unless there is a drastic occurrence you have to be optimistic and know that rainy days are followed by sunshine. Always.

Jonathan has not been trading for long, but he has come to an important and mature insight: How we trade depends on how we assess the environment. Are we experiencing a normal market environment or an abnormal one? If we hear a weather forecast predicting a rainstorm, we do not panic and refuse to go outdoors. We dress appropriately and go about our business, understanding that there is some small possibility that the storm could become something truly ugly and dangerous. If, however, we notice very ominous clouds and very low air pressure and hear a weather alert, we may very well decide to take precautionary measures and batten down the hatches.

Jonathan mentions data releases and international events as indicators of uncertainty in the world. In markets, we can also gauge uncertainty by looking at realized and implied volatilities—how much markets are moving and how much volatility is priced into markets via options. I find that historical analyses of markets also provide a useful gauge of uncertainty. When we look at where the market stands today and then go back in time and examine all similar occasions, we can get a sense for the variability of forward outcomes. Sometimes, those prospective outcomes contain a directional edge; sometimes they are random. Sometimes those outcomes are highly variable; other times they are more constrained. By examining the range of past outcomes under the present set of conditions, we can sensitize ourselves to the uncertainty of the immediate future.

One exercise that is useful when planning a trade is asking, "What would I expect to see if I am dead wrong?" This may sound odd, because in a sense, it's planning for failure. That, however, is what preparation is all about. If we have not consciously thought through the possibility we are wrong and planned our actions in that eventuality, then we really have not accepted uncertainty. Defining and planning for worst-case scenarios is a very effective way of taking the fear out of uncertainty.

Best Practice #31: Becoming Rule-Governed in Your Trading Practice

Think of the successes of great sports teams or businesses. In so many cases, consistency in execution is a common feature. The great football team doesn't just block and tackle well on a given occasion; they do so every play, every game. Businesses like FedEx or UPS don't just deliver on time; they hit their time targets consistently. How can traders achieve high levels of consistency amid markets that are ever-changing?

The answer is by turning trading practices into trading rules. Rules are what turn best practices into habits—and habits are what give us consistency. Contrary to popular conception, discipline is not about forcing yourself to do the right thing. It's about turning right things into habit patterns so that no force is needed to perform at a high level.

The idea of becoming rule-governed as a best practice comes to us from reader Markham Gross (@MarkhamGross), who is the founder of Anderson Creek Trading, LLC. He explains how the use of rules and systems brings consistency to trading:

> A trader or investor cannot control markets or the outside world. All that is under the trader's control is his or her reactions to what is happening in markets or what is perceived to be happening in markets. Therefore, systems should be applied. The best systems are often simple. Spreadsheets can work as an implementation tool and some light programming skills will also go a long way. Systems should be comprised of specific rules for when to enter, exit for loss, exit for profits, and size of the positions. These rules can match the trader's personality and temperament. They should be testable. Although there are limits to backtesting, performing some backtests will help the trader know what to expect so they are not surprised by normal drawdowns. To approach the market without rules on a daily or weekly basis would be a mistake.

What I find in my work with traders is that many of the best work in a hybrid fashion. They make decisions on a discretionary basis *and* their decisions are guided by explicit and tested rules. For example, one trader I worked with years ago examined price breakouts that tended to continue in the direction of the breakout versus those that reversed back into the prior range. He found several factors differentiated breakouts from fakeouts, including the volume of the move; where the move stood with respect to longer time frame activity; and the time of day of the breakout. He turned these factors into a checklist, so that he only took breakout trades that scored highly on his criteria. Those rules not only helped him find winning trades but kept him out of many losers.

Yet another tested rule that has been effective in guiding discretionary trading has been examining the market's early trading on a given day and adapting the day's trading to the level of participation being observed. From the opening minutes, we can observe if we are transacting more or less volume than recently, which gives us an indication of likely volatility and the degree of directional participation in the market. If I observe significantly below-average volume and very little buying or selling pressure in the opening minutes of trade, I become much more selective about trade location and much more opportunistic in taking profits. In many cases, I'll opt to not trade that day. The rules regarding volume and directional skew of participation help me act on opportunity and avoid being chopped up in slow markets.

When that earlier-mentioned trader first generated his rules, he used the checklist daily to guide his actions. Eventually, the criteria became sound trading habits and were implemented routinely. The same has been the case for my tracking of volume and buying/selling pressure. Repetition is the mother of habits, and habits are the backbone of discipline. Turning successful strategies into rules is a great way to ensure that best practices become robust processes.

Best Practice #32: Managing Trading Stress with Biofeedback

The body's flight-or-fight response that we know as stress is typically a reaction to perceived threat. When we care about an outcome that is uncertain—and especially when we perceive a threat to that outcome—our bodies mobilize for action. That leaves us with adrenaline pumping, muscles tensing, and heart rate accelerating. Such arousal is an adaptive response for dealing with physical threats, such as avoiding an oncoming car, but often gets in the way of careful, deliberate action when the threats we perceive are coming from the trading screen. It is ironic that, just as we most need to be grounded in the rational activities of our frontal cortices, we typically activate our motor areas and risk acting before thinking.

Key Takeaway

Biofeedback is a training tool for physical and cognitive self-mastery.

How we react to what we perceive plays an important role in determining whether stress brings disorganization and distress. A relevant best practice comes from TraderFeed reader Daniel Hunter, who outlines his use of biofeedback in dealing with trading stress. Earlier in the book, we took at look at how biofeedback can help us achieve optimal cognitive and emotional states. Here's what Daniel has to say about biofeedback as a strategy for coping with stress:

> I am a scalper in the forex markets, so anxiety, excitement, and apprehension can creep into the trading day. I combat this with a device that measures heart rate variability. The device I use is the Emwave2. It has an earlobe attachment that I use during trading. I use it along with the computer program provided and have a visual, real-time status of my current state. If my emotions start to waver and my breathing starts to change, it alerts me, often before I realize my state. With breathing exercises, I can bring my emotions back under control and focus on what is actually happening in the market. It is also a fantastic practice before bedtime, as you fall asleep faster and your quality of sleep is much improved. It is basically an objective meditation monitor.

Because the monitor gives us real-time feedback about whether we are in or out of our performance zone, it can be useful as a tool for mindfulness. Once we are aware of our stress responses, we can channel them in constructive ways and prevent them from driving our next trading decisions. The readings from the biofeedback application enable us to become observers to our states, so that we can see when we are in a state of flow and when we are responding to markets with those fight-or-fight reactions. Everyone falls out of the zone during performances. The key is becoming aware of those lapses, so that it is possible to take corrective action.

When we choose to trade, we elect to operate in an environment where there is risk and uncertainty. That ensures that we will experience stress. Our challenge is to turn stress into a stimulus for self-mastery—to control our responses rather than allow them to control us. Biofeedback is a best practice because it serves as an alert and also as a training tool for maintaining calm, focused concentration.

Best Practice #33: Building a Learning Network via Social Media

One of the greatest psychological challenges of trading is a cognitive, not an emotional, one. It is the challenge of bandwidth: our limitations in processing large amounts of information at any given time. Many portfolio managers I've worked with have developed ways of expanding their bandwidth, including building out teams to help with research and execution; connecting with savvy peers to discuss market ideas; and staying in touch with colleagues on the trading floor. Turning trading into a team sport increases the number of eyes and ears on markets and is valuable in spotting emerging trading ideas. How many times have I observed traders so focused on their particular trades that they miss what is happening in the broader market? Tunnel vision is a great way to get blindsided in markets. Turning trading into a team sport enables us to process a greater range of information during those occasions when we need to be highly focused.

Social media is accomplishing a leveling of the bandwidth playing field for individual traders. Most independent traders do not have a trading floor to turn to for market color and cannot afford to build out teams of analysts. Through social media, however, they can turn their trading into a virtual team sport. Cultivating a focused network of insightful peers adds to the eyes and ears on markets and sparks thinking about fresh sources of opportunity.

This is why building a social learning network is a best practice in trading. This is a network of peer traders who value your input and who also provide you with valuable observations and insights into markets. The key to creating an effective social learning network is selectivity. A great deal of the commentary we encounter via tweets, blog posts, and chat is high on noise, low on signal. You want a network that provides very high signal value.

A great place to start a learning network is Stock Twits. The Stock Twits feed is a curated stream of tweets with high information value. Via the feed, you'll notice certain contributors come up again and again. These are often high-value sources of information you will want in your network. Of particular value are the Saturday $STUDY sessions from the Stock Twits feed that select specific tweets and links for their valuable content. In general, the $STUDY postings offer a broad range of observations, analyses, and information. You'll find particularly good links via founder Howard Lindzon and head of community development Sean McLaughlin.

Yet another place to build your learning network is through sites that comb through content on the financial web and curate selections. Abnormal Returns offers a broad range of links daily and each week selects top podcasts and highlights the most popular links of the week. This also is a great way to discover valuable sources of information that can become your regular listening and reading. On the podcast side, there are the offerings from Michael Covel and Barry Ritholtz that feature interviews with top professionals in finance. Other excellent sources of links are Josh Brown via The Reformed Broker blog and Barry Ritholtz's The Big Picture site. An absolute treasure trove of writings in quantitative finance can be found on The Whole Street aggregator site. Curated blog selections are also available from the feed at Finviz.com.

A very promising strategy for building a learning network is starting with traders who are committed to training other traders. An excellent start would be to look up the traders who have contributed best practices to this book and check out their blogs and tweets. If you like what you see, find out who they link to and follow: The odds will be good that those will also be sources helpful to you. All of those represent potential contacts who can be useful resources for your trading development.

The acid test for any addition to your learning network is that what you read or listen to actually must contribute fresh and useful perspectives to your understanding and trading of markets. There is much to be said for entertainment—it's easy to get into surface readings of many sources—but what is ultimately valuable is what feeds your head. You can't solve fresh puzzles unless you have the right pieces. And you won't get all the pieces if you're locked inside your head. Through social media, you can move from research to building a virtual research team. It doesn't matter how emotionally controlled and disciplined you are: You can't trade the opportunities you never see or hear about.

Best Practice #34: Finding and Focusing on Your Trading Edge

Two kinds of traders fail to find success: those who cannot adapt to changes in markets and those who cannot focus and exploit their potential edges in markets. Very often, traders become frustrated with losses and abandon what they are doing, seeking ever better ideas and methods. This makes it very difficult to ever master any particular opportunity or skill set in markets. The lack of focus ensures that there is no ongoing deliberate practice: The trader who continually changes his or her approach remains a relative novice, lacking cumulative learning.

Key Takeaway

Once you've explored and expanded, success comes from simplifying and focusing on essentials.

An important best practice submission comes from David Blair (@crosshairtrader). Readers will recognize him from the Crosshairs-Trader site and blog and his ongoing work in training traders. David's best practice is all about focus: eliminating what is nonessential in markets and developing a very specific market edge and expertise:

> When I first started trading, I decided to be a sponge, soaking up all the stock market information I could, free or otherwise. After sponging it for a few years I realized I created a monster devoid of creativity, replaced by anxiety, confusion, fear, and impatience, all of which were a result of a lack of focus. I traveled in a black hole with a flashlight and didn't know it.
>
> During these years I was trading with a partner: a friend who introduced me to the business. Each day he would have a new topic for us to study. As a result, our trading room began to look like a war room. Eight monitors, two big-screen TVs, two color printers for printing charts, cases of books, CDs, seminar manuals, etc. The problem was, the more we added, the worse our performance, the worse our performance, the more we added, creating a vicious cycle of spoiled intentions. As my partner continued to add, I began to subtract. I began practicing minimalism by getting rid of all the things I thought were so important, realizing that stock prices cannot be predicted no matter how much I learned or added to my charts.
>
> My process now involves a very simple, easy to understand price pattern wherein I look for stocks breaking from price boxes to either (1) continue the previous trend or (2) reverse the previous trend. I have a well-defined method for locating these trades when they trigger on two time frames, the weekly and daily. I have prepared a watch list of stocks and have developed indicators specifically designed to alert me when there is a potential trade opportunity. In other words, I have become a "process specialist." I have developed a specific process that helps me manage the uncertainty of future stock prices. I no longer feel the need to study everything or watch anything other than the stocks on my watch list.

David's methodology makes sense: Stocks trading in a box are ones that have consolidated. Both directionality and volatility are at reduced levels. He identifies opportunities in which breakouts place him on the right side of both direction and volatility. This not only means that the market moves his way, but that it moves his way with a degree of impulsivity. Psychologically, having a specific methodology like this reduces distraction and enables a trader to become a true specialist, building skills in a particular kind of trading. Perhaps most important of all, specializing in a type of trading enables David to make trades truly his own, so that he will have the confidence to act decisively when that is required. Expertise in a particular type of trading also helps him quickly recognize when setups are not working and limit his losses.

Many successful physicians are not only specialists but sub-specialists. They find their "edge" by knowing one area in great depth. This can be a very helpful approach for traders as well. Once you master a single pattern, you can move on to others, developing a diversified array of opportunities.

Best Practice #35: Improving Your Workflow

We put thought into what we need to get done, but often don't reflect on the ordering and organization of what we do. Relatively simple changes in our workflow can yield profound benefits in our work effectiveness and efficiency. I recently spoke with a trader who conducted the lion's share of his market review immediately prior to the New York open. This occurred after a lengthy commute into the city and after numerous conversations on the trading floor on his arrival. By the time he got around to figuring out what he was doing for the day, he felt a mixture of distraction, fatigue, and time pressure—none of which helped him focus on market opportunity. His reduced concentration early in the day led to silly trading mistakes, which in turn built frustration. Quite simply, his workflow was not setting him up for success.

A worthy best practice is organizing your workflow as a trader. TraderFeed reader Rahul Rijhwani describes the organization of his trading workflow and how he separates tasks to maintain his effectiveness. Here is what he has observed:

> I analyze my stocks only after market hours. During market hours, the focus is only on execution. This way there is a lot of clarity since there is only one task at hand at any

given point. Also, there is a sense of calm and clear thought process when analyzing and executing.

To explain the process briefly, when the markets are closed, I open charts in my watchlist, then analyze them, and set alerts at important price points based on the trading strategy. Then I calculate the position size and note it in a diary. When the market is open the next day, when price comes close to the point where I have set an alert, there is a beep. I then open the chart, calculate risk/reward, and punch the order if the risk/reward is favorable.

The key takeaway here is that Rahul uses his workflow to separate the process of generating ideas from the process of following markets and executing trades. By preparing his trades in advance, down to the details of price level and sizing, he helps ensure that his decision making is controlled and planned and not reactive to the situation of the moment. This enables him to stay clear-headed without the need to resort to psychological techniques during the trading session.

The organization of our time helps us stay mentally organized. If I need to be open-minded and creative at one point in the trading day, I will make sure that the preceding activities are not ones that are taxing and stressful. If I need to tackle stressful and detailed work, I will make sure that I do so at times when my concentration and willpower are at high levels. A good workflow creates a rhythm during the day between activities that require energy and those that give energy. Most of all, organizing our workflow means that we control our work and it doesn't control us. That is a great psychological benefit.

Best Practice #36: Developing Trading Rituals

A ritual is an activity that has special meaning and that we perform the same way at the same time. A family might have its Thanksgiving meal rituals; most religious services are anchored by rituals; we have rituals for such special events as births, weddings, and funerals. Rituals are more than mere habits—they set time apart to focus us on what is meaningful. When we enter a ritual, we shift psychological gears to participate in the significance of the occasion.

A fascinating best practice in trading is developing trading rituals. These are activities that focus us on what is most important in trading. TraderFeed reader Yvan Byeajee, an active, full-time trader, has written a book called *Paradigm Shift* (2014) that stresses the importance of organization and preparation for trading success. Yvan explains, "The book is essentially a statement of the work ethic that is required to make it in this business. Without it, even the most robust system is doomed to failure. I strongly believe that this applies to almost anything in life."

Here is the daily schedule of rituals laid out by Yvan (all times Pacific):

Monday to Friday:

5:30 AM–5:50 AM: Read my list of positive affirmations. (Positive Expectancy Mind + Positive Expectancy Model = Success)

5:50 AM–6:30 AM: Breakfast while glancing over market related news.

6:30 AM: Market opens. Watch how price action unfolds.

8:00 AM: By that time I'm usually done watching the markets. I am out of any daytrades I took for the day. I also placed my orders to open any new swing trading ideas and placed my orders to close any existing ones

8:00 AM–8:30 AM: I read trading blogs.

8:30 AM–9:00 AM: I listen to a trading-related podcast.

9:00 AM–12:00 N: I'm usually out during that time period for a run, followed by a 1-hour yoga session.

12:00 N–1:00 PM: At that time, I'm back in front of my screen to watch the final hour prior to the market close and I look to close or initiate new positions if there are any.

1:00 PM–2:00 PM: I update my trading journal and trading log. I also save the charts of the setups I took or exited for later review.

2:00 PM–3:30 PM: Research and homework for the next trading day (scanning through hundreds of charts, noting possible entries, exits, position sizing, and risk management parameters to minimize decisions during market hours)

9:30 PM–10:00 PM: Book: Trading-related lectures. I will typically read one chapter per day.

10:00 PM–10:20 PM: Meditation

Saturday:

9:30 PM–10:00 PM: Book: Trading-related lectures. One chapter as usual.

10:00 PM–10:20 PM: Meditation

Sunday:

1:00 PM–2:30 PM: Read journal, logs, and saved charts. The goal is not only to learn something about the market's behavior, but also mine: What I did right, what I did wrong, and where I could have done better.

2:30 PM–4:00 PM: Backtesting (statistical analysis of previous chart patterns and their occurrences, updating of my positive expectancy model and possible new models).

9:30 PM–10:00 PM: Book: Trading related lectures. One chapter.

10:00 PM–10:20 PM: Meditation.

Yvan explains, "My best practices have evolved over time to fit my needs at the moment, so new traders should expect theirs to do the same. They should test, modify, and ultimately find something that suits them the best. Once they have set up a task to perform as part of their routine, they should try their best to stick to it and be done with it within the set time frame. Every time we participate in a ritual, we are expressing our beliefs, either verbally or implicitly, so we should be focused on the process, one small step at a time, and the results will take care of themselves."

Key Takeaway

Your rituals define the essence of your success.

Yvan offers a great example of how he has turned best practices into robust processes. Particularly striking is how much time he *doesn't* spend in front of trading screens. I think this is very important. He prepares his trades the night before and conducts extensive homework in the evenings and during weekend hours. That allows him to use active trading hours to simply execute his plans. Such planning and time away from screens prevents overtrading and also enables Yvan to work on himself.

The ritualistic aspect of Yvan's schedule is reflected in the way he segments time to work either on his trading or on himself. Note how he uses reading, affirmations, meditation, and yoga to keep his mind and body in shape. Each time period has a sacred purpose, devoted to a valued cause. This makes each time period special—and helps keep Yvan anchored in what is most important to his personal and professional development.

Your rituals may differ from Yvan's but the important takeaway—as he points out—is the consistency of your activities. It is that consistency that turns a worthwhile practice into a meaningful ritual. I strongly suspect that Yvan's edge in markets comes both from the work he performs daily and weekly and also his ability to turn best practices into rituals that hold emotional significance.

Best Practice #37: Adapting to Markets Through Scenario-Based Preparation

In trading, as in sports, the game is often won or lost before the competition formally begins. It's the preparation for winning that leads to winning and the failure to prepare that prepares for failure. Coach Bob Knight famously observed that many have the will to win, but not many have the will to prepare to win. Elite performers love the preparation, not just the performance—and that's what enables them to move to ever-higher levels of performance.

TraderFeed reader Paul Landry has contributed a valuable best practice: a scenario-based preparation routine. By anticipating a variety of possible market scenarios and clearly outlining how he'd respond to each, Paul helps ensure that he will not be surprised by market developments. It is very difficult to emotionally overreact to situations that we have anticipated and prepared for. In that sense, mental preparation is one of our best tools for emotional self-control. Here's how Paul explains his routine:

> I come from a military background. Before an operation, rehearsals are crucial to getting things right before we face decisions in the heat of battle. I find I also need to conduct rehearsals before the trading day. I rehearse seven possible scenarios with four parts for each one.
>
> The seven scenarios are: a bullish move that turns into a long trend upward; a bullish move that turns into a short trend upward; a bearish move that turns into a long trend downward; a bearish move that turns into a short trend downward; a return to the mean move where the market reverses; the most likely move that I could experience; and the most dangerous move I could experience.
>
> The four parts are: the likelihood of each scenario; what the charts and indicators will show to identify each scenario; what is the likely near term direction for each scenario; and what my reaction should be when faced with each scenario.

The rehearsals help me in two ways. First, the decision making is faster and of higher quality because I have been in the situation before. Also, the second-guessing during and after the trade is minimized because the decisions were rehearsed beforehand, when trading stress was minimal.

Notice that Paul's preparation routine is really an exercise in open-mindedness. He does not start the market day locked into any one particular scenario. Rather, he rehearses and prepares for all likely situations, staying flexible as markets unfold. During the day's session, certain scenarios will come to the fore and others will not play out, enabling Paul to focus on his preparation for the day's most likely outcomes.

My experience with this kind of preparation is that detail is important. It's not just visualizing a situation that is important, but concretely rehearsing the specific steps you would take in that situation. Preparing through multiple modalities is more effective than through a single channel. For example, visualizing a scenario and desired responses; talking out the scenario and responses; and writing them both out are different ways of processing trading plans. Spending more time on the exercise—and drawing on multiple ways of processing the plans—results in a deeper and more effective preparation.

"What-if" planning is essential not only in military actions but in most competitive games and sports, from chess to football. As Paul emphasizes, one cannot count on accurately and thoroughly processing a situation in the heat of battle. Anticipating and planning actions before things heat up is a great way to make sure we trade well, regardless of curve balls the market may toss our way.

Best Practice #38: Balancing Your Job with Your Trading Career

What if you want to develop yourself as a trader, but you need to bring in income right here, right now? In that case, you probably work a day or night job while you learn the ropes as a trader. Balancing your job with your hoped-for trading career can be a challenge, but it can be done.

A best-practice perspective comes from Sam Awad, who describes—tongue firmly in cheek—some of the strategies that help traders who have to make ends meet from 9 to 5:

> In my mind, the real unsung heroes of the trading world are people like me: people who love markets, are invigorated

by the intellectual pursuit of extracting money from the market; people who are willing to put up their hard earned capital against Ivy Leaguers, former Division 1 athletes, Ph.D. mathematicians and computer scientists; and who are just nutty enough to do it—while at work.

That's right. We're the guys who work 8 hours a day, every day. And when do those 8 hours occur every day? Oh yeah, at the exact same time as market hours. And yet for the love of the game and the dream of a new, free life, we persevere. ... Over the years, I've become an expert at this. I have faded liquidity spikes while yawning through Monday morning meetings; navigated Fed speeches and pylons during forklift training; caught a lucky bounce off a morning support level during a conference call; and given it all back rolling the dice on Non-Farms on casual Friday.

Through it all, I've compiled quite a few methods by which to achieve Trading at Work mastery:

1. Negotiate an earlier starting time: Arriving at work before your co-workers may seem like an opportune time to work on company work, since you will spend the rest of the day trading, but really you'll use this time to research and generate your day's trading ideas.
2. Volunteer for special projects: This is the best way to ensure you always have an excuse for not getting day-to-day work done, and you look like a hero volunteering. What do you do when those special projects come due? Don't concern yourself with that right now. When that day comes let Future You curse Present-Day, Money-Making You. It'll be worth it.
3. And this is the piece de resistance: If at all possible, find a software program that looks similar to your trading platform. It could be software that charts productivity analytics, or sales, or in my case, temperature and humidity monitoring. Just get everyone in your office used to seeing those nice red and blue bars on your monitor, and boom! You've just bought yourself valuable screen time!

Sam's advice may not work well for job longevity, but it captures a challenge that many people face when they are first learning how to trade. When I began trading intraday, I was teaching and running a student-counseling program at a medical school. Fortunately, students were engaged in courses during morning hours, which allowed me to follow markets early in the trading day. I developed a trading approach that only traded opening setups. To this day, if I trade intraday, my feel is best at and immediately following the market open. Day after day of focusing on the early trade provided an unusual intimacy with the dynamics of the market open—and its relevance for the trading day.

The need to maintain normal working hours is where simulated trading and the ability to replay the market day can be extremely useful. Once I finished work, I replayed the market day on my platform and practiced trading with real prices. That permitted me to gain a feel for markets without jeopardizing my work during the day, which I loved. I was also able to use evening hours to print and review charts, observe market patterns, and learn valuable lessons that have stuck with me to this day. The use of market replay to simulate trading is a great way to practice trading new patterns and learn from mistakes without jeopardizing either your capital or your job.

Creatively integrating the work you do to bring in a paycheck with the work you do to learn markets is a best practice. Whether it's by extending your time frame and making decisions at the market close or rehearsing shorter-term trading by using replay to see how patterns set up and recur, it is possible to make trading fit into an existing job and career.

Best Practice #39: Developing Self-Control Routines During the Trading Day

During market hours, it can become easy to focus on trading and neglect the person who is doing the trading! Once we lose self-awareness, we can make decisions that we would never make if we were calm and focused. Self-control is easy when we are not facing stressful situations and dealing with fight-or-flight responses. During periods of emotional, cognitive, and physiological arousal, however, our state shifts can take us very far from our initial planning. That is why self-control strategies that can be employed during trading hours are a best practice.

Key Takeaway

Self-mastery itself can be mastered.

Several self-control methods are offered by TraderFeed reader Gus Joury, a short-term trader of crude oil futures. Here are some of the daily best practices that aid his trading:

1. I start my day with 15–20 minutes of meditation/mindfulness. I practice breathing meditation and or TM to clear my mind and keep me focused and aware of my emotions before I start trading. During this time, I use the inner balance app with a heart rate variability monitor to measure my performance for that session and I record my score.
2. I go over my checklist to make sure I had a good night's sleep, protein breakfast, and workout. I also rate my physical condition, distraction level, and overall emotional and mental state for trading.
3. Before I start trading, I look at market conditions and rhythms at different time frames to try to evaluate whether the market is tradable, whether it is trending or choppy, etc. This helps me decide which tools and setups to use and whether it is worth trading or not.
4. I start my first trade with small size (1–2 contracts) to test the waters and see if I am in tune with the market and to get a feel for the overall market environment.
5. Once I start with a winning trade, I start increasing my size in the following trade by adding to the winners. I like to start small and if the market goes in my direction, I add to my position using buy/sell stops and then scale out at the first target and second target and then trail my last position with one tick below/above the previous bar low/high to maximize my profits in the trade after having pocketed earlier profits. This strategy makes me less anxious to take profits and helps me hold my position longer with a trailing stop. It gives me good risk management and allows my winners to be much larger than losers.
6. During my trade, if I experience any anxiety or discomfort, I take deep breaths in and out in order to maintain my focus and stick to my plan.
7. After closing my trade, if I feel any anxiety, regret, or discomfort, I take a breathing session break for 5–15 minutes until I clear my mind and refocus. I also do some EFT tapping (emotional freedom techniques) with breathing to release negative energy. I sometimes take a break by walking out of the trading office.
8. Once I hit my daily stop loss, I stop trading. I also stop trading if I lose 50–75 percent of intraday profits.

Notice how Gus combines methods for physical and emotional control, such as the breathing, with methods of money management. He attempts to stay in winning trades, exit losing trades with modest size, and regulate the losses he can incur on any given trading day. All of these are methods of self-control, and all of them help him stay focused on markets rather than focused on P/L. A number of traders I've worked with utilize breaks during the trading day—and especially around midday—to regain emotional equilibrium and refocus their efforts. The unwillingness to leave the screens and take a break often reflects an emotional attachment to trading that easily morphs into overtrading. Once we notice a need to trade, particularly when there is not a clearly perceived and articulated opportunity, that is a great time to pull back and regain control.

Gus recognizes that money management is an essential part of self-management in trading. As I've mentioned previously, I never want to lose so much money in a day that I cannot have a profitable week; I never want to lose so much in a week that I cannot come back for the month; and I never want a losing month to ensure a losing year. A major aid to optimism and positivity is ensuring that you always have enough dry powder to mount a comeback after a losing period. Controlling risk and placing risk/reward in our favor is one of the most powerful psychological interventions available to traders.

Best Practice #40: Breaking Negative Cycles of Behavior

The first step in changing any damaging behavior pattern is recognizing and interrupting it. When we interrupt a pattern, we necessarily stand apart from that pattern. We control it and refuse to let it control us. When our problem patterns appear during trading—patterns of negative thinking or impulsive trading—a surprisingly powerful response is to pause what you're doing, identify the negative pattern, consciously acknowledge and feel the potential consequences, and then refuse to let it control you.

This is what alcoholics learn to do in their recovery work: Recognize the "stinkin' thinkin'" and emotional triggers that lead to drinking; interrupt the urge to drink by emotionally connecting with the consequences of alcohol abuse; and then redirect themselves to a more constructive outlet.

One implementation of this best practice idea comes from TraderFeed reader Eldad Nahmnay, a daytrader who shares his five-minute rule:

> After reviewing my trading, I saw that I had a lot of repetitive trades. By this I mean that less than five minutes after I had closed a trade, I was back in a new one. Usually, this occurred after a losing trade. This made me realize that I hadn't accepted the loss completely and was looking for a sort of revenge. After understanding this, I added the five-minute rule. After a trade, I close the system for five minutes when I ask myself the following questions: What have I done well for this trade? What can I take away to help with later trades? Do I have any open emotions that can affect me later? Did I do anything that violated my trading rules?
>
> After answering these questions, I take a minute or two away from the screen to come back fresh. The number of poor trades that I took was reduced by more than 70 percent after I implemented this rule.

Notice that Eldad's rule is actually a routine to develop mindfulness in the midst of the trading day. By taking a break after closing each trade, he is able to stand apart from markets (and his reactions to markets) and ask himself key process questions. The five-minute break interrupts any negative patterns that may have leaked into his trading and helps ensure that a single bad trade doesn't become a series of bad trades. By instituting the break after every trade, the trader turns mindfulness—and the breaking of negative cycles—into a positive habit pattern. That provides both perspective and control. So often, it's the time spent not trading that effectively prepares us for the next trade.

Best Practice #41: Conducting Structured Performance Reviews

It's easy to become so consumed with trading and preparing for trading that we fail to review—and learn from—our trading performance. The successful money managers I've worked with have had structured processes for previewing markets, viewing markets during trading hours, and reviewing trading once the day and week are finished. Previewing brings preparation and rigor to trading; reviewing allows us to stand back from our decisions and take a coaching perspective, turning ordinary performance into true deliberate practice.

A powerful best practice is conducting a structured performance review to evaluate yourself and your trading. One example is offered by Ryan Worch, principal at Worch Capital. He explains:

> I always want to be confident that I'm operating with an appreciation for the larger picture. It's easy to get bogged down in the day-to-day action so I make a point to create a series of monthly goals and observations.
>
> At the end of each month, I perform a post-analysis on all of my trades. This is where the real work is done. I assess every trade and figure out what worked and why it worked. By doing so, I'm hoping to see what is being rewarded in each environment. From this, I can set goals for the next month. Sometimes breakouts are working, or mean reversion, or pullback trades. The only way to determine this is by breaking down every trade at the end of each month. This process loop and feedback is critical to staying engaged and adapting to ever changing markets.
>
> I'm challenging myself and asking questions during this process. What characteristics did the winners have? What did the losers have? Is there a pattern to be recognized? I record all of this for future reference. This is a feedback loop that makes me a better trader and helps me break down information more quickly in future markets and trades.
>
> Some quantitative examples are: percent winners vs. losers; average win vs. loss; percent of equity risked; percent of equity gained/lost; percent gain/loss on each trade, etc.
>
> From a qualitative standpoint: What caused the position to move (surprise, upgrade, downgrade)? What was the surrounding market environment like? Were outside forces at play (geopolitical event, monetary policy event, etc.)?

Key Takeaway

We will most consistently develop if our learning is structured.

Note that Ryan reviews both the market environment and his specific trades. By seeing which trades are and aren't working, he gains insight into the market that can be fed forward into future decisions. That insight can also help him take more risk in favorable environments and pull back his risk in murky ones. The structured review is both a learning tool regarding markets and a tool for improving trading performance.

Best Practice #42: Screening for Market Opportunity

Think of overtrading as a compromise of our best trading. Good trading is selective, delegating risk to opportunities that have a positive expected value. When we lose that selectivity, we not only court losing trades and periods in markets but also undercut our judgment and compromise the basis for our success. Losing trades are inevitable; no one can predict the future with certainty. Bad trading, on the other hand, is controllable. When we place trades for noneconomic reasons, we reinforce the very factors that can undermine performance.

Screening for trading opportunities is a way of ensuring that we take the right kinds of risk in markets and avoid marginal trades. A framework for screening as a best practice comes from TraderFeed reader Steve Ryan (@iamtrading) who describes his process for locating promising stocks and trades for the day session. Steve explains:

> My strategy is to find stocks that will move the most even during a choppy market day. Therefore, stocks with news and momentum stocks are two groups I trade the most.
>
> Moreover, I am also concerned about liquidity. Primarily a day trader and a swing trader, I cannot afford to let the market makers eat away my profits. Slippage and huge spread are two silent killers for short-term traders.
>
> Therefore I create a scan (using the free Finviz.com version) described below to get the stocks I want to look for the next day. The stocks must be:
>
> - Liquid, with an average volume traded per day of 1 million or more
>
> - Volatile enough with average true range of 1.5 or higher
>
> - Priced over $20
>
> - Price is above SMA 50 (for momentum up) *or* below SMA 50 (for momentum down)

- Simple moving average 20 is above SMA 50 (for momo up) or below SMA 50 (for momo down)

This scan usually returns anywhere between 150 and 210 stocks every night. From there, I look at Daily, Hourly, 15-minute, and 5-minute charts to find the best stocks to trade the next day.

One can alter the average volume per day, the price threshold, or the ATR to get more stock results.

The best practice here is having a robust process for separating greater opportunity from lesser opportunity. Once you filter potential trades based on screening and then further filter that list, you have taken a large step toward avoiding overtrading and focused yourself on the trades that are best for you. Notice how Steve places both volatility/liquidity and trend in his favor in his screening, increasing the likelihood that he'll capture the magnitude and direction of moves during the day session. With repetition, we can become ever better at screening, culling a wide range of possible stocks or markets into a smaller number of valid opportunities.

Best Practice #43: Organizing Your Trading Business

If you run your trading as a business, then you inevitably function as both the worker and manager. You are the researcher developing trade ideas; you are manager of your positions and risk; and you are also a self-manager. Many times trading does not succeed because the business is not well run. Traders jump from one role and function to another, without grounding each of these in productive routines and best practices. A solo shop owner has distinct processes for selecting and ordering merchandise, displaying the products, serving customers, and managing the finances. The success of the shop hinges on executing each of those functions efficiently and effectively. Each trader runs his or her shop—and the organization of that business will be a major factor in its success or failure.

One vision of organizing the trading business as a best practice is offered by Bryan Lee, a full-time futures trader from Malaysia. He describes how he divides his work into three components:

> I trade several futures markets in the US and Asia, which includes crude oil, gold, bonds, mini Dow futures, soybean, wheat, corn, palm oil, soybean oil, etc. My trading

approaches are long term trend following and swing trading. My trading is system-based, meaning all trading decisions are based on signals generated by my trading systems. I integrate my own risk management algorithms in all the products in my portfolio.

I divide my trading into three parts:

1. *Research and Development*—This includes study of trading methodologies and research, development, and back-testing of new trading strategies. Risk management for the entire portfolio is also included in this section.

2. *Trade Execution*—I wake up at 5 AM (Malaysia time) to run my trading system. Since my systems use end of day data, they will only generate trading signals before the market open each day. Then my job is to place the signals as trade orders in the trading platform. When a trade order is triggered, I am informed by the platform. I will then jot down the time, price, lots, and other trade information in my trading logbook.

3. *Auditor*—The job of an auditor is to verify and audit all trades done for the day. This is typically done at the end of each trading day. I trade on a GLOBEX platform, where many futures markets are open for almost 24 hours. I wake up at 5 AM and check for all the trades done for the day. I will verify the record in the trading log with the statement sent by the broker.

I perform three roles, a researcher, a trade executor, and an auditor, all by myself, but I only perform one role at a time. I can't be a researcher and a trade executor at the same time. This will create conflicts and affect my trading.

The key idea that Bryan highlights is that he clearly delineates the major functions of his trading and has a distinct time—and clearly defined processes—for each. Although Bryan is a systematic trader, his best practice applies to discretionary traders as well. Time needed for research and market observation must be separate from time spent actually trading and managing positions—and both must be separate from time spent working on oneself and improving one's performance. It's not merely that successful traders follow a process. Rather, they divide and conquer the many responsibilities of trading, creating separate processes for each part of their business.

What makes you a successful idea generator? A successful risk manager? A successful self-manager? If you don't have distinct time devoted to each, it is unlikely that you can perform and grow in each of those functions. Trading well ultimately means running your trading business well—and that means attending to each portion of the business in a hands-on manner.

Best Practice #44: Using Movement to Achieve Cognitive and Emotional Control

We know from research that exercise has a number of health and emotional benefits, including increased well-being and improved concentration. In spite of this, most traders work in a highly sedentary fashion, seated at desks and watching screens for hours at a time. The lack of movement keeps us restricted to a narrow state of mind and body and makes it difficult to shift our state when we enter periods of frustration or discouragement.

Using movement to shift our states of body and mind is an unappreciated best practice. A particularly effective way to incorporate movement into trading comes from TraderFeed reader Scott Garl. He explains how creating movement at one's workstation can provide multiple personal and trading benefits:

> My best practice is absurdly simple, yet I haven't seen a comment on your blog or any other trading related blog or resource regarding the benefits of a stand-up workstation and/or treadmill workstation versus the traditional sit-down workstation. I do know that some traders complain about the health problems associated with sitting all day long.
>
> Since purchasing a treadmill workstation eight months ago (to supplement my sit-down workstation), I can't say that my trading results have exploded to the upside, but there have been noticeable improvements from using it 2 to 3 hours per day. Staring at the screens at a brisk 2.4 miles per hour (as I'm doing now) has helped to alleviate two problem areas: frustration trading and trading out of boredom. It's just plain difficult to spiral into negative emotions after a stop-out or two while so physically active and breathing deeply. And it's nearly impossible to feel bored and fall prey to looking to the market for action.

Additionally, I feel a significant creative boost, as I never forget to turn on my Focusatwill.com feed, which I always forget to do while sitting for some reason. That helps to increase my mood, focus, and creativity even more. The treadmill has even helped with procrastination, as I tend to tackle many to-do's that normally get put off. I've lost significant weight, have noticeably stronger abs, and have gained muscle mass as a result of also using a dumbbell while reading or evaluating market patterns.

Key Takeaway

We can control mind and emotions by working on the body.

Scott's combination of work and exercise keeps him energized while trading. His use of the Focus At Will music and the weights also keeps him mentally and physically active, making it less likely that he will become bored during the trading day. His insight that it is difficult to lapse into negative emotions when staying physically energized is an important one. Controlling our bodies can be powerful ways to achieve cognitive and emotional control. Scheduling periods of exercise during the trading day can be a great way to renew energy and reset our minds. Integrating movement into the actual trading process takes that idea to the next level, keeping us at peak condition as we're making decisions and managing risk.

Best Practice #45: Creating Trading Checkups

There's a lot to be said for a periodic checkup from the neck up. It is easy to talk ourselves into trades, veering from our edges in markets. How do we know if we're truly aligned with our best practices? That's where checklists and checkups can be very helpful.

A structured process for conducting checkups is a best practice from Mike Bellafiore (@MikeBellafiore) and Steve Spencer (@SSpencer) from SMB Capital. They hold a twice-weekly checkup that helps ensure that junior traders are truly rigorous in their selection of trading ideas. Mike and Steve describe the process that occurs on their trading floor:

> Each Tuesday and Thursday at 1:30 PM EST we meet in our firm training room in midtown Manhattan for ... The Play-Book Checkup. The PlayBook Checkup? What, is someone

sick? No, there are no doctors or nurses present; just traders and developing traders. This is a best practice that has helped our traders identify and maximize their trading edge.

Here's how it works. A junior trader on our desk prepares a trade in template form—an SMB PlayBook trade—of a setup that makes sense to him or her. Then, he/she presents this trade to other traders in our training room. I host this learning session with tough questions to the trader regarding stock selection, a trade catalyst of lack thereof, preparation or lack thereof, thinking, and execution. Here I "check up" on the favorite trades of our new traders—their edge.

The junior trader breaks down a favorite trade into five variables for their presentation (the SMB PlayBook Template):

a. The Big Picture
b. Intraday Fundamentals
c. Technical Analysis
d. Reading the Tape
e. Intuition

Each day our new traders archive a setup that made the most sense to them before they leave the trading floor. From these PlayBook trades they choose one to present under the pressure of constructive scrutiny during the PlayBook Checkup. They know to choose wisely and be ready to defend their trade.

Some phrases heard in our training room during these sessions:

- Yeah, don't make that trade again. You are not going to make money trading plays like that.

- Where could you have been bigger in that trade?

- How the heck did we allow a Boston Red Sox fan into this firm?

- You have to be bigger in this trade. You are leaving money on the table by not being bigger.

- If you are not going to properly prepare for a trade, what makes you think the market will let you succeed?

- This is exactly the type of trade you can build a career around.

Here's what the PlayBook Checkup helps traders accomplish:

1. Defines their favorite setups
2. Eliminates setups not worth their intellectual, financial, and emotional capital
3. Guides traders to internalize their trading edge with their PlayBook
4. Helps traders learn good risk/reward trades from their peers
5. Offers them a trade review by a trading partner with a deep dive into a specific trade setup
6. Provides a forum where standards of quality trades for our desk are set
7. Teaches them how to think through their setups like a pro
8. Builds an opportunity for us to bond, joke, and share a common learning experience

---

Key Takeaway

A trading checkup with teammates keeps us aligned with sound practices.

This is a great example of how trading can become an effective team sport. Steve and Mike institute the checkup as part of their training program, but this is a process that any trader could implement with one or more trading buddies. It enables traders to think about their thinking, hone their edges, and learn from each other. The cumulative impact of engaging in such a checkup review each week is significant, as traders keep each other honest about strengths and weaknesses. A physician conducts a checkup to make sure the patient is healthy. Trading checkups can be effective ways to ensure that our trading is on a healthy footing.

Best Practice #46: Organizing Your Daily Routines

There aren't many hard-and-fast formulas for success in trading, but one that comes close is taking your best practices—what you do when you are successful—and turning those into positive habit patterns. This is accomplished is through the creation of routines. When we establish a routine—and then make it routine—we exploit our strengths by making them automatic.

Each trader's routines will differ, but the effective ones capture and organize the essence of the trader's best decision making. A good example comes from money manager @MPortfolios, who describes his process as blocks of routines:

> I've found a very beneficial component to the workday is having an organized routine, or blocks of routines, synced to the priorities of managing my practice.
>
> I have an end of day routine that is investment management focused, where I perform a scan of all positions vs. their various "by rule" stop levels to determine if any have triggered, if any have risen above maximum allocation levels, etc. and determine if replacement positions are indicated and what they will be. This routine sets up the following morning's initial actions.
>
> I start my day [second routine if I did have market open transactions to complete] by: (1) checking notifications and scan prior day's transactions (dividends, inflows, withdrawals) to know what's on my plate from an administrative standpoint; and (2) looking at macro spread charts of asset classes, regions, and market sectors for signs of underlying changes in the landscape. (I use relative strength as a basis for a large part of my approach.)
>
> I've found that a really helpful byproduct of this, besides the obvious benefit of being organized, is that it fosters calm, systematic decision making.

I like the idea of blocks of routines, where to-do items are clustered based on their mutual relevance and then placed in sequence to aid the running of the trading business. In my own trading, one block of routines would capture my morning workout; another would describe my review of markets, indicators, and quantitative studies; another would involve trade planning; and so on. Each of those blocks in turn captures a sequence of specific activities that I have found to be useful in preparation and trading. Other traders would organize their preparation into different blocks, perhaps including consultation with other traders, reading research, and reviewing charts.

@MPortfolios observes that this organization is a psychological tool as well as an aid to work flow. When we are grounded in sound routines, we can work efficiently and effectively, allowing us to devote our attention to the unique challenges that markets always seem to present. A modular organization of the trading day, dividing time into blocks and blocks into best practices, is an unusually powerful way to sustain a sense of control over our trading.

Best Practice #47: Developing Your Trading Framework

Too many traders justify poor trading and overtrading by appealing to "intuition." True, intuition and implicit learning are cornerstones of pattern recognition. That doesn't mean, however, that any trade one feels like executing is a good trade! Intuition is the result of extensive exposure to a field. Without prolonged immersion and study, there is no building of pattern recognition skills. The experienced trader learns to differentiate intuitive knowing from emotional impulses: One reflects understanding; the other reflects a need.

An effective way of ensuring that your trading truly represents sound trading is to construct a framework for your good trades that captures their essential elements. This is a best practice offered by Awais Bokhari (@eminiplayer), the co-founder and CEO of the Open Trader training program and the eminiplayer.net trading site. Awais has been involved in training over 1000 traders, so he has worthwhile insights into the building of trading skills. He describes the framework he employs to aid trade execution and screen for valid trade ideas:

> After working with numerous traders, one common challenge I've noticed is that even after they have developed a solid understanding of the market and its mechanics, they still struggle with trade execution, and can't objectively determine the quality of a trade setup in real time. So, even after they've developed a good trade plan, they're unable to execute that plan in real time.
>
> To improve execution, I provide our students with an Execution Framework and teach them The Anatomy of a Valid Trade Idea. The concept here is to break down the trading methodology/strategy and determine the common components that are at the base of every good setup. We then track those components in a trade journal/spreadsheet with simple Yes/No values. It's important that we're able to measure and track each component objectively. This means we can't include or track anything that relies on intuition.

For our discretionary trading methodology, we follow four key components that make up a valid trade idea:

1. *Good trade location*: For a majority of trade setups, trade location is going to be important. In many situations, trade location alone can be enough of a reason to enter a trade. To make this an objective determination, you simply answer whether you took the trade at a predetermined support/resistance zone.

2. *Intraday control/bias* (short-term directional bias): We can assess which side is in control on the day time frame by seeing where the market is trading in relation to the first hour high/low, midpoint, VWAP, VPOC (volume point of control), overnight high/low, and previous day's high/low. Trades in the direction of the intraday control have a higher probability of reaching their profit targets. When entering a trade that is counter to the intraday control, you should be more conservative with your trade location.

3. *Momentum*: We gauge momentum by monitoring the NYSE TICK in conjunction with price action. Trades in the direction of momentum have a higher probability of reaching their profit targets. When entering a trade that is counter to momentum, you should generally be more conservative with your trade location.

4. *Larger time frame control/bias (trend)*: For the purpose of day trading, we assess the larger time frame control based on the 30-minute and daily charts. Trades in the direction of the larger time frame have a higher probability of reaching their profit targets. And, again, trades that are counter to the larger time frame/trend should usually be taken at more conservative trade location.

5. *Confluence*: These four key components make up a valid trade idea. The more of these you stack in your favor, the higher the odds of the setup working out. As a rule, at least two of these components should be in your favor on every trade.

6. *Reward-to-risk*: R/R is used as a filter and is a prerequisite to entering any trade. Because R/R is subjective and

every single trade must meet our minimum R/R crite-
rion of 2:1, R/R can never be used as the only reason
to enter a trade. It is necessary, but not sufficient on
its own.

We've found that this execution framework allows our
traders to be more objective and quickly determine the
quality of a trade setup in real time. Another benefit is that
it allows the trader to objectively assess trades at the end of
the day.

Key Takeaway

The best way to avoid overtrading is to clearly define the qualities of good
trades.

Awais has created a guide to trade selection that can assist traders in
real-time decision making and also facilitate review of winning and losing
trades. By applying these criteria to all trades consistently, the trader
internalizes the basics of good decision making and turns excellence in
execution into a positive habit pattern.

One exercise I've found to be useful is to go back in time and identify
the trades I ideally would have entered and examine how those set up
with respect to the various measures I follow. I then contrast the patterns
I find with those that appeared during the trades I regret having entered.
These repeated observations have greatly assisted in the generation of
personal theories regarding why markets trend and reverse, which in
turn has greatly aided the selectivity of my trading. It is very helpful to
be able to very clearly identify when and why to trade: Your framework
is what keeps you honest during times when it's tempting to pursue
movement rather than opportunity.

Best Practice #48: Adding to Your Process Through the Power of Elimination

When I first tried my hand at developing quantitative models of markets,
I was impressed by the seeming predictive power I could gain by adding
more predictors to my equations. Of course, that worked just fine on
an in-sample basis, but completely fell apart when applied out-of-sample
and especially in real time. Why? Because the complicated equations

were custom fit to the historical data and thus not well suited to adapt to new data. That overfitting created a false sense of security. The equations with fewer, but powerful predictors were almost always the most robust—most able to provide predictive value going forward. They were simple in their sophistication.

A valuable best practice comes from a longtime mentor of traders, Charles Kirk (@TheKirkReport). He follows markets daily via The Kirk Report and conducts mentorship programs for groups of subscribers. Charles describes his best practice as "elimination," and his insight fits well with my early quant experience:

> Over 20 years I studied about every possible thing you can imagine about trading and investing. I accumulated so much knowledge, but eventually realized that the path toward greater profits and success was figuring out what to eliminate so I could focus on the things that really helped me when I was trading at my very best. All of us go through a period where we add more factors in our strategy. More things to watch, more indicators to use, more screens to run, more backtesting research to review, more people to listen to, and so on. The problem with doing that is that once you've been doing it for a while, the complexity itself becomes a huge distraction. Much of trading well is figuring out what things truly add value and which are actionable and then having the courage to eliminate everything else. There is a lot of noise and unhelpful factors out there that may be very interesting, but in reality are not helpful and often can present yet another obstacle for you to overcome.
>
> Once you understand the steps you must take and information you need that leads you most often to successful trades, the next step is to eliminate everything you can that isn't absolutely necessary. In addition, once you have a strategy that works, as a rule you never add anything else into it unless you can at the same time take something away. That rule will prevent you from making things far more complicated than they need to be and allow you to focus on what truly matters. The best practice of all, in my view, is one of elimination.

Charles offers a great piece of insight when he points out that it takes courage to eliminate the nonessentials. In other words, you have to have confidence in the few, essential components of your success to lean on those exclusively. Too often, when we seek the crutches of things to add to our strategies, it's because we lack confidence in those strategies. Stripping down our performance to bare essentials forces us to commit—and then to put our money on that commitment.

The same wisdom holds true for how we present ourselves in public. If we are comfortable in our own skin, we can present ourselves as we are—simply and straightforwardly. If we are not comfortable with ourselves, we will add layers to our social presentation to try to appeal to anyone and everyone. We might adopt clothing or attitudes that aren't truly ours, or we may try to adapt our presentation to the social setting of the moment. In each case, adding layers of complexity is a confession of low self-confidence and low self-acceptance.

When we trade who we are, we reinforce who we are; we don't undercut it. As Kirk wisely observes, that's a great reinforcer of confidence. Placing bets against our own best judgment is one of the most corrosive actions we can take.

Best Practice #49: Maximizing Your Information Processing

The typical trader works from multiple screens and each of the screens carries multiple pieces of information updated in real time. Some screens update charts; some update news; some are for messaging; some track quotes across many markets. No trader wants to miss a fast-breaking development, so the temptation is to add screens and add more data to each screen. Can traders really process all that information in real time? How much of what appears on our screens truly is information—and how much is distraction?

A valuable best practice in the cognitive process of trading comes from Terry Liberman (@windotrader) from WindoTrader. He emphasizes the importance of understanding and owning your trading information processing system. Years of experience in developing effective trading platforms have taught Terry quite a bit about how traders process information. His key point is that we cannot maximize our processing of market information unless we understand our information processing strengths and play to those. One of the unusual features of WindoTrader is the ability to overlay information displays on one another, so that the trader can visualize price action on several time frames simultaneously. For a highly visual information processor, this can provide a significant cognitive efficiency.

As Terry points out, the best practice of streamlining information to fit your processing style is increasingly important, given the explosion of data available to traders:

> As we know, there is no shortage of information because this is the Era of Information Overload on Steroids. The important thing for those of us who trade is to be able to quickly and easily find the information that meets our requirements as to relevance, usefulness, applicability, and fit.
>
> One way to think about information processing is to recognize that data are not information and must first be converted into information through your filters of relevance, importance, and applicability. Once they become information and meet your criteria as information, you now have knowledge and some understanding of it so you can make some decisions about it. And then, once it meets your requirements, decide how you're going to act on it in alignment with your performance criteria.
>
> To increase your ability to collect the information you require and process it, begin with the information you need, why you need it, and the benefit it will specifically provide you at this moment in time. Next, determine both the context and the content of the information as well as its validity overall and its validity for you. And finally, plan the specifics for using it and gaining the most from it in your pursuit of achieving your goal or goals. To read something fun as well as thought provoking, check out the book *Information Anxiety*.

Terry makes a very important point: Trading is, at root, a cognitive process. It is all about taking in data, assembling data into information and insight, and making decisions based on the ongoing streams of processing. How much of what is on our screens is truly essential to our decision making? How many screens would we employ and how cluttered would each screen be if we only focused on the data most relevant to our trading decisions?

We can optimize our trading if we optimize our cognitive processes.

Streamlining our information processing forces us to think about our thinking and follow our chains of reasoning in generating sound trading decisions. Terry's best practice is not just optimizing our screens; it's optimizing our thought processes and then adapting our screens to the best of our processing. More is not better; many times, fast information processing is as important to trading as deep processing. By carefully organizing what is on our screens and how it is displayed, we can improve the efficiency as well as the effectiveness of our thought processes.

Best Practice #50: Planning Your Trading Business

A little while ago, I met with some traders and asked them to bring to the meeting everything they had prepared for the new year of trading. All of them brought a list of goals for the coming year. Most of them brought lists of what they had done right and wrong during the previous year. None of them laid out concrete plans that detailed how they would take the learning from the previous year and use it to work toward their new year's goals.

In other words, they took the time to set goals, but didn't drill down to create plans for achieving those goals. How likely do you think they were to achieve their ideals for the year to come? Yet all of them felt that they were working on their trading.

The idea of planning as a best practice comes from an experienced observer of both markets and traders, Tadas Viskanta (@AbnormalReturns), author of the well-known Abnormal Returns blog. In this excerpt from his *Abnormal Returns* book, he emphasizes the importance of planning in trading and highlights the use of checklists in the planning process:

> One of the problems novice traders have is that they don't treat their trading with the same rigor and seriousness that they do with any other sort of business endeavor. However, trading is just like any other business in that it has revenues, overhead, variable expenses, etc. Trying to trade off the cuff without a plan or a means for measuring your performance is a recipe for disappointment.

Many traders balk at the idea of formulating a trading plan because they feel it might stifle their creativity or ability to react to rapidly changing market conditions. As well, in the wider world of startups, the detailed business plan seems to have gone into disfavor. In the world of trading, it never really seemed to catch fire. However, traders are well served to think about how they plan to go about generating profits. A trading plan that lays out the instruments they will trade, when they will trade them, and the methodology they will use to enter and exit trades is essential. Maybe even more important is a strategy to limit losses both on individual trades and in an overall portfolio. And as important as an overall trading plan might be, a trade-by-trade plan might be even more important.

Some traders find it useful to have a checklist they consult on an ongoing basis when they trade to ensure they are not missing anything along the way. As Atul Gawande, author of *The Checklist Manifesto*, writes: "In aviation, everyone wants to land safely. In the money business, everyone looks for an edge. If someone is doing well, people pounce like starved hyenas to find out how. Almost every idea for making slightly more money—investing in Internet companies, buying tranches of sliced up mortgages—gets sucked up by the giant maw almost instantly. Every idea, that is, except one: checklists." *Checklists don't dictate what a trader does; rather they ensure that what a trader is supposed to do actually gets done.*

The hallmark of a well-designed trading system may be the actuality that a checklist can be created. The more experienced and successful the trader, the simpler his or her trading system becomes over time. ... Experienced traders have spent a lifetime whittling down ideas into a plan that works for them—and maybe nobody else.

Tadas makes a key point here: You don't have a robust trading process unless it can be captured via checklists—and you can't truly claim to be process-driven if you have not codified those checklists and used them to guide decision making. Airline pilots check all systems before taking off and follow a well-laid-out flight plan. Physicians check their patients' systems before developing and following an evidence-based treatment plan. In both cases, winging it with unstructured decisions would lead to catastrophic consequences. The best trading plans are grounded in best trading practices—and those become templates for best performance.

Best Practice #51: Priming the Mind for Performance

One of the challenges of preparation is ensuring that what you've drilled when you're in practice mode will actually stick in the mind when you're in the heat of battle. It is not at all uncommon for students to prepare hard for big tests, only to have the material they studied fly out of their heads during the exam. What we process in a calm, focused manner and what we can access when we are hypercharged in flight-or-fight mode can be very different things. That is why processing information more frequently and deeply (encountering the information in different ways) is essential to cognitive performance. What we need to know is most likely to stick if we rehearse it well.

A clever cognitive best practice comes from TraderFeed reader Daniel Martin Schulz from Hamburg. He describes a priming strategy that he has found effective in his trading preparation:

> Thinking back to high school and university times, one technique that often provided me with a welcome boost before important tests the next morning was to review particularly important material right before going to sleep (and I mean right before the head hits the pillow, virtually the last thing before sleeping, except maybe kissing your significant other good night). It continues to amaze me how the material thus reviewed "sticks." It must be something about how our brain consolidates information and learned content during sleep (I am sure others have written about it but I have no link or article ready).
>
> I do not review a huge amount of charts—only a handful of printouts of the markets I followed very closely during the day, that I traded and/or that I intend to trade the next session. I use 4 time frames for each market (daily, hourly, 15 min, 5 min—but these details are unimportant and the time frames will vary from trader to trader). What will not vary is that we can "seed" our unconscious/sleeping brains with something to work with during the night that way. A small advantage for sure—but ours is a business of hunting the ever so slight edge.

Daniel's review strategy is effective because it reduces the impact of interference from the processing of subsequent events. Research suggests that an important part of creativity is an incubation process in which we relax our focus following intensive immersion in a problem. Daniel uses sleep as that incubation period, achieving a kind of seeding of the mind. This can aid both the recall of information studied and the integration of that information into fresh trading ideas. When we're faced with a difficult choice, we sometimes hear the advice to "sleep on it." From the vantage point of information processing and incubation, that can be valuable advice for traders.

Best Practice #52: Constructing an Effective Trading Journal

One of the challenges of any performance field is that peak performance requires immersion in an activity, but improving performance requires the ability to stand apart from that activity. That is why elite performers always engage in three broad processes: practice/preparation; real-time performance; and reviews of performance to guide future practice and preparation. That three-part cycle captures the essence of deliberate practice and ensures that we learn from experience and expand our expertise.

A key ingredient of that threefold process for many traders is maintaining a journal. TraderFeed reader Danny Shcharinsky emphasizes the role of journaling in working on oneself as well as working on markets:

> Among the many practices and routines traders recommend following on a daily basis, there is one that stands out the most in my trading. This one has nothing to do with actual trading (read: "cutting losses" or "letting profits run"). This one has to do with *you*. That's right: journaling. Good ol' pen-to-paper-write-your-heart-out type of journaling. While many successful market practitioners will always advise on how to do this, the one truth is that there is no right or wrong way to go about this. And I also don't mean the type of journaling where you get your trading platform to spit out a bunch of general statistics. While statistical analysis is certainly important to the improvement of your edge and intuition in your trading, I'm talking about the real

hearty stuff —writing down your feelings about a particular trade, pattern, general market, even right down to what you had for breakfast. In a world where neuroscience has overwhelming evidence that our mind shapes our bodies and physical actions, do you think it may be a good idea to have a clear record of your thoughts? I would vote yes. So go ahead, complain about the losses, get mad, angry, happy, excited, and inspired, but do it on paper, so you can move past it and grow.

Reviewing last night's journal entry first thing in the morning (prior to starting your trading day) would put you in the right frame of mind to do whatever it is that needs to be done. In addition, it would further crystallize concepts, ideas, and best actions that you have been practicing and thinking about for the past week, month, year. Repetition is the mother of Skill, right? Taking all of the above into consideration, I would add that this has to be done and reviewed consistently. Yes, every day, or at least consistently enough that it makes a difference.... Being consistent about your journaling will lead to a better and more clear flow in the way you feel and think. You will also find out things about yourself that will allow you to change, improve, and grow in ways you have not imagined.

As Danny points out, journals can be used in many ways: to vent frustrations, prepare for the coming day, and crystallize one's longer-term market views. Reviewing journals enables us to encounter our thoughts and experiences from a fresh perspective, as we now read what had previously been stuck in our heads. This creates a kind of dialogue in which the journal helps us carry on a conversation between ourselves as traders and ourselves as trading coaches. Through the journal we can observe ourselves, but also guide ourselves. That is why I am a big fan of journals that contain observations (what we did right and wrong); goals for improvement (extending what we did right, correcting what we did wrong); and concrete plans for implementing that improvement.

Journaling at its best is real-time business planning. It is a way of observing our trading business and managing it effectively. If we are spending our time either doing things worth writing about or writing things worth doing, we are most likely to be productive and successful— and managing our trading business well.

Best Practice #53: Conducting Video Reviews of Your Trading

One of the limitations of reviewing our trading and constructing plans based on those reviews is that our look back can be tainted by what we recall and what we do not. Particularly if we trade actively during a day, it's unlikely that we will recollect all the factors that went into good and poor trades. We may even forget our specific rationale for a given trade. Our memories are biased by our emotions, as well as hindsight and the salience of particular events. It is difficult to effectively review our trading if we can't accurately recall our trading!

Key Takeaway

We can't improve the details of our trading if we don't review our trading in detail.

The way sports teams get around that, of course, is by video recording each play and examining the video in detail to spot best and worst practices. TraderFeed reader Chris Britton, who video records his own trading and uses the review to work on his performance, describes this as a best practice:

> I am a discretionary day trader and I trade the 10 year note and 30 year bond futures. My pre-market analysis consists of identifying key support/resistance levels (yesterday's value area high, low, vpoc, etc.). For actual trading and getting a feel for the market action, I watch the depth of market with support from a chart to watch for emerging support/resistance levels.
>
> What I find helpful in doing trade reviews is recording my trading session (using Camtasia or the like). At the end of the day, I cut down the video to the important parts that consist of trades that I make and trades that I missed or whatever I feel may make an important point. Then I add in notes on the video that point out interesting clues that I keyed in on or missed. The finished video is anywhere from 10 to 30 minutes long, depending on how many trades I make. The key points in the video present the context of the price action, the order flow on the depth of market that

show why I entered (or did not enter), and, in some cases, why I exited when I did.

How does this help me? First, the recording helps me identify strengths and weaknesses in my ability to correctly read the order flow. From that, I have built a library of my own "best setups" or "avoidable pitfalls." For example, I can review trades that had a successful breakout at some resistance level and compare the order flow from those to trades that had a failed breakout. The key element is spotting what the order flow was doing that made the difference between the two. If my skills can't explain it, then at least I have the library to review in the future for when my order flow reading skills will be improved.

Second, the trade reviews at the end of the day are actually enjoyable. Even if a trade is a loser, I enjoy watching the video. That is because in some way, I improve my depth of market reading skills. Before I was making recordings, I dreaded the losing trade reviews and trying to remember what I did wrong. That opened the door for bias to creep in, which makes learning from the mistakes harder. With the recording, I learned that I can't escape my own accountability in making errors.

Finally, playback reviews during slow periods or on the weekends actually help keep my mind sharp and prepare me for the next trading session. I have found that while watching these reviews, the dialogue in my mind takes on an instructor-type role where I try to explain the play-by-play action.

I particularly like Chris's latter observation, where he notes that watching the videos places him in an instructor role. That reflects the impact of self-coaching. When Chris goes over the videos, he is like a coach reviewing game film with players. Going to specific portions of the video, reviewing the elements of performance in detail, and noting what could be done differently adds a level of detail to review that is impossible to replicate with a retrospective journal. As Chris notes, the reviews become enjoyable, because they are constructive—they teach and don't merely harp on negatives.

If pattern recognition is a function of cognitive focus and amount of exposure to instances of patterns, then a focused, video-based review is a great way to accelerate a trader's learning curve. The trader who has watched markets during the trading session and then focused on patterns in post-market review simply has more learning exposure per unit of time than the trader who fails to conduct review. For that reason, the video review is a powerful tool for learning and self-coaching.

Best Practice #54: Organizing Your Trading Morning

One of the best ways to ensure a sound trading routine during the day is to construct a sound routine during the morning. How we start our day so often sets the tone for that day. That means we can either start the day focused or distracted; disciplined or lax; prepared or unprepared. I have long maintained that one of the best ways of identifying successful traders is to observe what they are doing when they're not trading.

Following a detailed routine is a best practice from Steve Spencer (@sspencer_smb) of SMB Trading. His routine is valuable in that it prepares both the trader and the trading. Here is how Steve explains it:

> I have a routine that begins from the moment I walk into the office each morning. It is designed to both have me focused and prepared to trade the US equities market open at 9:30 AM. It has evolved over the past few years as my responsibilities have broadened outside of my own personal trading to include preparing the desk for the day and dealing with nontrading matters as well.
>
> Here is the current list of things I do each morning after arriving at the office:
>
> 1. Fill up my water jug (hydration is one of the keys to mental alertness).
> 2. Restart computer.
> 3. Open Gr8Trade (proprietary equities platform).
> 4. Open LiveVol (options platform); if any options trade ideas, open related Level II boxes.
> 5. Open eSignal (external charting software).
> 6. Login to SMB RT (proprietary trading tools).
> 6a. Open game plan (form used to enter my trading ideas).
> 6b. Fill in 2nd day and technical plays (ideas based on prior research and preparation).
> 7. Enter alerts for 2nd day plays into Gr8Trade (pop up alerts if stock trades at key prices).

8. Open SMB Scanner (research tool for finding stocks in play).
9. Complete game play sheet with Stocks in Play ideas.
10. Enter top trading ideas into journal (important for later review process).
11. Ideas must include entries/stops/targets/risk amount.
12. Options ideas are entered in margin at the top of the page.
13. Conduct AM meeting (discuss market and top trading ideas for the day).
14. Enter orders for Stocks in Play ideas discussed at AM meeting; input ideas into autoscripts to assist entries if market busy on open.

The following items help bring me back into focus for the market open:

15. Two minutes of breathing exercises.
16. Put on RT microphone (audio feed for desk and SMB community).
17. Discuss top trading ideas and plan via audio.
18. Share any stocks/important levels from the chat that are interesting.

So that is my entire morning routine. The thing that has changed the most recently is my ability to enter various scripts that will allow me to trade a variety of trading setups during busy market times that I otherwise might have missed. I find that in today's market, if you miss certain entries right at the open, it can impact your risk taking for the rest of the day. The scripts are also a great tool to support me on days where other responsibilities pull me off the desk.

| Key Takeaway |

Disciplined trading begins with a daily discipline.

Notice how Steve's morning routine accomplishes two purposes. First, it organizes his day and decision making. He identifies and prioritizes opportunities during his preparation and thus is able to act quickly and decisively when trades set up. Second, the routine enables Steve to process an unusually large amount of information in a concentrated period of time. Note his use of custom tools for much of his preparation. These enable him to screen for opportunities and program them for action (via scripts and alerts).

I find it interesting that Steve's routine is a combination of individual information processing and processing in a group. His preparation enables him to bring ideas to other traders, but also sets up conversations that bring him ideas. Over the course of a single day, Steve is simply encountering more potential trading opportunities than most traders—and that makes it more likely that he can focus on the best ones and maximize his results.

Best Practice #55: Scenario-Based Planning

A good rule is that we cannot be prepared for a situation that we do not anticipate. Many times, we become so focused on our base case—and locked in confirmation bias—that we fail to contemplate alternate scenarios and how we would respond to these. In those situations, emotional overreactions to trading events follow from our lack of preparation: We are surprised by events that were entirely foreseeable as possibilities. That element of surprise places us in a stress mode, impairing our perception and reducing our ability to calmly act on prior planning. Think of a situation in which you violated a trading plan and the odds are good that it's a situation in which lack of planning led to surprise, frustration, and emotional disruption.

A useful best practice comes from reader Jitender Yadav (@jitenderyadav07) from India, who points out the value of building alternate scenarios as part of planning for the trading day:

> One of the interesting characteristics of the markets is that they never fail to surprise us with their actions and catching us off the guard. Often these surprises prove to be costly. Although no one can know for sure market's next course of action, still we can prepare ourselves to face the surprise. In the evening before the trading day we can imagine about all the possible scenarios that can play out next day regardless of their actual probability to occur. We can, for example, imagine the ideal conditions we would like to see before making a long entry or the worst conditions to make a trade at all. We can imagine about our response to breakout

failure or our plan of action during a short squeeze. It won't take much time to think of so many other possibilities and we can do it in our free time like during the evening walk, etc. Again the markets have their own minds and even after this scenario building exercise they can have something different in store for us but then if one of our imagined scenarios actually plays out, we are ready with our plan.

Note that such scenario planning requires an open-mindedness, as we can only anticipate a range of situations if we are open to multiple possibilities. For this reason, scenario planning is a great tool to maintain cognitive flexibility. It is very common that traders will take actions during the day that seem unfathomable in retrospect: "How could I have possibly done that?" Generally, such boneheaded actions are the result of becoming so focused on short-term action and so locked into a single market scenario that we fail to step back, assess the entire situation, and plan for multiple possibilities. Jitender's observation is that such perspective can be an ongoing part of preparation for trading, enabling us to act decisively in the face of multiple possible outcomes. It is such planning that allows us to make sound decisions in the heat of battle, as we remove much of the market's ability to fill us with shock and awe.

Best Practice #56: Elaborating Your Trading Processes

Who are we as traders? The reality is that we fill many roles and engage in a variety of activities. It's rare to find traders who work diligently on becoming better traders. It's even rarer to see traders break down what they do into components and work on bettering themselves in each of those.

Dividing trading into component processes as a best practice comes from Pier Luigi Pellegrino (@PLPAR) from Paris, France. He breaks down trading into four basic areas and then breaks down each of those into two sub-domains and each of those into three specific performance elements. This creates a catalog of 24 performance functions of trading. Pier explains, "The daily trading routine is focused on a structured and regular implementation of the 24 performance elements."

Here is Pier's breakdown:

1. Vision (The Fund Manager)

   INNER DRIVE

   1. *Focused vision*: Create regularly the images of the financial goal to achieve.

2. *Intensity of purpose*: Feel with intensity the will to succeed and the expectation to win.
3. *Intrinsic motivation*: Being driven from within to reach high standards of performance.

ELITE MASTERY

4. *Self-efficacy*: Act with self-confidence and self-efficacy and belief in winning.
5. *Rage to mastery*: Sustain the conviction of being an elite performer driven to reach mastery.
6. *Implicit action*: Execute the trading strategy by accessing implicit and intuitive knowledge.

2. Strategy (The Portfolio Manager)

PATTERN RECOGNITION

7. *Portfolio ranking*: Scan, select, and rank the best trend stocks with the proprietary screening tool.
8. *Pattern monitoring*: Monitor price action and pattern development among the filtered stocks.
9. *Setup recognition*: Detect playbook setups through implicit pattern recognition.

MONEY MANAGEMENT

10. *Risk analysis*: Perform due diligence and risk analysis of potential trades.
11. *Capital allocation*: Determine the capital allocated to the trade (shares and stop level).
12. *Trading frequency*: Trade only the best setups with the greatest opportunity.

3. Execution (The Head Trader)

CONSISTENT ROUTINE

13. *Mental toughness*: Develop a strong and competitive mindset.
14. *Rituals*: Replicate consistently a structured and coherent daily routine.
15. *Zone state*: Enter on demand a zone state of focus and concentration during trading.

FLAWLESS EXECUTION

16. *Trade implementation*: Execute the trade flawlessly with clarity and intuition.

17. *Order management*: Utilize adaptive exit tactic with trailing stops and profit targets.
18. *Performance niche*: Focus relentlessly on your strategy and discard other methods.

4. Feedback (The Performance Coach)

DELIBERATE PRACTICE

19. *Performance training*: Train key performance skills with structured deliberate practice
20. *Mental rehearsal*: Isolate, rehearse, and integrate critical skills and optimal behaviors
21. *Laboring instinct*: Develop a mindset of continuous improvement and skill refinement.

PERFORMANCE ENHANCEMENT

22. *Continuous debriefing*: Debrief, monitor, and measure performance.
23. *Performance diagnosis*: Detect factors limiting performance and enhancing success.
24. *Feedback implementation*: Correct weaknesses and repeat winning actions.

Your breakdown of trading process might look different from Pier's (mine would be heavier on research processes and—ironically for a psychologist—less geared toward sustaining positive mindset), but the principle still holds: Dividing trading into component actions enables you to look under the performance hood and observe *in detail* what you're doing well and what could stand improvement.

Key Takeaway

If you don't break down what you do when you trade well, you won't be able to replicate the essential ingredients of success.

Indeed, a breakdown such as Pier's 24 performance functions could anchor an effective end-of-day or end-of-week report card that would guide goal setting for the next day or week. That would be a best practice that embraces best practices: a continuous set of trading diagnostics and tuneups.

Best Practice #57: Save

This is the shortest best practice, but perhaps the most important. I have worked in markets for years, and I have seen developing traders become successful traders and successful traders become struggling traders. When flush with success, traders so often believe it will last forever. They stop adapting. They no longer feel the need for reviews and practice. Then markets change and what used to work no longer works. What was once successful now brings losses and frustration.

What makes this scenario particularly sad is that, flush with success, traders rarely save their money. They spend freely, they pyramid winnings into ever-bigger trades—and then the time comes when their edge erodes. They are not prepared in their trading; they are not prepared mentally and emotionally; and they are not prepared financially.

If I were to place a single note on my trading screen to promote good trading, it would be, "This, too, shall pass." You're never as bad as you feel after losses and you're never as good as you believe after wins. The flush times will be followed by lean times and the lean times can become prosperous once more. That can't happen, however, if you don't save the money from the flush times to finance the times of relearning and adaptation. Too often, once-successful traders become former traders because they can't finance their new learning curves.

The best practice is to hope for the best, plan for the worst, and always keep yourself in the game by saving for the day when this success, too, shall pass. Markets are ever-changing, and your income will change as a result. If you're financially prepared for the lean times, you're best positioned to find your new success.

■ Summary

We've just seen 57 best practices. Some will apply to you more than others, but the odds are good that at least a few can make a meaningful difference in your trading. Here are a few thoughts about the practices as a whole:

1. *Look at the common themes.* Many of the practices describe ways of organizing trading, reviewing trading, and maintaining a positive mindset. These are key challenges for traders. If so many experienced traders cite best practices in these areas, it's a good bet that these are areas that you should prioritize.

2. *Take one thing at a time.* You can't work on everything at once. When you make multiple changes, it's difficult to know precisely what is working and what is not. One process improvement at a time helps you build your trading continuously and learn from your experience in a deliberate practice fashion.

3. *Focus on strengths, not just weaknesses.* If there is one key theme to this book, it's that success is a function of identifying and leveraging your strengths. Some of your best practices may remedy weak areas or help you avoid them, but the *best* best practices are those that extend the best of you.

Your development as a trader is best approached as an adventure. It's an opportunity to learn from every day's experience and move closer and closer to your ideals. There is no meaningful development of trading without self-development. Working on trading is working on you—and that's the most fulfilling adventure of all.

"Men are like grandfather clocks driven by watchsprings."

Colin Wilson, *The Black Room*

Let's recapitulate the major ideas from the book:

1. *Markets are ever-changing, across every time frame.* This means that success at trading is not a function of finding and exploiting a fixed edge. Rather, success comes from adapting to market changes and constantly renewing sources of edge.
2. *Performance is a function of cognitive and personality strengths, inborn talents, and acquired skills.* Elite performance requires concerted efforts to deepen our strengths.
3. *The most neglected area of development among traders is creativity.* We focus on executing trades and managing risk, but rarely work on expanding our creative capacity to generate ideas.
4. *A best practices framework enables traders to identify their strengths in each facet of trading and join those practices into robust processes.* We succeed when we turn our best practices into positive habits.

The previous pages have been grounded in four best processes that we've identified by ABCD:

A   Adapting to ever-changing markets
B   Building social, emotional, cognitive, and personality strengths
C   Cultivating creativity
D   Developing best practices across each facet of trading

We've seen that there is much more to a process orientation than simply following a set of routines. If you want to get started moving from best practices to best processes, divide your trading into seven basic activities:

1. *Research*—gathering information relevant to markets
2. *Idea generation*—synthesizing information into trade ideas
3. *Trade structuring*—finding sound risk/reward expressions of trade ideas
4. *Position/risk management*—managing stops, profit targets, trade sizing, scaling into or out of trades
5. *Portfolio/risk management*—combining uncorrelated or negatively correlated trades to diversify and smooth returns; managing risk across multiple trades
6. *Self-management*—keeping yourself in a peak mental, emotional, and physical state for optimal decision making
7. *Performance management*—reviewing performance in each of the above areas, learning from good and poor performance, setting goals for future performance, and following plans to achieve those goals

For each of these areas, track what you do best, capture those best practices in checklist form, and link them into routines that can be followed religiously. You won't be following a process. Rather, you'll follow sequences of processes for each aspect of trading, with each sequence anchored by your best practices. If you define these rigorously, you should be able to generate a flowchart that describes what you do and how you do it.

CONCLUSION: FROM BEST PRACTICES TO BEST PROCESSES

Key Takeaway

Improving your trading starts with creating a flowchart of how you trade at your best.

Most traders fall quite short of creating flowcharts of best practices linked into best processes. That, however, is how you build on your strengths, adapt to changing markets, and sustain performance success over time. *You can't improve performance if you don't clearly identify the drivers of your performance.* It's not about discipline, and it's not about robotically following setups that someone has taught you. It's about understanding how markets work and defining strategies that exploit that understanding. In your trading business, you work on generating ideas; you work on managing trades; and you work on managing yourself and your performance. What we've seen in this book is that everything in life is *use it or lose it.* You either cultivate your strengths and leverage those or you allow them to atrophy. Your work on your trading is your work on yourself—and that is the work that brings you ever closer to the person you're meant to be. Building the best within us gives us energy, allowing us to persist beyond the inevitable setbacks and frustrations. Energized by tapping into our deepest values and greatest capacities, we become more than grandfather clocks powered by watchsprings. We become truly self-sustaining.

I wish you well in your trading adventure.

It is March 5, 2015, nearly four months since Mia Bella and I sat together as I constructed a new way of charting. Price remains on the y-axis, but the x-axis represents events—not time. The simplest example of looking at markets through event time rather than chronological time is point-and-figure charting. In a P&F chart, it is price movement that is the event: You create a new bar every time the market moves by a certain threshold.

But there are many potential events that can anchor the x-axis. Price change is an event, as is relative price change. Volume traded is an event; so are upticks and downticks and trades transacted. Once we free ourselves from the clock and define time in event terms, fresh relationships become clear.

The stock market does not spend the same amount of days, months, and years rising and falling. Those who watch the market know that it typically falls quickly and rises more gradually. Suppose, however, we measure time in terms of price movement or transacted volume. Rises and declines begin to show more similarity in duration. Cycles appear with greater regularity.

When Mia came home after having been rescued from the high-kill shelter in Kentucky, she spent a good amount of time exploring. She learned that standing on her back legs and placing her front paws on a door would open the door. So now, if I'm in a room with the door partially closed, Mia simply stands, opens it, and walks in. She explores, she tries things, and she learns. We as traders are not so different. On my to-do list is a new measure of implied volatility that removes the impact of realized volatility; a new measure of sentiment that combines readings from equity and index options; and a revised way of looking at the buying activity and selling activity of separate groups of market participants. Some will pan out, others won't. All I know is that if we explore enough places and look at enough things, eventually we'll be like Mia and figure out how to open doors.

REFERENCES

Andreasen, N. C. *The Creative Brain*. New York: Plume, 2006.

Argyle, M. *The Psychology of Happiness*, 2nd ed. New York: Taylor & Francis, 2001.

Barber, B. M., Lee, Y-T., Liu, Y-J., and Odean, T. "Just How Much Do Individual Investors Lose by Trading?" *The Review of Financial Studies* 22 (2009): 609–632.

Baumeister, R. F., and Tierney, J. *Willpower*. London: Allen Lane, 2011.

Berkman, L. F., and Syme, L. "Social Networks, Host Resistance, and Mortality: A Nine-Year Follow-up Study of Alameda County Residents." *American Journal of Epidemiology* 109 (1978): 186–204.

Buckingham, M., and Clifton, D.O. *Now, Discover Your Strengths*. New York: Free Press, 2001.

Byeagee, Y. *Paradigm Shift: How to Cultivate Equanimity in the Face of Market Uncertainty*, Amazon Digital Services, 2014.

Catmull, E. *Creativity, Inc*. New York: Random House, 2014.

Chrysikou, E. G., Hamilton, R. H., Coslett, H. B., Datta, A., Bikson, M., and Thompson-Schill, S. L. "Noninvasive Transcranial Direct Current Stimulation over the Left Prefrontal Cortex Facilitates Cognitive Flexibility in Tool Use." *Cognitive Neuroscience* (2013): 81–89.

Coates, J. *The Hour Between Dog and Wolf*. London: Penguin, 2012.

Colvin, G. *Talent Is Overrated*. London: Penguin, 2008.

Compton, W. C., and Hoffman, E. *Positive Psychology*, 2nd ed. Belmont, CA: Wadsworth, 2013.

Csikszentmihalyi, M. *Creativity*. New York: Harper Perennial, 2013.

DeVries, M., Holland, R. W., Corneille, O., Rondeel, E., and Witteman, C. L. M. "Mood Effects on Dominated Choices: Positive Mood Induces Departures from Logical Rules." *Journal of Behavioural Decision Making*, 2012, 25: 74–81.

Dewan, M. J., Steenbarger, B. N., and Greenberg, R. P. (eds.) *The Art and Science of Brief Psychotherapies*, 2nd ed. Washington, DC: American Psychiatric Publishing, 2012.

Diener, E., and Suh, E. "Measuring Quality of Life: Economic, Social, and Subjective Indicators." *Social Indicators Research* 40 (1997): 189–216.

Diener, E., Sandvik, E., and Pavot, W. "Happiness Is the Frequency, Not the Intensity, of Positive versus Negative Affect." *Assessing Well-Being Social Indicators Research Series* 39 (2009): 213–231.

Duckworth, A. L., Peterson, C., Matthews, M. D., and Kelly, D.R. "Grit: Perseverance and Passion for Long-term Goals." *Journal of Personality and Social Psychology* 92 (2007): 1087–1101.

Duhigg, C. *The Power of Habit*. New York: Random House, 2012.

Dunker, K., and Lees, L.S. "On Problem-solving." *Psychological Monographs* 58 (1945): i–113.

Emmons, R.A. *Thanks!* New York: Houghton Mifflin, 2007.

Ericsson, K.A. *The Road to Excellence*. Mahwah, NJ: Lawrence Erlbaum, 1996.

Fordyce, M.W. "A Program to Increase Happiness: Further Studies." *Journal of Counseling Psychology* 30 (1983): 483–498.

Fredrickson, B. L. *Love 2.0*. New York: Plume, 2013.

Fredrickson, B. L. *Positivity*. New York: Three Rivers Press, 2009.

Fredrickson, B. L. and Branigan, C. "Positive Emotions Broaden the Scope of Attention and Thought-Action Repertoires." *Cognition and Emotion* 19 (2005): 313–332.

Fredrickson, B. L., Cohn, M. A., Coffey, K. A., Pek, J., and Finkel, S. M. "Open Hearts Build Lives: Positive Emotions, Induced through Loving-Kindness Meditation, Build Consequential Personal Resources." *Journal of Personality and Social Psychology* 95 (2008): 1045–1062.

Gompers, P. A., Kovner, A., Lerner, J., and Scharfstein, D.S. "Performance Persistence in Entrepreneurship." *Harvard Business School Working Paper* 09-028, 2008.

Grant, A. *Give and Take*. New York: Penguin, 2013.

Hammond, D. C. "Hypnosis in the Treatment of Anxiety- and Stress-related Disorders." *Expert Reviews in Neurotherapy* 10 (2010): 263–273.

Heath, C., and Heath, D. *Decisive*. New York: Crown Business, 2013.

Heath, C., and Heath D. *Switch*. New York: Random House, 2011.

Ilmanen, A. *Expected Returns*. Chichester, UK: Wiley, 2011.

Ivanov, I. *The Five Secrets to Highly Profitable Swing Trading*, Amazon Digital Services, 2014.

Jackson, J. J., Wood, D., Bogg, T., Walton, K. E., Harms, P. D., and Roberts, B. W. "What Do Conscientious People Do? Development and Validation of the Behavioral Indicators of Conscientiousness (BIC)." *Journal of Research in Personality* 44 (2010): 501–511.

Kahneman, D. *Thinking, Fast and Slow*. New York: Farrar, Straus, and Giroux, 2011.

Kelley, T. *The Art of Innovation*. New York: Currency.

Kohn, M. L., and Schooler, C. "Job Conditions and Personality: A Longitudinal Assessment of Their Reciprocal Effects." *American Journal of Sociology* 87 (1982): 1257–1286.

Kok, B. E., and Fredrickson, B.L. "Upward Spirals of the Heart: Autonomic Flexibility, as Indexed by Vagal Tone, Reciprocally and Prospectively Predicts Positive Emotions and Social Connectedness." *Biological Psychology* 85 (2010): 432–436.

Kok, B. E., Coffey, K. A., Cohn, M. A., Catalino, L. I., Vacharkulksemsuk, T., Algoe, S. B., Brantley, M., and Fredrickson, B.L. "How Positive Emotions Build Physical Health: Perceived Positive Social Connections Account for the Upward Spiral between Positive Emotions and Vagal Tone." *Psychological Science* 24 (2013): 1123–1132.

Kotter, J. *Leading Change*. Boston, MA: Harvard Business Review Press, 2012.

Kotter, J., and Cohen, D. S. *The Heart of Change*. Boston, MA: Harvard Business Review Press, 2002.

Kuhn, T. S. *The Structure of Scientific Revolutions*, 3rd ed. Chicago: University of Chicago Press, 1996.

Lahti, E. *What Is Sisu?* http://www.emilialahti.com/#!what-is-sisu/c1b3m, 2015.

Leutner, F., Ahmetoglu, G., Akhtar, R., and Chamorro-Premuzic, T. "The Relationship between the Entrepreneurial Personality and the Big Five Personality Traits." *Personality and Individual Differences* 63 (2014): 58–63.

Linker, J. *Disciplined Dreaming*. San Francisco, CA: Jossey-Bass, 2011.

Livingston, J. *Founders at Work*. Berkeley, CA: Apress, 2008.

Lo, A.W., and Repin, D.V. "The Psychophysiology of Real-Time Financial Risk Processing." *Journal of Cognitive Neuroscience* 14 (2002): 323–339.

Locke, E. A., and Latham, G. P. "New Directions in Goal-Setting Theory." *Current Directions in Psychological Science* 15 (2006): 265–268.

Loehr, J., and Schwartz, T. *The Power of Full Engagement*. New York: Free Press, 2003.

Lopez, S. J., Pedrotti, J. T., and Snyder, C. R. *Positive Psychology*, 3rd ed. Thousand Oaks, CA: Sage, 2015.

Mauboussin, M. J. *The Success Equation*. Boston, MA: Harvard Business School Publishing, 2012.

Ichiro Kawachi in collaboration with the Allostatic Load Working Group, "Heart Rate Variability." San Francisco: University of California, McArthur Research Network on SES and Health, 1997.

McClusky, M. *Faster, Higher, Stronger*. New York: Hudson Street Press, 2014.

McGonigal, K. *The Willpower Instinct*. New York: Penguin, 2012.

Michalko, M. *Cracking Creativity*. Berkeley, CA: Ten Speed Press, 2001.

Nettle, D. *Happiness*. Oxford: Oxford University Press, 2005.

Niederhoffer, V. *The Education of a Speculator*. Hoboken, NJ: Wiley, 1997.

Park, J., Konana, P., Gu, B., Kumar, A., and Raghunathan, R. "Confirmation Bias, Overconfidence, and Investment Performance." McCombs Research Paper Series No. IROM-07-10.

Peterson, C., and Seligman, M.E.P. *Character Strengths and Virtues*. Oxford: Oxford University Press, 2004.

Posner, M. I. *Cognitive Neuroscience of Attention*, 2nd ed. New York: Guilford, 2012.

Prochaska, J. O., Norcross, J. C., and DiClemente, C. C. *Changing for Good*. New York: William Morrow, 1994.

Ratey, J. J. *Spark*. New York: Little, Brown, 2013.

Ratey, J. J. *A User's Guide to the Brain*. New York: Vintage Books, 2001.

Root-Bernstein, R. S., and Root-Bernstein, M. M. *Sparks of Genius* Boston: Mariner, 2001.

Sawyer, K. *Group Genius*. New York: Basic Books, 2007.

Sawyer, R. K. *Zig Zag*. San Francisco: Jossey-Bass, 2013.

Sawyer, R. K. *Explaining Creativity*, 2nd ed. Oxford: Oxford University Press, 2012.

Sawyer, R. K. *Explaining Creativity*. Oxford: Oxford University Press, 2006.

Schwager, J. D. Market Wizards. *Hoboken*, NJ: Wiley, 2012.

Scott, J., Stumpp, M., and Xu, P. "Overconfidence Bias in International Stock Prices." *Journal of Portfolio Management* (2003): 80–89.

Seelig, T. *inGenius*. New York: HarperOne, 2012.

Seligman, M. E. P. *Flourish*. New York: Free Press, 2011.

Simonton, D. K. *Creativity in Science*. Cambridge: Cambridge University Press, 2004.

Simonton, D. K. *Genius, Creativity, and Leadership*. Cambridge, MA: Harvard University Press, 1999.

Steenbarger, B. N. "A Hard Look at Our Trading Edge." *TraderFeed, August 2*, 2014.

Steenbarger, B. N. *The Daily Trading Coach*. Hoboken, NJ: Wiley, 2009.

Steenbarger, B. N. *Enhancing Trader Performance*. Hoboken, NJ: Wiley, 2007.

Steenbarger, B. N. *The Psychology of Trading*. Hoboken, NJ: Wiley, 2003.

Tang, Y. "Mechanism of Integrative Body-Mind Training." *Neuroscience Bulletin* 27 (2011): 383–388.

Teasdale, J., Segal, Z.V., Williams, J. M., Ridgeway, V. A., Soulsby, J. M., and Lau, M. A. "Prevention of Relapse/Recurrence in Major Depression by Mindfulness-based Cognitive Therapy." *Journal of Counseling and Clinical Psychology* 68(4) (2000): 615–623.

Torrance, E. P. The Nature of Creativity as Manifest in Its Testing. In R. J. Sternberg (ed.), *The Nature of Creativity*. Oxford: Oxford University Press, 1988, 43–75.

Wadlinger, H. A., and Isaacowitz, D. M. "Positive Mood Broadens Visual Attention to Positive Stimuli." *Motivation and Emotion* 30 (2006): 89–101.

Zabelina, D. L., and Robinson, M. D. "Child's Play: Facilitating the Originality of Creative Output by a Priming Manipulation." *Psychology of Aesthetics, Creativity, and the Arts* 4 (2010): 57–65.

■ Further Resources from Brett Steenbarger

Enhancing Trader Performance (Hoboken, NJ: John Wiley & Sons, 2006): The process of developing expertise as a trader.

Positive Psychology Forbes blog, http://www.forbes.com/sites/brettsteen barger/: Positive psychology and peak performance articles.

The Daily Trading Coach (Hoboken, NJ: John Wiley & Sons, 2009): A cookbook of self-help methods for coaching yourself as a trader.

The Psychology of Trading (Hoboken, NJ: John Wiley & Sons, 2002): A solution-focused perspective on mastering performance psychology.

TraderFeed blog, http://www.traderfeed.blogspot.com/: Trading psychology, psychology of markets, and more.

And, of course, check out the resources offered by many of the contributors to the best-practices section of this book!

Brett N. Steenbarger, PhD, is a Clinical Associate Professor of Psychiatry and Behavioral Sciences at SUNY Upstate Medical University in Syracuse, New York. He has worked since 2004 as a performance coach for proprietary trading firms, investment banks, and hedge funds. The author of three previous books on trading psychology and the popular TraderFeed blog, Dr. Steenbarger has written over 50 peer-reviewed journal articles, book chapters, and books on the topic of short-term approaches to behavior change. He also writes a blog for *Forbes* that covers the field of positive psychology as it relates to peak performance.

C

Carstens, Henry, 22
Catmull, Ed, 274, 417
change, 54–74, 411
  crisis and, 60–63
  emotions and, 61–65
  mirroring and, 68–70
  motivation and, 67–68
  in psychotherapy, 65–66
  readiness for, 54–60, 79
  translation and, 65–66
  urgency and, 56–61, 66
chart review, 359–361
Chrysikou, Evangelia, 227, 417
coaching, 342–344
Coates, John, 77, 417
cognitive bias, 195–196, 215
cognitive control, 384–385
cognitive journal, 339
Colvin, Geoff, 139, 417
Commodity Channel Index, 335
Compton, William, 145, 151–152, 417
confirmation bias, 30, 231
conscientiousness, 149, 165–167,
    169–170, 201, 268
contemplation, 54–56, 58, 60–63,
    66–67, 69–71, 74, 79–83
contentment, 97, 143 *see also* life
    satisfaction
core motivations, 33–36, 87
correlation, 311–315, 319–320
  of asset classes, 313–315
  of stock sectors, 311–313
Covel, Michael, 367
creativity, ix–x, xiv-xv, 42, 86, 93,
    96–97, 132, 134, 138, 143,
    155, 193, 197, 199, 201, 207,
    267, 270–271, 273, 275, 291,
    297, 334, 411
  and analogy, 255–261
  automatic writing and speech,
    254–255
  becoming more creative, 235–237,
    335–337
  brainstorming, 266–271, 274

chart review, 359–361
combinations and, 250–257, 337
crisis of, 215–219
and discipline, 275
and entrepreneurship, 207–208, 210
and failure, 274–275
in groups, 263–266, 271–273
immersion and, 235
incubation and, 225–227, 337
insight and, 228–230
and lifestyle, 261–262
and problem finding, 230–235
process, 222–235
and productivity, 237, 247–250
reading in parallel and, 350–351
reframing problems and, 240–244
and strengths, 219–222
switching modalities and, 244–247
trading failure and, 237–240
and verification, 230–231
Csikszentmihalyi, Mihalyi, 96, 225,
    233–234, 248, 418
cycles, 8–9, 49–50, 319–320, 415

D

The Daily Trading Coach, x, 167, 173
Darwin, Charles, 1
day structure, 347–350
deliberate practice, x, 129, 131, 139,
    142, 165, 167, 193, 358
DeVries, Catherine, 195–196, 418
depression, 38, 71–72, 74, 143, 155,
    166, 190, 305, 338
discipline, ix, xi, 5, 9, 25, 30, 36–38,
    41, 43, 45, 47–49, 51, 70, 79,
    92, 100, 107, 110, 114–116,
    125, 149, 153, 165–166, 173,
    176, 199, 211–212, 217–219,
    239, 247, 253, 261–262, 267,
    275, 288 - 290, 297, 300, 329,
    341–342, 351, 359, 362, 364,
    367, 402–403, 413
Dewan, Mantosh, 418
Diener, Ed, 96, 146, 151–152, 418
Dow TICK, 317–320
Duckworth, Angela, 14, 130, 418